# The Fraudulent Transfer of Wealth

## Unwound and Explained

David J. Slenn

ABA
AMERICAN BAR ASSOCIATION
Business Law Section

Cover design by Catherine Zaccarine.



Printed in the United States of America.

26 25 24 23 22 5 4 3 2 1

ISBN: 978-1-63905-193-9

# Table of Contents

# Acknowledgements

I would like to thank my wife, Mindy, and children, Simone, Brielle, Elliot, and Audrey for all their encouragement, loving support, and patience while writing this book. I would also like to thank my father, Richard Slenn, for his support and inspiration, as well as Jay Adkisson and Ken Kettering for countless hours of discussion and guidance. I am grateful for the much needed energy provided by Buddy Brew Coffee (Kennedy location). My special thanks are extended to the ABA Business Law Section publishing team (Rick Paszkiet, Katrina Krause, and Caitlin McCauley) for their encouragement and assistance in publishing this book.

# Introduction

> "Probably the most severe trial to which an honest man can be subjected is the inability to pay his debts, even by the application of all his means. He is assailed by temptations of interest, of shame, of affection, to wander from the straight line of duty, while at the same time he is intrusted by the law with dominion over property which equitably and in justice belongs to his creditors. The quantity of litigation engendered by fraudulent conveyances is appalling, and the cunning devices and intricate schemes resorted to by debtors to elude the vigilance of creditors would, if no moral turpitude was involved, challenge admiration. The condition of the body of our law upon this subject is far from satisfactory and may be said to still be in a formative and unsettled state."[1]

As the United States continues to recover from the effects of a global pandemic, the Biden administration proposed legislation that aims to help strengthen American infrastructure as well as grow the economy "from the bottom up and middle out." The source of funding for these changes would come in part from increases in certain federal taxes. These changes have prompted many who have amassed great wealth to engage in sophisticated planning to reduce the contemplated increase in taxes they would otherwise pay. And while many facing the prospect of mounting creditors must liquidate assets to pay debts, the wealthy who face creditor claims can rest easier knowing that not only have they minimized amounts otherwise due to tax authorities, that same wealth may have been immunized from all other non-taxing creditors though intricate planning structures.

Consequently, at a time where the principle "those who owe must pay" holds especially true, the spotlight shines even brighter on those who have arranged their affairs to pay what they decide should be paid, if anything at all. The morality of dodging legitimate creditors becomes more pronounced during a pandemic, as do the economic consequences for a credit-based society.

Fortunately for creditors, an important legal tool exists that provides relief from the transfer of wealth structured in a fashion that hinders creditors. That tool is the centuries-old fraudulent conveyance law. Regardless of the degree of sophistication used to transfer wealth, the scope of fraudulent transfer law is broad

1. Frederick S. Wait, *A Treatise on Fraudulent Conveyances and Creditors' Bills, with a Discussion of Void and Voidable Acts* 4 (1884).

enough to permit a creditor relief where transactions range from the simplest to the most sophisticated. Fraudulent conveyance law provides a creditor with remedies to counteract a debtor's transfer of an asset, or the incurrence of an obligation, that impact the creditor's ability to collect a debt. The underpinnings for this ancient law are fairness and support for a system of credit. But some jurisdictions, including some U.S. states, altered or eliminated these policies to attract wealth and bolster the local economy. This discrepancy between jurisdictions has created complex conflict of law issues in fraudulent conveyance litigation.

Although the fraudulent conveyance law provides a creditor with remedies if a debtor makes a transfer of an asset under certain circumstances, there have been divergences among the states in providing such relief. These differences motivated a uniform act, which was first promulgated by the National Conference of Commissioners on Uniform State Laws in 1918 and referred to as the Uniform Fraudulent Conveyance Act (UFCA).[2] The Uniform Law Commission (ULC) then drafted an overhaul to the UFCA in 1984. The new uniform act was entitled the Uniform Fraudulent Transfer Act (UFTA). Finally, the ULC amended the UFTA in 2014, which included a name change—the Uniform Voidable Transactions Act (UVTA). The terms "voidable transaction," "fraudulent transfer" and "fraudulent conveyance" will be referred to collectively as a "fraudulent transfer" throughout this book, unless context requires otherwise. Aside from a choice of law provision and provisions related to series limited liability companies, the UVTA did not substantially change the UFTA and thus, references to the UFTA will be to the UVTA, unless context requires otherwise. References will also be made to the UFCA (still in force in Maryland) and non-uniform act state laws (e. g., South Carolina and Alaska) where context is required.

This book will examine the intersection between fraudulent transfer law and its application to modern day wealth transfer planning transactions. Although wealth transfer planning is a legitimate service and should be free from avoidance if done properly, some forms of wealth transfer are more prone to avoidance. Consequently, all parties impacted by the transfer of wealth can benefit from understanding the scope and application of fraudulent transfer law. Debtors can take steps to minimize a transaction's exposure to avoidance. Creditors can take proactive measures to reduce the chance of losing assets, or legal measures to restore the creditor.[3] Also, attention will be given to the scenarios where advisers face liability for their role in facilitating the transfer of wealth meant to frustrate a creditor's ability to collect a debt.

Ultimately, this book should provide a better understanding of how the broad reach of fraudulent transfer law can impact all parties to the modern transfer of wealth. But before applying fraudulent transfer law to modern transfers of wealth, one should consider historical applications of fraudulent transfer law.

---

2. The National Conference of Commissioners on Uniform State Laws adopted the name "Uniform Law Commission" as an alternative name in 2007, but also retained the former name.

3. *See* N. Boeke and W. Fendrick, *Fraudulent Transfers, Creditors' and Debtors' Practice in Florida*, Eighth Edition (2022). ("Florida's fraudulent transfer law provides a creditor with a powerful (but often underused) right to set aside many transactions by its debtor that reduce the creditor's chances of getting paid.")

CHAPTER 1

# Roots of Fraudulent Transfer Law

> In Roman law itself, the action, whatever it was called, as it appears in the legislation of Justinian is indubitably an amalgam of various forms of relief, which began perhaps with a *restitutio in integrum* and was later combined with an *interdict* and a personal action. This last was usually quasi-contractual in character, but might have penal elements, and thus have sometimes sounded in tort, i.e. delict. All these things were fused into what in the Code and Digest is commonly called just "the action," and characterized as "*utilis,*" i.e., "adapted" or "on the case."[1]

Centuries ago, debtors who did not pay their debts faced severe punishment, from excommunication from the Catholic church, to incarceration, and even death. In his 1897 treatise on fraudulent conveyances, Frederick Wait identified the "barbarous practice which prevailed among the ancient Romans of putting in insolvent to death, or selling him into slavery" and reflected the "strong legal and moral foundation which a pecuniary obligation had in the minds of the people in early times."[2] Eventually, punishment became a bit more debtor friendly as slavery was abolished by the second century, although imprisonment continued until the twentieth century.[3] Although incarceration for failure to pay

1. Max Radin, *Fraudulent Conveyances at Roman Law,* 18 VA. L. REV. 109, 130 (1931–1932).

2. Frederick S. Wait, *Fraudulent Conveyances and Creditors' Bills* 2 (3rd ed. 1897). Wait also noted a quote from Holmes' Common Law, p.14, which provided, "According to that law [referring to the law of the "Twelve Tables"], if a man was indebted to several creditors and insolvent, after certain formalities they might cut up his body and divided it up among them. If there was a single creditor he might put his debtor to death or sell him as a slave." *Id* at 2. *See also,* Thomas Moers Mayer, Will the Lawyers Pay? Counsels Ethical, Civil and Criminal Exposure For Creating Asset Protection Trusts, in Domestic Asset Protection Trusts: Effectiveness and Ethics, ALI-CLE Course Materials (May 4, 2015) (available on Westlaw).

3. See David L. Buchbinder, *A Short History of Bankruptcy,* Norton Bankruptcy Law Adviser. ("[B]y the second century A.D., debtor slavery had been abolished in the empire. Debtor imprisonment continued to exist, but this was distinguishable from slavery in that creditors could not use the services of an imprisoned debtor. The debtor could merely be held ransom until friends or family, or the debtor repaid the debt. *Merrick, supra*; *Radin, supra*; *Ford, supra*. (Debtor imprisonment has existed throughout history, including the twentieth century. *** During the Dark Ages, the financial system of western Europe receded as an important factor of daily life. Debtor imprisonment returned to vogue, prevailing throughout the period. (*Riesenfeld, supra* at 439, citing Justinian's Code VII, 71, 8.) The church proclaimed debt and insolvency sinful. Debtors

debts has been abolished,[4] debtors may be incarcerated for refusing to obey court orders. The Catholic Church has taken a more lenient view on debts in modern times, although the Church's call for leniency is directed more toward those who are poor and vulnerable.[5]

Although modern fraudulent transfer law can be traced to Roman law,[6] fraudulent transfer law in the United States more closely reflects the law as it developed in England. Fraudulent transfer law's historical roots as a contravention of public policy, and historical characterization as a crime or tort, manifests itself today in the wide array of relief granted by courts. In fact, defrauding creditors is still considered a crime in several states. With roots in tort and criminal law, it should not be surprising that courts will appeal to principles retributivism and utilitarianism when awarding fraudulent transfer relief.

## English Laws

The early English sanctuary laws reflect the tension between debtors and creditors and what could be described as an early form of exemption law. According to Professor Ross, "[t]aking sanctuary was another part of the time-honored method of seeking to escape financial liabilities. The early Roman comedies of Plautus typically feature a slave or prostitute seeking protection in the temple of a god. During the Middle Ages, canon law and the Church in England provided havens for harried debtors. King Edward, I tried to counter this practice by passing a law to limit the use of sanctuaries for fraudulent debtors."[7]

---

were subject to excommunication while alive or to denial of a Christian burial upon death. *Ford supra* at 23; *Radin, supra* at 34. As had been the case in early Rome, religious sanctions were once again utilized as an incentive to the repayment of debt.").

4. *See, e.g.,* Florida statute section 56.011, which abolished capias ad satisfaciendum. ("A capias ad satisfaciendum may not be issued upon a judgment, nor may the body of any person be subject to arrest or confinement for the payment of money, except for fines imposed by lawful authority."); *see also, Minor v. Heimbach*, 157 So.2d 95 (Fla. 3d DCA 1963). ("It appears that the sum of $817.05 is based upon an award in a workmen's compensation case. This action was commenced by appellee-plaintiff pursuant to [s] 440.24, F.S. A., to enforce payment of compensation due him by virtue of that award. We are satisfied that the appealed order violates [s] 55.14, F.S.A. and therefore must be, and is hereby, reversed.")

5. *See, e.g.,* "What Does the Church Say About Debt and Jubilee," United States Conference of Catholic Bishops, *available* at https://www.usccb.org/resources/what-does-church-say-about-debt-and-jubilee. ("In the case of international debt, then, justice involves co-responsibility on the part of debtors and creditors, who must seek to relieve the suffering caused by debt while promoting sound political, social, and economic policies. These principles and themes from Catholic social teaching make a compelling case for debt relief for the world's poorest countries. In his recent journey to America, Pope John Paul II renewed his call for solidarity and his appeal to forgive the debt of the poorest nations. He challenged us to speak out and to work for a new measure of justice and compassion. The Catholic Campaign on Debt is a response to his call.")

6. *See In re Kelton Motors, Inc.*, 130 B.R. 170 (Bankr. D. Vt. 1991). ("Under Roman law, a defrauded creditor could bring a tort action, known as a 'Paulian Action,' to void a fraudulent conveyance by an insolvent debtor. The policy underlying the Paulian Action was to benefit the public at large by facilitating and encouraging the payment of just debts." Radin, Fraudulent Conveyances at Roman Law, 18 Va.L.Rev. 109 (1931).)

7. Charles Ross, *Elizabethan Literature and the Law of Fraudulent Conveyance: Sidney, Spenser, and Shakespeare* 8 n. 10 (2003), citing 50 Edw. III, c. 6, which Ross provides was "aimed at those who, to avoid creditors, gave their tenements and chattels to friends, who agreed to pass on the profits, and then sought

The sanctuary and the Statute of 50 Edw. III, c. 6 were addressed by Professor Glenn in his 1915 treatise on fraudulent conveyances:

> The recitals in the Statute of 50 Edw. III, c. 6, would almost precisely apply to some present-day practices: "Diverse people (it states) do give their tenements and chattels to their friends, by collusion thereof to have the profits at their will, and after do flee to the franchise of Westminster, of St. Martin's Le Grand of London, or other such privileged places, and there do live a great time with an high countenance of another man's goods and profits of the said tenements and chattels, till the said creditors shall be bound to take a small parcel of their debt, and release the remnant." Of course, in those days it was necessary for the debtor to flee to sanctuary in order to escape imprisonment for debt. Nowadays, a fraudulent debtor does not need the protection of Westminster, because imprisonment for debt has been abolished. So far as his personal liberty is concerned, he can, to quote the words of the old Statute, "live a great time with an high countenance of another man's goods," wherever he pleases, instead of being bound by the jail liberties.[8]

Medieval sanctuary abuse has many similarities to some forms of modern-day wealth transfer planning, although the sanctuary lacked the formalities evidenced by a trust agreement. Numerous other English statutes addressed other creditor abuses near the end of the Middle Ages. The most relevant of such statutes to wealth transfer were enacted in 1376[9], 1379,[10] 1487,[11] 1571,[12] and 1601.[13] The laws dealt not only with the rights of creditors, but also of

sanctuary in the 'Franchise of Westminster, of S. Martin Le Grand of London, or other such privileged places.' The Parliament of Henry VII repeated the injunction of 50 Edw. III, c. 6 against deeds of gift made to defraud creditors by those who seek 'sanctuary, or other places privileged." (3 Hen. VII, c. 4.)

8. Garrard Glenn, *The Rights and Remedies of Creditors Respecting Their Debtor's Property*, 52 (1915).

9. 50 Edw. III, c. 6. (1376).

10. *See generally*, Frederick S. Wait, A Treatise on Fraudulent Conveyances and Creditors' Bills 33 (1884). (Describing 2. Rich. II, stat. 2, c.3.) ("The statute, 2 Rich. II, stat. 2, c. 3 (1379), contained provisions on the same subject [sanctuary abuse], and from its recitals was evidently framed to repress the hypocritical religious zeal of fraudulent debtors, and to furnish a method of substituted service of process. The quaint provisions of these early statutes show conclusively that fraudulent conveyances are not entirely the offspring of our modern civilization.")

11. *See Wilson v. Cheshire*, 6 S.C. Eq. 233, 238–39 (S.C. App. L. & Eq. 1826). (Referring to 3 Hen. VII. c. 4. (1487)) ("The chapter is in the following words: "Item, that where oftentimes deeds of gift of goods and chattels have been made, to the intent to defraud their creditors of their duties, and that the person or persons that maketh the said deed of gift, goeth to sanctuary or other places privileged, and occupieth and liveth with the said goods and chattels, their creditors being unpaid: It is enacted, that all deeds of gift of goods and chattels, made or to be made, of trusts to the use of that person or persons, that made the same deed of gift, be void, and of none effect." Now, it is clear from the language of the statute, that it was intended to protect the rights of creditors . . . ")

12. 13 Eliz., c. 5 (1571) (Eng.).

13. *See* Charles Ross, *Elizabethan Literature and the Law of Fraudulent Conveyance Sidney, Spenser, and Shakespeare* 15 (2003). (``In 1601 Elizabeth's Parliament passed a statute that reflects the wider association of fraud and waste. 43 Eliz., c. 8, 'an act against fraudulent administration of Intestates goods,' targeted estate administrators who managed to give away goods before creditors could be paid because the creditors "for lack of knowledge of the place of habitation of the administrator cannot arrest him, 'or if they find him and sue him, learn he is unable to pay 'the value of that he hath conveyed away of the Intestates' goods, or released of his debits, by way of wasting' (emphasis added).")

purchasers.[14] The 1376, 1379, and 1487 statutes took aim at debtors attempting to "have their cake and eat it, too." The ability to rearrange wealth by transferring wealth to friends and family via secret trust and seeking refuge in a sanctuary,[15] such that one could avoid creditors but still maintain the enjoyment of the transferred wealth, was fraudulent and greatly abhorred.

> Fraud, which the common law so greatly abhorred, was so much practiced by debtors upon creditors in early times as to attract the attention of Parliament, and to constitute a subject of frequent legislation. "These statutes," said Lord Mansfield, "cannot receive too liberal a construction, or be too much extended in suppression of fraud." It may be observed in explanation of this early legislation against fraudulent transfers that these statutes were enacted to more clearly formulate the common law with a view to suppress voluntary conveyances and secret trusts made by debtors who had escaped arrest for debt or avoided service of process by fleeing to sanctuaries or holy ground.[16]

But out of all those creditors' rights statutes, it was the 1571 statute, the Statute of 13 Elizabeth, that served as the main precursor to modern fraudulent transfer jurisprudence in the United States.[17] About 30 years after the enactment of the Statute of 13 Elizabeth, *Twyne's Case* was decided in the Court of Star Chamber. There, the court held that a debtor's transfer of sheep made with the

14. *Id.* at 103. citing 27 Eliz., c. 4 (1585) and Gerrard Glenn in his treatise, Fraudulent Conveyances and Preferences. ("'In the old days,' Glenn admits, 'every discussion of fraudulent conveyances includes the rights of purchasers as well as creditors. There was, indeed, another Elizabethan enactment which was called the Statute of Conveyances in Fraud of Purchasers.' Since Glenn dealt only with the rights of creditors, he mentions this statute 'only for purposes of elimination.'")

15. *See* Frederick S. Wait, A Treatise on Fraudulent Conveyances and Creditors' Bills 35 (1884). ("Sanctuaries, or cities of refuge for fraudulent and absconded debtors, do not seem to have been wholly abolished until during the reign of James I, and one such sanctuary, the noted White-friars, which flourished in the reign of that monarch, has been immortalized by Sir Walter Scott in his 'Fortunes of Nigel.'"); *See also*, Ross, *Elizabethan Literature and Fraudulent Conveyances*, 31.("The most glaring loophole of these statutes [50 Edw. III, c. 6 (1376), 2 Rich. II, 2, c. 3 (1379) and 3 Hen. VII, c. 4 (1487)] is that they only covered fraudulent conveyances where the debtor actually entered a legally defined safe haven. Parliament corrected the problem by passing 13 Eliz., c. 5.")

16. Frederick S. Wait, *A Treatise on Fraudulent Conveyances and Creditors' Bills* 41-42 (1884).

17. *See Roberts v. Anderson*, 1818 WL 1914 (N.Y. Ch. 1818), rev'd, 1820 WL 1759 (N.Y. 1820) ("In the revision of our statute law, the statutes of the 13th and 27th of Eliz. are connected together in one act, and the provisos in these statutes are consolidated in the 6th section of the act; but I have taken it for granted, as being a settled rule, (and one which was established by the Court of Errors,) in respect to our revised laws, that the construction of those different provisions in connection with the general proviso, remains the same since as before the revision."); *In re Kelton Motors, Inc.*, 130 B.R. 170 (1991). ("Fraudulent conveyance laws were also adopted in England as an attempt to curtail resort to ancient 'sanctuary law'" as a means of defrauding creditors.' "A sanctuary was not merely the interior of a church, but certain precincts defined by custom or royal grant. Debtors could take sanctuary in one of these precincts, live in relative comfort, and be immune from execution by their creditors." Baird and Johnson, Voidable Preferences, 38 Vanderbilt Law Review 713, at 829 (1985). Thus, debtors could sell or collusively transfer their property, take sanctuary, and leave their creditors without recourse except, perhaps, to receive a small payment from the debtor in return for release from the obligations. Reacting to this abuse, Parliament passed a 1376 statute that allowed creditors to execute upon lands and chattels collusively conveyed, and, again, in 1476, passed another statute voiding fraudulent gifts and chattels made in trust. Zinman, Houle & Weiss, Fraudulent Transfers According to Alden, Goss and Borowitz: A Tale of Two Circuits, 39 The Business Lawyer 988 (May 1984). )

intent to "delay, hinder, or defraud" could result in penal sanctions.[18] *Twyne's Case* has been described as the "creditor's beacon-light in suits to annul covinous transfers."[19] In *Twyne's Case*, the debtor, P (Pierce), owed sums to two creditors, T (Twyne) and C. The debtor transferred assets (which included the infamous sheep) to Twyne while a writ was pending in favor of C. In addition to making a preferential transfer to Twyne, Pierce continued to enjoy possession of the transferred assets.[20]

*Twyne's Case* was about more than a debtor preferring a creditor. It was also about the act of transferring assets with retained enjoyment, to the exclusion of creditors. "[T]he problem in *Twyne's Case* was not simply that the debtor had transferred property or that the debtor had preferred one creditor, Pierce, over another, C. Rather, the problem was that the debtor actively hid the transfer from his creditors and, in addition, seemed to set up the transaction so that the debtor could retain the benefit of the property and, eventually, probably recover the property from the transferee."[21]

But recall the Statute of 13 Elizabeth was penal in nature. Instead of providing the creditor with relief, the Star Chamber imposed a penalty and perhaps imprisonment.

> According to the statute of 13 Eliz. c. 5, Pearce and Twyne should have been fined the entire value of the goods conveyed, with one half going to the Queen and the other half "to the party or parties grieved by such feigned and fraudulent" conveyance, plus suffer imprisonment for six months without the possibility of bail. We have, however, no evidence that the Court imposed this penalty. If the 1599 deeds in fact represented goods worth somewhere near the value of the debts Pearce owned Audley, then the fine should have amounted to around £1000. Instead, the Court ended up reducing Pearce and Twyne's fines to £100 each. The mitigating of fines was common practice in the Star Chamber, where large fines were often said to be "ad terrorem, non ad ruinam" to create fear, not ruin. In addition, Twyne and Pearce likely did not serve their six months in prison. Normal Star Chamber practice was to imprison defendants only until they could provide sureties for the payment of the fine. They lined up their sureties and presumably went free.[22]

---

18. *Twyne's Case*, 3 Coke's Reports 80 (1602).

19. Frederick S. Wait., Fraudulent Conveyances and Creditors' Bills 48, (3rd ed. 1897).

20. *Id.* at 49. ("P was indebted to T. in L400 and was indebted also to C in L200. C brought an action of debt against P, and pending the writ P, being possessed of goods and chattels of the value of L300, secretly made a general deed of gift of all his goods and chattels, real and personal whatsoever, to T, in satisfaction of his debt; notwithstanding which P continued in possession of the goods, some of which he sold again, sheared the sheep, and marked them with his own mark.")

21. Barry L. Zaretsky, *Fraudulent Transfer Law as the Arbiter of Unreasonable Risk*, 46 S. C. L. Rev. 1165, 1170 (1995).

22. Emily Kadens, *New Light on Twyne's Case*, 94 Am. Bankr. L.J. 1, 77 (2020). (Internal citations omitted). (Citing Les Reportes Del Cases in Camera Stellata, 1593 TO 1609. From the original Ms. of John Haward 126 (William Paley Baildon ed., 1894)

It was not until 1623 that a private cause of action due to a fraudulent transfer arose under English law.[23] However, courts permitted creditors to utilize the penal statute to obtain relief before 1623.[24]

Over the course of centuries, the rule governing transfers made with the intent to hinder creditors, sometimes referred to as the "primordial rule,"[25] would evolve to deal with the transfer of wealth in all its forms. As Wait noted, ever since *Twyne's Case*, the principles of fraudulent transfer law have been extended "to avoid covinous conveyances not only as to existing creditors, but in certain cases as to subsequent creditors and even as to contingent subsequent creditors." This development would continue not only in England but also on a separate course in the new English colonies that would eventually establish their own republic and legal system, where fraudulent transfer law would develop both in court and statute.

The United States Supreme Court has decided many cases involving fraudulent transfers. Among the most notable of these decisions involve issues as to whether a fraudulent transfer can be the type of fraud sufficient to trigger denial of discharge,[26] whether a court lacked authority, prejudgment, to enjoin a defendant from transferring unencumbered assets,[27] whether the price paid at a foreclosure sale conclusively establishes reasonably equivalent value,[28] whether a state statute that authorizes prejudgment attachment of real estate without prior notice or hearing satisfies the Fourteenth Amendment's Due Process Clause,[29]

23. *See Springer v. Nohl Electric Products Corp.*, 2018 WI 48 (May 15, 2018). ("Moreover, although the 1571 Parliament designed this statute to be penal in nature, the 1623 Parliament gave it a civil application." *See also* Bruce A. Markell, *Toward True and Plain Dealing: A Theory of Fraudulent Transfers Involving Unreasonably Small Capital*, 21 Ind. L.Rev.469, 473 (1988) (citing 13 Eliz. c.5, §1 (1571) and 21 Jac. 1,c.19, §7 (1623)).)

24. *See* Bruce A. Markell, *Toward True and Plain Dealing: A Theory of Fraudulent Transfers Involving Unreasonably Small Capital*, 21 Ind. L. Rev. 469, 473 (1988). "Defrauded creditors soon turned this penal statute to their personal ends. Since such transfers were illegal, and thus presumable void, creditors reasoned that they could ignore the conveyance and follow the transferred property into the hands of the party receiving the goods. In short, passage of title was ignored, and the party receiving the goods had to give them up if the debt was just. Courts adopted this reasoning, and in 1603 Parliament followed suit and made fraudulent conveyances a part of the English bankruptcy laws. In 1623 Parliament completed the process and made these laws civil in nature.") (Internal citations omitted.)

25. *See* Kenneth C. Kettering, *Codifying a Choice of Law Rule for Fraudulent Transfer: A Memorandum to the Uniform Law Commission*, 19 Am. Bankr. Inst. L. Rev. 319 (2011). (``Although differing in detail, the UFCA, UFTA, and section 548 are quite similar, to the degree that cases applying any of those statutes freely rely upon cases applying the others. The core of each remains the primordial rule that declares avoidable any transfer of property made by a debtor with intent to "hinder, delay, or defraud" the debtor's creditors.")

26. *Husky Int'l Elecs., Inc. v. Ritz*, 136 S. Ct. 1581, 1586 (2016) ("The term 'actual fraud' in §523(a)(2)(A) encompasses forms of fraud, like fraudulent conveyance schemes, that can be effected without a false representation.")

27. *Grupo Mexicano de Desarrollo, S. A. v. Alliance Bond Fund, Inc.*, 527 U.S. 308, 333 (1999) ("Because such a remedy was historically unavailable from a court of equity, we hold that the District Court had no authority to issue a preliminary injunction preventing petitioners from disposing of their assets pending adjudication of respondents' contract claim for money damages.")

28. *BFP v. Resolution Trust Corp.*, 511 U.S. 531, 545 (1994) ("For the reasons described, we decline to read the phrase "reasonably equivalent value" in §548(a)(2) to mean, in its application to mortgage foreclosure sales, either "fair market value" or "fair foreclosure price" (whether calculated as a percentage of fair market value or otherwise). We deem, as the law has always deemed, that a fair and proper price, or a "reasonably equivalent value," for foreclosed property, is the price in fact received at the foreclosure sale, so long as all the requirements of the State's foreclosure law have been complied with.")

29. *Connecticut v. Doehr*, 501 U.S. 1, 4 (1991) ("This case requires us to determine whether a state statute that authorizes prejudgment attachment of real estate without prior notice or hearing, without a showing of

whether a person who has not submitted a claim against a bankruptcy estate has a right to a jury trial under the Seventh Amendment,[30] whether a bankruptcy trustee may utilize a single creditor's claim to avoid and recover the full value of a fraudulent transfer for the benefit of all bankruptcy estate creditors, even if the amount recovered exceeds the single creditor's claim,[31] and whether Congress intended "creditors" be given the meaning usually attributed to it as it pertains to fraudulent transfers.[32] As shown throughout this book, the Supreme Court, along with all the lower courts, often look to the fraudulent transfer common law to determine the scope of terminology.

---

extraordinary circumstances, and without a requirement that the person seeking the attachment post a bond, satisfies the Due Process Clause of the Fourteenth Amendment. We hold that, as applied to this case, it does not.")

30. *Granfinanciera, S. A. v. Nordberg*, 492 U.S. 33, 35 (1989) ("Since petitioners here have not filed such claims, respondent's suit is neither part of the claims adjudication process nor integral to the restructuring of debtor-creditor relations. Congress therefore cannot divest petitioners of their Seventh Amendment right merely by relabeling a pre-existing, common-law cause of action to which that right attaches and assigning it to a specialized court of equity, particularly where there is no evidence that Congress considered the constitutional implications of its designation of all fraudulent conveyance actions as core proceedings.")

31. *Moore v. Bay*, 284 U.S. 4, 5, 52 S. Ct. 3, 4, 76, L. Ed. 133 (1931). ("The Circuit Courts of Appeal seem generally to agree, as the language of the Bankruptcy Act appears to us to imply very plainly, that what thus is recovered for the benefit of the estate is to be distributed in 'dividends of equal per centum * * * on all allowed claims, except such as have priority or are secured.'")

32. *American Surety Co. v. Marotta*, 287 U.S. 513, 518 (1933) ("There being nothing to indicate any other purpose, Congress must be deemed to have intended that in §3a (1) "creditors" should be given the meaning usually attributed to it when used in the common law definition of fraudulent conveyances. *See* Coder v. Arts, 213 U.S. 223, 242. *Lansing Boiler Engine Works v. Ryerson*, 128 F. 701, 703. *Githens v. Shiffler*, 112 F. 505. Under the common law rule a creditor having only a contingent claim, such as was that of the petitioner at the time respondent made the transfer in question, is protected against fraudulent conveyance.")

CHAPTER 2

# Early U.S. Law

> "[W]e suspect there is absolutely nothing new about debtors' trying to avoid paying their debts, or seeking to favor some creditors over others—or even about their seeking to achieve these ends through "sophisticated... strategies," *ibid.* The law of fraudulent conveyances and bankruptcy was developed to prevent such conduct."[1]

The Statute of 13 Elizabeth and English common law were applied by American territories[2] and eventually by the states. This is evident in early state statutes such as Florida Statute Section 2.01, enacted in 1829 and entitled, "Common law and certain statutes declared in force." Section 2.01 provides "[t]he common and statute laws of England which are of a general and not a local nature, with the exception hereinafter mentioned, down to the 4th day of July 1776, are declared to be of force in this state; provided, the said statutes and common law

---

1. *Grupo Mexicano de Desarrollo S.A. v. All. Bond Fund, Inc.*, 527 U.S. 308, 322, 119 S. Ct. 1961, 1970, 144 L. Ed. 2d 319 (1999). The Supreme Court found a preliminary freeze order impermissible principally because injunctions of such kind were not "traditionally accorded by courts of equity" at the time the Constitution was adopted.

2. *See Butler v. Wilkinson*, 740 P.2d 1244, 1261 (Utah 1987). ("Since territorial days, we have held to that rule, although the common law rule is of even more ancient origin. Later, the common law rule was codified. *** The Uniform Fraudulent Conveyance Act, which was enacted in this state in 1925, codified the common law. 37 Am.Jur.2d, Fraudulent Conveyances §88, at 772 (1968). See 1925 Laws of Utah ch. 42."); *see also Ocklawaha River Farms Co. v. Young*, 73 Fla. 159, 174–75, 74 So. 644, 648–49 (1917). ("The history of the law of fraudulent conveyances shows that from the earliest times transfers of personal property in fraud of creditors have been deemed void at common law. *** The first statutes were aimed at the fraudulent gifts of chattels, St. 13 Elizabeth, c. 5, at conveyances of land as well as chattels to defeat creditors, and St. 27 Elizabeth, c. 4, against fraudulent conveyances to defeat subsequent purchasers. *** These statutes were adopted by the territory of Florida in 1823, and have been continued upon the statute books of this state to the present time. There are some slight variations in the language of our statutes, sections 2513–2515, General Statutes of Florida, of 1906, from that of the English originals, due, perhaps, to a laudable ambition to improve upon the English model. It is conceded that the statutes are highly remedial, beneficial in their nature, entitled to a liberal interpretation, are in pari materia, and should be construed together. The words 'utterly void' in each of these statutes, 13 and 27 Elizabeth, sections 2513, 2514, General Statutes, have not been given by the courts the full significance which they seem to imply. The word is construed to read 'voidable' and voidable only at the instance of those embraced within the meaning of the terms 'creditors and others' or 'purchasers.'")

be not inconsistent with the Constitution and laws of the United States and the acts of the Legislature of this state."

Notwithstanding the similarities between modern U.S. fraudulent transfer law and the English law, differences emerged between the two versions of the same body of law,[3] especially with respect to creditors' rights and the use of trusts as wealth transfer vehicles.[4] These developments would reflect various public policy concerns, including variances from the English common law.

## Public Policy

Why are there fraudulent transfer laws providing creditors with relief? The answer is based partly on the public policy that every man should pay his debts. This principle is an underpinning through which courts have and continue to construe fraudulent transfer law.[5] Transfers that are made with the actual intent to hinder creditors have been referred to as moral fraud, in contrast to transfers made by debtors while insolvent, which have been referred to as legal fraud.[6]

It goes without saying that the extension of credit is critical for a strong economy. For example, there would be negative economic consequences if

---

3. *See, e.g., Fox v. Hills*, 1 Conn. 295, 298 (Conn. 1815). ("The conveyance was valid as against the plaintiff's claim. Our statute relates only to fraudulent and deceitful conveyances made to avoid 'a debt or duty;' and from the proviso or saving at the close of the 2nd section, it appears that the debt or duty must be due to 'a creditor.' The plaintiff's claim was in no sense a debt. Nor was any duty due to him as a creditor. His right was not ascertained; and it was matter of contingency whether it ever would be. It may be admitted, that this case would come within the statute 13 Elizabeth. But there is a great difference between the provisions of that statute and ours; and the difference in language imports a difference in the intention of the legislature. Our statute bears more resemblance to some of the earlier English statutes against fraudulent conveyances, as 50 Edw. 3. c. 6. and 3 Hen. 7. c. 4.") *See also, Irving v. Robertson*, 40 S.C.L. 228, 240–41 (S.C. App. L. 1853). ("It is a mistake to suppose that the entire body of the common law was imported by the first settlers.")

4. *Nichols v. Eaton*, 91 U.S. 716 (1875). Professor Gray observed the degradation of creditors' rights with respect to the third-party trust. See John Chipman Gray, Restraints on the Alienation of Property xiii (2nd ed. 1895) (preface to the second edition). ("How far the law will allow a man to enjoy rights in property which he cannot transfer, and which his creditors cannot take for their debts, is a question becoming more and more frequent in this country. In 1876 I shared the surprise, common to many lawyers, at the opinion of the Supreme Court of the United States, in the case of Nichols v. Eaton, 91 U.S. 716, containing, as it did, much that was contrary to what, both in teaching and practice, I had hitherto supposed to be settled law.")

5. *See O'Neill v. Kilduff*, 81 Conn. 116, 70 A. 640, 642 (1908). ("Our state early adopted as a part of its common law the broad principle of public policy that "every man should pay his debts with his estate, be it what it will be, either real or personal," and, if his estate be insufficient to pay all creditors, each one shall have a "suitable proportion to his debt." This principle has influenced the course of our legislation and judicial decisions in respect to insolvency and underlies our statute against fraudulent conveyances as well as against preference of creditors with a view to insolvency. It is in view of this principle that our statute against fraudulent conveyances, first enacted in 1702, has been construed, extended, and applied. *Curtis v. Lewis*, 74 Conn. 368, 50 Atl. 878; 1 Swift's Dig. 266, 281, 282; *Trumbull v. Hewitt*, 62 Conn 448, 455, 26 Atl. 350. Our law is now settled that a voluntary conveyance by an insolvent is void as against his creditors as obnoxious to the principles of our common law and to the construction we have given to our statute against fraudulent conveyances. *Quinnipiac Brewing co. v. Fitzgibbons*, 71 Conn. 80, 85, 40 Atl. 913, and cases there cited; *Whittlesey v. McMahon*, 10 Conn. 138, 142, 26 Am. Dec. 389; *Abbe v. Newton*, 19 Conn. 20, 27; *Clarke v. Black*, 78 Conn. 467, 471, 62 Atl. 757.")

6. *See* Judy v. Judy, 742 S.E.2d 672 (2013). ("Actual moral fraud involves "a conscious intent to defeat, delay, or hinder [one's] creditors in the collection of their debts." First Carolinas Joint Stock Land Bank of Columbia v. Knotts, 191 S.C. 384, 409, 1 S.E.2d 797, 808 (1939).")

borrowers and guarantors could simply rearrange their assets to avoid paying debts. In 1888, the Supreme Court acknowledged the role fraudulent transfer law plays in promoting the extension of credit:

> The object of the statute of Elizabeth was to prevent debtors from dealing with their property in any way to the prejudice of their creditors; but dealing with that which creditors, irrespective of such dealing, could not have touched, is within neither the letter nor the spirit of the statute. In the view of the law, credit is extended in reliance upon the evidence of the ability of the debtor to pay, and in confidence that his possessions will not be diminished to the prejudice of those who trust him. This reliance is disappointed, and this confidence abused, if he divests himself of his property by giving it away after he has obtained credit.[7]

At the time of *Hume*, it was not commonplace for individuals to tie up wealth for their own benefit in asset protection trusts and for good reason—as self-settled spendthrift trusts were not permitted.[8] Importantly, *Hume* involved a situation where a debtor-creditor relationship was already established; it did not venture into the more controversial matter of the rights of future creditors.

In 2004, the Wisconsin Supreme Court similarly acknowledged, "[t]he Uniform Fraudulent Transfer Act reflects a strong desire to protect creditors and to allow for the smooth functioning of our credit-based society. It is a creditor-protection statute. Without such protection for creditors, '[c]reditors would generally be unwilling to assume the risk of the debtor's fraudulent transfers.'"[9]

Fraudulent transfer remedies help support a strong system of credit by preventing debtors from cheating creditors.[10] These remedies also support the

7. *Cent. Nat. Bank v. Hume*, 128 U.S. 195, 203–04, 9 S. Ct. 41, 43–44, 32 L. Ed. 370 (1888).

8. *See, e.g.*, *Mackason's Appeal*, 42 Pa. 330, 338-39 (1862); *Ghormley v. Smith*, 139 Pa. 584, 591 (1891); *Patrick v. Smith*, 2 Pa. Super. 113, 119 (Super. Ct. 1896).

9. *See Badger State Bank v. Taylor*, 2004 WI 128, ¶ 41, 276 Wis. 2d 312, 330, 688 N.W.2d 439, 448. *See also*, Frank R. Kennedy, *Involuntary Fraudulent Transfers*, 9 Cardozo L. Rev. 531 (1987). ("If an economic system employing credit is to function efficiently, creditors must be able to enforce obligations assumed by or imposed on their debtors. The law of fraudulent and preferential transfers consists of rules that have developed to enable creditors to enforce the duty of a debtor to be fair to all creditors.") *See also*, Arthur Joseph Hunt, in his English treatise *The Law Relating to Fraudulent Conveyances, Under the Statutes of Elizabeth, The Bankruptcy Acts, and the Voluntary Conveyances Act*, Second Edition, 1897, noted the tension between an individual's ability to transfer wealth versus the rights of creditors, "[w]hile it is not the policy of the law to hamper the transfer of property, or restrain, or in any manner interfere with the free and unlimited exercise of the rights of every one to deal with his own as he pleases and in his own way, due regard being had to public rights and interests, yet the law will not permit transfers to be made in violation of the rights of creditors. A man must be just to his creditors before he is generous to those who are nearer to him by ties of relationship. Hence it is that the law will not permit a debtor who is insolvent to purchase property and pay for the same, and have the title conveyed to his infant son, leaving creditors unpaid, and if he does so, such property may be reached and applied to the satisfaction of debts due his creditors.")

10. *See Schmidt v. HSC, Inc.*, 136 Haw. 158, 165, 358 P.3d 727, 734 (Ct. App. 2015). ("The purpose of the UFTA is to stop a debtor from deliberately cheating a creditor by placing property beyond his or her reach." *See, e.g.*, *Gilchinsky v. Nat'l Westminster Bank* N.J., 159 N.J. 463, 732 A.2d 482, 488 (1999).) *See also*, *Warchol v. Dynamic Control Int'l, Inc.*, No. 322029, 2015 WL 6161709, at *3 (Mich. Ct. App. Oct. 20, 2015). ("The Uniform Fraudulent Transfer Act reflects a strong desire to protect creditors and to allow for the smooth functioning of our credit-based society. It is a creditor-protection statute. Without such protection for creditors, '[c]reditors would generally be unwilling to assume the risk of the debtor's fraudulent transfers.'")

nation's collection of revenue, as the IRS may turn to fraudulent transfer law remedies in its attempt to enforce revenue laws. The ability for some to avoid paying their fair share of taxes was recently highlighted by controversies involving taxes paid (or not paid) by the ultra wealthy. The U.S. Senate conducted a hearing on the so-called tax gap, where Senator Sheldon Whitehouse identified a difference between taxes owed and taxes collected—to the tune of $441 billion per year.[11] However, IRS Commissioner Charles Rettig testified this amount was more like $1 trillion in recent years. The reason for such a large discrepancy was due, in part, to wealth transferred (and hidden) offshore.

In addition to the long-standing principle that those who owe must pay, there has been bipartisan support for measures to prevent wealthier debtors from achieving results not available to their less wealthy counterparts. For instance, Republican Governor Nathan Deal rejected Georgia's adoption of asset protection trust legislation due to the potential negative impact on the economy.[12] Democrat Senator Elizabeth Warren proposed consumer bankruptcy reform legislation, which is premised on, among other items, the fact that "well-counseled, affluent debtors can avoid repaying creditors through asset protection planning."[13]

Public policy varies quite widely at the state level. In some cases, lawmakers are, perhaps unwittingly, passing laws that weaken creditors' rights, including fraudulent transfer law. Often, these new laws overturn long-standing public policy that those who owe must pay. These relatively new laws may offer the opportunity for wealthy debtors to reduce federal and state taxes as well as avoid general creditors. Generally, states with higher gross domestic product (GDP) find their residents utilizing these debtor-friendly laws in lower GDP states, much to the dismay of general creditors as well as taxing authorities.[14] Even within the higher GDP states, legislation often pops up that significantly redefines property rights in various contexts. One such example is the trend for some non-community property states to allow for individuals to elect community property status to certain property to enable such individuals to achieve

11. Senator Whitehouse acknowledged that even though there might be disagreement between political parties on how to achieve fairness, both sides of the political aisle agree that those who owe must pay, especially in the current environment. "This is an important and timely hearing on the "tax gap" and the related role of offshore tax evasion. My Republican colleagues and I may disagree on what makes a fair tax code, but we very much agree that everyone should pay what they owe." (Emphasis added.)

12. *See* Governor Nathan Deal 2018 Veto Statements, available at https://nathandeal.georgia.gov/press-releases/2018-05-08/deal-issues-2018-veto-statements/. ("As a state, we want to ensure that the creditor-debtor relationship is an equitable one that facilitates economic prosperity and mobility, and self-settled spendthrift trusts—without proper safeguards—have the potential to negatively impact this balance. For the foregoing reasons, I VETO HB 441.")

13. Consumer Bankruptcy Reform Act of 2020, S. 4991, 116th Cong. § 101(a)(12)(2020). The proposed legislation would address such planning by "closing bankruptcy loopholes that allow the wealthy to exploit the bankruptcy process."

14. Some states may provide increased "privacy" as to transactions within the state, thereby attempting to prevent creditors with access to information. *See United States of America v. Delaware Department of Insurance*, No. 21-3008 (3rd Cir. Nov. 1, 2021)., where the State of Delaware argued state privacy laws prevented the IRS from discovery certain documents within the captive insurance division of Delaware's Department of Insurance. The IRS sought records with respect to a transaction of interest (micro-captive insurance) and its investigation of a promoter of the transaction.

a double step-up in basis on the death of one spouse. Not surprisingly, the IRS has refused to rule on whether individuals can achieve this result for federal tax purposes, at least in non-community property states that offer this community property election.[15] The pro-debtor legislation in certain states may significantly hinder a creditor's ability reach the assets pursuant to judgment enforcement measures, including relief under fraudulent transfer law.

15. *See* IRS Publication 555 (03/2020). ("The states of Tennessee and South Dakota have passed elective Community Property Laws. This publication does not address the federal tax treatment of income or property subject to the "community property" election.")

CHAPTER 3

# Uniform Acts

The first uniform law governing fraudulent transfers was the Uniform Fraudulent Conveyance Act (the UFCA), promulgated by the National Conference of Commissioners on Uniform State Laws in 1918.[1] The UFCA represented a codification of the "better" cases applying the Statute of 13 Elizabeth. Notwithstanding the adoption of a uniform act, as will be seen throughout this book, the fraudulent transfer common law did not disappear and continues to assist with the interpretation of the fraudulent transfer statutes.[2] Further, causes of action may exist separately under the common law and are often pleaded along with causes of action under fraudulent transfer statutory law.

> DeYeso also argues that enactment of a statute by the post-Revolution Commonwealth abrogates prior English statutes and she traces the origins of fraudulent conveyance law back from the Uniform Fraudulent Transfer Act (UFTA), through the Uniform Fraudulent Conveyance Act (UFCA), to the Statute of Elizabeth, which was adopted by custom and usage into the common law of Massachusetts. *See* Pearce v. Atwood, 13 Mass. 324, 354 (1816) (preexisting English statutes are repealed when Legislature enacts similar statute). DeYeso's chronology appears to be correct. See Kennedy, The Uniform Fraudulent Transfer Act, 18 UCC L.J. 195, 196, 200 (1986) ("The [UFCA] was a codification of the 'better' decisions applying the Statute of 13 Elizabeth of 1571" and "[t]he basic structure and approach of [UFCA] are preserved in [UFTA]"). *See also* Drake v. Rice, 130 Mass. 410, 412–413 (1881) (noting 13 Eliz., c. 5, applies in Massachusetts and was "but declaratory of the law as it was before"). However, Cavadi's claim is not a common-law claim of fraudulent conveyance that would be, in part, a

1. The National Conference of Commissioners on Uniform State Laws (NCCUSL) changed its name over time. All references herein to the NCCUSL will be to the Uniform Law Commission (ULC).

2. *In re* Seitz, 400 B.R. 707, 713 n.8 (Bankr. E.D. Mo. 2008) ("The Missouri fraudulent transfer statute (an enactment of the Uniform Fraudulent Transfer Act (the "UFTA")) was enacted August 28, 1992 and consists of Mo.Rev.Stat. §§428.005-428.059. Prior to the enactment of the UFTA, the Missouri fraudulent transfer law was codified at the substantively similar Mo.Rev.Stat. §428.020. Much of the pre-UFTA case law remains applicable on the issues related to fraudulent transfers, including the application of the badges of fraud, and often is cited without distinction between pre-UFTA and UFTA circumstances.")

> creature of English statute. Rather, Cavadi's claim is a creditor's bill that is a creation of the Courts of Chancery and does not originate in an English statute. DeYeso's argument is thus beside the point.[3]

Currently, forty-five states have adopted the UFTA (promulgated by the ULC in 1984) with or without further amendments effected by the UVTA, and some states retained their own statutes, such as South Carolina, which is modeled after the Statute of 13 Elizabeth.[4]

South Carolina's fraudulent transfer statute, Section 27-23-10 entitled, "Conveyances to defraud creditors; transfers of income and property to avoid paying child support" immediately precedes its statute addressing defrauding purchasers, Section 27-23-20 which is also modeled after 27 Elizabeth c. 4. Surprisingly to some, South Carolina Statute Section 27-23-30, entitled "Punishment of parties to fraudulent conveyances" reflects the *penal element* of fraudulent transfer law. Instead of "amounts paid to the crown," amounts due under the South Carolina statute would be payable to the State. Further, like the Statute of 13 Elizabeth, the South Carolina statute contemplates incarceration.

> All parties to such feigned, covinous and fraudulent gifts, grants, leases, charges or conveyances, or being privy to and knowing of them, or any of them, who shall wittingly or willingly put in use, avow, maintain, justify or defend them, or any of them, as true, simple and done, had or made bona fide or upon good consideration, of or to the disturbance or hindrance of the purchaser or purchasers, lessees or grantees, their heirs, successors, executors, administrators or assigns or such as have or shall lawfully claim anything by, from or under them, or any of them, <u>shall incur the penalty and forfeiture of one year's value of such lands, tenements and hereditaments so purchased or charged, the one moiety whereof shall be for the use of the State and the other moiety to the party or parties grieved by such feigned and fraudulent gift, grant, lease, conveyance, encumbrance or limitation of use, to be recovered by action in any court of competent jurisdiction; and also, being thereof lawfully convicted, shall suffer imprisonment for one-half year</u>.

---

3. *Cavadi v. DeYeso*, 458 Mass. 615, 629, 941 N.E.2d 23, 35 (2011).

4. South Carolina's version of the Statute of 13 Elizabeth obviously does not contain the penal provision payable to the Crown, but does recite an amount payable to the State. Louisiana permits creditors to bring a revocatory action to void transfers. *See Colbert v. Brennan*, United States District Court, E.D. Louisiana. (June 21, 2013.) ("Under Louisiana law, the revocatory action is the "civil law analogue to the common lawsuit to set aside a fraudulent conveyance." LA. CIV. CODE art. 2036 cmt. (c). Article 2036 states that "[a]n obligee has a right to annul an act of the obligor, or the result of a failure to act of the obligor, made or effected after the right of the obligee arose, that causes or increases the obligor's insolvency." Thus, in order for an obligee to annul an act of the obligor, the obligee must establish two elements: (1) an act or failure to act on the part of the obligor that causes or increases the obligor's insolvency; and (2) that the act occurred after the obligor's rights arose. *See Parish Nat'l Bank v. Wilks*, 04-1439 (La. App. 1 Cir. 8/3/05); 923 So.2d 8, 10. As such, "anteriority of the debt and insolvency of the debtor are prerequisites to the revocatory action." LA. CIV. CODE art. 2036 cmt. (f); *see also Lewis v. Hood*, 97-2118 (La. App. 1 Cir. 11/6/98); 721 So.2d 1078, 1080. For purposes of the revocatory action, "[a]n obligor is insolvent when the total of his liabilities exceeds the total of his fairly appraised assets." LA. CIV. CODE ANN. art. 2037.)

These penal roots are important to remember when viewing remedies granted in especially offensive fraudulent transfer cases. Given the historic criminal roots associated with defrauding creditors, it is not unusual to see courts impose secondary liability on those who assist with the "commission" of a fraudulent transfer, as well as disciplinary action against lawyers for their role. As will be seen herein, the degree of exposure for parties associated with effectuating a fraudulent transfer will depend heavily on the facts and circumstances surrounding the transaction.

## Characterization

A fraudulent transfer action may be characterized as sounding in tort or contract, as either an action at law or equity,[5] or as either a substantive or remedial cause of action. The ultimate characterization, in turn, may determine the choice of law, the right to a jury trial, as well as when and how the fraudulent transfer action may be brought.

The characterization of a fraudulent transfer as an action at law or equity will depend on the relief requested. The Supreme Court noted this distinction in *Granfinanciera v. Nordberg*, where the issue was whether a person who did not submit a claim against a bankruptcy estate had a Seventh Amendment right to a jury trial when sued by the trustee in bankruptcy to recover an allegedly fraudulent monetary transfer. The Supreme Court found the relief requested, a monetary judgment, to be legal in nature, thereby guaranteeing the transferee a right to a jury trial.

> Indeed, in our view *Schoenthal v. Irving Trust Co.*, 287 U.S. 92, 53 S.Ct. 50, 77 L.Ed. 185 (1932), removes all doubt that respondent's cause of action should be characterized as legal rather than as equitable. In *Schoenthal*, the trustee in bankruptcy sued in equity to recover alleged preferential payments, claiming that he had no adequate remedy at law. As in this case, the recipients of the payments apparently did not file claims against the bankruptcy estate. The Court held that the suit had to proceed at law instead, because the long-settled rule that suits in equity will not be sustained where a complete remedy exists at law, then codified at 28 U.S.C. §384, "serves to guard the right of trial by jury preserved by the Seventh Amendment and to that end it

5. *See* David Gray Carlson, Fraudulent Transfers: Void and Voidable, 29 Am. Bankr. Inst. L. Rev. 1, 4 (2021). ("At the heart of the procedure attendant to fraudulent transfers is a stubborn ambiguity. Hearkening back to the days when law and equity were the provinces of different courts, law courts and equity courts virulently disagreed on the nature of a fraudulent transfer. 'Law' (Esau to equity's Jacob) viewed fraudulent transfers as void ab initio. On this view, a fraudulent transfer is not a transfer at all, at least insofar as C is concerned. C could treat X's thing as if it were still D's thing. C's judicial lien attached to X's thing accordingly. Equity, however, viewed fraudulent transfers as 'voidable.' On this view, when D fraudulently transfers a thing to X, D's act of alienation is complete. D no longer has any title in the item transferred. Rather, X has title. X, however, holds the property in trust for the creditors of C. The conveyance being fraudulent, C is invited to have the conveyance set aside. What once was D's property is D's property again, and C is able to obtain the coveted judicial lien on X's thing. The lien implies that C may liquidate X's thing in order to satisfy C's judgment against D. Thus, to the law lords, a fraudulent transfer is no transfer. It is void. It never happened. To the chancellor, the transfer is absolutely effective until it is avoided or "set aside."")

> should be liberally construed." 287 U.S., at 94, 53 S.Ct., at 51. The Court found that the trustee's suit indistinguishable from respondent's suit in all relevant respects could not go forward in equity because an adequate remedy was available at law. There, as here, "[t]he preferences sued for were money payments of ascertained and definite amounts," and "[t]he bill discloses no facts that call for an accounting or other equitable relief." *Id.*, at 95, 53 S.Ct., at 51. Respondent's fraudulent conveyance action plainly seeks relief traditionally provided by law courts or on the law side of courts having both legal and equitable dockets. Unless Congress may and has permissibly withdrawn jurisdiction over that action by courts of law and assigned it exclusively to non-Article III tribunals sitting without juries, the Seventh Amendment guarantees petitioners a jury trial upon request.[6]

Justice White dissented, finding the decision "calls into question several of our previous decisions, strikes down at least one federal statute, and potentially concludes for the first time that the Seventh Amendment guarantees litigants in a specialized non-Article III forum the right to a jury trial."[7] Justice White believed the analysis should turn on both the nature of the claim *and the forum*, citing Supreme Court precedent in describing bankruptcy courts to be "by their very nature, courts of equity" and "forums in which a jury would be out of place."[8]

It is worth noting the decision's extensive amount of historical research pointing to secondary sources in the 1800's. As will be shown throughout this book, reference to legal history is necessary to fully understand the application of fraudulent transfer statutory law given its deep roots in the common law.[9]

While some courts may assume a default characterization for a fraudulent transfer action as legal in nature, that default determination may change based

---

6. *Granfinanciera v. Nordberg*, 492 U.S. 33, 109 S.Ct. 2782, 106 L.Ed.2d 26, 19 BCD 493 (1989).

7. *Id.*

8. *Id.*

9. The majority countered Justice White's assertion that fraudulent transfer relief is equitable in nature. ("This assertion, however, lacks the support it claims. With the exception of Justice Gray's opinion in *Drake v. Rice*, 130 Mass. 410, 412 (1881), and Roberts' treatise, none of the authorities cited so much as mentions 18th-century English practice. Although Collier offers as its opinion that actions to set aside fraudulent transfers are equitable in nature, 4 Collier on Bankruptcy ¶ 548.10, p. 548-125 (15th ed. 1989), it refers only to recent cases in defending its opinion, while acknowledging that some courts have disagreed. Bump and Wait both limit their citations to state-court decisions, refusing to analyze earlier English cases. *See* O. Bump, Conveyances Made by Debtors to Defraud Creditors §532 (4th ed. 1896); F. Wait, Fraudulent Conveyances and Creditors' Bills §§56-60 (1884). To be sure, in Drake v. Rice, 130 Mass., at 412, Justice Gray says that, "[b]y the law of England before the American Revolution, . . . fraudulent conveyances of choses in action, though not specified in the statute [of Elizabeth], were equally void, but from the nature of the subject the remedy of the creditor must be sought in equity." But the reason why suits to recover fraudulent transfers of choses in action had to be brought in equity, Justice Gray points out, is that they could not be attached or levied upon. *Id.*, at 413. *See also* O. Bump, *supra*, §531 ("[T]here is no remedy at law when the property can not be taken on execution or by attachment"). Justice Gray's summary of 18th-century English practice does not extend to cases, such as those involving monetary transfers, where an adequate remedy existed at law. The passage Justice White cites from Roberts' treatise is obscure and does not speak squarely to the question whether 18th-century English courts of equity would hear cases where legal remedies were sufficient." *See* W. Roberts, Voluntary and Fraudulent Conveyances 526-527 (3d Am. ed. 1845).) *Granfinanciera v. Nordberg*, 492 U.S. 33, 109 S.Ct. 2782, 106 L.Ed.2d 26, 19 BCD 493 (1989).

on the actual relief requested.[10] It follows that courts may consider a fraudulent transfer action as one in equity where the goal is to restore a creditor to pre-transaction status involving title to real property.[11]

Finally, one should not ignore any other relief requested in conjunction with monetary relief under a fraudulent transfer action. If the creditor seeks intertwined legal and equitable remedies, a court may choose to characterize all relief as legal to preserve constitutional rights.

> Regarding Plaintiff's fraudulent transfer claims that reference Defendant Fenwall, Counts XVII and XVIII, the Supreme Court has determined that courts of law and equity had concurrent jurisdiction over fraudulent transfer claims in 18th-century England, depending on the nature of the subject matter of the lawsuit. *Granfinanciera*, 492 U.S. at 43-44. In this case, the remedies sought by Plaintiff in relation to the alleged fraudulent transfer of tangible and intangible property—including avoidance, attachment and execution, and injunctive relief—are arguably equitable. However, the facts necessary to establish the fraudulent transfer claims are intertwined with those set forth in Plaintiff's request for declaratory judgment. (Doc. 105 at 30-34, ¶¶ 162-176, 177, 182). *See* Lincoln v. Board. of Regents of University Univ. System Sys. of Georgia., 697 F. 2d 928, 934 (11th Cir. 1983) ("When legal and equitable actions are tried together, the right to a jury in the legal action encompasses the issues common to both."). Therefore, the undersigned recommends the Court find that Defendant Fenwall retains a right to trial by jury on the issues common to both the declaratory judgment claim (Count XVI) and the fraudulent transfer claims (Counts XVII and XVIII).[12]

---

10. *See Schaufenbuel v. InvestForClosures Fin., L.L.C.*, No. 09 C 1221, 2009 WL 10699766, at *2–3 (N.D. Ill. Aug. 5, 2009). ("Plaintiffs' citation to the Illinois Uniform Fraudulent Transfer Act (IUFTA) does not seem to help their cause because "[a]ctions to recover fraudulent transfers, even when based on a modern statute, are deemed actions at law, though the ultimate classification depends on what remedies the plaintiff requests." *In re Teknek, LLC v. Hamilton*, 343 B.R. 850, 868-69 (Bankr. N.D. Ill. 2006). Suits to recover fraudulent conveyances are actions at law if the plaintiff is attempting to recover a cash/money judgment. *Id.* at 869. Because Plaintiffs do not detail the final forms of relief they request under the IUFTA, the Court declines to conclude on the current record that their fraudulent conveyance claim seeks equitable relief.") *See also*, *Hitachi Med. Sys. Am., Inc. v. Branch*, 2010 WL 3941824, at *6 (N.D. Ohio Sept. 14, 2010), *report and recommendation adopted*, 2010 WL 3941912 (N.D. Ohio Oct. 7, 2010), citing Shorten v. Woodrow, 34 Ohio St. 645, 649, 1878 WL 71 (Ohio 1878.) ("It should first be noted that an action to set aside a fraudulent transfer is equitable in nature.")

11. *See Van v. Asset Ventures, LLC*, No. 215CV01401JADPAL, 2015 WL 13424530, at *3 (D. Nev. Sept. 8, 2015). ("The Ninth Circuit expressly 'restricted' its holding in Estate of Ferdinand Marcos to 'only extraordinary cases in which equitable relief is not sought.' But the Vans seek equitable relief with their fraudulent transfer claim: to void and rescind the transfer of real property in Virginia from Asset Ventures to JBY. As the Nevada Supreme Court recently explained in *Cadle Co. v. Woods & Erickson, LLP*, '[c]reditors do not possess legal claims for damages when they are victims of fraudulent transfers. Instead, creditors have recourse in equitable proceedings in order to recover the property, or payment for its value, by which they are returned to their pre-transfer position.' 'Nevada's fraudulent transfer statute creates equitable remedies including avoidance, attachment, and, subject to principles of equity and the rules of civil procedure, injunction, receivership, or other relief.' Because the Vans seek equitable relief with their fraudulent transfer claim, the narrow holding of Estate of Ferdinand Marcos does not apply in this action.")

12. Bank of America, N.A., Plaintiff, v. Florida Glass of Tampa Bay, Inc., et al., Defendants. Additional Party Names: Am. Prod. Prod. Co. of Pinellas Cty., Inc., Fenwall, LLC, Joseph C. Muraco, Kevin T. Mullan, Muraco & Mullan Properties, Inc., Lynmar Commerce Park Ass'n, Inc., No. 8:16-CV-02104-27AAS, 2017 WL 11017883, at *8–9 (M.D. Fla. Aug. 18, 2017).

## Procedural Issues

Relief under the fraudulent transfer act may be sought either before or after a judgment.[13] A party's rights to transferred property might turn on whether a transfer was void or voidable as well as applicable law.[14] Whether a creditor has been injured will require looking at the elements under either an actual or constructive fraud argument, and the relief afforded may be dependent upon the creditor's position in the litigation process.

> Finally, although the failure to demonstrate insolvency is fatal to Residents' fraudulent transfer claim insofar as it is based on constructive fraud, the District Court erred in dismissing this claim insofar as it is based on actual fraud, which the District Court noted does not require a showing of insolvency. *Compare* Cal. Civ. Code §3439.04(a) (actual) with *id.* §3439.05 (constructive) and Del. Code Ann. tit. 6, §1304(a) (actual) with *id.*, §1305 (constructive). It is undisputed that CC-PA has previously required financial infusions from CC-DG in order to satisfy debts and that CC-DG has also disclaimed a duty to repay outgoing residents their owed refunds. Residents are not in privity with CC-DG, but with CC-PA. Residents are prejudiced by the transfer of funds to an entity beyond their reach and the resulting insecurity that they may not be repaid when owed. *See Mehrtash v. Mehrtash*, 112 Cal. Rptr. 2d 802, 805 (Cal. Ct. App. 2001) ("It cannot be said that a creditor has been injured unless the transfer puts beyond her reach property she otherwise would be able to subject to the payment of her debt.") (*citations omitted and alterations accepted*). Although Residents may not be able to demonstrate monetary loss at this juncture, they may still be entitled to an order limiting future transfers or other equitable relief. *See* Cal. Civ. Code §3439.07; Del. Code Ann. tit. 6, §1307; *see also* Cal. Civ. Code §3439.01(b) (noting that a claim "means a right to payment, whether or not the right is . . . fixed, contingent, matured, unmatured, disputed, undisputed, legal, equitable, secured, or unsecured"); Del. Code Ann. tit. 6, §1301(3) (same). We express no opinion as to the merits of Residents' actual fraud claim, but

---

13. *American Surety Co. v. Conner*, 251 N.Y. 1, 7 (N.Y. 1929) ("We think the effect of these provisions is to abrogate the ancient rule whereby a judgment and a lien were essential preliminaries to equitable relief against a fraudulent conveyance. The Uniform Act has been so read in other States ( Gross v. Penn. Mtg. Co., 101 N.J. Eq. 51; United Stores Realty Corp. v. Asea, [N.J.] 142 Atl. Rep. 38; Morse v. Roach, 229 Mich. 538; Lipskey v. Voloshen, 155 Md. 139).")

14. *See Matter of Hardin*, No. AP 19-05221-LRC, 2021 WL 4484875, at *8 (Bankr. N.D. Ga. Sept. 30, 2021). ("Professor Carlson posits that the void nature of fraudulent transfers and the ability of a judicial lien creditor to ignore the fact that the debtor conveyed property to a third party is inherent in the Uniform Fraudulent Conveyance Act, which provides a remedy to creditors with a matured claim—the option to "[d] isregard the conveyance and attach or levy execution upon the property conveyed." Carlson, at 11. He concludes that transfers under the UFTA, and now the UVTA, are both "void" and "voidable," as the more modern uniform law retained the remedy of disregarding the transfer. He notes, however, that a court must now order a levy against the transferee's property, supporting the argument that such transfers are merely voidable. Id.; see also UNIF. VOIDABLE TRANSACTIONS ACT §7(b) (Unif. L. Comm'n 2014) ("If a creditor has obtained a judgment on a claim against the debtor, the creditor, if the court so orders, may levy execution on the asset transferred or its proceeds."); O.C.G.A. §18-2-77(b).")

simply hold that it was error to dismiss this claim at summary judgment on the basis that Residents failed to demonstrate harm.[15]

Where a purported creditor has not yet filed a lawsuit articulating a right to payment, issues arise as to whether a "claim" exists that would permit seeking relief under fraudulent transfer law. Here, the purported creditor may seek provisional relief (such as an injunction) to prevent dissipation of assets prior to a lawsuit. Generally, where prejudgment relief has been requested, the purported creditor will need to show a reasonable likelihood of success on the merits of the case. This will require looking at the underlying substantive action that gives rise to a claim and thus, the fraudulent transfer action (e.g., breach of contract.)[16] Although the Supreme Court ruled in *Grupo Mexicano de Desarrollo, S. A. v. Alliance Bond Fund, Inc.*, that a prejudgment asset freezing order was not permissible under federal common law, such provisional relief may be awarded under fraudulent transfer law.

In the case of pre-suit relief, equitable remedies may protect a creditor until the underlying claim has been adjudicated. As reflected in *Burkhart v. Genworth Financial, Inc.*, this scenario may require the creditor to show the existence of a tort or contract that creates a debtor-creditor relationship, and satisfy state law requirements for injunctive relief.

Under TUFTA, the trial court may find substantial likelihood of success on the merits when it is "presented with evidence of intent to defraud the

15. Linda C. Cork, et al., Plaintiffs-Appellants, v. CC-Palo ALTO, Inc, et al., Defendants-Appellees,. Additional Party Names: CC-Dev. Grp., Inc., Classic Residence Mgmt. Ltd. P'ship, No. 19-15441, 2020 WL 3046720, at *3 (9th Cir. June 8, 2020)

16. *See Burkhart v Genworth Financial, Inc.*, No. 2018-0691-JRS, 2019 WL 6218633, at *1 (Del.Ch. Nov. 20, 2019), where the Vice-Chancellor denied a Status Quo Order, which was essentially a request for a preliminary injunction. *See also*, Defendant's Brief explaining why the Status Quo Order should be denied. Richard F. Burkhart, William E. Kelly, Richard S. Lavery, Thomas R. Pratt and Gerald Green, individually and on behalf of all others similarly situated, Plaintiffs, v. Genworth Financial, Inc., Genworth Holdings, Inc., Genworth North America Corporation, Genworth Financial International Holdings, LLC and Genworth Life Insurance Company, Defendants., 2019 WL 5864431 (Del.Ch.) ("As shown in the Defendants' briefing, courts consistently dismiss claims under the UFTA when plaintiffs fail to plead an actual or imminent injury in fact. See Reply in Support of Motion to Dismiss at 6-8. While these dismissals (properly) were based on a lack of standing, none of them would have been granted if the courts believed that an "increased risk" of future non-payment on a contingent claim constitutes a legally cognizable claim under UFTA. Cf., e.g., Infant Swimming Research, Inc. v. Faegre & Benson, LLP, 335 F. App'x 707 (10th Cir. 2009); Barry v. Bryan, 2017 WL 5973352, at *2 (D. Minn. Mar. 31, 2017).6 Jurisprudence in other areas also rejects risk-based theories of standing. These "risk-based theories of standing ... rest on a highly speculative foundation lacking any discernible limiting principle." David v. Alphin, 704 F.3d 327, 338 (4th Cir. 2013); Williams v. Lew, 819 F.3d 466, 473 (D.C. Cir. 2016); Taylor v. Bernanke, 2013 WL 4811222, at *6 (E.D.N.Y. Sept. 9, 2013). Thus complaints alleging "increased risk" of future default based on the alleged inadequacy of life insurance reserves have been dismissed for failure to allege a current injury.7 The Fourth Circuit has rejected claims that an increased risk of future identity theft is an actual or imminent injury, finding it to be based on "the same 'attenuated chain of possibilities' rejected by the Court in Clapper." Beck v. McDonald, 848 F.3d 262, 275 (4th Cir. 2017). ERISA and RICO decisions also have rejected "increased risk" as a cognizable claim. Krauter v. Siemens Corp., 725 F. App'x 102, 108 (3d Cir. 2018) ("a risk of future adverse effects on benefits is not an injury in fact"). Plaintiffs' "novel theory of injury," based on their allegedly taking on "additional risk," is not only incorrect but also "a prescription for ceaseless litigation." First Nationwide Bank v. Gelt Funding Corp., 820 F. Supp. 89, 94 (S.D.N.Y. 1993), aff'd, 27 F.3d 763 (2d Cir. 1994) (RICO action). The Defendants request the Court to decline Plaintiffs' argument to adopt this novelty here.")

creditor." *See* Tanguy v. Laux, 259 S.W.3d 851, 858 (Tex. App.–Houston [1st Dist.] 2008, no pet.); Tel. Equip. Network, Inc., 80 S.W.3d at 609. Therefore, we conclude the temporary injunction was not an improper pre-suit attachment of property. We overrule Rocklon's first issue and affirm the order of the trial court granting temporary injunction.[17]

Precisely how the fraudulent transfer action should be brought depends on applicable local law. Not surprisingly, parties might dispute the appropriate process for seeking fraudulent transfer relief.

Defendants argue that NobelBiz is prohibited from making a claim for fraudulent transfer in post-judgment proceedings. *Id.* at 7. Defendants state that, under Utah law, a claim of fraudulent transfer must be brought in its own civil action. *Id.* Defendants claim that they must be afforded the full scope of due-process rights that accompany a civil action when defending a claim of fraudulent transfer. *Id.* at 8. Therefore, Defendants' argue, it is inappropriate to make a claim for fraudulent transfer in these abbreviated post-trial motions. *Id.*[18]

Parties have disputed whether the fraudulent transfer law provides a substantive right, and if not, whether its use is prohibited unless an underlying substantive claim is brought.[19] An example of this scenario is the leveraged buyout.

We see no force in the argument that UFCA is inapplicable because it confers no substantive rights. It does not. It is not intended to. What plaintiffs seek by use of UFCA is not the substantive right of a claim as creditor, but a remedy to assist in the satisfaction of that substantive claim.[20]

A court is more likely to provide pre-suit relief if a relationship between the parties exists either under contract or due to the commission of a tort. If relief is not permitted, it may be that the statute begins to run to the detriment of the creditor.

---

17. *Rocklon, LLC v. Paris*, No. 09-16-00070-CV, 2016 WL 6110911, at *14 (Tex. App. Oct. 20, 2016).

18. NOBELBIZ, INC., Plaintiff, v. GLOBAL CONNECT, L.L.C., Defendant. NOBELBIZ, INC., Plaintiff,, No. 6:12-CV-244, 2017 WL 11190016, at *4 (E.D. Tex. Feb. 7, 2017).

19. See Janik v. City of Dallas, No. CIV.A.3:95-CV-2594-D, 1998 WL 292368, at *3–4 (N.D. Tex. May 26, 1998), aff'd sub nom. Janik v. City of Dallas, Texas, 226 F.3d 641 (5th Cir. 2000), and aff'd sub nom. Janik v. City of Dallas, TX, 226 F.3d 641 (5th Cir. 2000). ("Finally, the IAS/Nobel defendants move for summary judgment as to plaintiffs' claim based on the Texas Uniform Fraudulent Transfer Act ("TUFTA"), Tex. Bus. & Com.Code Ann. §§24.001–.012 (West 1987 & Supp.1998). Defendants assert that TUFTA does not appear to provide an independent cause of action and that TUFTA is inapplicable because plaintiffs and defendants are not in a debtor/creditor relationship. The court disagrees. *4 Plaintiffs may bring a cause of action under TUFTA "merely by virtue of a legal action, pending and unliquidated at the time of transfer, against the transferor." Colonial Leasing Co. of New Eng., Inc. v. Logistics Control Group Int'l, 762 F.2d 454, 458 (5th Cir.1985) (citing Hollins v. Rapid Transit Lines, Inc., 440 S.W.2d 57, 59–60 (Tex.1969)). TUFTA applies to tort claimants. They may maintain an action to set aside a fraudulent transfer "regardless of whether or not his claim has been by judgment reduced to a liquidated and definite amount in dollars and cents." Hollins, 440 S. W.2d at 59.7 The court denies summary judgment as to this claim.")

20. *Int'l Ass'n of Machinists & Aerospace Workers, IAM Local 437 v. U.S. Can Co.*, 150 Wis. 2d 479, 496–98, 441 N.W.2d 710, 718–19 (1989).

> It has been held under statutory enactment allowing a simple creditor to set aside a fraudulent conveyance that the statute of limitations runs from the time the creditor could first assail it. **668 Combs v. Watson, 32 Ohio St. 228; Ramsey v. Quillen, 73 Tenn. 184, 5 Lea 184. We do not think these cases should be followed because they bring about a result entirely inconsistent with the underlying *41 objective of the uniform act, which is to enhance and not impair the remedies of the creditor. Why should the creditor be compelled in every case to commence suit against the grantee to set aside a transfer under penalty of having the statute of limitations run until he is certain of being one in fact? Often the asserted claim against the principal obligor might well be uncertain, and even speculative, or at least one in which the amount of recovery is very uncertain. A construction should not be adopted compelling a creditor who claims to be such to institute proceedings of this nature until the debtor's liability has been established by final judicial determination. It is apparent that such compulsion will exist in many cases if the creditor cannot proceed by the old method. In many cases, the third-party grantee will be saved the burden of defending a suit by one whose cause of action failed against his grantor.[21]

Particularly offensive fraudulent transfers have been viewed as legal wrongs; this quasi-tort characterization may transform a fraudulent transfer into a cause of action which can support a claim of conspiracy or aiding and abetting against those who assist with such transfers, described in more detail in chapter nine. However, in these cases, the fraudulent transfer typically occurs near or after the commencement of a lawsuit. Post-judgment characterization as a quasi-tort makes even more sense because the transfer of assets to hinder judgment creditors is considered either a misdemeanor or felony in some states, although some states do not distinguish between judgment and post-judgment creditor status. The characterization of a fraudulent transfer may also be relevant for choice of law purposes, discussed in chapter five.

Remember, any creditor of the debtor may bring a claim for relief. Consequently, a situation may arise where one creditor may seek relief thanks to the existence of another creditor. "Hartford has standing under the UFTA even though the alleged fraudulent transfer (the transfer of $400,000.00 into the Partnership) involved a different creditor, Mr. Crowe. In Perkins v. Brunger, the Tennessee Court of Appeals addressed standing requirements under the UFTA. 303 S.W.3d 688, 691 (Tenn. Ct. App. 2009). In Perkins, the court recognized that if a party qualifies as a creditor (before or after the alleged fraudulent transfer), that party has standing to challenge any alleged fraudulent transfer involving a creditor, *even if the fraudulent transfer involved a different creditor.* In other words, if Hartford currently qualifies as a creditor, it may assert a claim under the UFTA even though the alleged fraudulent transfer involved a different creditor, Mr. Crowe."[22] Essentially, the existence of at least one creditor may trigger rights for any another creditor. A similar situation exists in

21. *Lind v. O.N. Johnson Co.*, 204 Minn. 30, 40–42, 282 N.W. 661, 667–68 (1938).

22. *Hartford Fire Ins. Co. v. CMC Construction Co.*, No. 3:06-CV-11, at *33 (E.D. Tenn. Aug. 24, 2010). (Emphasis added.)

bankruptcy, where a bankruptcy trustee may pursue a fraudulent transfer based on the existence of at least one unsecured creditor.[23]

Regardless of the requirements for bringing a claim for relief, generally, the elements must also be proven should be supported,[24] otherwise a creditor's claim for relief may be dismissed on summary judgment.

> The Court finds [the] Defendants' first point persuasive. It is unclear what exactly the Puntillos are claiming as fraudulent transfers. Instead, the Puntillos vaguely and generally assert that most everything related to Northridge had been transferred to Dave Knecht Homes, and that those transfers were likely fraudulent due to the judgment Northridge owed to the Puntillos. In other words, the Puntillos have merely restated the applicable rules as conclusions specific to the facts of this case. That does not suffice. See United States v. Thornton, 642 F.3d 599, 606 (7th Cir. 2011) ("Undeveloped and unsupported arguments may be deemed waived."). This Court is not obliged to research and construct legal arguments for the parties, especially when they are represented by counsel. Nelson v. Napolitano, 657 F.3d 586, 590 (7th Cir. 2011).
>
> *8 The Puntillos also briefly mention "the many transfers to the Knechts through the direct payment of personal expenses." (Pls.' Reply to Pls.' Mot. for Summ. J. at 5, Dkt. No. 84.) This point, however, was raised in Plaintiffs' reply brief. Since Defendants did not have an adequate opportunity to respond, the argument is waived. Judge, 612 F.3d at 542. It bears mentioning though that the specification is still undeveloped since the Puntillos do not do much by way of elaborating on its significance or relevance to the applicable standards. Summary judgment is the "put up or shut up moment" in litigation. *Johnson v. Cambridge Indus., Inc.*, 325 F.3d 892, 901 (7th Cir. 2003) (*citation omitted*). Plaintiffs have neither put up enough evidence nor

---

23. *See in re* Heritage Organization, L.L.C., 413 B.R. 438, 459-60 (Bankr. N.D. Tex. 2009) ("A trustee's right to avoid a transfer is derivative of an actual unsecured creditor's right and, therefore, to establish standing under §544(b), the Trustee must show the existence of an actual unsecured creditor holding an allowable claim that could avoid the challenged transfer. *See Ries v. Wintz Props., Inc.* (In re Wintz Cos.), 230 B.R. 848, 858-59 (8th Cir. BAP 1999) (citing *Sender v. Simon,* 84 F.3d 1299, 1304 (10th Cir.1996)); *Smith v. Am. Founders Fin., Corp.*, 365 B.R. 647, 659 (S.D.Tex.2007). While the Trustee must demonstrate the existence of this "golden creditor," *see Turner v. Phoenix Fin., LLC* (In re Imageset, Inc.), 299 B.R. 709, 715 (Bankr.D. Me.2003), the Trustee need not specifically identify the creditor by name; as long as the Trustee establishes that such unsecured creditors exist, he can assume the mantle of any one of them. *Leibowitz v. Parkway Bank & Trust Co.* (*In re* Image Worldwide, Ltd.), 139 F.3d 574, 577 (7th Cir.1998); *see also Stalnaker v. DLC, Ltd.* (In re DLC, Ltd.), 295 B.R. 593 (8th Cir. BAP 2003), *aff'd*, 376 F.3d 819 (8th Cir.2004). Only one triggering creditor is required, and the amount of its claim is unimportant. *Abramson v. Boedeker*, 379 F.2d 741, 748 n. 16 (5th Cir.1967) ("[I]f the transfer is avoidable at all by any creditor, it is avoidable in full for all creditors regardless of the dollar amount of the prevailing claim."); *Acequia, Inc. v. Clinton* (In re Acequia), 34 F.3d 800, 809-10 (9th Cir.1994). Moreover, the unsecured creditor need not exist at the time the avoidance action is filed, so long as that creditor existed on the date the bankruptcy petition was filed. *See*, e.g., In re DLC, Ltd., 295 B.R. at 605 ("we hold, as have other courts analyzing this issue, that the trustee must identify *See* a creditor with an allowable unsecured claim who had an allowable claim against the debtor on the date the bankruptcy petition was filed.") (citing Acequia, 34 F.3d 800, 807 (9th Cir.1994)).")

24. A court may relax the evidentiary requirements in situations involving self-settled trusts, as described more fully in chapter seven.

raised adequate arguments to establish that a reasonable jury could find that fraud in fact or fraud in law occurred. Defendants are thus entitled to judgment as a matter of law on Count I.[25]

# Actual Fraud

The UVTA provides three categories of avoidance provisions that give the creditor the ability to avoid transfers or obligations. The first category, sometimes referred to as fraud in fact, is where a debtor makes a transfer with the actual fraud to hinder, delay, or defraud any creditor of the debtor. The actual fraud analysis requires a creditor examine a debtor's state of mind when ascertaining whether a debtor had actual intent to hinder, delay, or defraud. "Under the framework set forth in MCL 566.34(1)(a) [Michigan's version of Section 4(a)], the debtor's state of mind in making a transfer determines whether a transfer qualifies as made with an actually fraudulent intent."[26] The phrase "hinder, delay, or defraud" is disjunctive, meaning a creditor does not need to show evidence of intent to defraud.[27]

Under this so-called primordial rule,[28] a creditor may use direct evidence (e.g., statements indicating the debtor's intent) or indirect evidence (e.g., timing of the transfer, solvency of the debtor, etc.) to prove a debtor made a transfer with the actual intent to hinder, delay, or defraud any creditor of the debtor.

Because direct evidence of actual fraud often is hard to obtain, creditors will resort to indirect evidence of actual fraud. Such indirect evidence has often involved the same hallmarks of fraud acknowledged in *Twyne's Case* and has been incorporated into the UVTA in Section 4(b). It is important, however, to note that the factors listed in UVTA Section 4(b), sometimes referred to as the "badges of fraud," are not exhaustive and other facts and circumstances may be considered.[29] Certain badges or factors have a tendency to routinely arise in

25. Anthony Puntillo & Mary Carol Puntillo, Plaintiffs, v. Dave Knecht Homes, LLC, David J. Knecht, & Karen M. Knecht, individually & as Tr. of the Karen M. Knecht Trust, Defendants., No. 15 CV 11839, 2019 WL 2225987, at *7–8 (N.D. Ill. May 23, 2019).

26. *Dillard v. Schlussel*, 865 N.W.2d 648, 657 (Mich. Ct. App. 2014).

27. See, e.g., Shapiro v. Wilgus, 287 U.S. 348, 354 (1932); Means v. Dowd, 128 U.S. 273, 288 (1888); Consove v. Cohen (In re Roco Corp.), 701 F.2d 978, 984 (1st Cir. 1983); Empire Lighting Fixture Co. v. Practical Lighting Fixture Co., 20 F.2d 295, 297 (2d Cir. 1927) (L. Hand, J.); Lippe v. Bairnco Corp., 249 F. Supp. 2d 357, 374 (S.D.N.Y. 2003), aff'd, 99 F. App'x 274 (2d Cir. 2004); Plotkin v. Pomona Valley Imports, Inc. (In re Cohen), 199 B.R. 709, 715-16 (B.A.P. 9th Cir. 1996); *see also* Kenneth C. Kettering, *The Uniform Voidable Transactions Act; or, the 2014 Amendments to the Uniform Fraudulent Transfer Act*, 70 Bus. Law. 777, 807 (2015). ("As innumerable cases have observed, those words say that a transfer that "hinders" or "delays" creditors violates the rule, even if it does not "defraud" them.")

28. *See* Kenneth C. Kettering, *The Uniform Voidable Transactions Act; or, the 2014 Amendments to the Uniform Fraudulent Transfer Act*, 70 Bus. Law. 777, 778 (2015). ("Its primordial rule, set forth in its modern American codifications in the Uniform Fraudulent Transfer Act ("UFTA") and the Bankruptcy Code, renders voidable any transfer of property by a debtor made with "intent to hinder, delay, or defraud" creditors.")

29. *See Janvey v. Dillon Gage, Inc. of Dallas*, 856 F.3d 377 (5th Cir. 2017). ("The district court instructed the jury that "[i]n determining actual intent, consideration may be given, among other factors, to" the badges of fraud. This instruction closely mirrors the Texas Pattern Instruction. See Texas Pattern Jury Instruction,

wealth transfer planning techniques, such as gifts (historically referred to as "voluntary conveyances") to friends and family.[30] The use of a trust is common in wealth transfer planning and was also one of the original badges of fraud in *Twyne's Case*. Multiple badges of fraud are often present when planning with trusts, where gifts are made to a trustee to hold for the benefit of beneficiaries who are often related to the settlor (and thus, qualify as insiders), and may also involve the settlor's retention of some benefit or control.

Fraudulent intent might also be inferred, or is more likely to be found, due to the nature of the transaction. Some examples of this scenario would be transfers in furtherance of a Ponzi scheme,[31] vendors in possession,[32] retention of collection benefits on assigned receivables,[33] fraudulent

Business, Consumer, Insurance & Employment §105.25 (2016) ("In determining actual intent, you may consider, among other factors [the badges of fraud]."). The use of the term "may" instructed the jury that they could, but did not have to, consider any of the badges of fraud. Bryan Garner, Black's Law Dictionary 1068 (9th ed. 2009) (defining "may" as "to be permitted to"). Similarly, the use of the phrase "among other factors" instructed the jury that the badges of fraud were a nonexhaustive list. The charge therefore properly instructed the jury that they could, but were not required to, consider the badges of fraud and that they could also consider any other relevant factor.")

30. *See Weathersbee v. Dekle*, 107 Fla. 517, 522, 145 So. 198, 200 (1933). ("Where the conveyance from husband to wife is voluntary, it matters not whether the intention of the parties was to hinder and delay creditors. When such hindrance and delay is the result of a voluntary conveyance between husband and wife, the real motive of the parties is immaterial. *McKeown v. Allen, supra; Gainer v. Russ*, 20 Fla. 157; *Gibson v. Love*, 4 Fla. 217. *But see Russ v. Blackshear*, 88 Fla. 573, 102 So. 749, as to the effect of the presumption of fraud which attaches.") See also, Vaughn v. Christian, 472 S.W.2d 337, 338 (Mo. 1971). ("The initial contention advanced by the Vaughns is that the transaction between the Christians and the Chamberlains was a voluntary conveyance. A conveyance that lacks valuable consideration is voluntary, Gentry v. Field, 143 Mo. 399, 45 S.W. 286, 287. A voluntary conveyance is presumptively fraudulent against existing creditors, Scharff v. McGaugh, 205 Mo. 344, 103 S.W. 550, 556; Harrison v. Harrison (Mo.App.), 339 S.W.2d 509, 516.")

31. See Thomas L. Taylor III, solely in his capacity as Court-appointed Receiver for Robert A. Helms, et al., Plaintiff, v. Grady H. Vaughn III. Defendant., No. A-15-CV-648-LY-ML, 2016 WL 11588707, at *4 (W.D. Tex. July 25, 2016). ("In the Fifth Circuit, the existence of a Ponzi scheme creates the presumption that a transfer is made with actual intent to defraud the transferor's creditors. Byron, 436 F.3d at 558. This is because a Ponzi scheme is, "as a matter of law, insolvent from its inception." Id. "'[T]he transferee's knowing participation is irrelevant under the statute' for purposes of establishing the premise of . . . a fraudulent transfer." Brown, 767 F.3d 439 (quoting SEC v. Res. Dev. Intern., LLC, 487 F.3d 295, 301 (5th Cir. 2007)). Accordingly, if the Receiver can establish by a preponderance of the evidence that Vendetta operated as a Ponzi scheme, the undersigned will presume that any transfers from Vendetta were made with the requisite fraudulent intent. Byron, 436 F.3d at 558.")

32. *See Superior Partners v. Pro. Educ. Network, Inc.*, 138 Ill. App. 3d 226, 231–32, 485 N.E.2d 1218, 1221 (1985). ("Notwithstanding the foregoing principles, however, subsection 2–402(2) of the Code provides that "[a] creditor of the seller may treat a sale * * * as void if as against him a retention of possession by the seller is fraudulent under any rule of law of the state where the goods are situated * * *." (Ill.Rev.Stat.1983, ch. 26, par. 2–402(2).) In Illinois, an absolute sale of personal property must be evidenced by the purchaser taking possession of the property. A transfer of personal property, unaccompanied by a corresponding change of possession, is fraudulent per se, and void as to creditors and subsequent bona fide purchasers. Wellington v. Heermans (1884), 110 Ill. 564, 575; Rozier v. *232 Williams (1879), 92 Ill. 187, 189; Allen v. Carr (1877), 85 Ill. 388, 389; Ticknor v. McClelland (1877), 84 Ill. 471, 474; Thompson v. Wilhite (1876), 81 Ill. 356, 358.") *See also*, Mooney, Mystery and Myth, at 774, Alabama Law Review (1988). ("The remnants of *Twyne's Case* manifested in the 'vendor in possession' doctrine continue to cast a shadow over the retention of possession by sellers in many jurisdictions.")

33. *Benedict v. Ratner*, 268 U.S. 353, 360–61, 45 S. Ct. 566, 568, 69 L. Ed. 991 (1925). ("Under the law of New York, a transfer of property as security which reserves to the transferor the right to dispose of the same, or to apply the proceeds thereof, for his own uses, is, as to creditors, fraudulent in law and void. This is true whether the right of disposition for the transferor's use be reserved in the instrument or by agreement in pais, oral or written; whether the right of disposition reserved be unlimited in time or be expressly terminable by

loans,[34] bulk transfers,[35] leveraged buyouts, and transfers to self-settled spendthrift trusts. Statutory carveouts might negate fraudulent intent.[36]

The key, with actual fraud, is proving intent, unless a transaction obviates the necessity. Once the intent is proven, the creditor may seek relief, unless a defense exists.

In his 1884 treatise, Frederick Wait cites *Covanhovan v. Hart*, 21 Pa. 495 500 (1853), where Chief Justice Black observed, "If a debtor, with the purpose to cheat his creditors, converts his land into money, because money is more easily shuffled out of sight than land, he of course commits a gross fraud."[37] Note that a debtor, with fraudulent intent, who converts an asset, such that the asset can be more easily dissipated, was enough to constitute a fraudulent transfer as early as 1853.

Today, wealth advisers might be surprised to see a creditor challenge the conversion of a corporation to an LLC, which has the effect of hindering creditors due to a charging order statute. While it is true that in the *Covanhovan* example, property was sold for cash, and in the conversion example, the company remains the same, other than a change to its legal form. The change in a creditor's legal rights with the change in entity form may be viewed as hindering creditors. Consequently, changing the nature of an asset can be a transfer, and the change in legal rights effectuated to hinder creditors can rise to the level of fraudulent intent.

# Constructive Fraud

The second category of avoidance provisions involves a transfer of an asset by a debtor in exchange for less than reasonably equivalent value and the existence of certain conditions where the debtor is left with insufficient assets.[38] The

---

the happening of an event; whether the transfer cover all the property of the debtor or only a part; whether the right of disposition extends to all the property transferred or only to a part thereof; and whether the instrument of transfer be recorded or not.")

34. *See, e.g.*, Florida Statute Section 726.201.

35. In 1989, the ULC recommended the repeal of Article 6 of the Uniform Commercial Code. *See, Why States Should Repeal Article 6 of the Uniform Commercial Code.* ("[C]reditors no longer face the choice of extending unsecured credit or no credit at all. Retaining an interest in inventory to secure its price has become relatively simple and inexpensive under Article 9 of the UCC—adopted in every state. If a bulk sale is fraudulent and the buyer is a party to the fraud, creditors have remedies under the Uniform Fraudulent Transfer Act.")

36. *See, e.g.*, Uniform Commercial Code Section 2-402(b) (vendor in possession), Bankruptcy Code Section 546(e) (potential safe harbor for leveraged buyout), Uniform Commercial Code Section 9-205 (use or disposition of collateral permissible), and state statutes expressly permitting self-settled spendthrift trusts.

37. Frederick S. Wait, *A Treatise on Fraudulent Conveyances and Creditors' Bills, With a Discussion of Void and Voidable Acts*, pg. 281, (1884).

38. *See Rudy v. Austin*, 56 Ark. 73, 19 S.W. 111, 113 (1892). ("Mere indebtedness is no evidence of fraud as to such creditors. But the insolvency of the grantor at the time of the conveyance is at least *prima facie* evidence of a fraudulent intent as to them, "because a transfer of property under such circumstances affords a reasonable ground of presumption that the intent with which it was made was to put beyond the reach of creditors, future as well as present, the property to which they had a right to resort for the payment of their debts." This presumption would necessarily arise if the grantor contracted debts immediately or so soon

pre-uniform act cases focusing on certain financial conditions demonstrates how courts applied presumptions to find the requisite intent to hinder, delay, or defraud creditors. The first condition, sometimes referred to as the unreasonably small assets[39] test, involves a transfer where the debtor had an unreasonably small amount of assets left after entering into a transaction.[40] The second condition, sometimes referred to as the equity sense[41] of insolvency, involves a transfer where the debtor knew or should have known that the debtor did not have enough remaining assets to pay debts as the debts come due.[42] The third condition, sometimes referred to as the balance sheet[43] test, involves a transfer where a debtor is either insolvent or rendered insolvent with respect to the transfer.[44] The solvency test does not examine reasonableness or state of mind; it is a mechanical test that must be applied by reference to various forms of evidence.[45]

Solvency is such a critical factor it appears as a badge of fraud under Section 4(a)(2) as well as an element in a Section 5 claim. At one time, there was disagreement as to whether one who had mere indebtedness and made a transfer for less than reasonably equivalent value was presumed to have made a fraudulent transfer, versus one who was insolvent and made a transfer for less than reasonably equivalent value. The former test was referred to as the Hardwicke-Kent doctrine,[46] and the latter rule, sometimes referred to as the

---

thereafter as to show that he reasonably had in contemplation the contracting of such debts at the time the transfer was made. From his inability to pay and the voluntary alienation the conclusion would naturally follow that he did not intend to pay such debts when they were contracted, and that the conveyance of the property was intended to delay or prevent the collection thereof by the sale of the property under due process of law.")

39. *See In re* Adelphia Commc'ns Corp., 652 F. App'x 19, 21 (2d Cir. 2016). ("The term "unreasonably small" is not defined in PUFTA, but courts have interpreted the term to describe a situation where a transaction leaves a debtor "technically solvent but doomed to fail." MFS/Sun Life Tr.-High Yield Series v. Van Dusen Airport Servs. Co., 910 F.Supp. 913, 944 (S.D.N.Y. 1995) (citing Moody, 971 F.2d at 1070 & n.22). The test for whether assets are "unreasonably small" focuses on reasonable foreseeability, see Moody, 971 F.2d at 1073, and is satisfied if at the time of the transaction the debtor had such minimal assets that insolvency was inevitable in the reasonably foreseeable future.")

40. UVTA Section 4(a)(2)(i).

41. *See Finn v. Meighan*, 325 U.S. 300, 303, 65 S. Ct. 1147, 1149, 89 L. Ed. 1624 (1945). ("Moreover, insolvency in the equity sense has always meant an inability of the debtor to pay his debts as they mature.")

42. UVTA Section 4(a)(2)(ii).

43. *See In re Opus E. LLC*, 698 F. App'x 711, 715 (3d Cir. 2017). ("Under the balance sheet test, a debtor is insolvent if the sum of its liabilities is greater than the sum of its assets, at fair valuation. 11 U.S.C. §101(32)(A); In re R.M.L., Inc., 92 F.3d 139, 154–55 (3d Cir. 1996). 'Fair valuation' is determined by valuing the debtor's assets on either a going concern or liquidation basis; the latter is only appropriate where bankruptcy is 'clearly imminent' and the 'business is on its deathbed.'")

44. UVTA Section 5(a).

45. *Humanigen, Inc. v. Savant Neglected Diseases*, LLC, C.A. N17C-07-068-PRW CCLD, at *14-15 (Del. Super. Ct. July 9, 2021) ("In support of its contention that Humanigen was insolvent when it transferred the benznidazole assets, Savant highlights: (1) a statement by the Court in its August 17, 2020 opinion; (2) a statement by Nomis Bay in Savant's request for admissions; (3) Humanigen's consideration of bankruptcy; (4) Humanigen's financial statements; and (5) Humanigen's inability to pay its obligations, including to its lawyers and board members. Given this record evidence, there is a material fact in dispute—i.e., whether Humanigen was insolvent—that must be developed more thoroughly.")

46. *See Hunters v. Waite*, 44 Va. 26, 43–44 (1846). ("The strong current of American decisions is certainly against the conclusive presumption of fraud from mere indebtedness. 1 Story's Eq. p. 350 to 360, notes; 2 Kent's Comm. 5 edit. p. 442, notes; cases cited in opinion of senator Allen, in *Seward v. Jackson*, 8 Cowen's *44

American rule, was eventually adopted as part of the uniform statute. In either case, courts permitted the transferee to rebut this presumption, and this right follows through under the uniform acts.[47] Under the UVTA, insolvency may be shown where a debtor stops paying debts as they come due; however, the transferee may, under Section 2(b) of the UVTA, rebut this presumption. No other provision of the UVTA permits a transferee to rebut evidence if proven by the creditor, although voidable transaction common law might provide otherwise.

## Insider Preference Rule

The third category of avoidance provisions is where where an insolvent debtor makes a transfer to an insider for an antecedent debt.[48] A common example of this would be a distribution from a limited liability company to an insider (e.g., a member or manager of the LLC) to repay a debt owed to the insider, despite the presence of a claim.

## Burdens and Presumptions

The creditor has the burden of proving, generally by a preponderance of the evidence, the elements of both actual and constructive fraud for relief. Once this burden has been met, relief may be awarded, with exceptions for defenses, equitable set-off, and insolvency (where a defendant has an opportunity to rebut.) Insolvency may be presumed when a debtor stops paying debts as the

R. 450, &c. But that matter need not be pursued further. Chancellor Kent himself, in the latest editions of his Commentaries, thus gracefully though reluctantly surrenders the question, so far as it rests at the present day upon authority. He says, "Judge Story evidently settles down upon the conclusion, under the stat. of 13 Eliz. that mere indebtedness at the time would not per se establish that a voluntary conveyance is void, even as to existing creditors; unless the other circumstances of the case justly created a presumption of fraud, actual or constructive, from the condition and rank of the parties, and the direct tendency of the conveyance to impair the rights of creditors. I have no doubt that such is the tendency of the decisions, both in England and America; and that the conclusions of fraud are to be left as matters of fact to a common jury. The doctrine in *Reade v. Livingston*, and of the English Chancellors on whom it rested is, as I greatly fear, too stern for the present times." Stern indeed! for any times, when it has the effect of converting an innocent into a fraudulent intent, and creditors at large into incumbrancers. The remark of the learned author, that the conclusions of fraud are to be left as matters of fact to a common jury is, of course, not intended to import the exclusion in common law trials of proper instructions from the Court to the jury, upon the nature and effect of the legal presumptions applicable to the case.")

47. *See Harkins v. Holt*, 124 Fla. 774, 778, 169 So. 481, 482 (1936). ("In cases of insolvency or of failing circumstances, the presumption of fraud follows the showing of insolvency, regardless of whether the conveyance was voluntary or otherwise. *Southern L. & S. Co. v. Verdier, supra; Weathersbee et ux. v. Dekle*, 107 Fla. 517, 145 So. 198, 199. However, this presumption or inference of fraud is not conclusive, but is rebuttable, and when so rebutted and put in equipoise, it is then the duty of the party having the affirmative, upon whose allegations the issues are founded, to go forward with the evidence.")

48. UTVA Section 5(b).

debts come due. Under the common law, a court may find that a burden may be rebutted by a defendant outside the context of solvency.[49]

In the wealth transfer context, courts have also presumed transfers as fraudulent where an insolvent debtor transfers an asset to a family member with the expectation of future support. "There can be no doubt that intrafamily transfers by an insolvent, in consideration of future support, are presumptively fraudulent at the time of the transfer. *See In re Skalski*, 267 B.R. 707, 710 n. 2, 711 (Bankr. W.D.N.Y., 2001)."[50] Intrafamily transfers based on past consideration may be subject to strict scrutiny.[51]

## Remedies

Regardless of the characterization of a fraudulent transfer, a court has wide latitude to "make things right" in situations where a creditor's rights have been impacted by a fraudulent transfer. A creditor may seek several remedies under fraudulent transfer law, and a judge has discretion as to the proper remedies.

> Although the UFTA does permit money judgments against fraudulent transferees, such judgments are only one available remedy. G.L. c. 109A, §§8, 9. The statute makes a full range of equitable remedies available to plaintiffs and commits the *642 form of remedy to the sound discretion of a trial judge. G.L. c. 109A, §8. Rivera, 77 Mass.App.Ct. at 27, 928 N.E.2d 348. Consequently, the judge had discretion to impose an equitable remedy permitting the plaintiff to reach Robert's one-half interest in the account, rather than ordering a money judgment against Madeline. *See Cavadi v. DeYeso*, 458 Mass. 615, 624, 941 N.E.2d 23 (2011). The judge did not abuse that discretion.[52]

The issue turns to when a creditor may seek relief, what relief a creditor may be afforded, and against whom a creditor may seek such relief. All of this depends on the facts surrounding the fraudulent transfer. Section 8 of the UVTA provides a creditor may seek relief not only against a transferee, but also "the person for whose benefit the transfer was made." The same approach was taken under the UFCA.

> A fraudulent conveyance claim seeking to recover money damages can only be maintained against a person who participates in the fraudulent transfer as either the transferee of the assets or the beneficiary of the conveyance."

49. *See Stephens v. Kies Oil Co.*, 386 So. 2d 1289, 1290 (Fla. Dist. Ct. App. 1980). ("These badges of fraud create a prima facie case and raise a rebuttable presumption that the sale was void. *Money v. Powell*, 139 So.2d 702 (Fla.2d DCA 1962); *Tornwall v. Carter*, 106 So.2d 96 (Fla.2d DCA 1958).") But see Comment 11 to UTVA Section 4.

50. *In re Walsh*, No. 05-26595 K, AP No. 06-2045 K, at *4 (Bankr. W.D.N.Y. Dec. 4, 2006).

51. *Id.* at *5. (The court rejected the transferee's argument that the transferee/wife had an equitable interest in the transferred property. "The Defendant seeks to transplant cases, arguments and theories, heretofore considered only in disputes within the marriage or within a nuclear or extended family, into the 'Statutes of Elizabeth' regarding fraudulent transfers, the focus of which has always been since ancient times the rights of creditors of the transferor.")

52. *Bakwin v. Mardirosian*, 467 Mass. 631, 641–42, 6 N.E.3d 1078, 1088 (2014).

> Fundacion Presidente Allende v. Banco de Chile, 2006 WL 2796793, at *3 (S.D.N.Y. May 29, 2006) (*citations omitted*); accord Stochastic Decisions, Inc. v. DiDomenico, 995 F.2d 1158, 1172 (2d Cir.), *cert. denied*, 510 U.S. 945, 114 S.Ct. 385, 126 L.Ed.2d 334 (1993); *In re Shore to Shore Realty Inc.*, 2011 WL 350526, at *5 (E.D.N.Y. Feb. 1, 2011); Sullivan v. Kodsi, 373 F.Supp.2d 302, 309 (S.D.N.Y.2005); RTC Mortg. Trust 1995–S/N1, 171 F.Supp.2d at 201. Thus, the transferor of the property—that is, the debtor—is not the proper defendant in a fraudulent conveyance claim. Nor may a claim be brought against parties who merely participated in the transfer but did not benefit from it. *See, e.g.*, Brenner v. Philips, Appel & Walden, Inc., 1997 WL 33471053, at *5 (S.D.N.Y. July 22, 1997).[53]

In making things right, the courts have resorted to not only restoring the status quo but sometimes adopting a utilitarian approach by awarding punitive damages to provide a deterrent effect.

> One policy of punitive damages is deterrence. 1 Dan B. Dobbs, Dobbs Law of Remedies §3.11(3), at 475–76 (2d ed. 1993). Without punitive damages, nothing other than costs would deter a debtor from attempting to fraudulently transfer his assets. If he gets caught, so be it: The cost would simply be what was owed in the first place. *See, e.g., SE Prop. Holdings, LLC v. Judkins*, No. 1:17-CV-00413-TM-B, 2019 WL 177981, at *10 (S.D. Ala. Jan. 11, 2019) ("Without an award of punitive damages or attorneys' fees, there would be no deterrence to a debtor weighing whether to make a fraudulent transfer. This is because the debtor would only lose the same asset he would have lost if he had not made a fraudulent transfer."); *Kekona v. Bornemann*, 349 P.3d 361, 372 (Haw. 2015) ("[A]t worst the fraudulent debtor is forced to pay what he or she already owed. Without the possibility of significant punitive damages, it would be difficult to deter this conduct."). It thus makes sense that the UFTA would permit recovery for punitive damages. *See Dobbs, supra*, §3.11(10), at 516 ("[T]he need for punishment or deterrence may be increased by reason of the very fact that the defendant will have no liability for compensatory damages.").
>
> In short, the absence of compensatory damages did not preclude the award of punitive damages.[54]

## *Prejudgment relief permitted*

A judgment is not required for a creditor to avail itself of the fraudulent transfer remedies. The Supreme Court has ruled that while an asset freezing order was

53. *Amusement Indus., Inc. v. Midland Ave. Assocs., LLC*, 820 F. Supp. 2d 510, 527 (S.D.N.Y. 2011).

54. Alliant Tax Credit 31, INC, a Fla. corporation, Alliant Tax Credit Fund XXVII, Ltd., a Fla. limited partnership, Alliant Tax Credit Tax Credit XXVII, Inc, a Fla. corporation, Alliant Tax Credit XI, Inc., a Fla. corporation, Alliant Tax Credit XI, Ltd., a Fla. limited partnership, Plaintiffs - Counter Defendants - Appellees - Cross Appellants, v. M. Vincent Murphy, III, Multifamily Housing Developers, L.L.C., a Georgia limited liability company, Community Management Services, Inc., a Georgia corporation, Gazebo Park Apartments of Acworth, LLC, a Georgia limited liability company, Defendants - Appellants - Cross Appellees, Marilyn Murphy, Defendant - Counter Claimant - Appellant - Cross Appellee., No. 15-14634, 2019 WL 2998107, at *10–11 (11th Cir. July 10, 2019).

not an available remedy under the federal common law, a creditor may still utilize the remedies under applicable fraudulent transfer law.[55] In *Henry v. Rizzolo*, the debtor argued that remedies were not available before judgment. The court rejected the debtor's argument:

> Defendant Rick Rizzolo's objections to Plaintiffs' discovery requests is premised on the argument that Plaintiffs must first obtain a judgment against him before they may conduct discovery regarding his assets. Plaintiffs, however, have asserted a cause of action against Defendants under Nevada's version of the Uniform Fraudulent Transfer Act (UFTA). The UFTA defines a "creditor" as a person who has a claim. NRS 112.150.4. "Claim" is defined as "a right to payment, whether or not the right is reduced to judgment, liquidated, unliquidated, fixed, contingent, matured, unmatured, disputed, undisputed, legal, equitable, secured or unsecured." NRS 112.150.3. Pursuant to NRS 112.210.1, a creditor may obtain certain UFTA remedies prior to obtaining a judgment on his claim against the debtor. These remedies include avoidance of the transfer or obligation to the extent necessary to satisfy the creditor's claim, attachment, an injunction against further transfers, appointment of a receiver to take charge of the asset transferred or of other property of the transferee; or "any other relief the circumstances may require."
>
> Courts interpreting these provisions have held that the UFTA does not require a creditor to reduce a claim to judgment before seeking to void a debtor's allegedly fraudulent transfer of property. As the Arizona Supreme Court states in Farris v. Advantage Capital Corporation, 170 P.3d 250, 251 (Ariz. 2007), "[t]he UFTA allows the levy of execution when a creditor has obtained a judgment, but does not require a judgment before a creditor may seek relief from an allegedly fraudulent transfer, including avoidance." In Friedman v. Heart Institute of Port St. Lucie, Inc., 863 So.2d 189, 193 (Fla. 2003), the Florida Supreme Court held that discovery on a UFTA claim should not be automatically stayed until a claimant obtains a judgment on his substantive claim against the debtor. The court noted that if a plaintiff was precluded from conducting discovery or prosecuting his UFTA claim prior to obtaining a judgment, "the goal of protecting creditors from wrongful asset transfers would likely be nearly entirely frustrated." *Id.* at 193. Obviously, the purpose of the UFTA is to protect creditors by ensuring that the debtor's assets will be available to satisfy an eventual judgment against the debtor. Friedman also recognized, however, that the court may exercise its discretion to limit discovery in such actions, including entering an appropriate protective order to prevent the disclosure of a defendant's personal and private financial information to third parties.[56]

In *New Falls Corp. v. Soni Holdings, LLC*, the court considered an argument that a prejudgment injunction violated the Supreme Court's decision in *Grupo*

---

55. *Grupo Mexicano de Desarrollo S.A. v. All. Bond Fund, Inc.*, 527 U.S. 308, 322, 119 S. Ct. 1961, 1970, 144 L. Ed. 2d 319 (1999).

56. Kirk and Amy Henry, Plaintiffs, v. Fredrick Rizzolo, aka Rick Rizzolo, et al., Defendants. Additional Party Names: Power Co., Inc., No. 208CV00635PMPGWF, 2009 WL 10692952, at *4 (D. Nev. Feb. 3, 2009).

*Mexicano*. Here, the characterization of the claim for relief plays an instrumental role in whether a preliminary injunction is available.

> Grupo Mexicano does not, however, preclude courts from entering asset-freezing preliminary injunctions in cases in which the movant seeks equitable relief. As the Second Circuit held in Gucci America, Inc. v. Weixing Li, 768 F.3d 122 (2d Cir. 2014), "[t]he Court's holding [in Grupo Mexicano] was limited to actions for money damages in which plaintiffs seek a preliminary injunction to prevent the defendant 'from transferring assets in which no lien or equitable interest is claimed.'" *Id.* at 130 (quoting Grupo Mexicano, 527 U.S. at 310). A court retains the authority to issue a prejudgment asset freeze where such authority is specifically authorized by statute, *id.* at 131 n.11, or "where such relief was traditionally available: where the plaintiff is pursuing a claim for final equitable relief, and the preliminary injunction is ancillary to the final relief." *Id.* at 131.
>
> ***
>
> Because the Court concludes that it has the authority to issue a preliminary injunction to grant the equitable preliminary relief sought by the Plaintiff, the Court proceeds to address whether Plaintiff has satisfied the prerequisites for a preliminary injunction.[57]

The court in *New Falls* went on to apply a test to determine whether it was fair to recommend the imposition of an injunction, ultimately concluding that an injunction was recommended. The availability of provisional relief will require applying local law; if these requirements are not met, the creditor will not obtain such relief.[58]

## Defenses, liability, and protection of transferee

In the wealth transfer context, it is common for the transferee to accept the transfer of property for no value, i.e., there is commonly a lack of value exchanged. For federal tax purposes, these are transactions treated as a gift, for which a federal gift tax exemption may apply, or the gift may be covered by the unlimited gift tax exemption applicable to gifts to spouses. However, there are also wealth transfer transactions that may not be treated as gifts for federal gift tax purposes but may be treated as lacking the exchange of reasonably equivalent value for purposes of fraudulent transfer law. A prime example of such a transaction is an intrafamily sale, where an asset is sold to a family member in exchange for a note requiring no payments for years. Another form of wealth

57. New Falls Corporation, Plaintiff, v. Soni Holdings, LLC, Kunal Soni, Anjali Soni & 632 MLK BLVD JR LLC, Om P. Soni, Soni Capital Resources, LLC, Kanwal Kapur, Weanona Hugie & Richard Spears, Defendants., No. CV19449ADSAKT, 2019 WL 4015170, at *9–12 (E.D.N.Y. July 5, 2019).

58. *See* Luis (Janer) Rullan, Plaintiff - Appellant, v. Jill K. Goden; Frederick I. Greenberg; Youth World International Company, Ltd; Youth World, Ltd, Defendants - Appellees, & Cacapon River Camps, Inc.; Cacapon Camps, Inc; Frederick I. Greenberg Revocable Trust; Alex Reece; John Doe; Eric S. Goden, Defendants, George William Liebmann, Tr.., No. 19-1037, 2019 WL 5095757, at *1–2 (4th Cir. Oct. 11, 2019).

transfer occurs when a debtor spouse directs funds into a tenancy by entirety account. The transferred funds are often wages, for which a debtor may attempt to assert a statutory exemption either as to the garnishment limitations (e.g., federal wage exemption) or exempt under state law, such that the wages would not be an "asset" and thus, there can be no transfer. Finally, capital contributions may be treated as non-taxable events for tax purposes, but constitute fraudulent transfers since the debtor's receipt of a membership interest may not have utility to creditors.

A wealth transfer adviser might become a transferee in some cases. For example, an attorney might be a transferee where a debtor-client transfers funds to the attorney to be held in a trust account. An attorney may be instructed to make further transfers out of the trust account to third parties, excluding the client's creditors. *In re Harwell* is a prime example of this scenario, where the law firm was targeted as a transferee in bankruptcy litigation that went to the Eleventh Circuit. It was in this legal saga that a Florida district court issued its infamous warning, "a warning bell has sounded for parties involved in 'asset preservation.'"[59]

Whether it be a spouse, a trustee or even a wealth transfer adviser, the transferee will look to available defenses to avoid or limit fraudulent transfer liability. In cases like the scenarios described above, the transferee may argue he or she should not be considered a transferee since he or she never had control over the transferred assets. This argument exists in the bankruptcy context, referred to as the "mere conduit" defense. Whether this defense exists outside of bankruptcy is a matter of state law.

> [Th]e mere conduit affirmative defense is a judicially created exception grounded in the equitable powers of the bankruptcy courts. *Id.* at 1322. It arose not under FUFTA, but in the context of an analogous fraudulent transfer provision in the Bankruptcy Code, which allows a bankruptcy trustee to avoid certain fraudulent transfers similar to those avoidable under the FUFTA and to recover the value of the transfers from the "initial transferee of such transfer." *See* 11 U.S.C. §§548(a)(1), 550(a)(1). Recognizing the inequity that would result if the court adopted a literal interpretation of the term "initial transferee," we crafted this equitable exception to exclude mere conduits or intermediaries who might otherwise be deemed "initial transferees" from being held liable for funds they never actually controlled or benefitted from. Custom Contractors, 745 F.3d at 1349, 1352; Harwell, 628 F.3d at 1322.
>
> Neither this Circuit nor the Florida courts have decided whether this equitable defense should also apply in statutory actions under FUFTA, and for the reasons set forth above we need not decide that question either. Nor must we decide whether JPMC would be entitled to the mere conduit affirmative defense if it did apply. Because Isaiah's complaint fails to allege an applicable FUFTA transfer, his complaint fails, as an initial matter, to state a claim of

59. *See* David J. Slenn, "Has the Warning Bell Sounded for Asset Protection Planners?", Prob. & Prop., March/April 2010.

> FUFTA liability. The District Court therefore did not err in dismissing his complaint under Rule 12(b)(6) on that basis.[60]

To the extent a transferee cannot assert a conduit defense, the transferee will either argue sufficient value was given (which likely will not work where the transfer of wealth was a gift) or appeal to equity based on the subsequent use of the funds. Where a transferee senses a fraudulent transfer and returns the asset, the transferee might be able to escape liability.[61]

## *Transferee Acts in Good Faith and Gives Reasonably Equivalent Value*

Section 8(a) of the UVTA provides a transferee with a defense if the transferee gives reasonably equivalent value and acts in good faith. This is an absolute defense that applies only in situations involving actual intent to hinder, delay, or defraud creditors. Obviously, this defense cannot exist in situations involving constructive fraud, because a prerequisite to relief under 4(b) and 5(a) requires a lack of reasonably equivalent value, and Section 8(a) requires the transferee give "reasonably equivalent value."

Under Section 550 of the BAPCPA, the trustee may recover against (1) the initial transferee or (2) any immediate or mediate transferee of such initial transferee. The trustee may not recover against anyone in the second category that takes for value and in good faith. Thus, while the UFTA provides an absolute defense for the transferee who takes for reasonably equivalent value and acts in good faith, the BAPCPA provides no such defense to the "initial transferee;" i.e., the initial transferee faces strict liability unless the equitable mere conduit defense applies.

## *Equitable adjustment*

In some cases, a spouse receives an asset (often as a joint tenant) but subsequently uses the asset for the benefit of the debtor spouse as opposed to the transferee spouse's benefit, or does not know about and receives no benefit from the asset. Here, a court may determine the spouse is not a transferee, and adjust the transferee spouse's liability downward.

---

60. *Isaiah v. JPMorgan Chase Bank*, 960 F.3d 1296 (11th Cir. 2020). (Internal citations omitted.)

61. The statute does not explicitly provide this result. *See Hickson v. Thielman*, 147 Cal. App. 2d 11, 15, 304 P.2d 122, 125 (1956) (finding a returning the asset does not necessarily protect the transferee.) ("Defendants contend that Medley testified that she returned the $1,500 to Harry and for that reason it was error to render judgment against her. The court was not required to believe her testimony and we must assume that the court did not believe it. But there was evidence to support the findings that Medley conspired with the others to defraud plaintiffs and if, as the court found, she received the money with that intention and purpose, returning the money to Harry would not have relieved her of responsibility. It is immaterial whether she entered into the scheme for the benefit of herself or for the benefit of Harry.")

> Here, the record establishes that the entire balance of the Subject Funds was paid by Donnelly to the debtor to pay for his everyday living expenses. Plaintiff does not dispute that the balance was used to pay for the debtor's "living expenses rather than for [the transferee's] own personal benefit." (Pl.' s Brief 16, ECF No. 440.) Based upon binding precedent and exercising its discretion, the Court holds that Plaintiff may not recover the balance of the Subject Funds because those funds were used to pay for the debtor's ordinary and necessary living expenses that he otherwise would have paid even if the fraudulent transfers had not occurred, rather than for Donnelly's benefit. *See In re* Kingsley, 518 F.3d at 878.[62]

A court may also permit the use of funds for the marital unit; a string of Pennsylvania cases illustrates this approach. If a court permits such a reduction for certain expenditures, a creditor may be forced to trace the expenditure of the funds to prove where the assets were used.

# Statute of Limitation/Repose

The time frame for a creditor to bring a claim for relief varies based on the type of fraudulent transfer.[63] A creditor has four years from the date of transfer to avoid a transfer made with actual fraud. In addition to the four-year rule, there is an additional one-year discovery rule permitted to bring a fraudulent transfer claim with respect to transfers made with actual intent, measured from the date the creditor reasonably should have discovered the transfer. Regarding constructive fraud, a creditor has four years from the date of transfer to bring a claim for relief, with no additional one-year discovery rule. Finally, a creditor has only one year to bring a claim for relief as to a transfer made in violation of the insider preference rule. Because these time frames are considered statutes of repose versus statutes of limitation, it is critical to identify the appropriate theory for relief clearly, as the right to bring a claim is extinguished if not made timely.[64]

> Thus, without exception, Petras must have brought his fraudulent transfer claim within one year from the date of transfer, Tex. Bus. & Com. Code §24.010(a)(3) and must have brought his intentional fraudulent transfer claim within four years after the date of transfer or within one year after he

62. *Branch Banking & Tr. Co. v. Hamilton Greens, LLC*, No. 11-80507-CIV, 2018 WL 6520928, at *1 (S.D. Fla. Dec. 4, 2018).

63. Many states that have adopted a uniform act have a non-uniform statute of limitation provision. *See generally*, Kenneth C. Kettering, *Codifying A Choice of Law Rule for Fraudulent Transfer: A Memorandum to the Uniform Law Commission*, 19 Am. Bankr. Inst. L. Rev. 319, 333–34 (2011). ("At least sixteen states have made substantive nonuniform changes to their enactments of section 9. Those changes are very diverse. Some states have lengthened the limitation period for some or all actual fraud, constructive fraud, or insider preference. Other states have shorted some of those periods. Some *334 states have narrowed or broadened in various ways the UFTA's discovery rule, which in the uniform text is applicable only to actual fraud. Others have made miscellaneous changes.")

64. *See In re* W.R. Grace & Co., 281 B.R. 852, 855 (Bankr. D. Del. 2002). ("At the outset, there appears to be some confusion in the arguments of counsel regarding which section or sections of the UFTA are at play here in light of the Court's limitation of the issue to constructive fraudulent conveyance.")

> did or reasonably could have discovered the transfer, *see* Tex. Bus. & Com. Code §§24.010(a)(1), (a)(2).
>
> The transfer that Petras alleges was fraudulent was the 2005 transfer of Franklin's assets to the Glacial Entities. Pl.'s First Am. Compl. ¶ 70. His section 24.006 fraudulent transfer claim is thus barred because the cause of action was extinguished in 2006. And Petras's section 24.005 intentional fraudulent transfer claim is also barred. At least by May 2010, Petras discovered that Franklin transferred its assets to the Glacial Entities. Pl.'s First Am. Compl. ¶ 48. Thus, his intentional fraudulent transfer claim was extinguished in May 2011. Petras filed suit in June 2011. So, this claim is also time barred. Accordingly, the Court dismisses Petras's fraudulent transfer and intentional fraudulent transfer claims (Counts 3 and 4).[65]

An issue may arise as to when the one-year clock starts ticking under the reasonable discovery rule. Debtors will argue a creditor's notice of the transaction is enough; creditors will argue that the fraudulent nature of the transaction must be disclosed.[66] Given the fraudulent transfer laws are creditors' rights laws, it is not surprising that many courts have found the required notice must include the fraudulent nature of the transaction.

> The third question is whether the one-year discovery period in Section 1309(1) of the Delaware Uniform Fraudulent Transfer Act starts when the mere existence of an allegedly fraudulent transfer is or could reasonably have been discovered, or whether it starts when the fraudulent nature of the transfer was or could reasonably have been discovered. Based on the reasoning and substantial weight of authority in other jurisdictions that have considered the issue, the court adopts the latter approach and finds that all of J.P. Morgan's fraudulent transfer claims (challenging both the dividends and other payments) were timely filed.[67]

A court might encounter an issue as to whether to apply the UVTA's statute of limitation or, for a state that has adopted one, a modified statute of limitation under an asset protection trust ("APT") statute.[68] This situation occurred in Utah, where the Utah version of the UVTA specifically directs for the application of the shorter period in situations involving a valid Utah asset protection trust.

65. Michael v. Petras, Plaintiff, v. Gary Mole, et al., Defendants. Additional Party Names: Andrew Marriner, Charles Kaplan, Don Bernard, Donald Bernard, Elizabeth Bernard, Generales Des Mines Au Congo, SPRL, Glacial Energy Holdings I, LLC, Glacial Energy Holdings II, LLC, Glacial Energy Holdings, Inc., Glacial Energy of New York, Inc., Glacial Energy of Texas, Inc., Glacial Energy, Inc., Julie Cannon, Kaplan & Assocs., LLP, Koby Bernard, Peter Koeck, Touchdown Properties, LLC, No. 3:11-CV-1402-N, 2012 WL 13103200, at *8–9 (N.D. Tex. May 17, 2012).

66. The Official Comments of the UVTA acknowledge this issue and suggest states adopt their own provisions reflecting a hard-line rule that notice is provided when the fraudulent nature of a transaction is disclosed.

67. *JPMorgan Chase Bank, N.A. v. Ballard*, No. CV 2018-0274-AGB, 2019 WL 3022338, at *1–2 (Del. Ch. July 11, 2019).

68. An asset protection trust is a self-settled spendthrift trust expressly permitted under the laws of certain jurisdictions.

The basic purpose of the UVTA is "to prevent fraudulent transfers of assets by debtors who seek to defraud creditors or avoid debts by placing assets beyond creditors' reach." Li v. Lewis, No. 1:20-cv-12-TS-JCB, 2020 WL 4346974, at *2 (D. Utah July 29, 2020) (*citation omitted*). Under the UVTA, a transfer is generally voidable as to a creditor "if the debtor made the transfer or incurred the obligation with actual intent to hinder, delay, or defraud any creditor of the debtor." Utah Code §25-6-202(1)(a). Generally, a claim for relief under section 25-6-202(1)(a) must be brought by the later of the following: "four years after the transfer was made" or "one year after the transfer or obligation was or could reasonably have been discovered by the claimant." *Id.* §256-305(1).

The UVTA contains distinct rules for trusts executed under Utah's asset protection trust laws. *Id.* §25-6-502. Notwithstanding the general statute of limitations outlined in section 25-6305(1), section 25-6-502(9)(c) provides a shorter statute of limitations for a claim that a debtor made a transfer to a Utah asset protection trust in order to defraud a creditor. To take advantage of the shorter statute of limitations, the asset protection trust must comply with the asset protection trust statute, including a set of conditions enumerated at section 25-6-502(5). If the trust qualifies as a proper asset protection trust, the statute mandates that the claim be brought "by a creditor of the settlor who was a creditor of the settlor before the assets in question were transferred to the trust" and the action must be brought by "the later of two years after the transfer is made, or one year after the transfer reasonably could have been discovered by the creditor." *Id.* §25-6-502(9)(c)(i). Where an asset protection trust provision conflicts with another provision of the UVTA, the provision in the asset protection trust subsection supersedes the conflicting general provision. *Id.* §25-6-502(13). Therefore, if the trusts in question fall under the asset protection trust statute, that subsection's shorter statute of limitations must apply.

***

The transfers on December 16, 2016, and November 14, 2016, fall outside of the two-year statute of limitations outlined for fraudulent transfers to asset protection trusts. Asphalt, therefore, was required to plead facts showing that the two-year statute of limitations does not apply to the transfers to the Trusts by pleading facts that demonstrate that the transfers to the Trusts do not fall under Utah Code §25-6-502 and should instead be subject to the general four-year statute of limitations in section 25-6-305(1). Although Asphalt now attempts to suggest that the two trusts are not proper asset protection trusts, it makes no such allegations in the operative complaint. Asphalt's complaint focuses exclusively on pleading causes of action under section 25-6-202 and thus fails to allege any facts in its complaint to overcome the two-year asset protection trust statute of limitations. Accordingly, the court GRANTS Defendants' motion to dismiss with respect to the claims based on the Rim to River and Stone Canyon transfers.[69]

69. *Asphalt Trader Ltd. v. Beall*, 1:20-cv-00155-JNP-CMR, at *1 (D. Utah Sep. 10, 2021).

*Asphalt Trader* makes it clear that, in a dispute between debtors and creditors in a state permitting asset protection trusts, creditors asserting a traditional statute of limitation will probably need to show why the trust at issue does not qualify for a shortened statute of limitation.[70] This type of analysis would be similar to the tests applied in *Erskine* and *Bertran*. "Analogous to the *Erskine* holding, the lack of the affidavit under AS 34.40.110(j) by Ms. Bertran before she transferred her interest in the Ranch to Toni 1 Trust debars the use of the protections against her creditors afforded by the Alaska Asset Protection Trust Act."[71]

70. Contrast with a fact pattern where a debtor attempts to import foreign law and reverse public policy of the debtor's state of domicile.

71. *In re* Bertran, No. F12-00501-HAR, 2016 WL 3411931, at *2–3 (Bankr. D. Alaska June 8, 2016).

CHAPTER 4

# Uniform Voidable Transactions Act

"Professor Kettering concludes by stating the obvious, and I paraphrase with my own take: the objectors cannot read English, and do not understand the legislative process behind uniform laws."[1]

In 2014, the Uniform Law Commission amended the Uniform Fraudulent Transfer Act to include a choice of law provision, requiring the law of the debtor's location to govern the debtor's fraudulent transfer of assets. This change is important because of the considerable amount of time and resources expended on litigation, including the choice of law. Like Article 9 of the Uniform Commercial Code,[2] the UVTA provides a fair choice of law rule that is easy to apply in a situation involving two or more potentially applicable fraudulent transfer laws.

## Official Comments

The Official Comments to the amendments to the UFTA drafted in 2014 were refreshed to account for, among other issues, developments in fraudulent transfer law since 1984, including addressing fraudulent transfer issues related to two prominent tools in wealth transfer planning, the limited liability company[3] and transfers to asset protection

1. Bruce A. Markell, *Comments on Selfishly Settled Trusts: Fulminations Over Fraud and Asset Protection Trusts*, 37 No. 11 Bankruptcy Law Letter NL 1 (November 2017.)

2. Unif. Commercial Code §9-301.

3. *See Limited Liability Companies in the Decade of the 1990s: Legislative and Case Law Developments and Their Implications for the Future*, 56 Bus. Law. 499, 499–500 (2001). ("The origins of LLC statutes were the partnership association statutes enacted by some states in the 1800s. These statutes never gained popularity, however, and it was not until 1977 that the modern version of the LLC came into existence with the enactment of legislation by Wyoming. Five years later, Florida followed Wyoming's lead after the Internal Revenue Service (IRS) issued a revenue ruling that classified a Wyoming LLC as a partnership for tax purposes. But, the IRS then proposed new regulations that would classify as a corporation any entity in which members were not liable for the entity's debts. This stemmed the growth of LLCs until a new IRS ruling in 1988 again recognized

trusts.[4] Both the APT and LLC, available in some jurisdictions with very debtor-friendly provisions, were either relatively uncommon or not available domestically in 1984.

Some planners took exception to the choice of law provision, together with a recital of the definition of creditor as not excluding future, unforeseeable creditors in the Official Comments. These two comments were seen as a potential hit to the asset protection industry, and more particularly, to the asset protection trust industry. Any hint of applying the law of the larger economy state where a debtor is domiciled and that follows traditional creditors' rights law (especially as it pertains to fraudulent transfers) would be detrimental financially to those who sell asset protection trust services that depend on the law of the asset protection trust jurisdiction. With the UVTA, a new battle between debtors and creditors emerged, with some asset protection service providers fighting hard to maintain asset protection trust business flowing without interruption. Regardless of whether a state adopts the UVTA, the choice of law issue still exists, and in many cases the courts are likely to adopt the common law approach that often results in the law of a debtor's domicile applying to prevent violation of public policy.

## Controversy Regarding Official Comments

The Official Comments make it clear what has been known for centuries; *all creditors* are potentially entitled to fraudulent transfer remedies if the creditor can satisfy certain requirements. Given the danger that judges might find the Official Comments persuasive (recall the case law citations in the Official Comments are all based on existing case law as of 2014), a strategy emerged amongst UVTA opposition where some states considering the adoption of the UVTA would be encouraged to incorporate language expressly disavowing certain statements contained in the Official Comments, or directing courts not to consider certain factors. These statements and factors embodied longstanding concepts that were always troublesome for asset protection planners, such as fraudulent transfer relief available to both present *and future* creditors where actual fraud is present.[5] The relevant statutory language simply did not change between the UFTA and the UVTA.

This "judicial straitjacket" approach is somewhat reminiscent of the Restatement of the Law (Third) Trusts treatment in South Dakota. The Third

---

that an LLC could be taxed as a partnership, thereby sparking a resurgence of legislative activity creating LLCs.") (Internal citations omitted.)

4. The first domestic asset protection trust legislation was enacted in Alaska in April of 1997. "Not to be outdone, the state of Delaware almost immediately thereafter adopted its own legislation on July 9, 1997, when it adopted the Delaware Qualified Dispositions in Trust Act." *See* Mario A. Mata, *Essential Tools and Techniques of Domestic and International Asset Protection Planning*, April 26, 2007, American Bar Association 18th Annual Spring Estate Planning Symposia.

5. It is not clear how this approach would work because the cases the Official Comments cited were merely comments; to truly eliminate the offensive comments, the cases cited would need to be overruled.

Restatement contained offensive language to some asset protection advisers, especially with respect to child support claims and the ability to reach a debtor-parent's assets in a South Dakota self-settled trust. The South Dakota legislature essentially told the courts to disregard such offensive language.[6]

> Our Legislature has placed formidable barriers between creditor claims and trust funds protected by a spendthrift provision. *See* SDCL 55-1-41 ("If the trust contains a spendthrift provision, no creditor may reach present or future mandatory distributions from the trust at the trust level."); SDCL 55-1-35 ("No trustee is liable to any creditor for paying the expenses of a spendthrift trust."). More to the point, the Legislature has emphatically rejected even the specter of an argument that would allow a child support creditor to reach trust funds protected by a spendthrift provision. Indeed, this precise legal theory is identified in §59 of the Restatement (Third) Trusts (2003) which states that "[t]he interest of a beneficiary in a valid spendthrift trust can be reached in satisfaction of an enforceable claim against the beneficiary for . . . support of a child. . . ." However, the Legislature anticipated such an argument in South Dakota courts and definitively foreclosed it with its 2007 enactment of SDCL 55-1-25 which provides in part:
>
> In the area of creditor rights, the Restatement of Trusts (Third) and the Uniform Trust Code create many new positions of law as well as adopts many minority positions of law. The provisions of §§55-1-24 to 55-1-43, inclusive, affirmatively reject many of these positions. Therefore, the Legislature does not intend the courts to consult the Restatement (Third) of the Law of Trusts . . . §59 . . . with respect to subject matters addressed by the provisions of §§55-1-24 to 55-1-43, inclusive.
>
> (Emphasis added); see also Richardson v. Richardson, 2017 S.D. 92, ¶ 16, 906 N.W.2d 369, 374 (stating that courts "must be mindful of the Legislature's public policy determinations. . . .").[7]

The UVTA opposition's literature accuses the UVTA Drafting Committee of recasting legitimate transactions (e.g., tax, business, or estate planning) as "voidable per se," so no professional who engages in legitimate planning should support the UVTA. However, this accusation lacks merit as the Official Comments make no such claim.[8] Upon reviewing the opposition's arguments,

6. Query whether the legislature's attempt to force courts not to look at certain sources of law violates the separation of powers.

7. Matter of Cleopatra Cameron Gift Tr. , Dated May 26, 1998, 2019 S.D. 35, ¶¶ 21-31, 931 N.W.2d 244.

8. See Kenneth C. Kettering, The Comments to the Uniform Voidable Transactions Act Relating to Self-Settled Spendthrift Trusts Are Correct, 42 Tax Mgmt. Est., Gifts & Tr. J. 267 (Sept. 2017). ("The first argument is that those cases should not be viewed as having precedential force today because the statutory codification of fraudulent transfer law today "does not provide that a transfer to [a self-settled spendthrift trust] is a voidable transfer per se." By this the Article means that no relevant statute today says in so many words that "a transfer to a self-settled spendthrift trust is avoidable per se." So what? The statutory language applied by the cases in question was exactly the same then as it is today. It is the time-honored language of the Statute of 13 Elizabeth that continues as the basic rule of the UFTA/UVTA today: "intent to hinder, delay, or defraud" any creditor. A transfer to a self-settled spendthrift trust was considered by the cases in question to contravene that language, and that language remains in force, unchanged, in the UFTA/UVTA today.") (Internal footnotes omitted.)

former bankruptcy judge and current professor of law, Bruce A. Markell, concluded that the opposition or "objectors" advancing such an argument "cannot read English."[9] Professor Markell also noted heated conversations during UVTA drafting sessions. "There were reports of shouting at drafting sessions in which a trust industry representative claimed to be both mainstream and ignored, and as a result, contended that the work of the Uniform Voidable Transactions Act drafting committee was intellectually suspect."

To understand why the opposition would make such a claim, one must understand the opposition's cast. Usually, the opposition has ties to those who sell, or otherwise profit from the sale of, asset protection trusts. The Official Comments do not state that all asset protection trusts will not work. To the contrary, the Official Comments go so far as assuming such trusts should not automatically violate Section 4(a) if used by persons who are domiciled in the state that provides for such trusts. "Suppose that jurisdiction X, in which this Act is in force, also has in force a statute permitting an individual to establish a self-settled spendthrift trust and transfer assets thereto, subject to stated conditions. If an individual Debtor whose principal residence is in X establishes such a trust and transfers assets thereto, then under §10 of this Act the voidable transfer law of X applies to that transfer. That transfer cannot be considered voidable in itself under §4(a)(1) as in force in X, for the legislature of X, having authorized the establishment of such trusts, must have expected them to be used."

The opposition's real concern is the potential impact of language in the Official Comments dealing with the terms "claim" and "creditor" in conjunction with Official Comments that address common asset protection techniques that are openly marketed to hinder creditors. The potential issue here is the application of the long-standing interpretation of the term "claim" (and thus, "creditor") under the common law, in conjunction with a choice of law pointer that prevents application of a foreign jurisdiction's modified fraudulent transfer law.[10]

The test for whether a transfer satisfies actual fraud is not determined solely by reference to all potential effects of a transaction (that is, could a creditor be hindered?) but requires examining the debtor's fraud (that is, did the debtor intend to hinder any creditor?) as well as the facts and circumstances. The fact that a debtor will choose to invest in an annuity, buy a home, or purchase life insurance, should not, by itself, result in avoidance merely because

---

9. Bruce A. Markell, Comments on Selfishly Settled Trusts: Fulminations Over Fraud and Asset Protection Trusts, 37 No. 11 Bankruptcy Law Letter NL 1 n. 17 (November 2017.)

10. UVTA opposition may attempt to insert a provision in legislative history or state statute that "disavows" Comment Number 2 to Section 4 of the UVTA. Comment Number 2 makes it clear that the term "creditor" includes present and future creditors, and that a creditor does not need to be "identifiable" at the time of the transfer. The statute does not impose any requirement that a creditor be "existing" or "identifiable" at the time of a transfer. This disavowal provision is then applied for purposes of the entire UVTA, which includes Section 2 of the UVTA, providing for the definition of "claim" and "creditor." It is highly unlikely that such an ambiguous approach will work to repeal the definition of "claim" to accomplish this result, however, state legislatures must be aware of any non-uniform provision to creditors rights law that is proposed by those representing debtors. Indiana and Arkansas legislatures made non-uniform modifications, but Alabama's legislature took a different approach, refusing to disavow the Comments, and asserting that the law cited by the Comments may or may not be consistent with Alabama law.

the debtor also knew there was creditor protection involved with each exemption.

> It is well established that under the Code, a debtor's conversion of non-exempt property to exempt property on the eve of bankruptcy for the express purpose of placing that property beyond the reach of creditors, without more, will not deprive the debtor of the exemption to which he otherwise would be entitled. Ford v. Poston, 773 F.2d 52, 54 (4th Cir.1985); *In re* Lindberg, 735 F.2d 1087, 1090 (8th Cir.), *cert. denied* sub nom. Armstrong v. Lindberg, 469 U.S. 1073 (1984); *In re* Reed, 700 F.2d 986, 990 (5th Cir.1983); Forsberg v. Security State Bank, 15 F.2d 499, 501 (8th Cir.1926). A leading bankruptcy commentator explains that this rule is just because "The result which would obtain if debtors were not allowed to convert property into allowable exempt property would be extremely harsh, especially in those jurisdictions where the exemption allowance is minimal." Collier on Bankruptcy ¶ 522.08[4], at 40 (15th ed. 1984). Nevertheless, this rule is not absolute. Where the debtor acts with actual intent to defraud creditors, his exemptions will be denied. Ford, *supra*, 773 F.2d at 55; *In re* Reed, *supra*, 700 F.2d at 990. Since fraudulent intent rarely is susceptible of direct proof, courts long have accepted extrinsic evidence of fraud. Absent extrinsic evidence of fraud, however, the debtor's mere conversion of non-exempt property to exempt property, even while insolvent, is not evidence of fraudulent intent as to creditors.[11]

As the Eighth Circuit noted in *Hanson*, intent can be gleaned from the effect, that is, the "badges of fraud" to prove intent at the time of the transfer, however, intent must still be proven. The mere fact an exemption has the effect of hindering creditors is not enough; the creditor must also prove intent to hinder.

The nature of the inquiry was summed up nicely by the Florida Supreme Court, citing Bump on Fraudulent Conveyances:

> On page 752, 14 Am. St. Rep., *supra*, the annotator, discussing the effect of a conveyance as against subsequent creditors, says: 'We apprehend that no general rule can be formulated equally applicable to all cases, and that such judicial declarations as have been made upon the subject must be interpreted with reference to the particular facts of the case in which they were made. If the subsequent debts were contracted long after the voluntary transfer was made, the presumption that it might have been made with a view of contracting them and of defrauding the subsequent creditors certainly becomes exceedingly weak, and may reasonably be treated as entirely destroyed, unless other circumstances appear to give *225 it renewed vitality. The evidence may, on the other hand, disclose that the subsequent debts have merely taken the place of prior ones, or that the debtor has continued or embarked in a business in which his becoming indebted was inevitable, or there may be other circumstances of the like persuasive character, creating or strengthening the presumption that, as the transfer was in fraud of prior, it was also in fraud of subsequent, creditors.' Bump on Fraudulent Conveyances (4th Ed.) §§293–296.

11. *Hanson v. First Nat. Bank in Brookings*, 848 F.2d 866, 868 (8th Cir. 1988).

> After a careful examination of many cases, this doctrine seems reasonable. We are unable to discover how constructive or even actual notice of the execution of a voluntary deed by a debtor could of itself inform a subsequent creditor of the secret purposes of the debtor in making the deed, of his insolvency, of his intention to contract large debts, or of his intention to engage in a hazardous enterprise, the risks of which he was seeking to avoid, or of other fraudulent and covinous purposes he might entertain, so as to shut off the subsequent creditor from attacking the voluntary deed for such or other sufficient causes. *See* Diggs v. McCullough, 69 Md. 592, 16 Atl. 453; Scott v. Keane, 87 Md. 709, 40 Atl. 1070, 42 L. R. A. 359; Baltimore High Grade Brick Co. v. Amos, 95 Md. 571, 52 Atl. 582, 53 Atl. 148. Our opinion is that, in so far as the instant case is concerned, where the bill is filed by a trustee in bankruptcy representing all classes of creditors, and where the facts are such as are here alleged, the bill is not obnoxious to the demurrer which was interposed.[12]

It should be noted that the circumstances identified in *Beasley v. Coggins* as particularly troublesome subsequently became part of fraudulent transfer statutory law.

Notwithstanding the foregoing, where intent must be proven to void a transfer, some courts have dispensed with the intent requirement as applied to a self-settled spendthrift trust or similar arrangement. The concept of "having your cake and eating it too" generally is premised on making a transfer with the intent to hinder creditors. By its very terms, such an arrangement creates a potential issue with fraudulent transfer law. Whereas one can argue a contribution of capital to an LLC that is engaged in business operations was made for business reasons and without a view to hinder creditors of the contributing member, the nature of the self-settled trust, or similar arrangement, is invariably marketed such that the debtor can enjoy the wealth but not the obligations that may arise with respect to creditors.

Despite the general prohibition on self-settled spendthrift trusts or similar arrangements, variations of the self-settled spendthrift trust have been upheld by courts where it is clear the primary purpose was not to hinder creditors. A prime example of this type of trust is a tax-driven arrangement that seeks to move value of a personal residence out of the homeowner's gross estate for Federal estate tax purposes. This trust, a so-called qualified personal residence trust or QPRT, along with other forms of trusts formed for estate and tax planning purposes, is discussed more fully in chapter seven. Suffice to say, a creditor will need to carefully examine both the trust agreement and the circumstances giving rise to the trust arrangement to determine if a transfer to the trustee of the trust is more aligned with the historically disfavored self-settled trust or is a variant that requires proof of intent at the time of the creation of the trust. Of particular importance is the retained term for the settlor. If a term over which the settlor retained an interest expires, the trust might convert to a

12. *Beasley v. Coggins*, 48 Fla. 215, 222–25, 37 So. 213, 215–16 (1904).

traditional irrevocable trust. But even in this scenario, the creditor should examine the facts and circumstances to determine whether the trust has truly changed to remove the settlor's retained interest.

The public policy behind the fraudulent transfer law is that a debtor should not be rewarded for creating an arrangement that permits him to quarantine assets in the event he should enter a transaction that was too risky, or to engage in a business without sufficient capital. That a debtor structured the arrangement more than four years before the claim arises should not make any difference based on the one-year reasonable discovery rule. Lastly, some courts have abandoned the per se approach with respect to self-settled trusts (or similar arrangements) and will require evidence of intent as with any other fraudulent transfer case. This does not mean a debtor wins, it means a creditor will need to carry the burden and prove the transfers to the self-settled trust or similar arrangement was done with the intent to hinder creditors.

By injecting more clarity to the matter, the UVTA helps clear the uncertainty surrounding choice of law for creditors, but simultaneously casts doubt as to whether an individual can engage in a fraudulent transfer and rely on weakened creditors rights laws in another jurisdiction. Consequently, it could be that the sale of asset protection trusts in non-asset protection trust states could wane, steering the client to more conservative investments in items such as a personal residence, annuities, and life insurance, all of which might enjoy creditor protection in the client's state of residence.

If the UVTA opposition cannot stop the enactment of the UVTA, the next best thing would be to attempt to weaken the non-asset protection trust state's UVTA so it would not interrupt the flow of wealth to the asset protection trust advisers.[13] Or, as to states with a DAPT statute, the UVTA could be modified to exist in harmony with the states' DAPT statute.[14]

---

13. Key battleground states are those that rank high in gross domestic product (GDP) and are a source of wealth to asset protection trust companies. These states include Florida and Texas, where any attempt for such state to enact the UVTA will most likely result in the opposition hiring lobbyists and conducting a grass roots campaign to generate enough opposition to the UVTA by identifying threats to planning. Such perceived threats involve loss of tax planning opportunities (e.g., "asset substitution") and limited liability companies that "disappear" if one member has fraudulent intent in a conversion transaction. The opposition will seek to tinker with any proposed UVTA bill in such a way that attempts to re-define the definition of "creditor" consistent with the asset protection industry's definition, thereby avoiding any real conflict between the two states. High GDP states must carefully consider the impact of cutting entire classes of creditors out of their fraudulent transfer law. The opposition has successfully implemented a non-uniform provision in Arkansas' legislative history, attempting to direct judges not to consider offensive provisions of the Official Comments. Query whether (a) a judge would refuse to acknowledge any cases cited by a creditor that are also contained within the "offensive" Official Comments, and (b) the constitutionality of such a direction essentially telling judges not to look at certain persuasive sources. The opposition attempted to implement such a provision in Florida's statute in 2018, however, such attempt was met with resistance from the Business Law Section of the Florida Bar.

14. *See* Legislative Analysis to Michigan House Bill 4618, which amends its UVTA to permit Michigan's version of an asset protection trust. ("House Bill 4618 would amend the Uniform Voidable Transactions Act to change provisions concerning jurisdiction and standards of proof with regard to qualified dispositions, as defined in the Qualified Dispositions in Trust Act. Generally speaking, the Uniform Voidable Transactions Act provides a creditor with the means to reach a debtor's assets when the debtor has transferred the assets to another person or incurred an obligation under circumstances considered fraudulent or unfair to the creditor,

The ability of a non-DAPT resident to utilize a DAPT state's pro-debtor provisions is questionable for creditor protection purposes, at least when the DAPT is funded via fraudulent transfer.[15] Demonstrably, given the number of courts that have already applied the law of the (non-DAPT) state of the debtor's residence under the Restatement (Second) of Conflicts of Law,[16] the choice of law result for debtors utilizing the asset protection trust outside a fraudulent transfer action is nothing new. Further, the recent decision of the Alaska Supreme Court in *Bertran* calls into question the validity of DAPT statutes that provide for exclusive jurisdiction over fraudulent transfer issues. The result in *Bertran* was downplayed by at least one commentator, who concluded the worst-case scenario is that a DAPT state would use a longer statute of limitations. This conclusion ignores other aspects of pro-debtor provisions in a DAPT statute that would also be lost, such as the burden of proof standard (typically heightened by the DAPT state), the ability to use a trust agreement as evidence of the debtor's intent (often prohibited by the DAPT state), and secondary liability for advisors who assist in the creation of a DAPT (often immunized by the DAPT state), etc.

Several courts have refused to permit a debtor to set the ground rules for a fraudulent transfer such that a creditor cannot seek relief. Although some advisers *insist* the Restatement's choice of law analysis should point to the governing law chosen in a trust agreement under Section 273, the courts have routinely ignored this argument.[17] This is because transfers made to self-settled trusts, especially those made with the intent to hinder, delay, or defraud creditors, may violate strong public policy of a state that has not reversed long-standing law. Instead, courts have applied Section 270 of the Restatement, which provides:

> Law designated by the settlor to govern validity of the trust. Effect will be given to a provision in the trust instrument that the validity of the trust shall be governed by the local law of a particular state, provided that this state has a substantial relation to the trust and that the application of its local law does not violate a strong public policy of the state with which as to the matter at issue the trust has its most significant relationship.

Some asset protection advisers continue to downplay decisions that take this approach, citing bad facts or questioning the court's ability to grasp trust law. Some quibble at whether a self-settled trust actually violates public policy of the law of debtor's domicile, but at the same time, argue that should be ignored in favor of the weakened fraudulent transfer law of the asset protection trust

---

and the Qualified Dispositions in Trust Act provides for the creation of irrevocable trusts whose assets cannot be reached by creditors if certain requirements are met.")

15. Consequently, there could be tax issues associated with an asset protection trust designed as a completed gift trust if is formed by a resident located in a non-DAPT state.

16. As discussed *infra*, the courts have been reluctant to permit an individual to arrange his affairs such that he may transfer wealth into trust, incur debt, and then force the creditor to play by the rules of the debtor's chosen domicile (which is often pro-debtor.)

17. There are two pending law reform efforts in this area: the American Legal Institute's project to draft a Restatement Third of Conflict of Laws, and the newly formed ULC project to draft a uniform or model law regarding choice of law for trusts and estates.

state. This begs the question: if no public policy is violated, why insist on using a weakened fraudulent transfer statute, and one that prohibits judges from considering the terms of the trust agreement, as well as immunizing the advisers who were involved in the transaction?

For these complex conflict of law reasons, the asset protection trust industry is seeking to implement asset protection trust statutes in high-GDP states, even though a proposed statute for a high GDP state most likely would not provide much creditor protection due to a large banking presence as well as an active creditors' rights bar (including strong family law and personal injury law bars).[18] Or, the governor might decide at the last second to veto such legislation. Such was the case with a proposed asset protection trust statute in Georgia. The win for the Georgia asset protection trust industry was not protecting assets through Georgia's new asset protection trust legislation because the protections were *diluted severely* in contrast to traditional asset protection trust legislation. Instead, the goal was presumably to reverse Georgia public policy (and avoid the adverse Restatement result discussed earlier) to permit the use of foreign laws that provide extensive debtor protections. Although banks were protected fairly under the proposed Georgia asset protection trust statute, it was primarily tort creditors who would be prohibited from reaching asset protection trust assets.

## Voidable per se

Generally, a creditor must prove intent under an actual fraud approach to void a transfer. However, the common law has recognized situations where the type of transaction will lead to an inference of the requisite intent to hinder, delay, or defraud. This is distinguishable from a creditor pointing to numerous statutory badges of fraud, which accomplish the same result. Examples of transactions that have satisfied the requisite intent historically include transfers pursuant to Ponzi schemes and to self-settled spendthrift trusts.

The Official Comments point to the established case law involving self-settled spendthrift trusts, which, unsurprisingly, has drawn great protest from those who profit off the sale and administration of self-settled spendthrift trusts. The presumption approach historically taken by some courts was limited to the use of self-settled spendthrift trusts, and has not included QPRTs, GRATs, and charitable trusts. The main difference between the foregoing being that the latter are presumed to be subject to creditor claims from the outset,[19] whereas the self-settled spendthrift trust attempts to immunize the trust corpus ab initio.

18. Ohio and Michigan are examples of high GDP states that adopted a DAPT statute.

19. Thus, if a settlor of a QPRT, GRAT or charitable trust dies during the retained interest term, the assets are (generally) included in the settlor's estate for federal estate tax purposes since the term interest is subject to creditor claims. In contrast, the APT is meant to exclude all assets from the settlor's estate in reliance on state law, which may or may not be the law of the decedent's domicile. For those who do not reside in an APT domicile, many suggest avoiding the APT for this reason (estate tax inclusion), among many others.

UVTA opponents have argued that because the common law includes decisions where courts have found transfers to self-settled spendthrift trusts to be voidable per se, all transactions identified in the Official Comments to the UVTA are voidable per se. However, transactions identified in the Official Comments, such as those involving corporations or limited liability companies in certain situations, are referred to as potentially voidable based on the circumstances. As discussed in chapter three, many transactions have given rise to an inference or presumption of fraudulent intent. Further, opponents assert the presumption case law has an expiration date for validity. Despite the numerous cases highlighting the exposure of transfers to self-settled trusts under fraudulent transfer law, the UVTA opponents have sought to suppress the Official Comments because the cases are "ancient".[20]

It is also worth noting that the phrase voidable per se does not appear anywhere in the Official Comments. Even if the Official Comments did make such a statement, it would conflict with the text of the UVTA (the creditor must prove actual fraud under the UFTA/UVTA). UTVA opposition advancing the presumption argument point to Official Comments dealing with circumstances that hinder, delay, or defraud, and may be voidable for that reason. Voidable, however, is not the same as per se void.[21] The opposition conspicuously ignores nearly five pages of comments dealing with intent to hinder, delay, or defraud.

Further, the fact that some courts have applied a per se approach to self-settled trusts should not be cited as support for preventing individuals from using business entities in a legitimate fashion or engaging in legitimate estate, business, or tax planning. Unlike the use of a self-settled trust, which has a special distinction in the history of creditors' rights, other forms of planning, by themselves, should not raise any fraudulent transfer suspicion. However, transactions made as part of any planning process are not immune from challenge automatically. Thus, although the contribution of property to a corporation should not, by itself raise red flags,[22] the circumstances may justify application of fraudulent transfer law. Further, the conversion of an entity to a

20. See Kettering, BNA. ("The comments merely point out that, for more than 150 years, courts have unanimously held that such a transfer is not consistent with fraudulent transfer law. The Article proposes to suppress mention of that fact.") *See also*, *United States v. Hooe*, 7 U.S. 73, 80–81, 2 L. Ed. 370 (1805). ("The 5th sign of fraud mentioned in *Twyne's case*, 3 Co. 81. (b) is, that there 'was a trust between the parties; for the donor possessed all, and used them as his proper goods, and fraud is always appareled and clad with a trust, and a trust is the cover of fraud.' And it is unimportant whether the trust be expressed or implied. Every gift made on a trust is out of the proviso of the act. Here it was part of the trust that Fitzgerald should raise money upon the deed to his own use; and a deed which covers the property from his creditors and gives the grantor the whole benefit and use of it, is the very kind of deed which the statute meant to avoid.")

21. *See Mayer v. Hellman*, 91 U.S. 496, 501, 23 L. Ed. 377 (1875). ("The assignment in this case was not a proceeding, as already said, in hostility to the creditors, but for their benefit. It was not, therefore, void as against them, or even voidable.") See Black's Law Dictionary, "That may be avoided, or declared void; not absolutely void, or void in itself. Most of the acts of infants are voidable only, and not absolutely void."

22. *See* Comment 6 to UVTA Section 4. ("The fact that a transfer has been made to a relative or to an affiliated corporation has not been regarded as a badge of fraud sufficient to warrant avoidance when unaccompanied by any other evidence of intent to hinder, delay, or defraud creditors.")

different form may be done without fear of challenge,[23] unless the conversion can be proven to have been effected with the actual intent to hinder, delay, or defraud creditors. In sum, the UVTA enactment concerns rest primarily with some (not all) asset protection proponents, who are attempting to extend the choice of law uncertainty surrounding APTs (uncertainty that has always existed) to legitimate planning transactions to garner support in opposition of the UVTA.

23. *Plantation Key Developers, Inc. v. Colonial Mortg. Co. of Indiana*, 589 F.2d 164, 172 (5th Cir. 1979). ("Courts are reluctant to label common business decisions as fraud. *Sponholtz v. Sponholtz*, 190 So.2d 572 (Fla.1966) (change of business organization from partnership to corporation does not support theory of fraudulent conveyance).")

CHAPTER 5

# The Fraudulent Transfer Iceberg: Application of Statutory & Common Law

If fraudulent transfer law is viewed as an iceberg, the fraudulent transfer statutory law would be the visible tip, and the fraudulent transfer common law would be the hidden body. Although the fraudulent transfer statutory law largely codified the fraudulent transfer common law, it did not completely displace the common law.[1] The operative terms of the fraudulent transfer statute may require judicial interpretation, and so, it should be no surprise that the common law has been applied to help interpret fraudulent transfer statutes.[2] Further, the fraudulent transfer statutory law does not displace other statutes that may apply to a fraudulent transfer.[3] All such law can potentially apply to various forms of wealth transfer, as well as secondary liability for assisting with fraudulent transfers as part of a wealth transfer plan.

It was recognized as early as 1933 that the modern statute's use of the phrase, "hinder, delay, or defraud" (present in the UFCA and UFTA/UVTA)

1. *See Phillips v. Phillips*, No.A13-0699, 2014 Minn. App. Unpub. LEXIS 190, *10 (Minn. Ct. App. Mar. 10, 2014) ("The MUFTA largely codifies claims that existed at common law and/or under its precursor, the Uniform Fraudulent Conveyance Act.")

2. *See Nat'l Auto Serv. Centers, Inc. v. F/R 550, LLC*, 192 So. 3d 498, 508 (Fla. Dist. Ct. App. 2016), reh'g denied (May 25, 2016), review denied sub nom. F/R 550, LLC v. Nat. Auto Serv. Centers, Inc., No. SC16-1045, 2016 WL 6299565 (Fla. Oct. 27, 2016). ("In *Freitag*, the court supported its claim about remedial purpose with the observation that both the common law and the statutory predecessor to the Uniform Act—the Uniform Fraudulent Conveyance Act—tied the timeliness of claims founded on fraud to the discovery of the facts constituting the fraud. 947 P.2d at 1189. The presumption, the court reasoned, should be that the Washington legislature was aware of this and must have shared that understanding when it codified the Uniform Act. The problem is that the understanding that the Freitag court presumed the Washington legislature to have shared varies markedly from the understanding conveyed by the actual words that its legislature—as well as Florida's—voted to adopt. Regardless of what the understanding at common law or under the Uniform Act's statutory predecessor was, "discovery of the transfer" means something that is unambiguously different from "discovery of the fraudulent nature of the transfer." *Cf. Samples v. Fla. Birth-Related Neurological*, 40 So.3d 18, 22 (Fla. 5th DCA 2010) (declining to apply principle that statutes in derogation of the common law are strictly construed where the statutory language was unambiguous). The language that the legislature enacted is "discovery of the transfer," and it is that understanding we are obliged to follow.")

3. As discussed in chapter six.

was merely the adoption of the Statute of Elizabeth, requiring examination of the common law to flesh out the scope and application of the phrase. "[D]etermination of the subject matter of the [Uniform Fraudulent Conveyance Act] would require reference to the general common law. The use of the words of art, 'conveyance . . . with intent . . . to hinder, delay or defraud . . . creditors,' gives the cue that this is a modernized Statute of Elizabeth and nothing else."[4] In the iceberg analogy, it is the hidden body of fraudulent transfer common law that provides creditors with numerous potential avenues for relief and potential danger for those who engage in transactional planning. This is because the common law demonstrates how courts will interpret and apply terms to provide a creditor with relief under the fraudulent transfer law and carries centuries of decisions with it.

> The UFTA, by its own terms, is consistent with this background. The Act states that "[u]nless displaced by the provisions of this chapter, the principles of law and equity, including . . . the law relating to . . . fraud . . . or other validating or invalidating cause, supplement[s] this chapter's provisions." R.I. Gen. Laws. §6–16–10. At the very least, this clause demonstrates a desire by the drafters to preserve the common law as a supplement to the UFTA unless precluded by the terms of the Act. Moreover, to find broad preemption in the UFTA, in the absence of language of preemption, would be at odds with the presumption that statutes should not be construed to alter common law principles absent an explicit statement of legislative intent to do so. *See, e.g., Shaw v. R.R. Co.*, 101 U.S. 557, 565, 25 L.Ed. 892 (1879) ("No statute is to be construed as altering the common law, farther than its words import."); *Knowles v. Ponton*, 96 R.I. 156, 190 A.2d 4, 6 (1963) ( "It is a well settled rule in the construction of statutes that legislative enactments will be construed to alter the common law only to the extent that the legislature has made that purpose clear."); Norman J. Singer, Sutherland Statutory Construction §61:1 (2001 Revision) ("Where there is any doubt about [statutes'] meaning or intent they are given the effect which makes the least rather than the most change.").[5]

The uniform fraudulent transfer acts (UFCA and UFTA/UVTA) both contain a provision confirming no intent to displace the remedies that are otherwise available for creditors.[6] This means that unless it is clear that fraudulent transfer statutory law replaces the common law, statute or rule (i.e.,

4. *See* McLaughlin, J. Angell, *Application of the Uniform Fraudulent Conveyance Act*, 46 Harv. L. Rev. 404 (1933).

5. *In re Valente*, 360 F.3d 256, 261 (1st Cir. 2004).

6. *See* UVTA §12. *See also, In re Kohner*, No. 2:13-BK-02159-DPC, 2014 WL 4639920, at *7 (Bankr. D. Ariz. Sept. 11, 2014). ("UFCA §11 provided that "[i]n any case not provided for in this Act the rules of law and equity including the law merchant, and in particular the rules relating to the law of principal and agent, and the effect of fraud, misrepresentation, duress or coercion, mistake, bankruptcy, or other invalidating cause shall govern." Similarly, the UFTA provides in §10 that, 'unless displaced by the provisions of this [Act], the principles of law and equity, including the law merchant and the law relating to principal and agent, estoppel, laches, fraud, misrepresentation, duress, coercion, mistake, insolvency, or other validating or invalidating cause, supplement its provisions.'") *See also, Gulf Ins. Co. v. Clark*, 2001 MT 45, ¶ 42, 304 Mont. 264, 275, 20 P.3d 780, 787. ("As §31-2-342, MCA, makes clear, by no means is an action under UFTA an exclusive remedy. *See* §31-2-342, MCA (providing that unless displaced by provisions under UFTA, "the principles of law and equity . . . supplement its provisions"). To this end we observe that although another remedy at equity or law

replace a remedy, cause of action, statute of limitation/repose, pleading standard, right to a jury trial, etc.), then all such items will exist independently of fraudulent transfer statutory law.[7] Throughout this book, the common law in the context of fraudulent transfer law will be referred to as the "fraudulent transfer common law."[8] Of prime importance for those who are involved with wealth transfer planning, is the common law that exists with respect to liability for those who assist with a fraudulent transfer.

## Broad Terminology

It should be noted that courts have interpreted fraudulent transfer statutory terms liberally in favor of creditors. This liberal interpretation has been applied to various terms, such as a "conveyance,"[9] a "claim,"[10] etc. The term "creditor" is especially important in the wealth transfer planning context as it pertains to transfers meant to safeguard assets from claims.

## Transfer

The term used to describe the passage of an asset from a debtor to a transferee has changed over time. Initially, the term used to describe a fraudulent transfer was a "conveyance." This was the term in use when the ULC promulgated the

---

may be available-one which may in fact accrue at the time judgment is entered-UFTA clearly stands on its own unambiguous terms.")

7. *See In re Valente*, 360 F.3d 256, 261–62 (1st Cir. 2004). ("Courts in other states evaluating claims in other contexts have also rejected UFTA preemption of existing remedies. *See, e.g., Macedo v. Bosio*, 86 Cal. App.4th 1044, 1051, 104 Cal.Rptr.2d 1 (Cal.Ct.App.2001) ("[T]he UFTA is not the exclusive remedy by which fraudulent conveyances and transfers may be attacked. They may also be attacked by, as it were, a common law action."); *262 *Cortez v. Vogt*, 52 Cal.App.4th 917, 929, 60 Cal.Rptr.2d 841 (Cal.Ct.App.1997) ("[T]he remedies of the UFTA . . . are cumulative to the remedies applicable to fraudulent conveyances that existed before the uniform laws went into effect."); *Freitag v. McGhie*, 133 Wash.2d 816, 947 P.2d 1186, 1189–90 (1997) (observing that the purpose of the UFTA was to "discourag[e] fraud" and that "within the UFTA itself lies a mandate to apply the common law to the extent it is not inconsistent with the provisions of the act"); *Bill Nay & Sons Excavating v. Neeley Constr. Co.*, 677 P.2d 1120, 1123 (Utah 1984) (imposing a resulting trust after concluding that the creditor did not satisfy the requirements for relief under the UFTA). *But see Moore v. Browning*, 203 Ariz. 102, 50 P.3d 852, 858 (App.2002) (concluding that the UFTA preempted the common law use of the statute of limitations regarding fraudulent actions). Given this precedent, both within and without Rhode Island, we conclude that Rhode Island's adoption of the UFTA did not preempt common law remedies applicable to fraudulent transactions.")

8. *See Kelleher v. Kelleher*, No. 13-CV-05450-MEJ, 2015 WL 5693726, at *13 (N.D. Cal. Sept. 29, 2015). ("California recognizes that fraudulent transfer common law causes of action are not preempted by CUFTA and remain available remedies. Fid. Nat. Title Ins. Co. v. Schroeder, 179 Cal. App. 4th 834, 849 (2009).")

9. *Butler v. Wilkinson*, 740 P.2d 1244, 1260 (Utah 1987). ("Given the purpose of the Act, [the term 'conveyance'] should be construed with liberality so as to reach all artifices and evasions designed to rob the Act of its full force and effect in preventing debtors from paying the just claims of their creditors.")

10. *Hullett v. Cousin*, 204 Ariz. 292, 297, 63 P.3d 1029, 1034 (2003). (The UFTA's definition of claim is unquestionably broadly worded. See A.R.S. §44-1001(2). As such, it includes unknown and unasserted claims. *In re W.R. Grace & Co.*, 281 B.R. 852, 862 (Bankr.D.Del.2002) ("This expansive language [defining a claim] must negate any residual inference that a right to payment must be known and asserted to be a claim.").)

first uniform act (the Uniform Fraudulent Conveyance Act) in 1918. Subsequently, the term "transfer" was used to clarify that not only could conveyances of real property be voided, but so too could transfers of other types of property. In 2014, the term "transaction" replaced "transfer" in the act's title. The change in title reflects the fact that fraudulent transfer law encompasses not only a change in legal rights to property via transfer (or conveyance) but also the incurrence of an obligation. The UVTA defines "transfer" to mean "every mode, direct or indirect, absolute or conditional, voluntary or involuntary, of disposing of or parting with an asset or an interest in an asset, and includes payment of money, release, lease, license, and creation of a lien or other encumbrance."

Despite the name change, however, "transfer" is still utilized in Sections 4 and 5. Over time, courts have construed the term transfer to include just about every machination one can invent to change an interest in an asset. Not only does transfer apply to a movement of title from the debtor to a transferee, but it also encompasses a change in the legal rights the debtor has in an asset. This liberal construction is afforded under the uniform acts as well as under the bankruptcy code.

> The definition of the term "transfer" as used in this Statute is basically identical to the definition of the term used by §101(58) of the Bankruptcy Code and is intended to cover any transaction whereby a transferor divested himself or herself, directly or indirectly, of any cognizable interest, legal or equitable, in the property of the transferor. Based on the broad definition of the term both by the Statute relied on by the Trustee as well as the definition of the Code, this Court is satisfied that the execution of the Trust Amendment was a transfer within the meaning of that term used in Florida Statute 726.102(12). By relinquishing her trust powers and relinquishing her dominion and control over the trust assets the Defendant "part[ed] with an . . . interest in an asset" and but for the Trust Amendment she could have invaded the assets in the trust at any time. Thus, it is without question that the Trustee could have seized the corpus of the trust before the Trust Agreement was amended, the funds in the Trust were the very funds she received through the transfer declared to be preferential and which is the basis of the judgment obtained by the Trustee. Having concluded that the execution of the amendment to the Trust Agreement did in fact effectively operate as a transfer of the Defendant's interest in the corpus of the trust, this leaves for consideration whether or not the Trustee established with the requisite degree of proof all the requisite elements of a viable fraudulent transfer claim under Fla.Stat. §§726.105 and 726.106(1).[11]

Consistent with other liberal interpretations of operative provisions, a court may broadly interpret "transfer" to include a multitude of ways a debtor can transfer an asset. The term can encompass changing an asset's characteristics (e.g., changing a business interest from corporate stock to a limited liability company interest) or exchanging one asset for another (e.g., cash for an

11. *In re Crawford*, 172 B.R. 365, 367 (Bankr. M.D. Fla. 1994).

annuity). Florida law specifically addresses the conversion of one asset into another and provides relief for a fraudulent conversion, separate and apart from the fraudulent transfer statute. Essentially, a conversion can be viewed as a transfer of an asset without the use of a third party. This might seem counterintuitive as one typically considers a transfer to require separate parties.

But a separate fraudulent conversion statute is not required due to the broad definition of "transfer." *In re Nagel*[12] illustrates how a court will find a transfer even with the lack of a third-party transferee. Here, the appellate court held that a debtor need not transfer an asset to a third party; it is sufficient for fraudulent transfer purposes that the debtor merely changed the nature of the asset.

> In the instant matter, Nagel alleges Lawson and Westen enlisted Westen's brothers, attorneys Derek and Peter Westen, to help them design and implement an "Asset Protection Plan" when it became apparent the arbitrator would rule in Nagel's favor. The plan had three components. First, they converted respondent Westen Family Group, LLC (WFG), of which Lawson and Westen held a 20.7 percent membership interest, from a California LLC into a Nevada LLC. Second, they placed a portion of the Brentwood sale proceeds into an annuity. Third, they bought a house in Texas and improved it with the balance of their sale proceeds. Nagel further alleges Lawson and Westen promptly moved to Texas upon receiving the arbitrator's preliminary award so they could invoke the state's unlimited homestead exemption to shield the new house and annuity from creditors.
>
> Nagel filed this action when she learned about these asset protection measures. She named Lawson and Westen as defendants along with Derek Westen, Peter Westen, WFG, and two Westen family trusts. Her first amended complaint included three causes of action at issue here: (1) to set aside fraudulent transfer of assets under both the UVTA3 and common law (as to WFG only); (2) civil conspiracy (as to all parties); and (3) aiding and abetting (as to Derek Westen, Peter Westen, WFG, and the family trusts).4 Nagel sought to annul the transfers and to restrain Lawson and Westen from disposing of their assets, among other remedies.[13]

As noted by attorney and Forbes columnist Jay D. Adkisson, "The Court of Appeals went on to note that nothing in the UVTA can be interpreted to prevent the debtor from being, essentially, the transferee of herself. This, the Court felt, furthered the public purposes of the UVTA which was to keep debtors from doing things to diminish the rights of their creditors or to "devise new and more creative ways to circumvent valid obligations."

The court also noted how a broad interpretation of the term "transfer" was consistent with case law interpreting the term.

> "PGA West, *supra*, 14 Cal.App.5th 156, 221 Cal.Rptr.3d 353 presented the Fourth District with a situation similar in concept (if not fact) to ours.

12. *Nagel v. Westen*, 2021 WL 58119 (Cal.App., Distr. 2, Jan. 7, 2021).
13. *Id.*

> Debtor recorded a deed of trust on his condominium. He named an unincorporated sham entity as the deed's beneficiary and then foreclosed to insulate his equity from a creditor's claims. Many years later the creditor tried to avoid the UVTA's seven-year period of repose by arguing a transfer did not occur until debtor incorporated the sham entity. Prior to then, the creditor argued, debtor had effectively given a property interest to himself. The Fourth District declined to adopt the creditor's rigid characterization of the term 'transfer' by focusing on the legal distinctions between the debtor and the purported transferee. The debtor's intent to insulate his assets and defraud creditors brought the transaction within the UVTA. (*See id.* at p. 174, 221 Cal.Rptr.3d 353 ["although Mork never incurred a real obligation to Hulven under the deed of trust and note, and Hulven apparently never really existed as a corporate entity, Mork's fraudulent attempt to transfer the equity in his condominium to Hulven to insulate that asset from potential creditors constitutes a 'transfer' as defined in section 3439.01, subdivision (m)"].) We agree. The creditor's interests should drive the court's interpretation of the term 'transfer' rather than the form of debtors' asset manipulations."

Finally, it is worth noting the court in *Nagel* overruled the trial court's ruling involving secondary liability to those who assisted with the transfer. This topic is discussed in more detail in chapter nine.

Not only may a creditor challenge the transfer of an asset, but the creditor may challenge the transfer of "an interest in an asset."[14]

> It is absolutely apparent from Creditor's petition, which was supported by overwhelming evidence at trial, that Debtor and Wife conspired to fraudulently convey, through the use of the corporate defendants DHBI and NCOI, the income Debtor would have received for his professional services as an orthopedic surgeon. Debtor did this "with an intent to hinder, delay, and defraud" Creditor of his obligations under the February 1996 judgment. As such, all of the income Debtor would have earned for his professional services as an orthopedic surgeon in his medical practice since Creditor obtained the February 2, 1996, judgment, which we find was fraudulently conveyed to Wife, DHBI and/or NCOI, shall be retransferred back to Debtor personally such that Creditor is able to collect his judgment from that income.[15]

A transfer can occur even if the debtor remains the technical owner of the asset. An Eleventh Circuit opinion confirms this result and provides more support for creditors to bring fraudulent transfer claims regardless of whether a debtor converts or transfers an asset.

---

14. *See Klatte v. Buckman, No. CV140699FLWLHG, 2016 WL 1090437, at *5 (D.N.J. Mar. 21, 2016).* ("Plaintiffs concede that Mercer Capital did not 'own' its customers' accounts, but rather that each account holder controlled their own account(s). Def.'s SOMF ¶ 37. However, under the MUFTA, a 'transfer' includes the disposition of both an 'asset' as well as 'an interest in an asset.' Minn. Stat. §513.41(12). Clearly, Mercer Capital had some 'interest' in its customers' accounts even if, technically, each account was 'owned' by the respective account holder. While a customer might choose to leave an investment company and take its account (and assets) elsewhere, it stretches the bounds of reason to argue that an investment company has absolutely no 'interest' in those accounts while they were managed by that same company, or that the interest could not be transferred to another investment company. Defendants' argument ignores the plain language of the MUFTA's definition of the term 'transfer.'")

15. *Fischer v. Brancato*, 147 S.W.3d 794, 801 (Mo. Ct. App. 2004).

> The FUFTA defines a "transfer" as "every mode, direct or indirect, absolute or conditional, voluntary or involuntary, of disposing of or parting with an asset or an interest in an asset." Fla. Stat. §726.102(14). While the definition of transfer is broad, the statute plainly requires a plaintiff to show that the debtor either disposed of his asset or relinquished some interest in that asset. *Nationsbank, N.A. v. Coastal Utilities, Inc.*, 814 So. 2d 1227, 1230 (Fla. Dist. Ct. App. 2002). As long as the debtor relinquishes some interest in or control over the asset a FUFTA transfer has occurred, even if he remains the technical owner of the asset. *In re Levine*, 134 F.3d 1046, 1050 (11th Cir. 1998). Accordingly, in Levine we held that the debtor's purchase of an annuity constituted a FUFTA transfer because, by purchasing an annuity, the debtor limited his ability to withdraw his money to the terms of the annuity contract, thereby relinquishing some interest in that money. *Id.* at 1049–50. The debtor no longer retained total control over or unfettered access to the full amount of his "property." *Id.* at 1050.[16]

One can glean from the foregoing cases that the broad definition of transfer may be particularly useful in situations where a debtor reorganizes a business entity to another entity form that restricts a creditor's rights. In the case of a reorganization from a corporation to a limited liability company, the debtor parts with interest in stock and replaces the interest with LLC interests (e.g., units) but remains the owner before and after the reorganization. Such reorganization may be viewed as a transfer and can be successfully challenged where such a transfer is done with the requisite intent to hinder, delay, or defraud any creditor.

## Voidable

Section 4(a) of the UVTA provides certain transfers or obligations are "voidable as to a creditor" if made with actual or constructive fraud. Early U.S. cases and statutes used the phrase "void as to creditors" or "utterly void."[17] "It will be shown that the term 'void' is constantly interpreted to mean nothing more than 'voidable,' and that this construction is especially true as applied to voluntary assignments. Though the statute, in characterizing assignments, constantly uses the term 'void as to creditors,' it is obvious that 'nothing more is intended than inoperative or voidable;' or, as was observed by Chief Justice Shaw, 'such conveyance is not absolutely void, but voidable only by creditors.' It is the distinguishing characteristic of a void act that it is incapable of ratification, but an assignment which is fraudulent upon its face is capable of confirmation by creditors, and is good between the parties, hence it is not, logically speaking, void."[18]

16. *Isaiah v. JPMorgan Chase Bank*, 960 F.3d 1296 (11th Cir. 2020).
17. *See Shipe, Cloud & Co. v. Repass*, 69 Va. 716, 725 (1877).
18. Frederick S. Wait, *A Treatise on Fraudulent Conveyances and Creditor's Bills*, 417, (1884).

Whether a transfer is viewed as void or voidable might have important consequences. In *Matter of Hardin*,[19] an issue arose as to whether a judicial lien obtained prior to a debtor's bankruptcy filing attached to real estate fraudulently transferred by the debtor prior to filing bankruptcy. If the transfer was void, the judicial lien was considered to have attached to the transferred property, notwithstanding the fact that the debtor did not own legal title at the time the judgment was obtained and recorded, because ownership of the property never actually transferred. But if the transfer was merely voidable, the judgment did not attach to the property because it was not owned by the debtor at the time judgment was obtained. In this case, the judgment lien did not attach to property recovered by a bankruptcy trustee.

## Asset

Where a fraudulent transfer involves a transfer, the transfer must involve an "asset." For this inquiry, the debtor must have an interest under state law for which a creditor can seek relief. The legal status of the asset vis-à-vis the debtor is critical, and often an issue in wealth transfer situations. Here, the nature of an interest in an asset, an applicable exemption under statute or a protected form of ownership under the common law, might mean the asset is not really an asset for fraudulent transfer purposes.

Some may structure a transaction where a debtor's interest is not readily apparent, such as a transfer of assets followed by the debtor retaining no beneficial interest, but the status as a permissible appointee.[20] Where a debtor is a trust beneficiary, the debtor might engage in conduct to avoid having a beneficial interest as to certain assets. This might occur where a beneficiary disclaims an interest in a trust, discussed in more detail in chapter seven. Alternatively, a trustee might attempt to withhold a distribution of trust assets to the beneficiary, calling into question whether the beneficiary's interest has vested such that it can be considered a constructive receipt by a debtor/beneficiary followed by a voidable transfer by the debtor/beneficiary to the trustee. Or a court may determine that the trust agreement sufficiently conditions the beneficiary's interest such that the interest never vested and remains a mere contingent interest.

The transfer of an asset that is exempt or immune from creditor claims does not hinder creditors; if the creditors could not reach the asset in the first place, they are no worse off if the asset is transferred. Often, the issue will be whether transferred property is an asset for purposes of the fraudulent transfer statute; if property is not an asset then a transfer of the asset is not subject to avoidance. Frequently, a debtor will claim the transferred property is not an asset by virtue of

19. *Matter of Hardin*, No. AP 19-05221-LRC, 2021 WL 4484875, at *7 (Bankr. N.D. Ga. Sept. 30, 2021).

20. *See*, for example, Florida Statute Section 736.0103(4). ("An interest as a permissible appointee of a power of appointment, held by a person in a capacity other than that of trustee, is not a beneficial interest for purposes of this subsection.")

the asset being protected under state exemption law (e.g., homestead, life insurance, annuity) or the common law (e.g., tenancy by the entireties).

# Exemption Creation

Where a debtor claims an asset is exempt or immune, and thus not an asset for fraudulent transfer purposes, a creditor will examine how the proposed exempt property obtained its alleged status. Where a debtor converts a non-exempt asset into an exempt asset, a creditor can challenge such conversion under either fraudulent transfer law or fraudulent conversion law. The key under either mode of recovery is the requirement of proving the debtor's intent with respect to the conversion.

> As a final comment, it should be noted that this Court is receding in part from its holding in *In re* Levine, *supra*, that converting non-exempt property to exempt property is not per se fraudulent and conversion of such property for the purpose of placing such property out of the reach of creditors will not deprive a debtor of an exemption to which the debtor would otherwise be entitled. After further research and consideration, this Court is satisfied that a showing that the conversion of a non-exempt asset into an exempt asset for the specific purpose of placing the asset out of the reach of creditors is sufficient to deprive a debtor of his right to claim that property as exempt.[21]

In some cases, the property itself will be tainted and subject to disgorgement, regardless of whether the property otherwise qualifies for exempt status. This scenario is typical in super creditor situations, discussed in chapter ten.

## *Community Property*

Community property is a form of ownership between husband and wife recognized by several states, mostly in the western half of the United States. The issues that typically arise with respect to fraudulent transfer and community property are whether the assets are protected initially in the community property form and whether a subsequent transfer out of such status is voidable. Unlike the laws of some states that provide creditor protection for a married couple's assets held in a tenancy by entirety (where tenancy by entirety assets are protected from the claims of one spouse's creditors), the same protection might not exist in some states for a couple's community property. Consequently, a spouse may wish to remove assets from community property status and transfer such assets into another format to provide creditor protection.

This process might involve the transmutation of assets from the community property status into the name of one spouse. Once transmuted into the name of a spouse, the spouse may then transfer the newly transmuted asset into

21. *In re Levine*, 134 F.3d 1046, 1050 (11th Cir. 1998).

a creditor protected format. A creditor may argue the transmutation was not valid or seek avoidance of the subsequent transfer by the spouse as a fraudulent transfer.[22]

Sometimes marital planning is done primarily for creditor protection but under the guise of tax planning. For example, an adviser may tell a wealthy spouse that she can move her community property to South Dakota and achieve a double-step-up in the tax basis of such assets upon the death of the first spouse. The driving force for this transaction might be creditor avoidance, because the South Dakota statute doubles as an asset protection trust statute. This statute also mysteriously refers to South Dakota community property law, however, under South Dakota's common law, community property is non-existent. It is unclear how a court would treat a law pointing to a form of legal ownership under the common law that does not exist, at least not without adopting a full community property regime. It is clear the IRS has reservations about how it intends to treat community property where the status was obtained by a mere election.[23]

## *Tenancy by entirety*

Tenancy by the entireties (TBE) property is recognized in several states, mostly on the East Coast. The concept of TBE property arose because women suffered from legal disabilities and were not able to own property in their individual name. "Tenancy by the entirety is a creature of the common law of feudal England. At common law, according to Blackstone, . . . the very being or legal existence of a woman had virtually no property rights, even in her own property. She could not own personal property, and had no right to earnings for her personal labor. In order to confine land tenure to those capable of performing feudal duties, the husband held a freehold estate in all land owned by the wife, which, in the event of children, became a life estate. He enjoyed exclusive right to possession as well as ownership of the rents and profits of the land. He could convey this estate without the wife's consent, and his creditors could levy it.*** [B]y the fourteenth century, they developed fiction that the husband and wife were a single entity, and any land conveyed or bequeathed to husband and wife was held not in joint tenancy, but by the entirety, with an indestructible right of survivorship. Personal property could not be held by the entirety."[24]

---

22. *See Safarian v. Govgassian*, No. B291387, 2020 WL 1921791, at *9 (Cal. Ct. App. Apr. 21, 2020). ("We note the Law Revision Commission studying transmutations reported that '[m]ost people would find an oral transfer of such property, even between spouses, to be suspect and probably fraudulent, either as to creditors or between each other.' (Recommendation Relating to Marital Property Presumptions and Transmutations (Nov. 1983) 17 Cal. Law Revision Com. Rep. (1984) p. 214.) Two provisions were enacted as part of the statutory scheme governing transmutations to specifically protect the rights of creditors and third parties. Section 851, former Civil Code section 5110.720, states that transmutations are subject to the laws governing fraudulent transfers. (§851.)")

23. *See* IRS Publication 550 (3/2020).

24. Preliminary Report and a Request for Guidance, Ad-Hoc Committee on Tenancies by the Entireties, Florida Bar Business Law Section (June 3, 1998.)

Whereas numerous English and American courts held that the entireties doctrine did not mesh with laws providing women could own property, some state courts held differently, permitting the doctrine to coexist with a woman's right to own property. Although the justification for TBE property has long since vanished, the protection afforded to assets held in this form of ownership has continued under the common law, and has flourished as a form of asset protection.[25]

In situations where property is claimed to be held as tenants by entirety (and consequently, not an asset), a creditor often will examine whether the TBE was created through a fraudulent transfer and if not, whether all the unities were established to create a tenancy by the entireties. In the case of a bank account alleged to be held as tenants by the entirety, the inquiry may require obtaining the original signature card that was used to open the account. Debtors may argue an erroneous signature card designation does not reflect the intent of the spouses upon opening the account but cannot point to inadequate counsel from a banker. "As it applies to the mechanics of the bank-customer relationship in the opening of accounts, *Beal Bank* does not require a bank to explain the legal ramifications of the various account options. Only a handful of attorneys in Florida are able to describe the differences between a tenancy by the entireties bank account and a joint account with right of survivorship. The bank's obligation is to clearly provide customers with the option of a tenancy by the entireties account, not to assist them in making a considered choice. To paraphrase the old proverb, a bank's duty under *Beal Bank* is to lead the horse to water, not to make him drink it."[26]

While proving proper creation of TBE over a bank account or real property may require locating a signature card or deed, evidence supporting the proper creation of TBE over personal property may be hard to identify, as noted by the Florida Supreme Court in 1971. "Another reason for the distinction is that the application of entireties concepts to personalty becomes exceedingly complex as the nature of the personalty increases in sophistication, and the judicial mind seeks to require greater safeguards lest the tenancy be abused."[27]

Today, the abuse contemplated by the Florida Supreme Court in 1971 often takes the form of an LLC interest owned as TBE. The creation and transfer of interests is not susceptible to discovery by use of third party or public records; the only evidence is within the domain of the party who seeks to defraud creditors. Notwithstanding the level of sophistication employed by crafty debtors some four decades after *Hector Supply*, the law of fraudulent transfer law is broad enough to provide a creditor with relief.

In *SE Property Holdings, LLC v. McElheney*,[28] the debtor, McElheney, defaulted on a loan. The plaintiff creditor, SE Property Holdings, LLC, brought

25. Delaware enacted a statute such that the TBE property could be transferred to a Delaware Statutory Tenants by the Entireties Trust, where the ownership protection would, at least under the Delaware statute, persist despite being transferred in trust.

26. *Wexler v. Rich*, 80 So. 3d 1097, 1101 (Fla. Dist. Ct. App. 2012).

27. *First Nat. Bank of Leesburg v. Hector Supply Co.*, 254 So. 2d 777, 780 (Fla. 1971).

28. *SE Property Holdings, LLC v. McElheney*, 2016 WL 7494300, US District Court, ND FLA, Not Reported in F.Supp.3d (2016)

a foreclosure action against McElheney, and sought to enforce the eventual judgment in its favor by way of writ of garnishment, charging order, or both, against ten business entities in which McElheney held interests. As the court put it, "SE Property had its judgment, and it came collecting."

The court was faced with a fact pattern where the debtor transferred his LLC interest to the debtor and his wife, as tenants by the entirety. If the LLC interests were truly held in a tenancy by the entirety, the LLC interests would be immune from creditors under Florida's common law.[29] However, the court determined it did not need to reach this decision because there was evidence of a fraudulent transfer when the debtor expressed intent to protect the LLC assets.

> Ultimately, though, this Court might not have to decide the issue. Lurking in the shadows of this case is the suggestion that McElheney has transferred his individual interests in the LLC entities to tenancies by the entireties with his wife in order to avoid his creditors. Indeed, SE Property argues that one reason to interpret Florida law as disallowing such transfers is that otherwise "at any time Mr. McElheney so elects, regardless of how long he has owned his shares, he could simply protect it from his creditors by re-titling the entity as TBE, and arguably do so even after a charging order is entered or garnishment is served." ECF No. 227, at 3.
>
> *11 This argument ignores the fact that Florida has various fraudulent transfer statutes that would not permit McElheney to take such actions. For instance, §726.106, Florida Statutes provides that "[a] transfer made or obligation incurred by a debtor is fraudulent as to a creditor whose claim arose before the transfer was made or the obligation was incurred if the debtor made the transfer or incurred the obligation without receiving a reasonably equivalent value in exchange for the transfer or obligation and the debtor was insolvent at that time or the debtor became insolvent as a result of the transfer or obligation." Section 726.105 covers transfers intended to avoid future as well as present creditors.
>
> These statutes may very well apply to the transfer of McElheney's individual interests in McElheney Properties and Coastalmed to himself and his wife as tenants by the entireties. If they do, those transfers would be invalid regardless of what Florida law says about the tenancy-by-the-entireties transfer issue. Moreover, some of the transfers of assets between McElheney and the LLC entities might fall under the fraudulent transfer statutes and allow SE Property to avoid those transfers and successfully execute the writs of garnishment and/or charging orders.
>
> Again, though, the parties have wholly failed to brief this issue, and this Court is not in the business of making the parties' arguments for them. The parties focused their energy on the tenancy-by-the-entireties issue, and this Court has partially resolved that issue. But to determine the fates of the

---

29. The fear among some planners that transfer LLC interests from one spouse to both spouses as TBE would presumably be that such LLC interests were not held TBE since the creation of the TBE interest lacked the unities of time and title. The Florida Bar Real Property Trust and Estate Law Section subsequently supported a bill that would eliminate the time and title requirements but the proposal was rejected by the Business Law Section of the Florida Bar.

charging orders and writs of garnishment, this Court will require further briefing from the parties on the issue of fraudulent transfers. The parties may need to engage in more discovery, as well.[30]

## Homestead

Some states provide creditor protection for a debtor's home. A frequent issue is whether a debtor who buys a home or pays down a mortgage has committed a fraudulent transfer. In these situations, it is important to understand the source of the creditor protection; if the state's constitution affords creditor protection, it is possible a statutory cause of action via fraudulent transfer will not trump the state's constitutional homestead protection.

One state that provides constitutional homestead protection is Florida. Not only does Florida law provide this broad protection with its own unique characteristics,[31] but its Supreme Court has ruled that fraudulent transfers involving a Florida homestead are not defeated by Florida's fraudulent transfer statute. However, this fraudulent transfer homestead exception is not without limits. In Florida, the equitable lien doctrine has been applied to prevent a debtor from using the homestead where equity demands otherwise.[32] In 2014, the Eleventh Circuit held a fraudulent transfer of funds used to purchase a homestead could satisfy the fraud or egregious conduct requirement necessary to trigger application of the equitable lien doctrine.[33] In addition to proving fraud, a creditor must also trace the fraudulently transferred funds into the

30. *SE Prop. Holdings, LLC v. McElheney*, No. 5:12CV164-MW/EMT, 2016 WL 7494300, at *10–12 (N.D. Fla. May 7, 2016). (Emphasis added.)

31. *See Snyder v. Davis*, 699 So. 2d 999, 1002 (Fla. 1997), where the court supported the homestead protection that passed free of creditor claims to a decedent's heirs as "protected homestead." ("Finally, it is important to note that creditors are aware of the homestead provision and its inherent protections. As we discussed in Public Health Trust, we will not narrowly interpret the homestead provision simply because 'financially independent heirs' may receive a windfall. 531 So.2d at 950. There we wrote: The homestead protection has never been based on principles of equity, see Bigelow [v. Dunphe, 143 Fla. 603, 197 So. 328 (1940)], but always has been extended to the homesteader and, after his or her death, to the heirs whether the homestead was a twenty-two-room mansion or a two-room hut and whether the heirs were rich or poor. Id. Creditors have been on notice for many years that the plain language of the constitution protects homestead property from most creditors. It is with these policy considerations in mind that we address the two major issues in this case. *** Homestead law in the United States has evolved over time and it is strictly an American innovation. In Florida, moreover, our case law surrounding the homestead provision has its own contours and legal principles. As a result, it is not susceptible to comparisons with similar provisions in other jurisdictions. Importantly, our courts have emphasized that, in Florida, the homestead provision is in place to protect and preserve the interest of the family in the family home.")

32. *See Havoco of America v. Hill*, 790 So. 2d 1018, 1028 (Fla. 2001), citing *Smith v. Smith*, 761 So. 2d 370, 373 (Fla. Dist. Ct. App. 2000) ("[T]he supreme court has limited the exception allowing an equitable lien on homestead to those cases where the owner of the property has used the proceeds from fraud or reprehensible conduct to either invest in, purchase, or improve the homestead.")

33. *In re Bifani*, 580 F. App'x 740 (11th Cir. 2014). ("The purpose of the lien is to prevent unjust enrichment. Allowing Bifani to fraudulently transfer property to LaMarca to avoid his creditors, allowing LaMarca to use the proceeds from the properties to purchase a home, and then allowing Bifani to live in that home with LaMarca rent free with no remedy for the bankruptcy trustee is entirely unjust. Accordingly, we conclude that the bankruptcy court properly imposed an equitable lien on the Sarasota property, and the district court erred by reversing. The district court's order is affirmed in part, reversed in part, and remanded for the district court to impose the equitable lien.")

homestead and show that the funds were used to "invest in, purchase, or improve the homestead." In *Roberts v. Hopkins (In re Hopkins)*, the bankruptcy court for the Middle District of Florida held a single mortgage payment would not suffice, but that there must be a substantial reduction in the mortgage balance (amounting to a purchase or investment) to trigger the equitable lien doctrine.[34]

Texas also has a strong homestead exemption, where a California court interpreting Texas law held that the fraudulent transfer of funds to purchase a home will not prevent a debtor from successfully raising the homestead defense.

> Like the Texas Constitution, Florida's Constitution provides that—outside of specifically enumerated exceptions—a homestead is exempt from forced sale by any court. Fla. Const. art. X, §4. In Havoco, a debtor from Tennessee purchased a property in Florida using nonexempt funds in an attempt to shield his assets from a judgment creditor. See 790 So. 2d at 1019. The Court first noted that Florida's homestead exemption had long been construed liberally given its public policy implications. *See id.* at 1020. In light of this, the court declined to broaden the exceptions to the homestead exemption beyond those expressly enumerated. *See id.* at 1028. It held that the homestead exemption still applies where a debtor transfers nonexempt assets into an exempt homestead with the intent to hinder, delay, or defraud creditors. *Id.* Given the similarities between the Texas and Florida homestead exemptions, the Court finds the reasoning of the Florida Supreme Court to be relevant and persuasive to the issue presented here. Accordingly, the Court finds that Texas's homestead exemption—like Florida's—applies even when a debtor acquires the homestead using nonexempt funds with the intent of hindering its creditors.[35]

One claiming homestead, like any other exemption, must truly be entitled to the exemption in the first place. For example, Florida's homestead protection requires equitable or legal ownership, causing many lawyers to counsel their clients to hold title individually, and not through a trust or business entity. While some forms of trust ownership have been ruled safe for purposes of Florida's homestead protection, protection has been lost where the home is owned by a business entity.

> While the judgment debtor in Callava had some ownership interest in the property—as a beneficiary of the trust that owned it—in the instant case Guillen has no ownership interest, either legal or equitable, in the property at issue. *See* In re Alexander, 346 B.R. 546, 547 (Bankr. M.D. Fla. 2006) ("To qualify for Florida's homestead exemption, an individual must have an

---

34. *Roberts v. Hopkins (In re Hopkins)*, 625 B.R. 791, 799-0 (Bankr. M.D. Fla. 2021) ("An equitable lien may only be placed on a homestead when funds obtained through fraud or egregious behavior are used to purchase, invest in, or improve the homestead. Even had Plaintiffs brought a claim for fraudulent transfer and traced the funds into the mortgage payments on the Homestead, Plaintiffs still cannot state a claim for an equitable lien because three regular mortgage payments do not satisfy the requirement of monies used to invest in, purchase, or improve the homestead. This does not mean the use of fraudulently obtained funds to pay a mortgage can never result in an equitable lien. A substantial principal reduction of the mortgage loan or payment of several mortgage payments may qualify as a purchase or investment in the homestead. That is not the case here.")

35. Hinds & Shankman, LLP, Plaintiff, v. Richard Lapides, et al., Defendants. Additional Party Names: Janis Lapides, No. CV 18-10731-CJC(SKX), 2019 WL 4956148, at *3–4 (C.D. Cal. Oct. 8, 2019).

> ownership interest in a residence that gives the individual the right to use and occupy it as his or her place of abode.").
>
> We also note that although Guillen is the president and sole shareholder of A.M.J.R.K., such status did not give her an interest in the corporation's property. *See* Mease v. Warm Mineral Springs, Inc., 128 So.2d 174, 179 (Fla. 2d DCA 1961) ("The stockholders do not have vested in them title in the corporate property."); *see also* Hackney v. Niedecken, 133 So.3d 1228, 1230 (Fla. 2d DCA 2014) (holding that status as a corporate stockholder did not entitle that stockholder to payment made on corporation's property). Accordingly, we must reverse the trial court's order and *882 remand for further proceedings consistent with this opinion.[36]

Where an asset is claimed as exempt homestead, creditors will examine how equity was established in the home or whether the homestead was subsequently abandoned, thereby causing loss of exempt status.

> The district court found that the homestead exemption was unavailable to appellants. The district court correctly noted that we have recognized exceptions to the exemption. *See* Maki v. Chong, 119 Nev. 390, 394, 75 P.3d 376, 379 (2003) (holding a homestead that was acquired with fraudulently obtained funds was not protected by the exemption); Breedlove v. Breedlove, 100 Nev. 606, 608-09, 691 P.2d 426, 427–28 (1984) (concluding the homestead exemption did not apply to a parent who owed child support arrears). However, neither exception has been shown to apply to the instant matter—there was no allegation that D'Haenens utilized fraudulently obtained funds to purchase the homestead or that he is in arrears for statutorily-mandated financial obligations to a dependent. The district court also relied upon Coppler & Mannick, P.C. v. Wakeland, 117 P.3d 914 (N.M. 2005), to find that the exemption was unavailable to shield appellants' fraudulent and malicious conduct. But Coppler involved a creditor who had an interest in the property, *see id.* at 918 ("[Debtor] caused significant damage to the property for the sole purpose of sabotaging the [creditors'] lawful interests."), and it is not clear from the record that respondents had a legal interest in the property. Lastly, the district court, relying upon out-of-state caselaw to find that there was nothing left to which the exemption could attach after the voluntary conveyance and the transfer of title, found that the homestead exemption should not apply because of abandonment. However, the cases relied upon by the district court address claims in the homestead exemption after the transfer of the property, not at the point of the transfer, the action which is the subject of respondents' complaint.[37]

## *Exemption tracing*

While property held in an exempt status and is not an asset, controversy may arise when exempt property undergoes a change in form. Here, the issue is

36. *DeJesus v. A.M.J.R.K. Corp.*, 255 So. 3d 879, 880–82 (Fla. Dist. Ct. App. 2018).

37. *Bizzaro v. Half Dental Franchise, LLC*, No. 72522, 2018 WL 3625725, at *2 (Nev. July 26, 2018).

whether the change is sufficient to cause a loss of the exempt status, thereby becoming an asset that has been transferred. In some cases, the proceeds from an exempt form will be protected, and in others, the protected status lost.

*In re Benzaquen* involved a fact pattern where the joint tenant husband transferred funds out of a tenancy by entirety account into an account (the Account) in the husband's sole name. The court held the transferred funds retained their exempt status since a tenancy by entirety can only be terminated by both spouses.

> Thus, the issue is whether, when the TBE funds were transferred to the Account, and assuming the Account was not a TBE account, did the TBE funds lose their status as TBE property. The answer is "no." Florida law is very clear. *69 Once it is determined that the property is held as TBE, the TBE can only be terminated by the divorce of the spouses, the death of one of the spouses, or an agreement between the spouses. Maxwell, 2012 WL 4078407 at *3; Passalino v. Protective Group Securities, Inc., 886 So.2d 295 (Fla. 4th DCA 2004). The TBE is not destroyed by placing TBE funds in an attorney's trust account, Passalino, 886 So.2d at 298; it cannot be destroyed by the unilateral act of one spouse without the other to put TBE funds into an account in only one spouse's name, Maxwell, 2012 WL 4078407 at *5; it cannot be destroyed when one spouse removes the other spouse's name from a TBE account, Sitomer v. Orlan, 660 So.2d 1111 (Fla. 4th DCA 1995). *See also* Beal Bank, 780 So.2d at 53; Aranda, 2011 WL 87237 at *3.
>
> In this case, the Debtor and his wife testified that as soon as they received the $1.1 million from the sale of their home, they were concerned about losing the money if the bank failed. They each testified that they were aware of the $250,000 per depositor per account FDIC insurance and that they opened the Account to take advantage of that protection. They each testified that it was their intent to use the money to buy a new home and to have some savings. They also testified that it was not ever their intent that the funds would be transferred only to one or the other of them. Bank of the West did not put on any evidence that contradicts this testimony.
>
> Consequently, under Florida law the funds held in the Account were, and continued to be, funds held TBE even if the Account does not qualify as a TBE account. Accordingly, the Debtor's motion is GRANTED. Bank of the West shall have fourteen (14) days from the date of this Order to take all steps necessary to release the garnished funds.[38]

*Benzaquen* makes sense when one considers it takes both spouses to consent to terminate a tenancy by entirety. The nature of the protection should not be lost if a spouse unilaterally moves funds without consent because the funds still are considered tenancy by entirety.

The result in *Benzaquen* can be contrasted with a debtor who removes funds from a retirement account, such as an individual retirement account. In that situation, a creditor can argue the nature of the funds loses its characterization as a retirement fund because the funds are no longer subject to the

38. *In re Benzaquen*, 555 B.R. 63, 68–69 (Bankr. S.D. Fla. 2016).

retirement rules, and thus, no longer qualifies for a retirement fund exemption. In *Zotto*, the court held funds voluntarily withdrawn from the debtor's IRA and subsequently deposited into a preexisting savings account as nonexempt and subject to garnishment. In finding in favor of the creditor, the court distinguished between distributions that were required by law to be distributed versus funds that a debtor voluntarily withdrew. These distinguishing factors suggest that one must be careful in moving retirement funds out of an exempt state without being confident about the subsequent treatment in a new account.

> Del Zotto contends that her funds held by Garnishee in a personal savings account are exempt from garnishment pursuant to Section 222.21(2), Florida Statutes. Specifically, Del Zotto contends that the funds were transferred from her IRA, making the funds exempt from Plaintiff's claims pursuant to Section 222.21(2), Florida Statutes, which provides that "any money . . . payable to an owner" of an account is exempt from claims of the owner's creditors if the account is maintained in accordance with the Internal Revenue Service's tax-exempt requirements. §222.21(2)(a). Her funds maintain this exempt status, Del Zotto argues, even though they are no longer held in her tax-exempt IRA and are now in a personal savings account. Plaintiff contends the opposite, arguing that the funds lost any exempt status upon Del Zotto withdrawing them from her IRA and depositing them into a nonexempt savings account. *** The Court recommends that the funds Plaintiff seeks to garnish are nonexempt and, thus, that the Motion should be granted. Therefore, the Court recommends that a final judgment of garnishment be entered against Garnishee in the amount of the lesser of $52,223.30 or the amount remaining unpaid on the Judgment. §77.083, Fla. Stat. (2016).[39]

## Transferee

The recipient of the transferred asset is a "transferee." Section 8 of the UVTA provides that a creditor may obtain a judgment against "the first transferee of the asset or the person for whose benefit the transfer was made." While this might seem straightforward, courts have declined to find transferee status where the recipient does not control the asset. A common example of this scenario would be a bank receiving a deposit of funds transferred by a debtor. Another example might be a law firm where it receives funds in its trust account. Yet another example could be the non-debtor spouse where the debtor-spouse transfers funds to a joint account with the other spouse. Finally, if a recipient further transfers funds to another recipient, a court may hold that the second recipient is not a transferee if the creditor cannot prove the first transfer was in fact a fraudulent transfer.

39. *Universal Physician Servs., LLC v. Zotto*, No. 8:16-CV-1274-T-36JSS, 2016 WL 6902354, at *3–5 (M.D. Fla. Nov. 2, 2016), *report and recommendation adopted*, No. 8:16-CV-1274-T-36JSS, 2016 WL 6879288 (M.D. Fla. Nov. 22, 2016).

> Because the Court finds that the trustee has failed to establish by a preponderance of the evidence that the debtor fraudulently transferred her one-half interest in the Arizona property to Mr. Ptacek in 2015, the Court need not address any claims regarding Mr. Ptacek's transfer of the Arizona property to the LLC in 2016. Whether Mr. Ptacek transferred the Arizona property to a separate LLC with an intent to hinder, delay, or defraud his own creditors is irrelevant. If the trustee cannot establish a fraudulent transfer claim against Mr. Ptacek under Sections 544 or 548, then the trustee has no claim against the LLC as a transferee under Section 550. Rather, Section 550(a) only permits recovery from a transferee "to the extent that a transfer is avoided under section 544, 545, 547, 548, 549, 553(b) or 724(a) of this title." Accordingly, the Court finds that the trustee has also failed to establish a claim against the LLC.[40]

But where a person is, in fact, a transferee, such person might be liable to the creditor. The relief can vary based on the circumstances. For instance, where a transfer is made with the debtor's actual intent to hinder, the transferee is liable unless the transferee acted in good faith and gave reasonably equivalent value.[41] As noted herein, the corresponding provisions dealing with actual fraud under the Bankruptcy Code strip this defense from the first transferee, essentially creating strict liability for the initial transferee.

Not only may a creditor obtain a judgment against the transferee who comes into possession of an asset (subject to the foregoing exceptions), but the creditor may also obtain a judgment against a person for whose benefit the transfer was made.[42] This analysis will require closely examining the facts to determine the extent to which a person benefitted from a transaction.

# Claim

The term "claim" is defined as a right to payment. Identifying the claim is necessary before a creditor can seek relief under fraudulent transfer law; the

40. *In re*: Mellise N. Ptacek, Debtor. Richard A. Baumgart, Trustee, Plaintiff. v. James Ptacek, 8641 East San Ardo Drive LLC, & Mellise N. Ptacek, Defendants., No. 16-10279, 2019 WL 4049842, at *13 (Bankr. N.D. Ohio Aug. 27, 2019).

41. *See* Regions Bank v. Kaplan, No. 18-14010, 2020 WL 820932, at *2 (11th Cir. Feb. 19, 2020). ("Kathryn challenges the district court's judgment against her for the amount she received from Triple Net, BNK, and R1A. When a debtor transfers property '[w]ith actual intent to hinder, delay, or defraud any creditor of the debtor,' creditors can hold the transferee liable. Fla. Stat. Ann. §§726.105(1)(a), 726.108(1)(b). Kathryn does not dispute the evidence at trial that supported the district court's finding that she and Marvin made the transfers to avoid an impending judgment against their companies. She instead contends that this evidence is 'wholly irrelevant' because she 'repaid' the money. We disagree. Even if returning a fraudulent conveyance could relieve a transferee of liability—and nothing in Florida's fraudulent transfer act suggests that it could—Kathryn has not established that the district court clearly erred when it found that she did not actually repay anything.") (Emphasis added.)

42. *Humanigen, Inc. v. Savant Neglected Diseases, LLC*, C.A. N17C-07-068-PRW CCLD, at *24-25 (Del. Super. Ct. July 9, 2021) ("A non-transferor or non-transferee can be liable for fraudulent transfer if it is a beneficiary of the fraudulent transfer. To detect beneficiary status, this Court engages the same three-factor test bankruptcy courts use. The Court must determine: (1) whether the benefit was received by the beneficiary; (2) whether the benefit is quantifiable; and (3) whether the benefit is 'accessible to the beneficiary.' Under this test (with its requirement that all three factors are present), Nomis Bay is not a beneficiary.")

existence of a creditor-debtor relationship triggers the potential application of fraudulent transfer law and remedies.

A claim does not need to be reduced to a judgment; the definition of claim expressly includes a right to payment that is contingent as to liability. The possibility that a claim might not result in judgment does not preclude standing to bring a fraudulent transfer action.

> As to the second, the record indicates that the fraudulent-conveyance claim could have litigation value. CIT and Sun, after all, settled the lawsuit for $3.7 million, which would make little sense if the action truly had no chance of success. The Bankruptcy Court could convert the case to Chapter 7, allowing a Chapter 7 trustee to pursue the suit against Sun and CIT. Or the court could simply dismiss the Chapter 11 bankruptcy, thereby allowing petitioners to assert the fraudulent-conveyance claim themselves. Given these possibilities, there is no reason to believe that the claim could not be pursued with counsel obtained on a contingency basis. Of course, the lawsuit—like any lawsuit—might prove fruitless, but the mere possibility of failure does not eliminate the value of the claim or petitioners' injury in being unable to bring it.
>
> Consequently, the Bankruptcy Court's approval of the structured dismissal cost petitioners something. They lost a chance to obtain a settlement that respected their priority. Or, if not that, they lost the power to bring their own lawsuit on a claim that had a settlement value of $3.7 million. For standing purposes, a loss of even a small amount of money is ordinarily an "injury." *See, e.g.*, McGowan v. Maryland, 366 U.S. 420, 430–431, 81 S.Ct. 1101, 6 L.Ed.2d 393 (1961) (finding that appellants fined $5 plus costs had standing to assert an Establishment Clause challenge). And the ruling before us could well have cost petitioners considerably more. *See* Clinton v. City of New York, 524 U.S. 417, 430–431, 118 S.Ct. 2091, 141 L.Ed.2d 393 (1998) (imposition of a "substantial contingent liability" qualifies as an injury). A decision in petitioners' favor is likely to redress that loss. We accordingly conclude that petitioners have standing.[43]

Where the alleged fraudulent transfer has occurred prior to an adjudication of a legal claim, the issue may arise as to whether a party may seek relief under the fraudulent transfer law as a "creditor." Here, the claimant is typically seeking equitable relief in the form of an injunction to prevent dissipation of assets prior to the commencement or adjudication of a lawsuit. Although the U.S. Supreme Court has ruled against an asset freezing order under federal common law, it expressly noted an exception for fraudulent transfer law and the availability of prejudgment relief. Typically, this prejudgment relief is injunctive relief or an attachment.

Where the claim is contingent in nature, the court will be tasked with identifying the value of the claim. In *Burkhart v. Genworth Financial, Inc.*, the Delaware Court of Chancery was faced with a class action lawsuit brought by policyholders and insurance agents. Specifically, the plaintiffs alleged Genworth

43. *Czyzewski v. Jevic Holding Corp.*, 137 S. Ct. 973, 983, 197 L. Ed. 2d 398 (2017). (Emphasis added.)

was siphoning off assets from a long-term care subsidiary to avoid paying future claims. This was due to evidence that the long-term care subsidiary would have problems paying claims and was not permitted to raise premiums. The plaintiffs alleged past transfers should be voided and sought relief to prevent future transfers. Since more than four years had expired with respect to the past transfers, the chancellor ruled such transfers were time barred. However, with respect to the cause of action seeking relief for a claim that had not yet matured, the chancellor ruled a claim did exist for which relief may be sought.

> In Section 1307, the DUFTA unequivocally provides that "in an action for relief . . . a creditor . . . may obtain: [] [a]voidance of the [fraudulent] transfer . . . to the extent necessary to satisfy the creditor's claim." Despite (or perhaps because of) the DUFTA's clear language, the question presented here—whether a creditor with an unmatured and contingent claim has standing to bring a claim under the DUFTA when her contractual right to payment is not yet mature—has not been addressed by Delaware courts. I asked the parties for supplemental briefing on this question. And after considering their briefs and supplemental materials, I am persuaded the answer to the question is yes—that is, a creditor with an unmature and contingent claim does have standing to bring a claim under the DUFTA even though her contractual right to payment is contingent and not yet mature.
>
> Creditors are not "required to stand by helplessly until a distant maturity date arrives while his debtor is fraudulently depleted of all assets." In short, the injury Plaintiffs have alleged is the quantum of prejudice creditors suffer when their debtors intentionally move assets to defraud them. To hold that this injury does not confer standing would be to contradict the DUFTA's plain language. As originally promulgated in 1918, Section 10 of the Uniform Fraudulent Conveyance Act provided, "[w]here a conveyance made or obligation incurred is fraudulent as to a creditor whose claim has not matured, he may proceed in a court of competent jurisdiction against any person whom he could have proceeded had his claim matured." Justice Cardozo interpreted this language to "abrogate the ancient rule whereby a judgment and a lien were essential preliminaries to equitable relief against a fraudulent conveyance." In doing so, he observed, "the act is explicit that a creditor may now maintain a suit in equity to annul a fraudulent conveyance, though his debt has not matured."[44]

Again, even though relief may be provided pre-judgment, there must be an underlying claim giving rise to ultimate damages creating a right to payment. "Unlike Counts I–IV, which are expressly predicated upon contractual rights to payment, Counts V–VII rest on claims which, if reduced to judgment, will not create any right to payment at all, but instead will result in the unwinding of certain transactions and the restoration of others. In short, because their DUFTA claims in Counts III–IV do not and will not themselves create a "right to payment," Plaintiffs are not "creditors" under DUFTA for purposes of

44. *Burkhart v Genworth Financial, Inc.*, 250 A.3d 842, 855(Del.Ch. 2020).

Counts V–VII and cannot, therefore, state claims under the statute with respect to those transfers."[45]

A court may also permit a prejudgment fraudulent transfer suit on the grounds that it is a tort—this particular characterization may also support the argument that it may be brought as a cause of action seeking relief prior to judgment.

Notwithstanding the availability of injunctive relief, a creditor must still satisfy constitutional requirements before an order for provisional relief will be entered in its favor.

> *6 Even if the Florida Uniform Fraudulent Transfer Act permits the requested asset freeze, Regions fails to show clearly either irreparable and imminent injury or a balance-of-the-equities that favors the injunction. In 2012 and 2015, the defendants purportedly conducted a series of fraudulent transfers to hinder Regions' ability to collect a future money judgment. Regions first received information about the transfers in May 2016 but waited until January 30, 2017, to request an injunction against the defendants' "further transfers." And Regions submits no evidence of a fraudulent transfer after 2015. The months-long delay in requesting an injunction counsels strongly against a finding of imminent and irreparable injury. Additionally, Section 726.109(2) of the Florida Uniform Fraudulent Transfer Act permits Regions to obtain a money judgment against a "subsequent transferee" if the defendants persist in the allegedly fraudulent transfers of money. Also, Regions fails to show clearly that the balance of equities favors the requested injunction.[46]

The threat of a lawsuit may also be enough to constitute a claim.[47] However, a court will not find a claim exists if the right to payment results in judgment for the debtor or the judgment expires or is vacated. "Similarly in this case, when the judgments on which the UFTA claim is based expired, plaintiffs were no longer creditors of defendants and their claims became moot."[48]

---

45. *Burkhart v. Genworth Fin., Inc.*, No. CV 2018-0691-JRS, 2022 WL 1468769, at *11 (Del. Ch. May 10, 2022). (Internal citations omitted.)

46. *Regions Bank v. Kaplan*, No. 8:16-CV-2867-T-23AAS, 2017 WL 3446914, at *2–6 (M.D. Fla. Aug. 11, 2017).

47. *See Tolle v. Fenley*, 2006 UT App 78, ¶ 14, 132 P.3d 63, 66–67. ("Based on the broad definition of a claim under the UFTA and the direction from our supreme court to construe the statute liberally, we hold that Jeanne was 'indeed, a creditor of [Robert], given that [her] claim to the [properties]—although not reduced to judgment [at the time]—had arisen through recent threats [of civil action].' Bradford, 1999 UT App 373 at ¶ 16, 993 P.2d 887. Jeanne's numerous threats of suit and Robert's awareness of probable legal action against him amount to a 'claim' for purposes of the UFTA. See *67 United States v. Green, 201 F.3d 251, 257 (3d Cir.2000) (citing Baker v. Geist, 457 Pa. 73, 321 A.2d 634 (1974), for the holding that mere 'awareness of a probable legal action against a debtor amounts to a debt' for purposes of the Pennsylvania Uniform Fraudulent Conveyances Act); Bradford, 1999 UT App 373 at ¶ 16, 993 P.2d 887; 37 Am.Jur.2d Fraudulent Conveyances and Transfers §3 (2001) ("The existence of a debt is a requirement for bringing a fraudulent conveyance action and generally speaking, the awareness of probable legal action against a debtor amounts to a 'debt.'" (footnotes omitted)). The trial court found that '[w]hile the Plaintiff, Jeanne Tolle, did not file civil suit until February 2002 in Florida and procure a judgment until September 24, 2004, the Plaintiff made her intentions clear to Robert Tolle and the other defendants prior to any transfers.' For purposes of the UFTA, Jeanne is therefore a creditor whose claim arose before Robert transferred the properties.)

48. *Oregon Recovery, LLC v. Lake Forest Equities, Inc.*, 229 Or. App. 120, 127, 211 P.3d 937, 942 (2009).

# Hinder, delay, or defraud

A creditor may avoid a transaction if the creditor can prove the debtor made a transfer, or incurred an obligation, with the actual intent to "hinder, delay, or defraud" any creditor of the debtor. This actual fraud avenue of relief is distinct from a creditor seeking avoidance under a constructive fraud analysis by proving a debtor made a transfer based on the presence of certain financial circumstances, where the debtor did not receive reasonably equivalent value.

However, although the phrase is sometimes referred to as actual fraud, no fraud, in the traditional sense, actually must be proven.[49] Instead, as provided under the terms of the statute, the creditor must prove a debtor intended to hinder, delay, or defraud any creditor. Here, the question becomes (a) whether a transaction had the effect of hindering, delaying, or defrauding a creditor, and (b) whether the debtor had the intent of doing so when engaging in the transaction. As one can imagine, there are an infinite number of ways an individual can hinder, delay, or defraud creditors; the issue becomes whether there was both a delay and the requisite intent. A court may consider a debtor's degree of sophistication when examining the debtor's intent. Whether a debtor has made a transfer with actual intent to hinder, delay, or defraud is relevant not only for fraudulent transfer purposes, but also as to whether a debtor in bankruptcy made a transfer to a self-settled trust for purposes of the ten-year prohibition against such transfers prior to filing bankruptcy, as well as whether a debtor's bankruptcy discharge should be denied.

> The words "hinder," "delay" and "defraud" used to describe the intent required under 11 U.S.C. §727(a)(2) are not defined terms under the Bankruptcy Code. *See* 11 U.S.C. §101. The meaning of these terms comes from the common law and is codified in the Uniform Fraudulent Conveyance Act, now the Uniform Voidable Transactions Act. *See In re* Woodfield, 978 F.2d at 518, citing inter alia, Evans v. Trude, *supra*, and Matter of Ayala, *supra*. The terms of hinder, delay, and defraud connote intentional actions by a debtor to frustrate or thwart collection by creditors and describe a continuum of intents that may differ temporally or in substance and effect, but each of which is impermissible for purposes of 11 U.S.C. §727(a)(2). The dictionary definitions of these words reinforce these observations. The word "hinder" has been defined as a transitive verb: "1. To be or get in the way of. 2. To obstruct or delay the progress of." The American Heritage Dictionary of the English Language at 830 (4th ed. 2006). The word "delay" has been defined as a transitive verb: "1. To postpone until a later time; defer. 2. To cause to be later or slower than expected or desired." Id. at 480. The word "defraud" has been defined as a transitive verb: "To take something by fraud; swindle." Id. at 477. The word "fraud", in turn, has been defined as a noun:

49. *See* Kenneth C. Kettering, *Codifying A Choice of Law Rule for Fraudulent Transfer: A Memorandum to the Uniform Law Commission*, 19 Am. Bankr. Inst. L. Rev. 319, 359 (2011). ("It should be kept in mind that the shorthand phrase actual fraud, and indeed the very name of the Uniform Fraudulent Transfer Act, are somewhat misleading in that they refer exclusively to fraud. The primordial rule of fraudulent transfer law applies to any transfer made with intent to 'hinder, delay, or defraud' the transferor's creditors, and that disjunctive language has long been held to apply to transactions that are untainted by fraud.")

> "1. A deception deliberately practiced in order to secure unfair or unlawful gain. 2. A piece of trickery; a trick. . . . " *Id.* at 699.[50]

A transaction that delays will not, by itself, constitute a debtor's attempt to hinder, delay, or defraud, unless the transaction is designed to accomplish such a result. The odds of voidability increase where the delay occurs under suspicious circumstances or where there is direct evidence of the intent to delay creditors.

There are several cases where courts have found intent to hinder creditors when a debtor articulated intent to engage in asset protection or sought the services of an asset protection advisor. In some cases, a debtor might testify to the effect that asset protection was a motivating factor.

> In his complaint filed in the December 2009 Seychelles Action, Dr. Xiao stated that he formed LSI to enter into the Woongjin contract because the Debtor faced potential liabilities due to, inter alia, (1) "claims by third parties that Michael Little had possibly infringed their intellectual property rights," and (2) Mrs. Little's claims related to Mr. Little's interests in the Debtor. *Id.* at 9. In his mind, and in his own words, "the formation of [LSI] was a routine transaction of asset protection," meant to keep money offshore. *Id.* at 2; Tr. 37, ECF No. 135. Ms. Chen was fully aware of the reasoning behind LSI's formation. Tr. 78, ECF No. 133.[51]

In one case, merely visiting with an asset protection attorney was enough to constitute a factor in finding intent to hinder future creditors.

> As indicated by Defendant's testimony that prior to filing his bankruptcy petition, he met with an asset protection firm, and one of his goals in doing so, was to potentially protect his assets from potential creditors, Trial Testimony of Joseph Ellison, November 19, 2015 at 10:58-10:59 a.m., and while he changed his mind about using the asset protection firm, the evidence of his consideration, meeting and paying the asset protection firm supports a finding that Defendant intended to hinder or delay his nonpreferred creditors.[52]

## Reasonably Equivalent Value

There are numerous cases where debtors have maintained the existence of reasonably equivalent value to prevent application of constructive fraud claims. Not surprisingly, there has been disagreement as to the value asserted for the

50. *In re Ellison*, at *10 (Bankr. C.D. Cal. Sept. 23, 2016), aff'd, No. 2:14-BK-24463-RK, 2017 WL 3976304 (B.A.P. 9th Cir. Sept. 8, 2017), aff'd, 758 F. App'x 615 (9th Cir. 2019).

51. In Re: Lxeng LLC, Debtor. Richard M. Coan, Trustee of Lxeng LLC, Plaintiff v. Xin Chen, Defendant., No. 13-51144 (JJT), 2019 WL 4146478, at *15–16 (Bankr. D. Conn. Aug. 30, 2019).

52. *In re Ellison*, 2016 WL 5349715, at *6 (Bankr. C.D. Cal. Sept. 23, 2016), aff'd, No. 2:14-BK-24463-RK, 2017 WL 3976304 (B.A.P. 9th Cir. Sept. 8, 2017), aff'd, 758 F. App'x 615 (9th Cir. 2019).

assets transferred; the value asserted by the debtor will tend to be higher than that asserted by the creditor. In analyzing the proper value, it is necessary to determine the point in time for valuing the value transferred, as well as the appropriate point of view as to the sufficiency of asset received. Traditionally, the answer has been that the asset the debtor received is valued at the time of the transfer, and that the value is determined from the creditor's perspective. "Whether a debtor obtained reasonably equivalent value in a particular transaction is determined from a reasonable creditor's perspective at the time of the exchange, without regard to the subjective needs or perspectives of the debtor or transferee and without the wisdom hindsight often brings."[53] This test has been described as well worn and is meant to be applied with the goal of preventing the depletion of a debtor's assets to the detriment of unsecured creditors.

> The Mickens' main argument in support of their claim they received reasonably equivalent value for the transfer is that the Bankruptcy Court erred by evaluating the question using the perspective of the creditors. In their mind, this means the Bankruptcy Court failed to consider several points in favor of the Mickens. The Court disagrees. The perspective of the creditors test is the well-worn test applied in constructive fraud claims. As the comment to the UFTA states, "'Value' is to be determined in light of the purpose of the Act to protect a debtor's estate from being depleted to the prejudice of the debtor's unsecured creditors. Consideration having no utility from a creditor's viewpoint does not satisfy the statutory definition." Uniform Fraudulent Transfer Act §3, cmt. 2.[54]

## *Necessities*

In some situations, a court might look to whether a transfer was made not for reasonably equivalent value, but whether it was made for a necessity.[55] Under this approach, Pennsylvania's courts have held that, "an insolvent debtor's deposits of his or her own funds into an entireties account are not fraudulent as to said debtor's creditors to the extent that said funds are then used to satisfy reasonable and necessary expenses for the maintenance of said debtor's family."[56] Although the test is commonly articulated as an expenditure on

53. *Spencer & Assocs., P.C. v. Harper*, No. 01-18-00314-CV, 2019 WL 3558996, at *14 (Tex. App. Aug. 6, 2019). *But see In re: Mellise N. Ptacek, Debtor. Richard A. Baumgart, Trustee, Plaintiff. v. James Ptacek, 8641 East San Ardo Drive LLC, & Mellise N. Ptacek, Defendants.*, No. 16-10279, 2019 WL 4049842, at *12 (Bankr. N.D. Ohio Aug. 27, 2019). ("The reasonableness of consideration supporting a transfer is evaluated from the standpoint of the debtor. *Id.* (citing Aristocrat Lakewood Nursing Home v. Mayne, 133 Ohio App.3d 651, 665, 729 N.E.2d 768 (8th Dist.1999)). The trustee has the burden of proving that the debtor received less than reasonably equivalent value in exchange for her transfer by a preponderance of the evidence. Simon v. Short (*In re* Oakland Physicians Med. Ctr., LLC), 596 B.R. 587, 610 (Bankr. E.D. Mich. 2019).")

54. *Hagan v. Mickens*, No. 1:17-CV-1013, 2018 WL 3913760, at *4 (W.D. Mich. Aug. 14, 2018).

55. Where funds are deposited into a joint account, there may be an issue as to whether the non-debtor account holder is a "transferee" or entitled to adjustment as the equities may require.

56. *See In re Meinen* 232 B.R. at 842.

necessities, in actuality, the receipt of a necessity would most likely be reasonably equivalent value. "Judge McCullough explained that this test is consistent with the PUFTA, 12 Pa.C.S.A. §5103(a), because the payment of necessary household expenses can be viewed as a receipt of reasonably equivalent value in that the funds are used to satisfy an antecedent debt."[57]

## Future Creditors

Planners must understand the definition of "creditor" to help clients avoid engaging in fraudulent transfers. The terms of the UFTA/UVTA provide that both present and future creditors can avoid a transaction.[58] Identifying those with existing claims is usually not difficult, although some mistakenly believe that a claim means a subjectively "valid" claim or a claim reduced to judgment. Aside from this misunderstanding, the more common misunderstanding applicable to wealth transfer planning involves the rights of creditors whose claim has not yet risen under a Section 4(a) analysis.

The Section 4(a) actual fraud analysis is particularly troublesome for some who aggressively pursue creditor avoidance transactions under the assumption that only future creditors who were reasonably foreseeable or identifiable at the time of the transfer may be considered future creditors who may seek relief. This controversial topic was addressed by New York attorney Thomas Moers Mayer.

> Mr. Engel, Mr. Sullivan, and Mr. Osborne carefully constructed arguments that not all creditors are "future creditors" entitled to the protection of the fraudulent transfer laws. But their arguments simply do not work, because they are aimed at the wrong issue.
>
> The issue is not what creditors are entitled to sue under the fraudulent transfer laws. Outside of Texas, all creditors—present and future— are so entitled: The statutes say so simply and clearly. Indeed, the Texas statute compels the conclusion that intent to defraud future creditors is fatal to a transfer. Moreover, such authority as this non-Texan has been able to unearth indicates that the Texas limitation is a statute of repose, not a requirement that the claim be reasonably foreseeable.
>
> Mr. Sullivan's argument that plaintiffs with unprecedented, or "bizarre," or "attenuated" claims are not "creditors" protected by the UFTA is based on faulty logic: he relies on cases holding that a person is not a creditor *as of a given date*, but those cases are irrelevant to the question of that person's

57. *Cardiello v. Arbogast*, 479 B.R. 661 (2012.)

58. *See SE Prop. Holdings, LLC v. McElheney*, No. 5:12CV164-MW/EMT, 2016 WL 7494300, at *11 (N.D. Fla. May 7, 2016). ("Section 726.105 covers transfers intended to avoid *future* as well as present creditors.") See also, §7. Conveyance Made With Intent to Defraud., Unif.Fraudulent Conveyance Act §7. ("Every conveyance made and every obligation incurred with actual intent, as distinguished from intent presumed in law, to hinder, delay, or defraud either present or future creditors, is fraudulent as to both present and future creditors.") *But see* Conn. Gen. Stat. Ann. section 52-552e. ("A transfer is made or obligation incurred by a debtor is fraudulent as to a creditor, if the creditor's claim arose before the transfer was made or the obligation was incurred . . .")

> rights under the UFTA *in the future when the person does have a claim.* The Second, Third, and Eleventh Circuits did indeed hold that such plaintiffs do not have claims, and are not creditors, during a bankruptcy case, but when those plaintiffs obtain their claims, and become creditors, the statute will apply and nothing in the holdings suggests otherwise. To use *Piper* as an example: The baby who is born the day after the bankruptcy case is over may not have a claim in the bankruptcy case, but it does have a claim when it dies in an air crash two years later. It will be entitled to the protections of the UFTA. That much is clear from the asbestos cases, where the plaintiffs' claims do not "arise" until their injury is manifest, which can be ten or twenty years after the manufacturer has finished using asbestos, and yet such plaintiffs are clearly protected by the UFTA.
>
> In addition, the logical integrity of Mr. Sullivan's argument has been seriously challenged, and his probability-weighted "Long Range Solvency Calculation" invalidated, by United States District Judge Wolin's prominent decision in *Committee of Asbestos Personal Injury Claimants v. Sealed Air Corporation (In re W.R. Grace & Co.).*
>
> As the case name implies, Grace is one many corporations forced into chapter 11 by the increase in asbestos litigation since 1999. However, in the mid-1990s asbestos lawsuits had been in decline, and Grace looked very solvent. So in 1998, Grace sold a $5 billion division to Sealed Air Corporation; all but about $1.3 billion of the proceeds went to Grace's shareholders. The transfer to Sealed Air was potentially a fraudulent conveyance if Grace was, at the time, insolvent. Grace does not believe it is insolvent today, since Grace believes that the vast majority of asbestos claims against it are meritless, but Grace surely did not believe it was insolvent in 1998.[59]

Some have argued that if a creditor is not identifiable or reasonably foreseeable, it is impossible for a debtor to have the intent to hinder, delay, or defraud the future creditor because intent could not have been formulated to that creditor at the time of a transfer. The asset protection trust viability is inextricably dependent upon the ability to intentionally shelter wealth with an eye toward hindering future unforeseeable creditors. Accordingly, the laws of the asset protection trust statutes expressly modify traditional fraudulent transfer law to provide this result.

The controversy over whether a creditor must be existing or foreseeable was addressed by Professor James White in his article on self-settled trusts:

> Whether "future creditors" include only those known to the settlor at the time of the transfer and those with a foreseeable connection to the settlor at the time of the transfer or also include others, not then known or foreseen, is a much-debated point. Section 4's title specifically refers to "**future**" **creditors**. The middle clause in Section 4(a) invites application "whether **the** creditor's claim arose before or after the transfer was made or the obligation

59. Thomas Moers Mayer, *Will the Lawyers Pay? Counsels Ethical, Civil and Criminal Exposure for Creating Asset Protection Trusts*, TSWB26 ALI-CLE 33 (May 4, 2015).

60. James J. White, *Fraudulent Conveyances Masquerading as Asset Protection Trusts*, 47 UCC L.J. 367 (2017).

> was incurred . . . " And 4(a) (1) requires actual intent to hinder . . . "**any**" creditor. (*Emphasis in original.*)[60]

If one applies an ordinary meaning approach, the text of the statute does not impose a temporal requirement as to the identity of a creditor. Instead, the focus is on the debtor's intent at the time of the transfer, whereby the creditor, whose claim arose before or after the transfer, may seek relief if the creditor can prove the transfer was made with intent to hinder, delay, or defraud any creditor.

To better understand this terminology utilized by the UFCA in 1918, it is helpful to examine the use of such terms in cases then in existence, with such cases forming a part of the common law that is used today in the United States and reflected in the UFTA/UVTA.

Prior to the use of the terms present and future creditors in the uniform acts, the Statute of 13 Elizabeth applied to creditors and "others." The fraudulent transfer law of South Carolina, first appearing in South Carolina law dating back to the 1700s, is like the Statute of 13 Elizabeth, also containing reference to creditors and others:

> Every gift, grant, alienation, bargain, transfer, and conveyance of lands, tenements, or hereditaments, goods and chattels or any of them, or of any lease, rent, commons, or other profit or charge out of the same, by writing or otherwise, and every bond, suit, judgment, and execution which may be had or made to or for any intent or purpose to delay, hinder, or defraud creditors and others of their just and lawful actions, suits, debts, accounts, damages, penalties, and forfeitures must be deemed and taken (only as against that person or persons, his or their heirs, successors, executors, administrators and assigns, and every one of them whose actions, suits, debts, accounts, damages, penalties, and forfeitures by guileful, covinous, or fraudulent devices and practices are, must, or might be in any ways disturbed, hindered, delayed, or defrauded) to be clearly and utterly void, frustrate and of no effect, any pretense, color, feigned consideration, expressing of use, or any other matter or thing to the contrary notwithstanding.[61]

Virginia's fraudulent transfer statute, enacted in 1919, also reflects the historical statutes, providing for creditors, others, and purchasers:

> Every gift, conveyance, assignment or transfer of, or charge upon, any estate, real or personal, every suit commenced or decree, judgment or execution suffered or obtained and every bond or other writing given with intent to delay, hinder or defraud creditors, purchasers or other persons of or from what they are or may be lawfully entitled to shall, as to such creditors, purchasers or other persons, their representatives or assigns, be void.[62]

The reference to others has been interpreted to refer to those who were not yet creditors but were viewed as subsequent creditors.

61. South Carolina Statute Section 27-23-10. (Emphasis added.)

62. §55-80. Void fraudulent acts; bona fide purchasers not affected. (Emphasis added.)

> The statute embraces not merely conveyances made with intent to delay, hinder, or defraud creditors, but conveyances made with the intent to delay, hinder, or defraud others. The word "others" is inserted to take in all manner of persons, as well as creditors after as before the conveyance, whose debts should be defrauded. The enacting clause is still stronger because the word "creditors" is not mentioned, but general words "person or persons." The words of the statute seem to be so general in order to take in all persons who shall be in any way hindered.[63]

U.S. courts have historically focused not on the type of creditor seeking relief (present versus future creditor), rather, the focus is on the debtor's intent at the time of transfer. The U.S. Supreme Court held that a transfer between husband and wife was not a fraudulent transfer where the husband was not insolvent at the time of the transfer, and the transfer was not made in contemplation of future creditors—with no delineation between future "unforeseeable" versus future "foreseeable" creditors:

> But it would be a very unjust conclusion from such facts that in 1871, when he made the conveyances to his wife, and in 1874, when he made the arrangement for the execution of the bonds and mortgages to his wife, anterior to any known or expected liability to Vanderbilt, he was acting with a view of subsequently going through bankruptcy, or defrauding Vanderbilt, or any other creditor.[64]

The Supreme Court's approach makes sense; unless creditors are harmed at the time of the transfer, or intent can be proven that the transfer was made to hinder, delay, or defraud future creditors, the transfer should be protected from attack.[65] In *Schreyer*, the creditor (Vanderbilt) was unable to show that the debtor made a transfer with intent to hinder, delay, or defraud Vanderbilt, or any other creditor.

In *Stockton v. Ford*, the Supreme Court commented on how a claim was not proper when brought two years after a transfer. In so holding, the Court noted that the transfer was made with full consideration and there was no evidence submitted showing the debtor had intent to hinder or delay creditors. Put differently, even though the plaintiff obtained a judgment two years after the transfer at issue, the Supreme Court still found it necessary to address whether the debtor had intent to hinder or delay creditors at the time of the transfer.

> The suit was not commenced by Way & Bainbridge against Pryor until 15 January, 1842, nearly two years after this assignment of judgment of Pryor

---

63. Orlando F. Bump, *A Treatise Upon Conveyances Made by Debtors to Defraud Creditors*, Fourth Ed. (1896), 4th ed., rev. and enl., with references to all American and English cases by James McIlvaine Gray.

64. *Schreyer v. Platt*, 134 U.S. 405, 417, 10 S. Ct. 579, 583, 33 L. Ed. 955 (1890). (Emphasis added.)

65. *See Brown v. Vandermulen*, 44 Mich. 522, 524, 7 N.W. 238, 238 (1880). ("The object is to set aside certain conveyances made by Peter Vandermulen, one of the judgment debtors, to or for the use of Mary A. Vandermulen his wife. The fact of the conveyances and that they were voluntary is admitted, but they were made some years before complainant became a creditor, and it therefore became a necessary part of his case that he should show the conveyances were made with intent to defraud either existing or subsequent creditors. *Herschfeldt v. George*, 6 Mich. 456; *Keeler v. Ulrich*, 32 Mich. 28.")

> against N. W. Ford to Jones. The assignment, as we have seen, was made upon full consideration, without any concealment, or, for aught that appears, intent to hinder or delay creditors; and was well known to the plaintiff long before he became the purchaser at the sheriff's sale. It passed the legal interest in the judicial mortgage out of Pryor, and vested it in Jones, as early as 12 March, 1840, and we are wholly unable to perceive any ground of equity in the plaintiff, or those under whom he holds, for disturbing it through a judgment against the assignor rendered nearly two years afterwards.[66]

Early U.S. decisions reflect how the courts did not find present creditors (those who had a claim at the time of the transfer) had superior rights to subsequent creditors (those who did not have a claim at the time of the transfer.)

> Numerous decisions may be cited to show that if the conveyance was in fact fraudulent as to existing creditors, although no existing creditor attempts to impeach it; it may nevertheless be done by the subsequent creditor, on the ground that it makes no difference against whom the fraud was directed if fraud was in the mind of the party at the time the conveyance was made, and the actual fraudulent intent was directed against any creditor, prior or subsequent, it is impeachable at the suit of a subsequent creditor.
>
> Walker v. Burrows, 1 Atk., 93; Stileman v. Ashdown, 2 Atk., 477; Russell v. Hammond, 1 Atk., 13; White v. Sansom, 3 Atk., 410; Kidway v. Conssmaker, 12 Ves., 136; Halloway v. Millard, 1 Madd., 225; Richardson v. Smallwood, 1 Jacob, 552; 4 Cond. Eng. Ch. R., 262; Sexton v. Wheaton, 8 Wheat., 229; Hindes' lessee v. Longworth, 11 Wheat., 199; Salmon v. Bennett, 1 Conn., 525; Reade v. Livingston, 3 Johns. Ch., 481; Hutchison v. Kelly, 1 Rob., 123; Bank of Alexandria v. Patton, *Ibid.*, 500; Hunters v. Waite, 3 Gratt., 26; Johnston v. Zane's trustee, 11 Gratt., 552; Pratt v. Cox, 22 Gratt., 330.
>
> The law does not restrain a man's domain over his own property so long as he acts with fairness and good faith, but it treats as null and void all fraudulent conveyances to secure it from the pursuit of his creditors; it is fraudlent [sic] to defeat them by reservations of benefits to himself; it is equally fraudulent to defeat them by benefactions conferred upon others. It is not the consideration, but the intent with which a conveyance is made that makes it good or bad as to creditors. Baldwin, J., in Hunters v. Waite.[67]

The court in *Lockhard* acknowledged that not all transfers are subject to avoidance, nor should the fraudulent transfer law be applied to prevent a man from dealing with his assets however he wishes. The key to relief under fraudulent transfer law, at least with respect to the primordial rule, is whether the debtor had the requisite intent when entering a transaction and the transaction's resulting effect on creditors. The early cases did not have the benefit of a clear set of rules governing voidability and burden of proof, so the tests were articulated in various forms over the years.

---

66. *Stockton v. Ford*, 52 U.S. 232, 245 (1850). (Emphasis added.)
67. *Lockhard & Ireland v. Beckley*, 10 W. Va. 87, 102–03 (1877).

## Future Unforeseeable Creditors

In some cases, the transfer of wealth is done primarily to avoid creditors. This goal may conflict with fraudulent transfer law. The adviser's documentation of intent to hinder future creditors might become evidence of actual intent to hinder creditors. Consequently, asset protection planners typically assert that future "unforeseeable" creditors may not seek relief under fraudulent transfer law. Perhaps because of their concern with such position, these planners utilize the laws of jurisdictions that prevents a creditor from using an asset protection trust agreement as evidence of fraudulent intent. Because many creditors are not able to expend, or do not wish to expend, the funds necessary to prove a debtor's intent, the asset protection planner usually can adopt an incorrect view on the definition of creditor, but realistically not have to defend that position in court.

Concern with the scope of fraudulent transfer law, exacerbated by the UVTA and its updated Official Comments, has driven the certain planners to hire lobbyists to advance legislation that is more debtor friendly. The same legislation may insulate those who assist with fraudulent transfers and remove future, unforeseeable creditors from the class of creditors who may seek relief. This approach has the effect of rewriting fraudulent transfer law. If a court still finds a way to apply traditional fraudulent transfer law, industry proponents might declare the case to involve bad facts to be ignored, accuse creditors of improper focus, or determine that a judge is attempting to invent new law.[68]

The test for actual fraud, according to some, should be more limited given modern advances in financial reporting.[69] It is true that the more time that passes between a transfer and a claim should work in favor of the debtor as not

68. *See* §2:2. Fraudulent transfer law and the asset protection debate, 1 Asset Protection: Dom. & Int'l L. & Tactics §2:2. ("Needless to say, the legal debate on this issue resonates at a higher emotional pitch than most financial laws. As stated in Chapter 1, our aim is not to settle this debate. Instead, our goal is to reorient our readers to the fact that creditors' interests are very well protected under modern fraudulent transfer law. However, it seems that creditors have not properly focused on fraudulent transfer as a strong remedy. Perhaps the debate over whether asset protection is a valid goal in estate and financial planning would not take on such a controversial tone if creditors would argue their cases under fraudulent transfer law as written rather than exerting their energies inventing new causes of action and attempting to penalize professionals who assist clients in protective planning.")

69. *See* §2:2. Fraudulent transfer law and the asset protection debate, 1 Asset Protection: Dom. & Int'l L. & Tactics §2:2. ("A strong argument can be made that the modern variants of the Statute of 13 Elizabeth should be interpreted in the current financial atmosphere, which abounds with creditor safeguards, unlike the markets of the 16th century when modern finance was still finding its legs. Without question, known and reasonably foreseeable creditors should be protected from fraudulent transfers. But is a creditor who is remote in time and events from the time of a transfer also entitled to such unlimited, broad-based protection? Historically, courts have not interpreted the statutes in this manner. Rather, they have focused on the relative proximity to known, or at least reasonably knowable, creditors. Unknown future creditors, removed in years and events from the transfer, have not been protected by the courts and, indeed, should not be. The law simply does not require individuals to put all of their assets at risk. Furthermore, if a client passes the 'balance sheet test' prior to implementing an asset-protective vehicle (i.e., the transfer does not render the transferor insolvent), and there is no claimant on the horizon and no misrepresentation to creditors or claimants, the client is merely positioning his or her assets in a prudent manner.") (Emphasis added.)

having the requisite intent to hinder, delay, or defraud. However, this conclusion is not absolute, and each case stands on its own.

The argument that actual fraud requires that a future creditor must be "reasonably foreseeable" can be traced to several sources. Courts have used the phrase "reasonably foreseeable" when applying the constructive fraud test with respect to whether the debtor was left with unreasonably small assets.[70] Here, the test is sometimes articulated as whether the transferor could have reasonably foreseen whether a transfer of assets would have left the transferor with unreasonably small assets. Note, this test has nothing to do with whether a debtor has intent to hinder, delay, or defraud creditors under an actual fraud analysis. It is merely a test to determine whether a particular form of constructive fraud has been satisfied.

The terms "causal connection" and "reasonably foreseeable" have been mentioned by a few courts that determined a debtor did not make a fraudulent transfer. Because some courts have mentioned these restrictive terms in decisions favoring a debtor in fraudulent transfer actions, asset protection proponents argue the terms modify the traditional definition of creditor. However, these restrictions are not supported by the bulk of traditional fraudulent transfer law, and their appearance is limited to few cases, some of which do not actually support the use of such restrictions. Instead, the terms predominately exist in certain articles, where authors cite other authors who support the use of the restrictions.[71] This industry commentary may sometimes appear as persuasive authority in a defendant's argument showing the lack of intent to hinder, delay, or defraud:

> Uniform fraudulent transfer laws divide creditors into two categories: present creditors and future creditors. Section 428.024, R.S.Mo, see also Elizabeth M. Schurig and Amy P. Jetel, Asset Protection: Domestic and International Law and Tactics §2:4 (2013). Although MUFTA only references "present" and "future" creditors, the class of "future creditor" should be divided into two further categories: "potential subsequent creditors" and

70. *See CB Richard Ellis, Inc. v. CLGP, LLC*, 251 P.3d 523, 535 (Colo. App. 2010). ("We conclude that, by referring to the reasonableness of the size of the asset, the trial court applied the proper legal standard when considering this form of constructive fraud. Further, we conclude that trial court's findings, including its finding that the size of the asset was reasonable, support its ultimate finding that the reserve asset was not unreasonably small. Applying the proper test, this means that the broker did not show that the garnishees should have reasonably foreseen that the distribution would create an unreasonable risk of insolvency. *See* ASARCO, 396 B.R. at 397; *In re* Healthco, 208 B.R. at 302.") (Emphasis added.)

71. *See* Robert T. Danforth, *Rethinking the Law of Creditors' Rights in Trusts*, 53 Hastings L.J. 287 (2002). ("In an action brought under UFTA section 4(a)(1)—in which the creditor must prove 'actual intent to . . . defraud'—a future creditor must typically establish that, as of the time of the transfer, the creditor held 'contingent, unliquidated, or unmatured claims,' or that the creditor held 'a claim that [could] reasonably [be] foreseen by the transferor.' Professor Peter A. Alces states that, in an action based on actual intent to defraud, a future creditor must 'establish a causal link between the fraudulent disposition and the injury suffered.' Regarding this same question Professor Alces further states that '[the] focus on causality provides a means to distinguish between the actions that operate directly to prejudice a particular creditor and those actions that in some remote, not foreseeable way, have after the *331 passage of considerable time or the occurrence of an intervening cause, compromised a creditor's financial interest.'")

> "unknown future creditors." *Id.* Uniform fraudulent transfer laws do not protect unknown future creditors. *Id.* Unknown future creditors are those whose specific claims were unforeseen by the debtor at the time the transfer was made. *Id.*
>
> Rather, in order to establish that a transfer is fraudulent, there must be evidence of a creditor who reasonably could be anticipated, and the creditor must have a foreseeable obligation. *Id.* citing Wantulok v. Wantulok, 67 Wyo. 22, 40, 214 P.2d 477, 21 A.L.R.2d 572 (1950); City of Philadelphia v. Stepan Chemical Co., 713 F. Supp. 1491 (E.D. Pa. 1989). Eurovest, Ltd. v. Segall, 528 So. 2d 482, 483 (Fla. Dist. Ct. App. 3d Dist. 1988); Hurlbert v. Shackleton, 560 So. 2d 1276, 1280 (Fla. Dist. Ct. App. 1st Dist. 1990); Bank of Montreal v. Malinski, 498 So. 2d 440 (Fla. Dist. Ct. App. 3d Dist. 1986). There must be a causal connection between the alleged fraud and the injury claimed by the creditor in order to find that the creditor may pursue an action for fraud. Peter A. Alces, Law of Fraudulent Transactions §5:85 (2013).
>
> We see this principle of foreseeability in Missouri's long line of cases pertaining to future creditors. The general rule in Missouri is that a subsequent creditor will not be heard to complain of what his debtor did with his property before the indebtedness accrued. Lehr v. Moll, 247 S.W.2d 686, 690 (Mo. 1952). The only exception is the debtor who at the time he conveyed his property harbored a fraudulent intent to become indebted and to so smuggle and hide it as to prevent the collection of a special debt. Coleman v. Hagey, 158 S.W. 829 (Mo. 1913); *see also* Clapp v. Kenley, 210 S.W. 10 (Mo. 1919); May v. Gibler, 4 S.W.2d 769 (Mo. 1928); Stierlin v. Teschemacher, 64 S.W.2d 647, 654 (Mo. 1933) Maender v. Breck, 159 S.W.2d 310 (Mo.App. 1943).[72]

Obviously, whether cited cases support the modified definition of creditor is all a matter of interpretation.[73] As mentioned, the lack of creditor foreseeability and passage of time between a transfer and claim should help a debtor's argument that actual intent was lacking. However, these two factors are not the only factors to be considered when determining intent. A transfer made with evidence of intent to hinder future creditors cannot be ignored solely due to the passage of time between a transfer and a claim. Creditors should scrutinize the cases cited as support because the analysis is at odds with centuries of fraudulent transfer law. For example, a bankruptcy court rejected the causal connection argument in a fraudulent transfer action, finding no evidence that such an argument even existed in the cited case law.

> LaSalle asserts that there was no causal connection was established at trial between the Hospital's bankruptcy in April 2000 and any of the challenged

72. Frost Bank, Plaintiff/Respondent, v. Thomas E. Howard, Jr., Janice K. Howard and Daniel Howard, Trustee of the Thomas E. Howard Jr. Irrevocable Trust #2, Defendants/Appellants., 2014 WL 462950 (Mo. App. W.D.), 33--34.

73. Thomas Moers Mayer, *Will the Lawyers Pay? Counsels Ethical, Civil and Criminal Exposure for Creating Asset Protection Trusts*, TSWB26 ALI-CLE 33 (May 4, 2015). Thomas Mayer, a creditors' rights lawyer, reviewed many of the pro-future foreseeable creditor cases and concluded, "I submit that these cases are not good authority for the proposition in question: whether a future, unanticipated creditor can complain of a transfer intended to put assets beyond the reach of creditors generally."

> payments. It contends, without further argument, that there is a requirement that there is a causal connection between the transfer called into question and the allegedly constructively fraudulent result. LaSalle cites *In re* Bergman,293 B.R. 580 (Bankr.W.D.N.Y.2003) but does not provide analysis of the issue. Bergman contains no reference to any requirement as stated by LaSalle. Without more, there is no basis to rule in LaSalle's favor on this argument.[74]

At least one litigator representing a creditor encountered some of the future foreseeable creditor cases and addressed each case in a motion filed with the South Carolina Supreme Court:

> Petitioner argues, however, that an additional element should be added to South Carolina case law to require that subsequent creditors must be "foreseeable" in order to have standing to set aside a past fraudulent conveyance based upon proof of actual moral fraud. In support of the argument Petitioner cites authorities from other jurisdictions. The proposition is argued by Petitioner out of context; the authorities cited do not say what Petitioner argues; and the proposition should not be adopted.

Petitioner cites six cases as follows:

> 1) *Leopold v. Tuttle*, 378 Pa. Super. 466; 549 A2nd 151 (1988). This Pennsylvania Decision was decided under Pennsylvania's statutory law, which is markedly different from South Carolina's.
>
> 2) *Wantulok v. Wantulok*, 214 P2d 477(Wyo 1950) is a Wyoming decision that addresses neither "foreseeable future creditors," nor others. In the case, the personal representative of a deceased grantor sought the re-conveyance on behalf of her decedent of lands allegedly fraudulently conveyed. The case does not address the issue of present or future creditors.
>
> 3) The same can be said of the third decision, *Weinhart v. Weinhart*, 193 Misc 424, 84 NYS2d 375 (1948). The Weinhart case was also brought by a grantor against the grantee, seeking a re-conveyance of property that had allegedly been fraudulently conveyed. The opinion says nothing about "foreseeable creditors."
>
> 4) *City of Philadelphia v. Stephan Chemical Co.*, 713 F.Supp. 1491 (ED Pa 1989) is another Pennsylvania case. However, it was not decided under Pennsylvania's Fraudulent Conveyance statute, but rather was decided under the Business Corporation Act of Pennsylvania, having to do with the winding down of a corporation. It says nothing about "foreseeable creditors."
>
> 5) *In re: Kusar's Estate* 5 Ohio Misc. 23, 211 NE2d 535 (1965) is an Ohio decision and, like others cited by Petitioner, does not discuss anything about "foreseeable creditors."

74. *Paloian v. LaSalle Bank Nat'l Ass'n* (*In re* Doctors Hosp. of Hyde Park, Inc.), 507 B.R. 558, 661 (Bankr. N.D. Ill. 2013). (Emphasis added.)

> 6) *In re: Oberst*, 91 BR 97 (BC CD Cal 1988), a 1988 California Bankruptcy Court decision, does not address the "foreseeable creditor" argument that Petitioner seeks to make.[75]

Ironically, the case often cited for the proposition that only foreseeable creditors may seek relief is *Schreyer*, which did not involve any delineation between future foreseeable creditors and future unforeseeable creditors. Instead, the Supreme Court held there was no evidence presented that the debtor intended to hinder, delay, or defraud the creditor at issue, or any other creditor.[76]

In *Sexton v. Wheaton*, the Supreme Court held subsequent creditors may seek relief just as present creditors. The key, for future creditors, is the intent of the individual at the time of the transfer.[77] In *Wallace v. Penfield*, the Supreme Court similarly held that subsequent creditors may seek relief as well, with the emphasis not on whether the subsequent creditor was identifiable at the time of the transfer, but whether the debtor had intent to hinder, delay, or defraud at the time of the transfer.

> Neither the conveyance to the wife nor the withdrawal of the husband's means from his business for the purpose of improving the land settled upon

75. James T. JUDY, Bobby R. Judy and Kevin Judy, Respondents, v. Ronnie F. JUDY, J. Todd Judy Ryan C. Judy and Wanda B. Judy, Defendants, of whom Ronnie F. Judy is,(4)27, Petitioner., 2013 WL 4790052 (S.C.), 6--7. (Emphasis added.)

76. *Schreyer v. Scott*, 134 U.S. 405, 417 (1890). ("It may be that Schreyer did not want to pay Vanderbilt's claim; and it may be, as claimed by counsel, that he improperly sought the assistance of the bankrupt court to be relieved from liability therefrom; but it would be a very unjust conclusion from such facts, that in 1871, when he made the conveyances to his wife, and in 1874, when he made the arrangement for the execution of the bonds and mortgages to his wife, anterior to any known or expected liability to Vanderbilt, he was acting with a view of subsequently going through bankruptcy, or defrauding Vanderbilt or any other creditor.")

77. *See Laughton v. Harden*, 68 Me. 208, 213 (1878). ("The leading case in this country on the effect of a voluntary conveyance upon the rights of subsequent creditors is *Sexton v. Wheaton*, 8 Wheat. 229. The court there place stress only upon the intent of the grantor. *Mattingly v. Nye*, 8 Wall. 370, sustains the same doctrine. *Parish v. Murphree*, 13 How. 92, is to the same effect. In Hitchcock v. Kiely, 41 Conn. 611, it was decided that 'a voluntary conveyance, fraudulent in fact, will be set aside in favor of creditors, whether the grantee participated in the fraud or not.' In that case, the contending party was a creditor subsequent to the conveyance.") (emphasis added); *Walter v. Lane*, No. 3251, 1874 WL 17273, at *5 (D.C. 1874). ("The Supreme Court has given its unqualified assent to this doctrine in *Sexton vs. Wheaton*, 8 Wheaton, 227, and the distinction between existing and subsequent creditors is clearly made; and it is held that as respects the latter the conveyance is not void unless there is intentional fraud contemplated by the grantor in the creation of future debts. This decision was made in the case of a subsequent **281 creditor seeking to have a voluntary conveyance in favor of a wife declared void; but that court has never had occasion to pass upon the question, where the conveyance is set aside at the suit of antecedent creditors, whether creditors whose debts have been contracted since its execution may not come in upon the fund thus created. *** We have expressed an opinion on this point because it seemed to be one of importance on the argument; but aside from this, we think that upon the facts of the case the subsequent creditors are to be let in on the ground that the settlement was made in contemplation of future debts. It has repeatedly been decided that in case of actual fraud as respects such creditors the deed will be declared void. *Chopin vs. Peare*, 10 Conn., 69; *Gunn vs. Butler*, 18 Pick., 248; *Reade vs. Livingston*, 3 Johns. Ch., 481; 1 American Leading Cases, 1; *Sexton vs. Wheaton, supra*; *Hinde vs. Longworth*, 11 Wheaton, 199."); *Mattingly v. Nye*, 75 U.S. 370, 372, 19 L. Ed. 380 (1869). ("The statute of 13 Eliz., ch. 5, is in force in the county of Washington, but it does not affect a conveyance like this as to subsequent creditors, unless fraud was intended when it was made. (*Sexton v. Wheaton*, 8 Wheation, 239; S. C. 1 American Leading Cases, 1.) The whole learning of the law upon this subject is so fully developed in the note to this case in the work last mentioned, that it would be a waste of time to do more than refer to it.")

> the wife had the effect and operation to hinder or defraud his then existing creditors. Nor does the evidence justify the conclusion that the conveyance was executed, or the improvements made, with an intent to hinder or defraud either existing or subsequent creditors. Giving full weight to all the circumstances, there is no reason to impute fraud to the husband.[78]

The Supreme Court in *Graham v. Railroad Co.*[79] held that if an individual is solvent and has no intent to hinder creditors, the individual's transfer should not be voidable.

> In Graham v. Railroad Co., a leading and important case, it is said to be a well settled rule of law, that if an individual, being solvent at the time without any actual intent to defraud creditors, disposes of property for an inadequate consideration, or even makes a voluntary conveyance of it, subsequent creditors cannot question the transaction. The argument advanced is that such creditors are not injured; they gave credit to the debtor in the status which he had after the voluntary conveyance was made.[80]

If foreseeability was an element of a fraudulent transfer, one must wonder why such a crucial requirement was never considered as part of the uniform acts beginning in 1918. Further, if such a requirement developed under the common law, a court would have addressed the nature of the test (e.g., standard to determine whether a creditor is reasonably foreseeable, who bears the burden of proving such foreseeability, etc.)

Notwithstanding the terms of the uniform acts and case law, a court might erroneously refer to foreseeability when determining whether a creditor can seek relief under fraudulent transfer law. In *Koffman v. Smith*, a bankruptcy court defined a future creditor as one who is reasonably foreseeable, citing *Leopold v. Tuttle.*[81] In so finding a foreseeability requirement for future creditors, the bankruptcy court in *Leopold* cited three cases interpreting the term "future creditor." The *Leopold* court first considered the Pennsylvania Supreme Court's decision in *Stauffer v. Stauffer*, 465 Pa. 558 (1976), which made no mention of a foreseeability requirement.

The *Leopold* court then considered other Pennsylvania decisions as supporting the foreseeability approach. The first case cited was *County of Butler v. Brocker*, 455 Pa. 343, (1974). However, in *Butler*, there is no mention of a foreseeability requirement in the majority decision. Instead, the test was articulated as follows, "Butler County need only show an intent to hinder, delay, or

78. *Wallace v. Penfield*, 106 U.S. 260 (1882).

79. *Graham v. La Crosse & M.R. Co.*, 102 U.S. 148, 26 L. Ed. 106 (1880).

80. Frederick S. Wait, *A Treatise on Fraudulent Conveyances and Creditor's Bills* (1884), pg. 158.

81. *See Koffman v. Smith*, 453 Pa. Super. 15, 25–30, 682 A.2d 1282, 1287–89 (1996), citing Stauffer v. Stauffer, 465 Pa. 558, as precedent for requiring foreseeability. ("Leopold v. Tuttle, *supra*, defines a future creditor as follows: *26 "[O]ne with a legal claim against a person at the time that person makes a conveyance, even one that has not yet been reduced to judgment or even filed, is a future creditor who is entitled to set aside the conveyance if he can show it was made with actual intent to hinder, delay, or defraud present or future creditors." *Id.* (quoting Stauffer v. Stauffer, 465 Pa. 558, 351 A.2d 236 (1976)). A future creditor is further defined as a creditor whose claim may foreseeably arise in the near future and exists when a conveying party can reasonably foresee incurring the costs of a judgment at the time of the conveyance. *Id.*")

defraud on the part of Dr. Brocker to make the conveyance fraudulent." The only support for a foreseeability requirement can be found in the dissenting judge's opinion. The dissenting judge would not have found a fraudulent transfer existed because, at the time the debtor made the transfer, there was only speculation as to what the county would do. In other words, the dissenting judge took the view espoused by some asset protection planners, which focuses not on the transferor's intent, but on the probability of the claim maturing.[82]

The second case cited in *Leopold* was *Iscovitz v. Filderman*, 6 A.2d 270 (Pa. 1939), where the debtor, Filderman, served as a guardian and engaged in transactions for which he would no doubt incur liability in a surcharge action. Although the court mentions the debtor being aware of the probability of a surcharge action,[83] this was evidence that supported the debtor's intent to hinder, delay, or defraud creditors.

## *Relevant State Case Law*

Numerous state courts have held that a future creditor may seek relief under the fraudulent transfer law, without any requirement that the future creditor be a foreseeable future creditor. For instance, the Supreme Court of Vermont did not interpret *Schreyer* as holding a future creditor seeking relief must have been foreseeable at the time of the transfer.

> Moreover, the plaintiffs, as subsequent creditors with notice of Martha's interest, are in no position to complain that they were hindered, delayed, or defrauded by a tenancy created long before their obligation accrued. As later creditors, their burden of proof is not discharged by suspicious circumstances. Constructive fraud will not take away her interest in the property. The fraud must be actual and intentional to avoid a voluntary conveyance that was prior to their claim. *Schreyer v. Scott*, 134 U.S. 405, 10 S.Ct. 579, 33 L.Ed. 955, 958; 37 Am.Jur.2d, Fraudulent Conveyances s 144; annotation 32 A.L.R.2d at 91.[84]

---

82. *County of Butler v. Brocker*, 455 Pa. 343, 349-350 (1974). ("I dissent. Section 357 of the Uniform Fraudulent Conveyance Act is not applicable to this case. The appellee conveyed an interest in property to his wife on August 22, 1966. On that date the petition asking that the appellee be held in contempt had not yet been filed. It was not filed until eight days later on August 30, 1966. Under such circumstances, the appellee's conveyance could not have been with actual intent to defraud a future creditor. At the time of the conveyance in this case, it was pure speculation as to whether a petition for contempt would be filed—it was pure speculation whether the appellee would be adjudged guilty of criminal contempt —it was pure speculation that a criminal penalty would be imposed in what was and had been a custody dispute between parents—it was pure speculation that the criminal penalty would be the exorbitant sum of $25,000. Under such circumstances there was no conveyance with actual intent to defraud a future creditor, even assuming that a legal liability for a criminal penalty is covered by the Uniform Fraudulent Conveyance Act and even assuming that such a criminal penalty can be imposed without a jury trial.")

83. *Iscovitz* at 272. ("As soon as the legality of the investment made by Filderman as guardian was questioned, he entered into the series of transactions that in a few months stripped him of all his assets.")

84. *Rose v. Morrell*, 128 Vt. 110, 114, 259 A.2d 8, 11 (1969). (Emphasis added.)

The Supreme Court of Texas did not find a foreseeability requirement for future creditors and instead focused on the debtor's intent at the time of the transfer:

> Where a person makes such a conveyance with a view to shield his property from future debts, it would be fraudulent as to such debts, notwithstanding he may have in his hands at the time property amply sufficient to pay all existing debts. If it is shown that the intent is fraudulent as to future liabilities, it would be void. Thomp. Trials, §2013; *Hutchison v. Kelly*, 1 Rob. (Va.) 133. As to subsequent debts the question of intent in executing a voluntary conveyance is one of fact, to be ascertained from evidence either circumstantial or direct, as in other cases; but no legal presumption of fraud would arise from the mere fact that debts were subsequently created.[85]

The Supreme Court of Arkansas took the same approach as the Supreme Court of Texas:

> A conclusion quite as favorable to subsequent creditors, if not more so than this, has been reached by many of the courts even when the statute does not expressly include the subsequent creditor within its terms. In *Day v. Cooley*, 118 Mass. 527, Morton, J., delivering the opinion of the court, said: "It is well settled that if a debtor makes a conveyance with the purpose of defrauding either existing or future creditors it may be impeached by either class of creditors;" citing *Parkman v. Welch*, 19 Pick. 231; *Thacher v. Phinney*, 7 Allen, 146; *Winchester v. Charter*, 12 Allen, 606; *Wadsworth v. Williams*, 100 Mass. 126. In the old case of *Reade v. Livingston*, 3 Johns. Ch. 481, Chancellor Kent, following the rule as laid down by the English courts, came to a conclusion on this question very similar to that now followed by the courts of Massachusetts; and Mr. Bigelow, in his work on Fraud, after making an historical examination of the cases upon this question, concludes that the weight of authority in this country is on the side of the English rule substantially as expressed by Chancellor Kent. 2 Bigelow, Fraud, 105; *Belford v. Crane*, 16 N. J. Eq. 265, 84 Am. Dec. 156, and note; *Bassett v. McKenna*, 52 Conn. 437; *Wyman v. Brown*, 50 Me. 139; *Lowry v. Fisher*, 2 Bush. 70; *King v. Wilcox*, 11 Paige, 589; *Dewey v. Moyer*, 72 N. Y. 70; *McLane v. Johnson*, 43 Vt. 48; *Claflin v. Mess*, 30 N. J. Eq. 211; *Kirksey v. Snedecor*, 60 Ala. 198; *Lawson v. Warehouse Co.*, 73 Ala. 293; *Williams v. Avery*, 38 Ala. 118; *Hutchison v. Kelly*, 1 Rob. (Va.) 130; *Sexton v. Wheaton*, 1 Am. Lead. Cas. 44; *Hagerman v. Buchanan*, 45 N. J. Eq. 292, 17 Atl. 946. The cases on this question, which are numerous and conflicting, are collated in a note to the above case of *Hagerman v. Buchanan* in 14 Am. St. Rep. 732. We do not undertake to decide what rule the weight of authority on this question supports, for the peculiar language of our own statute controls us.[86]

85. *Dosch v. Nette*, 81 Tex. 265, 269–70, 16 S.W. 1013, 1015 (1891). (Emphasis added.)
86. *May v. State Nat. Bank*, 59 Ark. 614, 28 S.W. 431, 433 (1894). (Emphasis added.)

The Supreme Court of California similarly held that all future creditors have rights:

> It is clear that under these circumstances, defendant and plaintiff were concerned with the possibility that the sales volume would undergo a further decrease and that additional indebtedness would accumulate so that defendant would be unable to pay the full amount of its indebtedness, which would include the claims of both present and future creditors. (4) Hence, even if it be assumed that the creditors at the time of the agreement could have been satisfied, the agreement would still have been fraudulent as impairing the rights of future creditors. Future creditors as well as present creditors are protected by the legislation relating to fraudulent conveyances. Such protection is extended not only under the Uniform Fraudulent Conveyance Act, which was adopted in this state in 1939 (Civ. Code, §3439.7), but under the law as it stood in 1938 when the agreement was made. (Former Civ. Code, §3439; *Sasaki v. Kai*, 56 Cal.App.2d 406, 410 [133 P.2d 18.].[87]

In *Kilker v. Stillman*, the California Fourth District Court of Appeal was presented with the issue of whether only some future creditors have rights:

> Appellants argue "that for fraudulent transfer purposes the world of creditors must be divided into three classes: 1) present creditors, 2) future creditors, and 3) future potential creditors." They argue: "There is no dispute between the parties or in the evidence presented that the Kilkers were not present creditors in 2004 the year that Mr. Stillman transferred his assets to the trust in question. The question actually turns on whether the Kilkers can be truly considered actual future creditors." Their argument continues: "A future creditor should be defined as a creditor whose claim arises after the transfer in question, but where there was a foreseeable connection between the creditor and the debtor at the time of the transfer."[88]

However, the court disposed of the foreseeable connection argument by reviewing the plain language of the statute in addition to *Severance v. Knight-Counihan Co.*:

> Appellants' argument is not supported by the language of section 3439.04, subdivision (a). The statute does not include the terms "future creditor" or "future potential creditors." Section 3439.04. subdivision (a) does not require that, from the debtor's perspective, a creditor who challenges a transfer as fraudulent under the UFTA to have been reasonably foreseeable as the debtor's creditor before pursuing remedies under the UFTA. Furthermore, the statute does not require that the debtor intended to hinder, delay, or defraud the specific creditor who challenges a transfer of an asset as violative of the UFTA. On the contrary, section 3439.04, subdivision (a) provides that a current creditor can challenge a transfer as fraudulent, regardless whether

---

87. *Severance v. Knight-Counihan Co.*, 29 Cal. 2d 561, 567–68, 177 P.2d 4 (1947). (Emphasis added.)

88. *Kilker v. Stillman*, No. G045813, 2012 WL 5902348, at *4 (Cal. Ct. App. Nov. 26, 2012). (Emphasis added.)

that creditor had a claim at the time of the transfer, if that creditor can prove, inter alia, the transfer was made to hinder, delay, or defraud any creditor.

* * *

In *Severance v. Knight-Counihan Co.* (1947) 29 Cal.2d 561, 567–568, the California Supreme Court held that a debtor's future creditors were protected against fraudulent conveyances under former section 3439.7 of the Uniform Fraudulent Conveyance Act (former §3439 et seq.), stating: "It is clear that under these circumstances, [the parties] were concerned with the possibility that the sales volume would undergo a further decrease and that additional indebtedness would accumulate so that defendant would be unable to pay the full amount of its indebtedness, which would include the claims of both present and future creditors. Hence, even if it be assumed that the creditors at the time of the agreement could have been satisfied, the agreement would still have been fraudulent as impairing the rights of future creditors. Future creditors as well as present creditors are protected by the legislation relating to fraudulent conveyances. Such protection is extended not only under the Uniform Fraudulent Conveyance Act, which was adopted in this state in 1939 [citation], but under the law as it stood in 1938 when the agreement was made." Appellants do not cite any legal authority showing the Legislature intended to change this unrestricted interpretation of "future creditors" with the passage of the UFTA in 1986.[89]

The Supreme Judicial Court of Massachusetts also made no such delineation between future creditors:

In other respects, the decree of the court below was right. The facts found by the master show that the conveyances to Joseph and Ernest were made with the actual intent to hinder, delay, and defraud creditors. It is true that in 1931, when the conveyances were made to Joseph, the liability on which the judgment was based had not arisen, but that is of no consequence. A conveyance made with actual intent to defraud either present or future creditors is fraudulent as to both present and future creditors. G.L.(Ter.Ed.) c. 109A, §7; *Themo v. Themo*, 296 Mass. 190, 192, 5 N.E.2d 26. And 'Where a conveyance * * * is fraudulent as to a creditor, such creditor, when his claim has matured, may, as against any person except a purchaser for fair consideration without knowledge of the fraud at the time of the purchase * * *' have the conveyance set aside to the extent necessary to satisfy his claim. G.L.(Ter. Ed.) c. 109A, §9. *See Service Mortgage Corp. v. Welson*, 293 Mass. 410, 413, 200 N.E. 278; *Walworth Co. v. Locke, Stevens & Sanitas, Inc.*, 300 Mass. 557, 559, 16 N.E.2d 1; *Buckley v. John*, 314 Mass. 719, 726-727, 51 N.E.2d 317.[90]

The Florida Supreme Court properly phrased the test as one of intent, not whether the creditor was present or a creditor to be:

A conveyance may be canceled for fraud whether present or creditors to be were in mind in its making. In the case at bar, when considered from the

89. *Id.* (Emphasis added.)

90. *David v. Zilah*, 325 Mass. 252, 256, 90 N.E.2d 343, 345 (1950). (Emphasis added.)

> standpoint of the whole record, we may reasonably infer that either class were in contemplation.[91]

The Florida Third District Court of Appeals similarly noted that even if a creditor is not in existence at the time of a transfer, the debtor must have intent to hinder, delay, or defraud for the creditor to seek relief:

> It is immaterial whether the actual fraudulent intent related to existing creditors or was directed exclusively against subsequent creditors. *Beasley v. Coggins*, 48 Fla. 215, 37 So. 213 (1904); *Malinski*; 13 Fla.Jur.2d Creditors' Rights and Remedies §253 (1979). However, where the creditor is not in existence at the time of the conveyance, there must be evidence establishing actual fraudulent intent by one who seeks to have the transaction set aside. *Beasley*, 37 So. at 215; 37 Am.Jur.2d Fraudulent Conveyances §67 (1968).[92]

Two years later, the First District Court of Appeals was confronted with a case where a physician began transferring assets to his wife *before* his malpractice insurance was cancelled and importantly, before the doctor committed any malpractice.[93] In a suit against the physician for malpractice by a patient who did not exist and could not have been identified at the time of the doctor's transfers to his wife, the trial court applied the foreseeable creditor approach, only to be overruled by the First District Court of Appeals:

> In its order, the trial court drew a distinction between "probable" and "possible" future creditors. Classifying appellant as a "possible" future creditor, the court said it found no cases holding a transfer of assets to be fraudulent as to "possible" future creditors. *** Though there is evidence in the record of Dr. Shackleton's intent with regard to the subject transfers, the trial court did not specifically rule on whether he intended to defraud appellant or anyone else in making the transfers. Its focus was instead on the nature of the subsequent creditor, *i.e.*, it focused on whether the subsequent creditor was "possible" or "probable". Appellant's argument is well taken that this is not the relevant inquiry and, as the trial court acknowledged, there is no case law pertaining to such a distinction between creditors. We reverse and remand for a finding on whether Dr. Shackleton had the requisite actual fraudulent intent at the time he transferred the affected assets. Because appellant was not an existing judgment creditor when Dr. Shackleton transferred the affected assets to a form of ownership by him and his wife, together, it is incumbent upon her to show that Dr. Shackleton har-

---

91. *Taylor v. Jones*, 112 Fla. 234, 237, 150 So. 254, 255 (1933).

92. *Eurovest, Ltd. v. Segall*, 528 So. 2d 482, 483–84 (Fla. Dist. Ct. App. 1988). (Emphasis added.)

93. *See Hurlbert v. Shackleton*, 560 So. 2d 1276, 1277-1278 (Fla. Dist. Ct. App. 1990). ("Dr. Shackleton used to practice obstetrics, gynecology, and surgery but in September 1983 he received notice that his medical malpractice insurance was to be cancelled effective January 1984. As a result, he began a part-time general medical practice confined primarily to doing physicals, x-rays and tests, eliminating riskier areas of practice. About this time Dr. Shackleton began transferring assets that were in his name alone to himself and his wife, either as tenants by the entireties, or as joint tenants with right of survivorship (w.r.o.s.) *** On February 20, 1984 Dr. Shackleton committed malpractice during the treatment of appellant.*** Subsequently, during a deposition, Dr. Shackleton was asked why he transferred his place of business to him and his wife jointly; he responded '[b]ecause I wasn't able to get malpractice insurance, and I wanted to cover all the bases.'")

> bored actual fraudulent intent at the time any of the asset transfers were made. *Bay View Estates Corporation v. Southerland*, 114 Fla. 635, 154 So. 894 (1934); *Eurovest, LTD., supra.* Since the affected assets were all originally owned solely by Dr. Shackleton, if any asset is found to be fraudulently transferred, it is subject to satisfying the judgment debt. Section 726.01, Fla.Stat. (1985).[94]

Although *Hurlbert* seems clear that the emphasis is not on the label one assigns to a creditor but a person's intent at the time of transfer, some have argued that *Hurlbert* is not clear, as noted by Thomas Mayer.

> In short, Hurlbert holds directly against the basic position of the asset protection bar: There is no difference between "probable" or "possible" creditors. The only question is intent. Indeed, that Hurlbert is somehow favorable to its view of fraudulent transfer law is one of the more outrageous positions taken by the asset protection bar.[95]

The same issue regarding the rights of future creditors arose four years later in New York under the Uniform Fraudulent Conveyance Act.

> The allegations of the complaint sufficiently set forth a cause of action based upon a fraudulent conveyance under Debtor and Creditor Law §276, which provides that "[e]very conveyance made and every *536 obligation incurred with actual intent, as distinguished from intent presumed in law, to hinder, delay, or defraud either present or future creditors, is fraudulent as to both present and future creditors". Thus, contrary to the appellants' contention, the plain language of the statute reaches conveyances intended to defraud future creditors, including conveyances which occurred prior to the time the obligation to the plaintiff arose (*see*, Kashan v. Kosoff, 112 A.D.2d 350, 491 N.Y.S.2d 801; Bein v. Baer, 7 Misc.2d 543, 162 N.Y.S.2d 676; *see also*, United States v. Cohn, 682 F.Supp. 209).[96]

The Alabama Supreme Court held that a transfer to a trust by a husband who did not retain a beneficial interest, but gave one to his wife,[97] could be voided by subsequent creditors if the transfer was tainted with actual fraud:

> In the instant case there was no reservation of benefit for the grantor, Billing; nothing placed in trust for his use or advantage. But it is contended for complainant that the reservation for Mrs. Billing was the same in fraudulent effect as if made for Billing himself. As to existing creditors this proposition

---

94. *Hurlbert v. Shackleton*, 560 So. 2d 1276, 1279–80 (Fla. Dist. Ct. App. 1990). (Emphasis added.)

95. Thomas Moers Mayer, *Will the Lawyers Pay? Counsels Ethical, Civil and Criminal Exposure for Creating Asset Protection Trusts*, TSWB26 ALI-CLE 33 (May 4, 2015).; *but see* John T. Rogers, 1 Asset Protection: Dom. & Int'l L. & Tactics. ("There have been and no doubt will continue to be a variety of views about the propriety and usefulness of asset-protection trusts and related ethics issues. For a well-researched, negative point of view, see Thomas Moers Mayer, *Will the Lawyers Pay? Counsels Ethical, Civil and Criminal Exposure for Creating Asset Protection Trusts*, TSWB26 ALI-CLE 33 (May 4, 2015).")

96. JR & J Holding Co. v. Rabinowitz, 201 A.D.2d 535, 535–36, 607 N.Y.S.2d 724, 725 (1994) (Emphasis added.)

97. Notably, the court refers to a settlor's retained interest as having a fraudulent effect. Creditors may focus on this analysis when reviewing transfers to trusts for the benefit of the debtor's family.

> is sound enough, if it be assumed that the reservation was a mere gift. *Huggins v. Perrine*, 30 Ala. 396, 68 Am.Dec. 131; 12 R.C.L. 543, §68. As to subsequent creditors, though it were a gift, such a reservation in trust would be void only in case it were made by the grantor with the intention of hindering, delaying, or defrauding such creditors; that is, it must be tainted with actual fraud. *Huggins v. Perrine, supra*; *Smith v. Pitts*, 167 Ala. 461, 52 South. 402; *Echols v. Orr*, 106 Ala. 237, 17 South. 677.[98]

In a late 1800s decision, the Maryland Supreme Court held that evidence of a debtor's solvency, although relevant, is not a determining factor under an actual fraud analysis.

> There is no doubt about the right of subsequent creditors to have a voluntary deed set aside if made with the intention and design of defrauding those who should thereafter become creditors,[99] although the grantor be solvent, or even free from debt, at the time the deed is executed; but the mere fact that the deed was voluntary does not give them the right to do so, but there must be something to convince the court that there was some fraudulent intent on the part of the grantor before it can be set aside on the ground of fraud. That fraudulent intent may, however, be ascertained in different ways.[100]

This intent-driven approach was also taken by the Tennessee Supreme Court, where the court focused not on the type of creditor, but intent at the time of the transfer. The court found it relevant as to whether the transferor made the challenged transfer in contemplation of future indebtedness:

> The rule in this state is well settled that, as against existing creditors, a voluntary settlement or conveyance will be presumed fraudulent; but, as to subsequent creditors, there is no such presumption, and fraud in fact must be established. If the conveyance is made with any design of fraud or collusion or injury to other persons in the future, it would be void. So if it is made with the intent to defraud existing creditors, it will, in general, be held void as to subsequent creditors. *Nicholas v. Ward*, 1 Head, 324; *Nelson v. Kinney*, 93 Tenn. 443, 25 S. W. 100; *Trezevant v. Terrell*, 96 Tenn. 528, 33 S. W. 109. The law on this subject is very clearly expressed in 8 Am. & Eng. Enc. Law, p. 751, viz.: "Subsequent creditors, as well as antecedent or existing creditors, may avoid a conveyance fraudulent as to them, and a voluntary conveyance may often be impeached by a future or subsequent creditor, even for fraud as to creditors existing at the time it was made. In case of an attack by existing creditors, however, they are aided by the presumption that the conveyance, if voluntary, was intended to defraud them, while the burden is upon subsequent creditors to show fraud in the transaction. This is usually done by showing that the gift, conveyance, or settlement was made by the debtor in contemplation of future indebtedness.[101]

---

98. *Greil v. Durr*, 203 Ala. 644, 648, 84 So. 743, 747 (1919). (Emphasis added.)

99. The court focuses on the transferor's intent at the time of the transfer, and disregards any limitation on classes of creditors, permitting those who thereafter become creditors.

100. *Scott v. Keane*, 87 Md. 709, 40 A. 1070, 1071 (1898). (Emphasis added.)

101. *Nelson v. Vanden*, 99 Tenn. 224, 42 S.W. 5, 7 (1897). (Emphasis added.)

The results have been the same in numerous lower court decisions. A Texas appellate court found voidability ultimately depends on intent.

> It must be conceded that, ordinarily, a subsequent creditor cannot set aside even a voluntary conveyance, on the ground that it was made in fraud of the rights of creditors. *De Garca v. Galvan*, 55 Tex. 53; *Lewis v. Simon*, 72 Tex. 470, 10 S. W. 554. If, however, the conveyance be made with the intention thereby to defraud future creditors, it is void as to them. *Cole v. Terrell*, 71 Tex. 550, 9 S. W. 668; *Dosche v. Nette*, 81 Tex. 265, 16 S. W. 1013.[102]

An Ohio appellate court decision also confirmed that a creditor does not need to be in existence at the time of the transfer, with no further requirement that such creditor be foreseeable:

> DiMarco argues that Prouse was not a creditor nor was he a debtor when the transfer was made. A "claim" means a "right to payment, whether or not the right is reduced to judgment, liquidated, unliquidated, fixed, contingent, matured, unmatured, disputed, undisputed, legal, equitable, secured, or unsecured." R.C. 1336.01(C). A "creditor" means a person who has a claim, R.C. 1336.01(D), and a "debtor" is a person who is liable on a claim. R.C. 1336.01(F). However, Prouse did not have to be a creditor when the transfer was done. Rather, anyone who now has a claim against a party and alleges that the transfer was done fraudulently to elude other creditors or obligations may step in and declare that the transfer was done fraudulently. The plain language of R.C. 1336.04 clearly provides that the claim of the creditor can arise after the transfer of the property.[103]

In *Poulous v. Poulous*, a North Carolina court dealt with the argument that only creditors who were then existing at the time of the transfer had rights:

> Poulos Defendants contend that G.S. §39-23.4(a)(1) must be interpreted as consistent with this principle and "therefore operates to allow a future creditor to attack a fraudulent transfer that occurred prior to the future creditor's standing as a creditor, but only if the transfer was intended to hinder, delay, or defraud a then-existing creditor at the time of the transfer." (Murray Br. Supp. Summ. J. 10 (*emphasis in original*).) *12 48. The Court is not persuaded by Poulos Defendants' argument. First, the principle cited in Norman Owen Trucking applies to transfers by the debtor that leaves the debtor with insufficient assets to pay "his debts then existing." 131 N.C. App. at 173, 506 S.E.2d at 271. A claim under §39-23.4(a)(1), unlike subsection (a)(2), does not require that the transfer make the debtor insolvent or potentially insolvent. Rather, it is sufficient if the creditor challenging the transaction shows that the transfer was intended to "hinder, delay, or defraud any creditor." The Official Comments to the UVTA make this conclusion clear, providing that "there is no requirement in §4(a)(1) that the intent referred to be directed at a creditor existing or identified at the time of

102. *Rives v. Stephens*, 28 S.W. 707, 708 (Tex. Civ. App. 1894), writ refused. (Emphasis added.)

103. *Prouse, Dash & Crouch, L.L.P. v. DiMarco*, 2008-Ohio-919, ¶ 48, 175 Ohio App. 3d 467, 480, 887 N.E.2d 1211, 1221. (Emphasis added.)

> the transfer" and "[d]iminution of the assets available to the debtor's creditors is not necessarily required to 'hinder, delay, or defraud' creditors." The Court rejects Dr. Poulos' argument that G.S. §39-23.4(a)(1) implicitly requires a then-existing creditor at the time of fraudulent transfer for a future creditor to void the transaction.[104]

Based on the foregoing, if a legislature truly wanted to abolish the ability of future, unforeseeable creditors to bring claims, then the legislature must alter the language of its fraudulent transfer statute to accommodate transfers made with the express purpose of hindering future creditors. In doing so, the modification should also articulate that the common law associated with future creditors is also eradicated.

Recognizing the conflict between self-settled trusts and traditional fraudulent transfer law, drafters of asset protection trust statutes (often asset protection lawyers) have included language in the asset protection statute that is meant to overrule state fraudulent transfer statute.[105] For example, the Utah legislature altered its fraudulent transfer statute with respect to transactions under its asset protection trust statute.[106] As a result of these modifications, the rights of creditors varies greatly between the DAPT state and the non-DAPT state.

## Substance over form

Similar to the common law regarding taxation,[107] fraudulent transfers have been analyzed using substance over form in favor of creditors. For example, a court may consider the substance of a transaction to determine if the one-year discovery rule was tolled. In *Scott v. Keane*, the court held that notice to creditors should be more than notice of a transfer; it should not defeat the subsequent creditor who had no idea of the intent behind a recorded transfer.[108] *Scott v. Keane* illustrates the concept of a creditor knowing about a transfer versus knowing about the *fraudulent nature* of a transfer which is often a distinction at issue for purposes of the one-year discovery rule.

---

104. *Poulos v. Poulos*, No. 15 CVS 1116, 2016 WL 5375649, at *11–12 (N.C. Super. Sept. 26, 2016). (Emphasis added.)

105. Query how a court would rule on statutory modifications given the fraudulent transfer law exists in both statute and the common law where the statutory law is expressly not meant to affect the common law. The drafters of asset protection trust statutes might acknowledge this dilemma and consequently, include language in the asset protection statute that addresses both sources of fraudulent transfer law.

106. Compare Utah Code Ann. §25-6-14(5)(m)(iii) ("(iii) the settlor does not intend to hinder, delay, or defraud a known creditor by transferring the assets to the trust;" with Tenn. Code Ann. §35-16-103(3) ("The transferor does not intend to defraud a creditor by transferring the assets to the trust;"). Here, two states permit self-settled trusts, but require affidavits for contributions to the trust. The cited sections illustrate how Utah makes it easier to sign the affidavit by limiting actual intent to a "known creditor" whereas Tennessee makes no such distinction. (Emphasis added.)

107. Economic substance is addressed in the Internal Revenue Code Section 7701(o).

108. The caselaw is mixed on this issue, however, the UVTA Official Comments invite the states to adopt their own provision providing clarity on this issue.

> But, in addition to that, if recording the deed gives constructive notice, as it may be admitted it does, is it to be said that it is only notice of the transfer, and not of the purposes declared on its face, which the law pronounces fraudulent, and hence makes the deed invalid against them? Such a doctrine would have the tendency to make the public records an asylum for fraud instead of means to avoid it, as they are intended to be. If such be the effect of recording a deed, why did not the record of the instruments in Warner v. Rice, 66 Md. 436, 8 Atl. 84, and Brown v. McGill (decided at the last January term of this court) 39 Atl. 613, protect the parties claiming under them? It is true the question involved in those cases was not the same as in this, but those deeds had been recorded, and gave notice, as well as this deed does, to subsequent creditors of the interests held by the parties. But the provisions in the deeds did not protect the parties, notwithstanding they had been recorded, because they were contrary to the policy of the law; and so must this deed be declared, because it is an attempt of the owner of property to retain control over it, although nominally settling it on others; and his setting apart a life estate for himself, which would be liable to creditors, while still holding such power over the whole property, cannot satisfy them, or the law which should protect them against such schemes and devices, the sanction of which by a court of equity must result in the increase of fraud and methods used to take advantage of honest people. Whatever Scott's real motives were in the execution of these deeds, we must judge of them by the terms of this trust deed, which the law declares fraudulent, and it cannot be upheld, but both deeds must be set aside, so far as they interfere with or affect the rights and claims of the appellee.[109]

Substance over form often may require a court to examine the totality of the transaction circumstances, essentially looking to (for example) the equivalent of the step-transaction doctrine to void a transfer disguised through multiple transfers and/or entities:

> This argument is creative but fundamentally misunderstands a basic precept of fraudulent-transfer doctrine: substance trumps form. As we have frequently noted in an analogous context, "fraudulent conveyance doctrine . . . is a flexible principle that looks to substance, rather than form." *Boyer v. Crown Stock Distribution*, Inc., 587 F.3d 787, 793 (7th Cir.2009) (quotation marks omitted); *see also In re Joy Recovery Tech. Corp.*, 286 B.R. 54, 74 (N.D.Ill.Bankr.2002) ("Courts will eschew appeals to form which obscure the substance of a transaction. Thus, a multilevel transaction will be collapsed and treated as a single transaction in order to determine if there was a fraudulent conveyance.")[110]

In the wealth transfer setting, the application of substance over form could be used to ignore a formal arrangement in favor of the substance of the transaction. For example, a transfer to a trustee under a trust agreement that does not expressly provide the settlor with a beneficial interest yet permits the

109. *Scott v. Keane*, 87 Md. 709, 40 A. 1070, 1073–74 (1898). (Emphasis added.)

110. *Cont'l Cas. Co. v. Symons*, 817 F.3d 979, 993 (7th Cir.), *cert. denied sub nom. Symons Int'l Grp., Inc. v. Cont'l Cas. Co.*, 137 S. Ct. 493, 196 L. Ed. 2d 403 (2016).

settlor to be part of a class of permissible appointees of a power exercisable by a third party, could be recast as the retention of a retained interest based on the facts and circumstances. Circumstances where the form is at odds with substance also tend to support the application of alter ego. Establishing alter ego means the creditor might not need to show a transfer of an asset by a debtor, as the debtor would be deemed the owner of the asset. Consequently, alter ego and fraudulent transfer are often plead in the alternative.

# Attorney fees

With roots in criminal law and occasional overlap with tort law when viewed as a legal wrong, it is no surprise that some fraudulent transfer situations will open the door for attorney fee considerations. One must recall an important public policy, that those who owe should pay their debts. If courts were to adopt an approach that fraudulent transfers always result in restoring parties to the status quo, it would create an incentive for every individual to engage in a fraudulent transfer as a prophylactic measure. This approach has developed as a mantra for the aggressive advisers, who often dismiss the consequences of fraudulent transfer law by taking the position that a client has nothing to lose as the worst that can happen is a creditor will simply reverse a transfer.

On the other hand, it should not be assumed that damages and attorney fees will always be awarded in fraudulent transfer cases.[111] Under the American Rule, for example, courts will not award attorney fees unless the parties agreed or a statute provides otherwise. As to the former, several states have done just that, with reasonable attorney fees awarded under the Texas[112] and Virginia fraudulent transfer statutes.[113]

---

111. *See Paul v. Avrahami*, 216 So. 3d 647, 649 (Fla. Dist. Ct. App. 2017). ("Following the fraudulent transfer final judgment, Appellee filed a motion for attorney's fees, where he 'move[d] the court for an award of attorneys [sic] fees against Defendants, Gerald A. Paul, The Gerald A. Paul Revocable Trust and Andrew Paul and to tax costs pursuant to Florida Rule of Civil Procedure 1.420.' In response, Appellants served Appellee their own motion for attorney's fees pursuant to section 57.105, Florida Statutes, wherein they asked Appellee to consent to an amendment of the final judgment and a withdrawal of his request for fees and costs against Appellants. Notably, Appellants cited to statutory and case law for the proposition that the trial court could not award attorney's fees against impleaded defendants in proceedings supplementary. Pursuant to the safe-harbor provision of section 57.105(4), Appellants gave Appellee twenty-one days to withdraw the motion. However, Appellee did not. Upon receipt of the email containing the motion, Appellee's counsel replied: 'Interesting. Perhaps you should file a 57.105 claim against Judge Barkdull as well. Good luck with that.' *** Appellee's motion for attorney's fees against Appellants (who were originally impleaded defendants) was without merit and clearly contrary to both statutory and case law. We reverse the trial court's denial of Appellants' section 57.105 motion for attorney's fees, and remand for the trial court to grant the motion. When calculating fees, the court must determine the amount of reasonable fees that Appellants' counsel incurred in defending Appellee's frivolous motion for attorney's fees—and order Appellee's counsel to pay those fees.")

112. Texas Statute Section 24.013. ("COSTS. In any proceeding under this chapter, the court may award costs and reasonable attorney's fees as are equitable and just.")

113. Virginia Statute Section §55-82.1. ("In any suit brought by a creditor pursuant to §55-80, 55-81, or 55-82 where a (i) gift; (ii) deed; (iii) conveyance, assignment, or transfer of or charge upon the estate of a debtor; (iv) suit commenced or decree, judgment, or execution suffered or obtained; or (v) bond or other writing is declared void, the court shall award counsel for the creditor reasonable attorney fees against the

Although the UFTA does not expressly provide for attorney fees, numerous courts have awarded attorney fees to the creditor. As noted, it is not unusual for a court to not only compensate a creditor through avoidance of a transfer, but given especially offensive conduct, award damages to deter such future conduct.[114] Often, the circumstances leading to an award involves a debtor engaging in a fraudulent transfer with actual intent to hinder, delay, or defraud an existing creditor. Courts have permitted this under either the catch-all[115] provision of the UFTA or the fraudulent transfer common law.[116]

## Statute of Limitations

Some states that have not adopted a uniform fraudulent transfer act (such as South Carolina), or have adopted a uniform act but not the uniform statute of limitations provision (such as California and Minnesota), will require either looking to a non-uniform statutory provision or the common law. It should be clear that the adoption of the UFTA statute of limitations will displace the UFCA statute of limitations.[117] However, such would not be the case where a

---

debtor. Upon a finding of fraudulent conveyance pursuant to §55-80, the court may assess sanctions, including such attorney fees, against all parties over which it has jurisdiction who, with the intent to defraud and having knowledge of the judgment, participated in the conveyance. Should there be a resulting judicial sale, any award of attorney fees shall be paid out of the proceeds of the sale, as other costs are paid, provided the award of attorney fees does not affect a prior lien creditor not represented by the attorney.")

114. *See Aristocrat Lakewood Nursing Home v. Mayne*, 133 Ohio App. 3d 651, 672, 729 N.E.2d 768, 783 (1999). ("Finally, the Ohio Supreme Court has also recognized that punitive damages and attorney fees may be awarded when appropriate in fraudulent conveyance cases. *Locafrance*, at 202-203, 6 OBR at 255-256, 451 N.E.2d at 1225-1226. In a case involving the former Uniform Fraudulent Conveyance Act, the court specifically recognized that merely '[s]etting aside the conveyance and other remedies set forth in R.C. 1336.10 and 1336.11 would not be a sufficient deterrent to discourage appellants and other debtors from making fraudulent conveyances to avoid creditors.' *Id.* The nursing home in the case at bar presented some evidence to support its claims.")

115. *See Johns v. A.T. Stephens Enterprises, Inc.*, 815 So. 2d 511, 516 (Ala. 2001). ("Citing Ala.Code 1975, §8-9A-7(a)(1), the defendants first argue that the normal remedy for a fraudulent conveyance is not damages, but rather a rescission or avoidance of the conveyance. Although the defendants are correct in arguing that a Code section provides creditors with avoidance as a remedy, the same section expands the remedial list to include '[a]ny other relief the circumstances may require.' Ala.Code 1975, §8-9A-7(a)(3)c. We conclude not only that the law permits damages awards in cases involving fraudulent conveyances, but that the facts of this case require such an award.")

116. See Mahavir Mehta, Plaintiff & Respondent, v. Activor Corporation et al., Defendants & Appellants. Additional Party Names: Actiogen Corp., Chanda LLC, Chanda Zaveri, No. B276151, 2018 WL 1391786, at *1 (unpublished opinion) (Cal. Ct. App. Mar. 20, 2018). ("Defendants first argue punitive damages are not recoverable in a UFTA action as a matter of law. They cite no authority for this contention, other than the absence of any language in UFTA that expressly provides for punitive damages. UFTA, however, authorizes '[a]ny other relief the circumstances may require.' *** Moreover, UFTA does not provide the exclusive remedy for fraudulent conveyances. (Macedo v. Bosio (2001) 86 Cal.App.4th 1044, 1051.) UFTA remedies 'are cumulative to the remedies applicable to fraudulent conveyances that existed before the uniform laws went into effect.' (Wisden v. Superior Court (2004) 124 Cal.App.4th 750, 758.) As a matter of law, punitive damages may be awarded in fraudulent transfer actions, whether under UFTA or common law.")

117. *See Gulf Ins. Co. v. Clark*, 2001 MT 45, ¶ 43, 304 Mont. 264, 275, 20 P.3d 780, 788. ("We therefore conclude that, contrary to Gulf and Security's argument, the legal remedy available to the creditor in Murphy, brought under the now repealed Uniform Fraudulent Conveyance Act, is no longer available because that right was displaced by UFTA, which carries a clear, explicit statute of limitations.")

state has not adopted any uniform provision, as was the case in Minnesota where a fraudulent transfer made with actual fraud received a longer statute of limitations under the state's fraudulent transfer *common* law.[118] In *Finn v. All. Bank*, the Minnesota Supreme Court did not hesitate to review fraudulent transfer common law dating back to 1868.

## Right to Jury Trial

The applicable fraudulent transfer common law may provide guidance as to whether a jury trial is available. This may require examining fraudulent transfer law as it existed at the time a state adopted its own constitution and identifying whether the remedy sought is legal or equitable in nature, essentially adopting the approach taken in *Granfinanciera, S.A. v. Nordberg* at the state level.

> Article I, Section 22 of the Florida Constitution simply provides that the "right to trial by jury shall be secure and remain inviolate." Yet the constitutional right to a jury trial does not extend to every type of civil action. The guarantee extends only to those categories of actions in which the right to a jury trial was enjoyed as of 1845, the date that Florida's first constitution became effective. *** Determining whether there were jury trials in particular types of actions at common law (and in particular in Florida prior to 1845) can be a daunting task because there is no single reliable historical source which neatly categorizes the causes of actions as they existed in the eighteenth and early nineteenth centuries. The task is further complicated by the evolution of causes of action over time and, more recently, by the merger of courts of law and courts of equity. *See generally* King Mountain Condominium Ass'n v. Gundlach, 425 So.2d 569 (Fla. 4th DCA 1982). However, because our Florida constitutional guarantee has been interpreted by our supreme court as predicated on whether the right to trial by jury existed for the particular cause of action as of 1845, we must endeavor to ascertain the historical status of the cause of action. *** When faced with the issue of whether there is a constitutional right to a jury trial for a particular cause of action, review is not limited to the search for an eighteenth-century analogy.

118. *See Finn v. All. Bank*, 860 N.W.2d 638, 657–58 (Minn. 2015). Minnesota did not adopt UFTA's four-year rule. ("Here, by contrast, the parties do not dispute that fraudulent-transfer claims *658 based on an actual intent to hinder, delay, or defraud creditors existed at common law as early as 1868, and likely earlier. *See Blackman v. Wheaton*, 13 Minn. 326, 330 (Gil. 299, 303) (1868). Setting aside whether constructive-fraud claims existed at common law—a question we need not answer—the fact that the Legislature has codified fraudulent-transfer liability does not change the underlying 'gist and essence' of fraudulent-transfer law. *McMillan v. Cheeny*, 30 Minn. 519, 521, 16 N.W. 404, 405 (1883). Nor does it transform it into a liability created by statute, which, as we made clear in McDaniel, does not apply 'to liabilities existing at common law which have been recognized by statute.' 469 N.W.2d at 85.In short, for the limited purpose of determining the applicable statute of limitations, we conclude that a claim against a transferee that receives an actually fraudulent transfer under MUFTA is for 'relief on the ground of fraud,' just as it was for a transferee that received a fraudulent transfer at the time of McMillan and Duxbury. Thus, we agree with the court of appeals that the district court erred when it dismissed the Receiver's actual-fraud claims under Minn. Stat §541.05, subd. 1(2), and therefore remand to the district court for consideration of whether the Receiver filed its action within six years of the discovery of the 'facts constituting the fraud.'")

> A second, and more important step, in the analysis requires a reviewing court to examine the remedy sought and determine whether it is legal or equitable in nature. *See* Granfinanciera, S.A. v. Nordberg, 492 U.S. 33, 42, 109 S.Ct. 2782, 2790, 106 L.Ed.2d 26 (1989).[119]

*Dexia Credit Local v. Rogan* provides guidance as to the availability of a jury trial in the context of a wealth transfer transaction. Specifically, the issue in *Dexia* was whether a fraudulent transfer to a trust, and the requested turnover of assets, was a legal remedy versus an equitable remedy. The *Dexia* court held the turnover of specific assets was not legal relief, but equitable relief, necessitating the court to strike a request for a jury trial, but uphold the request for a jury trial as to *monetary distributions* sought to be voided to beneficiaries:

> Acknowledging that there is no hard-line test for determining whether a remedy is equitable or legal, the Seventh Circuit has provided useful guidance in this regard:
>
>> It is possible, nonetheless, to draw general distinctions between the two forms of relief. Legal remedies traditionally involve money damages. Equitable remedies, by contrast, are typically coercive, and are enforceable directly on the person or thing to which they are directed. Traditionally, equitable relief is discretionary, whereas legal relief is not.
>>
>> Int'l Fin. Servs. Corp., 356 F.3d at 736 (internal citations and quotations omitted).
>
> In this case, Dexia seeks turnover of two categories of assets. The first are assets contained in the various trusts. Dexia contends that the assets in those trusts are in fact the assets of Peter Rogan, against whom Dexia has a judgment, and should be used to satisfy that judgment. The Rogan children are the putative beneficiaries of those trusts. As such, their interests in the trusts are intangible assets. Dexia is attempting to terminate the children's intangible interests and obtain a turnover of the assets of the trusts, which are held not by the children, but by the trustees of the trusts. Under the guidance provided by Granfinanciera and International Financial Services, it is clear that the children are not entitled to have a jury determine whether Dexia is entitled to the relief it seeks concerning the trusts. Among other reasons, Dexia is not seeking a monetary award from any of the Rogan children. Additionally, the Seventh Circuit has noted that a court order to turn over property during proceedings under Rule 69(a) "was an order in the nature of specific performance," which is an equitable remedy. *See* Ruggiero, 994 F.2d at 1225 (*affirming* district court order requiring judgment debtor's wife to turn over real estate to judgment creditor and imposing a resulting trust on the same property); Marseilles Hydro Power, LLC v. Marseilles Land & Water Co., 299 F.3d 643, 648 (7th Cir.2002) (holding that specific performance is an equitable remedy).
>
> The second category of assets that Dexia seeks to have turned over includes assets in the Rogan children's personal bank and securities accounts, which

119. *381651 Alberta, Ltd. v. 279298 Alberta, Ltd.*, 675 So. 2d 1385, 1388-1389 (Fla. Dist. Ct. App. 1996.)

Dexia claims were transferred from the various trusts. Unlike the relief with respect to the trusts, this involves turning over to Dexia assets in which the Rogan children have a direct, tangible interest. Though the question is not free from doubt, what Dexia seeks in this regard is somewhat akin to a money judgment against the children, which would be a legal remedy. *See* Granfinanciera, 492 U.S. at 44; Int'l Fin. Servs. Corp., 356 F.3d at 736. The Court concludes that Brian and Sara Rogan (who made jury demands in a timely fashion) are entitled to a jury trial with respect to Dexia's claim to recover the assets in their personal accounts.

Conclusion

*4 For the reasons set forth above, the Court strikes Robert Rogan's jury demand. The Court also strikes Brian and Sara Rogan's jury demand with respect to Dexia's request for turnover of the assets of the RPP Finance Trust, the Peter G. Rogan Irrevocable Trust, and the trusts domiciled in Florida and Belize that Peter Rogan created in the names of each of his children. Brian and Sara Rogan are entitled to a jury trial with respect to Dexia's attempt to recover transfers they received from the trusts.[120]

## Secondary Liability

Although a relatively rare occurrence, a court could impose liability on a person who assists with wealth transfer planning if the planning constitutes a fraudulent transfer that is considered a legal wrong sufficient to support causes of action based on aiding and abetting or conspiracy. Where a person who provides assistance with a fraudulent transfer and is also the mastermind of the planning that amounts to a fraudulent transfer with actual fraud (as opposed to constructive fraud), a court may be willing to entertain secondary liability as such planning can amount to an agreement sufficient to trigger conspiracy liability. Chapter nine addresses this issue in more detail as it applies to attorneys who assist with egregious fraudulent transfers.

## Choice of Law

Until the UVTA, no statute governed the choice of law for fraudulent transfers. Attempting to hardwire the choice of law via contract is not much help, either, because a fraudulent transfer often is viewed as a tort and relief under a fraudulent transfer action is one directed against the transferee-defendant, who most likely did not sign any contract with the creditor.

When faced with a conflict between the potential application of fraudulent transfer law in two or more jurisdictions, a court will need to decide how the fraudulent transfer claim is characterized. If the characterization of the action is

120. *Dexia Credit Local v. Rogan*, No. 02 C 8288, 2009 WL 528902, at *2–4 (N.D. Ill. Mar. 2, 2009).

to determine whether the transfer was fraudulent (versus whether a transfer was valid), the conflict of law principles may require the court view the conflict as one sounding in tort versus contract. This characterization is important as the conflict of law rules for a tort may differ than those for a contract.

> Plaintiff's claim under the Uniform Fraudulent Transfer Act (UFTA) is governed by Georgia's version of the UFTA, O.C.G.A. §§18-2-70 et seq. It is arguable that Delaware law should apply to Plaintiff's UFTA claim because the security agreements all provide that Delaware law should apply. But, the dispute here cannot be accurately described as one involving rights in the security agreement as between the parties. The issue framed by the Plaintiff is whether certain conveyances were fraudulent as to Defendant Derek J. Rials. Because the instant controversy actually concerns not the validity of the transfer, but whether that transfer was fraudulent vis-à-vis Defendants, it is one of tort law, not contract law. Accordingly, it should be determined by conflict of laws principles governing the selection of law in tort cases. North Carolina choice of law principles for tort cases dictate that the substantive law of Georgia be applied to Plaintiff's UFTA claim because Georgia is the state where the alleged fraudulent conveyance occurred.[121]

Tort characterization is also relevant when a court must decide whether a creditor's interest in seeking relief under fraudulent transfer law outweighs the choice of law in a document not signed by the creditor.

> In this case, application of the New York interest analysis test reveals that New York's interest in seeing its fraudulent conveyance law applied outweighs the interest of the Partnership in having its internal relationships governed by the law under which it is organized, especially in light of the fact that plaintiffs, though limited partners, are suing in their capacities as tort creditors. The alleged torts largely occurred in New York; all plaintiffs and the vast majority of the false profit defendants are domiciled in New York. None are domiciled in Delaware. In light of the foregoing, and considering the strong interest New York has in seeing its law applied when one of its domiciliaries alleges it has been defrauded, *see, e.g.*, Marenyi v. Packard Press Corp., 90 Civ. 4439(CSH), 1993 WL 227704, at *3 (S.D.N.Y. June 21, 1993) (M.J.Katz), the Court finds that New York law has a strong interest in seeing its fraudulent conveyance statutes applied, and declines to apply the internal affairs doctrine to this claim. *See* Stephens, 1996 WL 271789, at *4 (citing *428 Norlin v. Rooney, Pace Inc., 744 F.2d 255, 263-64 (2d Cir.1984) (rejecting use of internal affairs doctrine in matter of corporate governance of Panamanian corporation where public policy of New York weighed in favor of application of New York law) (parenthetical language in original)).[122]

Because the fraudulent transfer law statutes lacked guidance as to the choice of law, much time-consuming and costly litigation would ensue over

121. *Commercial Credit Grp., Inc. v. Falcon Equip., LLC of Jax*, 2010 WL 144101, at *5 (W.D.N.C. Jan. 8, 2010).

122. *Drenis v. Haligiannis*, 452 F. Supp. 2d 418, 427-28 (S.D.N.Y. 2006).

which jurisdiction's law would apply in cases with multijurisdictional implications. Consequently, this uncertainty and expense led to the creation of a Uniform Law Commission study and drafting committee, which ultimately resulted in amendments to the UFTA (including a name change to the UVTA) that provided a choice of law provision pointing to the location of the debtor.[123]

The conflict of law issue often arises in conflicts involving wealth transfer and fraudulent transfer law given the propensity for some wealth planners to forum shop for their clients. Forum shopping occurs in various wealth transfer contexts, such as utilizing foreign laws that permit perpetual trusts or the ability to avoid state or federal tax.[124] A fraudulent transfer conflict of law issue may also arise where a debtor residing in a non-asset protection trust state transfers assets to a state that permits asset protection trusts or provides other law that impairs a creditor's traditional rights. While asset protection trusts may violate important public policy in the state of the debtor's domicile, such public policy has been statutorily overridden in the asset protection state.

When faced with a fraudulent transfer issue involving a debtor's attempt to use debtor-friendly law of a foreign jurisdiction, courts have often ignored a debtor's choice of governing law. Instead, courts have applied the law of the debtor's domicile under a conflict of law analysis.

Additionally, courts have abandoned the choice of law analysis where the trust agreement is viewed as a sham.

> First State Fiduciaries also claims that the forum selection clause in the trust instrument, designating Delaware as the situs for resolving all disputes, is controlling here. If the Delaware irrevocable trust is void ab initio and unenforceable, however, the forum selection clause would be inapplicable in any event. *See* KI, Inc. v. KP Acquisition Partners, LLC, Superior Court, judicial district of Stamford-Norwalk, Complex Litigation Docket, Docket No. X05-CV-09-60027474-S (September 24, 2010, Blawie, J.); Powell v. Spruce Peak Realty, LLC, Superior Court, judicial district of Middlesex, Docket No. CV-09-5006181-S (September 17, 2009, Jones, J.).[125]

More courts have been willing to turn to equity to disregard certain wealth planning structures. For example, the application of alter ego may be an im-

123. *See* Kenneth C. Kettering, *Codifying a Choice of Law Rule for Fraudulent Transfer: A Memorandum to the Uniform Law Commission*, 19 Am. Bankr. Inst. L. Rev. 319 (2011).

124. State taxing authorities may discover its residents using loopholes provided under the laws of other states (to avoid tax) and take action accordingly. For example, New York Tax Law Section 612 modifies Federal income to address the use of non-grantor incomplete trusts that allow a resident to avoid state income tax. ("There shall be added to federal adjusted gross income . . . [i]n the case of a taxpayer who transferred property to an incomplete gift non-grantor trust, the income of the trust, less any deductions of the trust, to the extent such income and deductions of such trust would be taken into account in computing the taxpayer's federal taxable income if such trust in its entirety were treated as a grantor trust for federal tax purposes. For purposes of this paragraph, an 'incomplete gift non-grantor trust' means a resident trust that meets the following conditions: (i) the trust does not qualify as a grantor trust under section six hundred seventy-one through six hundred seventy-nine of the internal revenue code, and (2) the grantor's transfer of assets to the trust is treated as an incomplete gift under section twenty-five hundred eleven of the internal revenue code, and the regulations thereunder.")

125. *Day v. Seblatnigg*, No. FSTCV146021170S, 2015 WL 9871322, at *8 (Conn. Super. Ct. Dec. 23, 2015).

pediment to the effectiveness of a transaction. Given the danger and uncertainty of a court's application of equity, some pro-debtor jurisdictions have attempted to limit equitable remedies by including language in protective legislation.

Creditors seeking to void the transfer of wealth utilizing limited liability companies may encounter different choice of law rules based on the requested relief. For instance, if a creditor is seeking to enforce a charging order with respect to a debtor's interest in an LLC, a court may decide that the law of the LLC formation should govern.[126] This was the case in *Wells Fargo Equip. Fin., Inc. v. Retterath*, where the Iowa Supreme Court found Iowa law (that is, the state where the LLC at issue was formed) governed, and as a result, concluded that tenancy by entirety protection did not exist as to the debtor's ownership interest held with his spouse. It should be noted that the Iowa Supreme Court did not consider choice of law as it would have applied to Wells Fargo's relief under fraudulent transfer law.

> For the purposes of determining the enforceability of a charging order, we hold that a member's membership interest is located where the LLC was formed. Our holding aligns with the anomalous characteristics of a membership interest in an LLC, particularly because a charging order is directed to the LLC rather than the individual member since it requires the LLC to redirect the debtor-member's distributions to the creditor. *See* Iowa Code §489.503(1); *see also* Fla. Stat. Ann. §605.0503(1). Additionally, Iowa law governs an LLC's "internal affairs" and "[t]he liability of a member as member and a manager as manager for the debts, obligations, or other liabilities" of the LLC. Iowa Code §489.106. Locating the membership interest in the state in which the LLC was formed recognizes this authority and promotes uniformity. "To conclude otherwise (i.e., that the interest lies wherever the debtor happens to be domiciled) could result in substantial uncertainty and confusion," as an LLC could become subject to various and competing charging orders from differing foreign jurisdictions. JPMorgan Chase Bank, N.A., 393 P.3d at 959. Likewise, our holding creates certainty for creditors because it provides them with a fixed jurisdiction to pursue charging orders.
>
> *5 6 In this case, the Retteraths' interests in Homeland exist under Iowa law, and their creditor's remedies are also limited by Iowa law. Accordingly, we hold membership interests in an LLC are located in the state where the LLC is formed. The district court correctly concluded Iowa law applies to this case. Further, the district court correctly dismissed the Retteraths' petition to vacate the charging order since Iowa law does not recognize the ownership of property by a married couple as tenants in the entireties. *See* Fay v. Smiley, 201 Iowa 1290, 1294, 207 N.W. 369, 371 (Iowa 1926) ("Assuming for the purpose of this division of this opinion, that this deed, in the eyes of the common-law rule, would create an estate in entirety, we have to say that such a construction has never been recognized under the Iowa practice; and, when attempts have been made to induce the court to make such construction, it

126. *See generally*, J. Adkisson, The Charging Order Practice Guide, Ch. 20 (Am.Bar.Assoc. 2019).

> has refused to do so."). Given this lack of recognition of the doctrine of tenants in the entireties, the district court also correctly found the foreign judgments were properly registered and the charging order was properly issued. Similarly, we need not address Analia's due process claim since Iowa does not recognize her right to own Homeland interests jointly with her husband as a tenancy by the entireties. She was not entitled to notice since she is not a judgment debtor of WFEFI.[127]

Although the rationale in *Retterath* was favorable to the creditor (Wells Fargo), the extension of this rationale might not appear to be beneficial in a general sense. This is because other courts have determined the applicable law when it comes to judgment enforcement to be governed by local law. However, *Retterath* can still be consistent with the general approach of not permitting debtors to set the ground rules in advance of defrauding creditors. Consider a situation where the debtors formed an LLC in a state that both features charging order protection, as well as recognizes tenancy by entirety ownership (and its attendant creditor protection.) If the Retteraths instead chose Delaware, Wells Fargo would have encountered two states (Florida as the state of debtor's residence and Delaware as the state of formation) that recognized tenancy by entirety. Applying *Retterath*, the debtors might argue Wells Fargo could not seek a charging order as to tenancy by entirety property. The creditor would not be any better off had the Retterath's used a Florida LLC. However, if the Retterath's made a fraudulent transfer as to the LLC interests, strong precedent exists under fraudulent transfer law to apply the law of the debtor's domicile (here, Florida.) While this might not provide much benefit in comparison to Delaware's general fraudulent transfer statute (i.e., the fraudulent transfer statute that has not been modified in a pro-debtor fashion in conjunction with its asset protection trust statute), the benefit would be far greater in comparison to a jurisdiction, including foreign jurisdictions, that have weak fraudulent transfer laws.

## *Actual Conflict*

The first step in a fraudulent transfer choice of law analysis is to determine whether there is an actual conflict between two or more potentially applicable fraudulent transfer laws. For example, if State A follows one uniform act and State B features a different uniform act or body of law, differences may exist that could cause a conflict. One difference between the UFTA and the UFCA concerns the payment of an antecedent debt. "In comparison with the UFTA, which only allows the avoidance of 'insider' transfers in satisfaction of an antecedent debt made while the debtor is already insolvent, New York law potentially allows a much broader set of for-value transactions to be deemed constructive fraudulent conveyances, and the transfer would be set aside without any showing as to the transferor's intent. *** Hence, New York law and

127. *Wells Fargo Equip. Fin., Inc. v. Retterath*, No. 18-0599, 2019 WL 1574686, at *4–5 (Iowa Apr. 12, 2019).

the UFTA conflict in ways that are potentially relevant to this action. Consequently, a determination of which jurisdiction's law should govern must be made."[128] Another difference between the UFTA and UFCA that could cause a conflict is the statute of limitations. Further, the conflict could be between states that follow the same uniform act but have non-uniform differences or conflicts in the associated common law interpreting the terms.

In cases involving foreign laws, the debtor may need to prove foreign law as a precursor to the choice of law analysis.[129] Where a debtor does not prove the substance of the foreign law, the creditor may attempt to apply the law of the forum state.[130]

## *Jurisdiction Pointing Test*

When determining the law of which two (or more) jurisdictions may govern the fraudulent transfer, the court making the determination must employ a test that points to one jurisdiction. The test itself varies among the courts, resulting in unpredictable results for litigants. For instance, a court might apply the eleven-factor test (applicable to torts)[131] contained in the Restatement (Second) of Conflict of Laws. This approach points to the law of the jurisdiction having the most significant contacts in light of certain policy considerations and interests in the dispute. The choice of law in bankruptcy is also complicated, resulting in three different tests being employed to determine the appropriate governing fraudulent transfer law.[132]

---

128. *Taberna Preferred Funding II, Ltd. v. Advance Realty Group LLC*, 45 Misc. 3d 1204(A). (Unreported Disposition.)

129. *Nineveh Invs. Ltd. v. United States*, CIVIL ACTION No. 16-1068, at *20 (E.D. Pa. Aug. 13, 2019) ("Plaintiff's burden is to show that foreign law differs from domestic law, not to show that the laws conflict. The conflict of laws analysis is separate from the Rule 44.1 analysis and occurs only after the Court determines that parties have met their burden of proving foreign law. *See* Bel-Ray Co. v. Chemrite Ltd., 181 F.3d 435, 440 (3d Cir. 1999).")

130. *Nineveh Invs. Ltd. v. United States*, CIVIL ACTION No. 16-1068, at *20-21 (E.D. Pa. Aug. 13, 2019) ("The United States argues that the Court should apply the doctrine of depecage to this action. "'Depecage' refers to the use of the law of different states to resolve different issues in the same case." *See* Calhoun v. Yamaha Motor Corp., U.S.A., 216 F.3d 338, 342 (3d Cir. 2000). The United States contends that depecage should be applied in this case because plaintiffs have only provided the substance of Bahamian law as to issues related to interpretation of the Trust instrument. U.S. Mem. C.O.L. 6. It is the position of the United States that plaintiff has not met its burden of proving Bahamian law related to a number of additional legal issues, such as the law related to the doctrines of nominee/alter ego, fraudulent transfer, and sham/economic substance.")

131. *See* Restatement (Second) of Conflicts of Laws §§ 6 and 145 (Am. Law Inst. 1971). *See also*, Foisie v. Worcester Polytechnic Inst., 967 F.3d 27, 42 (1st Cir. 2020).

132. *See* Kettering, *Codifying a Choice of Law Rule*, 19 Am. Bankr. Inst. L. Rev. 319, The Supreme Court has not laid down a rule as to what choice of law rule a bankruptcy court should apply to issues governed by nonbankruptcy law, and lower federal courts are divided on the subject. Some hold that a bankruptcy court must apply the choice of law rules of the forum state, as in a diversity case. Others hold that choice of nonbankruptcy law is governed by a uniform federal common-law rule, generally applying for that purpose the approach taken by the Restatement (Second) of Conflicts of Laws ("Second Restatement") and looking to the state with the "most significant contacts" (which approach is discussed in part IV of this paper). Still others split the difference, treating choice of law in bankruptcy as being ultimately a federal question, but applying the choice of law rules of the forum state absent a federal interest that justifies use of a different rule.

To determine which jurisdictions have an interest in a dispute, a court may consider the various jurisdictions' contacts with the litigation. A false conflict exists if the jurisdiction with a potentially conflicting law does not have an actual interest in the dispute.[133] For example, in *Janvey v. Aguire*, a party argued that Antigua law should apply because investors in a Ponzi scheme purchased CDs from a Stanford entity in Antigua. However, the court determined that the Stanford entities operated as a single entity headquartered in Houston, Texas. Although investors made purchases from the Antiguan corporation, the corporation was a sham, existing solely to perpetuate fraud. "Antigua has no interest in applying its own law in such a scenario." The court also noted that none of the parties asserting Antiguan law should apply were Antiguan citizens and Antiguan law prohibited the corporation from serving Antiguans.

For purposes of handling matters between parties to a trust agreement, it is likely that a court will apply the law designated in the trust agreement. However, in fraudulent transfer actions or situations where public policy is violated, courts have been reluctant to permit a settlor-turned-debtor to force pro-debtor law on a creditor that is not a party to the trust agreement. Similarly, a court would probably be reluctant to permit an LLC member-turned-debtor to force foreign pro-debtor law on a creditor who did not sign the operating agreement. So, while it is true that parties to an agreement may choose the rules governing the agreement, a debtor should not expect to injure a third-party creditor and assume the debtor's choice of law will apply.

*In re Rensin* illustrates how an agreement may violate public policy and the impact of this violation will have on a choice of law provision. In *Rensin*, the settlor created a trust several years before a creditor action. Because the trust was a self-settled spendthrift trust, it violated Florida public policy. Consequently, the choice of law contained in the trust agreement was completely ignored, and instead, the bankruptcy court applied Florida law as to all aspects of the trust.[134]

> Under Florida law, the choice of law provided in a contract is binding unless it offends Florida public policy. *Se. Floating Docks v. Auto-Owners Ins. Co.*, 82 So. 3d 73, 80 (Fla. 2012); *Mazzoni Farms, Inc. v. E.I. DuPont De Nemours & Co.*, 761 So. 2d 306, 311 (Fla. 2000). Florida law strongly disfavors asset protection trusts, where the settlor is also the primary beneficiary and there are spendthrift protections. *Menotte v. Brown (In re Brown)*, 303 F.3d 1261, 1266 (11th Cir. 2002) (citing cases). While Florida law provides a broad set of exemptions designed to protect various assets from the collection activities of creditors, see Fla. Stat. ch. 222, Florida courts will not enforce a spendthrift trust designed to permit a person to place his or her assets beyond the arms of creditors. *See* Fla. Stat. §736.0107; *In re Brown*, 303 F.3d at 1266-67; *Barbee v. Goldstein (In re Reliance Fin. & Inv. Group, Inc.)*, No. 05-80625, 2006 U.S. Dist. LEXIS 82945, at *19-20 (S.D. Fla. Nov. 14, 2006). Mr. Rensin

133. *Janvey v. Aguire*, 2013 WL 2451738, at *4 (N.D. Tex. Jan. 22, 2013), vacated sub nom, 2018 WL 7051049 (N.D. Tex. Jan. 11, 2018).

134. As discussed herein, there could be significant repercussions for tax purposes if the choice of law fails in favor of a domicile that would not provide such tax benefits.

> does not contest that the law of Belize is contrary to Florida public policy on this point.
>
> The Joren Trust falls squarely within this category of trusts. To permit Mr. Rensin to rely on the law of Belize, to enforce an asset protection trust designed to offend his creditors, is contrary to Florida public policy. The Court will not apply Belize law but will apply the law of Florida to all aspects of the Joren Trust. *See Goldberg v. Lawrence (In re Lawrence)*, 227 B.R. 907, 917-18 (Bankr. S.D. Fla. 1998).[135]

As addressed more fully in chapter seven, self-settled trusts are especially prone to the claims of creditors for several reasons. For example, the trust agreement's applicable law governing creditors' rights may be ignored due to violation of public policy as illustrated in *Rensin*. With the application of traditional creditors' rights law, creditors may have the benefit of traditional fraudulent transfer law and utilize various theories to reach self-settled trust assets. Additionally, in non-DAPT states, there is most likely no statutory prohibition on a creditor using the trust agreement as evidence of actual fraud in proving a fraudulent transfer.[136] Finally, under a non-DAPT state law, a settlor's retained interest may be reached under the rule against self-settled trusts (RASST) (without any showing of fraudulent intent.)

---

135. In re: Joseph K. Rensin, Debtor. Nicole Testa Mehdipour, Chapter 7 Tr., Plaintiff, v. Joseph K. Rensin, Defendant., No. 17-11834-EPK, 2019 WL 2004000, at *7 (Bankr. S.D. Fla. May 6, 2019).

136. *But see* UVTA Official Comment, Section 4, n. 8. Note 8 acknowledges that a transfer to a self-settled trust by a DAPT state resident should not, by itself, constitute actual intent under Section 4. ("If an individual Debtor whose principal residence is in X establishes such a trust and transfers assets thereto, then under §10 of this Act the voidable transfer law of X applies to that transfer. That transfer cannot be considered voidable in itself under §4(a)(1) as in force in X, for the legislature of X, having authorized the establishment of such trusts, must have expected them to be used.")

CHAPTER 6

# Fraudulent Transfer Law and Other Law

Other laws may provide separate grounds for relief against the transfer of wealth. The Official Comments recognize how other laws may supplement, not supplant, fraudulent transfer law.

## Criminal statute

Recall the Statute of Elizabeth had a penal element to it. Some state statutes make it a crime to hinder, delay, or defraud creditors. Usually, these fraudulent transfer criminal statutes require that the creditor have a security interest in the transferred property.

> (a) A person commits the crime of defrauding secured creditors if he destroys, removes, conceals, encumbers, transfers, or otherwise deals with property subject to a security interest with intent to hinder enforcement of that interest.
>
> (b) "Security interest" means an interest in personal property or fixtures as defined in Section 7-1-201.
>
> (c) Defrauding secured creditors is a Class A misdemeanor.[1]

While a criminal statute does not typically create a private right of action for a creditor,[2] the existence of the statute is still a legitimate concern for debtors and their attorneys who advise them.[3] In light of these statutes, a lawyer should

1. Ala. Code §13A-9-46.

2. See Cain v. Fid. Nat. Title Ins. Co., No. 1 CA-CV 10-0858, 2013 WL 988106, at *9 (Ariz. Ct. App. Mar. 12, 2013), as amended (Apr. 3, 2013). ("Section 44–1211 is a criminal statute. Cain has not cited, nor has our research revealed, any authority suggesting that it allows for a private right of action. Therefore, the trial court did not err in dismissing Cain's complaint as to this claim.")

3. *See Stokes v. State*, 373 So. 2d 1211, 1213 (Ala. Crim. App.), writ denied sub nom. Ex parte Stokes, 373 So. 2d 1218 (Ala. 1979). ("The defendant was indicted and convicted under Alabama Code Section 13-4-2

consider his or her role when assisting a client in light of the ethical rule prohibiting a lawyer from counseling a client to engage, or assisting a client to engage in conduct the lawyer knows is criminal. This concern would most likely only exist in theory and only in the most egregious fraudulent transfer cases.[4] However, these statutes underscore the importance of advisers engaging in due diligence, discussed more fully in chapter nine.

## Proceedings supplementary

Relief under fraudulent transfer law is available both before and after a judgment. Post judgment, a creditor may find relief under a state proceedings supplementary statute. For example, under Florida statute section 56.29, if a debtor's property is held by a third party, a creditor may force the third party to prove why such property is not subject to execution. Essentially, if garnishment, levy, or attachment does not work, a creditor may use section 56.29 to obtain property held in the hands of third parties. Often, this may involve a fraudulent transfer action. However, under section 56.29(3)(a), the traditional fraudulent transfer burden shifting is altered in favor of creditors; if an asset was held by the debtor one year before service on the debtor, and the asset held by a third-party claims title, the debtor has the burden to prove the transfer was not fraudulent:

> When, within one year before the service of process on the judgment debtor in the original proceeding or action, the judgment debtor has had title to, or paid the purchase price of, any personal property to which the judgment debtor's spouse, any relative, or any person on confidential terms with the judgment debtor claims title and right of possession, the judgment debtor has the burden of proof to establish that such transfer or gift was not made to delay, hinder, or defraud creditors.

## Spousal Transfer Statutes

Law governing the transfer of a spouse's asset to the other spouse may apply to provide relief to a creditor. Such is the case in Georgia, where a statute requires a married couple prove fairness to creditors with respect to interspousal transfers. In one case, an issue arose between a couple and KeyBank regarding whether the debtor-couple had the initial burden of proving such fairness, given Georgia's adoption of the UFTA, which places the initial burden on the creditor.

> Longstanding Georgia law provides that "when a transaction between a husband and wife is attacked for fraud by the creditors of either, the onus shall be on the husband and wife to show that the transaction was fair."

(1975) for selling a truck to hinder, delay, or defraud the Peoples Bank of Frisco City, Alabama. The trial court fixed punishment at one year and one day imprisonment.")

4. See Section 1.2(d) of the ABA Model Rule of Professional Conduct. ("A lawyer shall not counsel a client to engage, or assist a client, in conduct that the lawyer knows is criminal or fraudulent, but a lawyer may discuss the legal consequences of any proposed course of conduct with a client and may counsel or assist a client to make a good faith effort to determine the validity, scope, meaning or application of the law.")

> O.C.G.A. §19–3–10 (2016). Georgia courts, interpreting this provision, have long held that "[t]he burden is on the husband and the wife to show that the transaction as a whole was free from fraud[, a]nd it is for the jury to say whether the husband and the wife carried their burden in this regard." *** In 2002, Georgia adopted the Uniform Fraudulent Transfer Act (UFTA) which, among other things, created a new cause of action for fraudulent conveyances.[5]

The court held that the UFTA did not implicitly repeal the burden established under another Georgia statute:

> As an initial matter, nothing in the UFTA clearly contradicts the provisions of section 19–3–10. We conclude that a Georgia court would read them in pari materia. Not until its non-retroactive amendment in 2015 did Georgia's UFTA contain any provision concerning the burden of proof. Thus, the version of the Uniform Act in effect at all times relevant to this appeal did not clearly contradict section 19–3–10's allocation of the burden of proof in the context of spousal transfers. Moreover, we believe that Georgia courts would reconcile the provisions of the two statutes. The special context of a spousal transfer might well have been intended to require greater scrutiny than allegedly fraudulent transfers in other contexts, even to insiders other than a spouse.[6]

In some states, the transfer of a marital asset might result in a breach of fiduciary duty by the asset-transferring spouse. In this event, a court may order avoidance of the transfer, like that provided under fraudulent transfer law.

> The potential remedies for breach of the fiduciary duty by one spouse include "an award to the other spouse of 50 percent, or an amount equal to 50 percent, of any asset undisclosed or transferred in breach of the fiduciary duty plus attorney's fees and court costs, with value of the assets "determined to be its highest value at the date of the breach of the fiduciary duty, the date of the sale or disposition of the asset, or the date of the award by the court. (§1101, subd. (g).) When the breach "falls within the ambit of Section 3294 of the Civil Code," the remedies "shall include, but not be limited to, an award to the other spouse of 100 percent, or an amount equal to 100 percent, of any asset undisclosed or transferred in breach of the fiduciary duty." (§1101, subd. (h).)[7]

*In re Walker*[8] provides another example of how existing statutes can coexist with fraudulent transfer statutes. In *Walker*, the bankruptcy court was faced with the application of two fraudulent transfer statutes; one was Tennessee's version of the UFTA (the TFTA), and the other, Tennessee Code Section 66-3-101, was language derived from the Statute of 13 Elizabeth, but not repealed. Section 66-3-101 was described by the court as "an old statute which has been

5. *Key Equip. Fin., Inc. v. Overend*, No. 15-15592, 2016 WL 6933309, at *2 (11th Cir. Nov. 28, 2016)

6. *Id* at 5.

7. *In re* Marriage of Darius Mohsenin & Denise Mohsenin. Darius Mohsenin, Appellant, v. Denise Mohsenin, Respondent., No. A156151, 2020 WL 6938032, at *6 (Cal. Ct. App. Nov. 25, 2020).

8. *In re Walker*, No. 1:13-BK-13184-SDR, 2017 WL 1239561, at *27 (Bankr. E.D. Tenn. Apr. 3, 2017).

used by creditors for over two hundred years to recover fraudulently conveyed property."[9] Whereas transfers in 2007 and 2008 would have been time barred under the TFTA, such transfers were not time barred under Code Section 66-3-101, "[t]he court finds that there is a seven-year statute of limitations for the recovery of the real property under Tenn. Code Ann. §66–3–101 and a six-year statute of limitations for the recovery of the value of the transfers."[10]

## Rule Against Self-Settled Trusts

The self-settled spendthrift trust has enjoyed a few statutes of its own over the years. The first variant of laws that limited its use was enacted during the reign of King Edward III, which addressed conveyances of lands by debtors to their friends, by collusion of having the profits thereof at their pleasure.[11] Approximately a century later, another statute, often referred to as the rule against self-settled trusts (RASST),[12] was enacted during the reign of King Henry VII, and is the forerunner to the provision found in Section 505(a)(2) of the Uniform Trust Code.[13]

---

9. *Walker* cited *In re Covington*, where Section 66-3-101 was described as follows, "Tenn.Code Ann. §66–3–101 derives from the Statutes of 13 Elizabeth (Ch. 5) and 27 Elizabeth (Ch. 4). *State v. Nashville Trust Co.*, 28 Tenn.App. 388, 416, 190 S.W.2d 785, 796 (1944). Its predecessor was first enacted in Tennessee in 1801. *See* 1801 Tenn.Pub. Acts Ch. XXV, §2. The current version first appeared in 1858. *See* Tenn.Code §1759 (1858). In 1919 the Tennessee legislature enacted a uniform fraudulent conveyance law. *See* 1919 Tenn.Pub. Acts Ch. 125 §2. Currently codified at Tenn.Code Ann. §§66–3–301–314, the uniform law supplements but does not replace its older relative. *United States v. Kerr*, 470 F.Supp. 278, 281 (E.D.Tenn.1978); *Scarborough v. Pickens*, 26 Tenn.App. 213, 218, 170 S.W.2d 585, 587 (1943)." *In re Covington*, 171 B.R. 294, 296 (Bankr. M.D. Tenn. 1994).

10. *Id.*

11. 50 Edw. 3 (1376-7).

12. *See, e.g., In re Montgomery*, 104 B.R. 112, 114–15 (Bankr. N.D. Iowa 1989). ("The Swanson court found that in spite of the substantial restrictions placed on the power of a teacher to transfer or assign his or her interests in the plan, the plan "would not be a valid spendthrift trust under Minnesota law." Swanson, 873 F.2d at 1124. The Swanson court reached this conclusion on two separate grounds. First, the court found that because a teacher, who was also the beneficiary of the plan, made contributions to the plan, the plan was self-settled. The court found that this arrangement violated Minnesota's common law rule which holds that where the settlor of a trust and beneficiary of a trust are the same person (i.e. the trust is self-settled), the trust is not a spendthrift trust. Swanson, *115 873 F.2d at 1124. The Swanson court noted that the rule against self-settled trusts being enforced as spendthrift trusts is the rule in "most jurisdictions."")

13. Official Comment to Uniform Trust Code Section 505(a)(2) provides a useful summary of the rule against self-settled trusts. "Subsection (a)(2), which is based on Restatement (Third) of Trusts Section 58(2) and cmt. e Tentative Draft No. 2, approved 1999), and Restatement (Second) of Trusts Section 156 (1959), follows traditional doctrine in providing that a settlor who is also a beneficiary may not use the trust as a shield against the settlor's creditors. The drafters of the Uniform Trust Code concluded that traditional doctrine reflects sound policy. Consequently, the drafters rejected the approach taken in States like Alaska and Delaware, both of which allow a settlor to retain a beneficial interest immune from creditor claims. *See* Henry J. Lischer, Jr., Domestic Asset Protection Trusts: Pallbearers to Liability, 35 Real Prop. Prob. & Tr. J. 479 (2000); John E. Sullivan, III, Gutting the Rule Against Self-Settled Trusts: How the Delaware Trust Law Competes with Offshore Trusts, 23 Del. J. Corp. L. 423 (1998). Under the Code, whether the trust contains a spendthrift provision or not, a creditor of the settlor may reach the maximum amount that the trustee could have paid to the settlor-beneficiary. If the trustee has discretion to distribute the entire income and principal to the settlor, the effect of this subsection is to place the settlor's creditors in the same position as if the trust had not been created. For the definition of 'settlor,' *see* Section 103(15)."

According to Professor Ross, these two statutes, 50 Edw. III, c. 6 (1376) and 3 Hen. VII, c. 4 (1487) (along with 2. Rich. II, St. 2, c. 3 (1379), covered fraudulent conveyances only in situations where the debtor entered a legally defined safe haven. "Parliament corrected the problem by passing 13 Eliz., c. 5." The Statute of Elizabeth was an improvement in creditors rights, because it "was designed to meet many issues that arose or might arise in court." Professor Ross notes Henry VII's statute applied only to deeds of gifts and goods and chattels, whereas the Statute of Elizabeth applied to "feoffments, gifts, grants, alienations, conveyances, bonds, suits, judgments, and executions." Further, Henry VII's statute applied only to duties owed to creditors, whereas the Statute of Elizabeth applied to creditors "and others" and not just to duties, but also to "lawful actions, suites, debts, accounts, damages, penalties, forfeitures, heriots, mortuaries, and releases." Put simply, the Statute of Elizabeth was an attempt to update creditors' rights.

The RASST was meant to apply strictly to transfers of personal property into trust for the exclusive benefit of the settlor.[14] The RASST provides that the creator or settlor of a trust, who transfers property in trust, is considered the owner of such property, to the extent the trustee can possibly transfer back to the settlor. "Self-settled trusts may be reached by creditors, even if the settlor was solvent at the time of the trust's creation and no fraud was intended."[15] A self-settled trust has special treatment for Medicaid qualification purposes.[16]

The main distinction between seeking relief under fraudulent transfer statutory law and the RASST is the RASST does not require any showing of intent, whereas fraudulent transfer statutory law requires intent, either presumed based on certain conditions or in other cases, proven based on facts and circumstances. However, under fraudulent transfer law, the entire transfer to a trustee is subject to avoidance, whereas with the RASST, as reflected under the Uniform Trust Code, only the maximum amount that may be distributed to the settlor may be subject to recovery.[17] This means that a debtor may successfully

14. *See Curtis v. Leavitt*, 15 N.Y. 9, 123 (1857). ("This statute, then, only avoids conveyances, &c., which are wholly to the use of the grantor. If we came to a different conclusion, if we held that it applied to transfers made for other objects but containing a residuary interest or partial use for the debtor, then the question would arise whether the whole is void, or only so much of the grant as is not sustained by the valid purposes for which it was made.")

15. *In re Brown*, 303 F.3d 1261, 1267 (11th Cir. 2002).

16. *In re Corn*, 493 S.W.3d 311, 317 (Ark. 2016) ("A 'D4A' trust is authorized under the Omnibus Reconciliation Act of 1993. Pub.L. No. 103–66, 107 Stat. 312 (1993). As a threshold matter, the Act provides that assets contained in a self-settled trust are countable or 'available' for the purposes of determining Medicaid eligibility. 42 U.S.C. §1396p(d)(1)-(3). That is, if a beneficiary places his own assets in a trust, those assets are counted against him. However, these rules do not apply to assets held in trusts that meet certain requirements. 42 U.S.C. §1396p(d)(4)(A). One of these requirements is that the trust is established by a parent, grandparent, legal guardian, or court. In other words, a 'D4A' trust cannot be self-settled. If Congress wanted to allow the trust to be self-settled (allowing the establishment of a 'D4A' trust by the intended beneficiary himself), it would have included the beneficiary in the list of those who could establish the trust . However, it did not. For a court to do so upon demand would virtually write an additional term into federal law, which in the same Act provided that assets in self-settled trusts were countable for purposes of Medicaid eligibility.")

17. Idaho has not adopted the Uniform Trust Code but addresses the RASST in Idaho Code Ann. §55-905. Idaho's version of the RASST, entitled "Fraudulent transfers of personalty," provides that any such transfer to a self-settled trust is void against all creditors. ("All deeds of gift, all conveyances, and all transfers

create third-party interests in transferred property and protect the property under the RASST, but the creation of third-party interests will not stop a creditor seeking relief under fraudulent transfer law.

If a settlor made a transfer into trust with intent to hinder, delay, or defraud, or was insolvent, the transfer may be subject to application of fraudulent transfer law, with the self-settled nature of the trust being a badge of fraud that could create a presumption of fraudulent intent.

> An assignment is void for actual fraud, if while assignor provides for only a part of his creditors he attempts in the instrument to reserve any portion of the fund to himself. Such an attempt has been regarded as establishing what is sometimes termed a fraud in law, but more accurately it affords a conclusive presumption of an active, fraudulent design on the part of assignor (*Collumb agt. Caldwell*, 16 N. Y., 484).[18]

The modern interpretation of the RASST provides that a self-settled trust does not need to be for the exclusive benefit of the settlor, nor is its application limited to personal property. For example, if the settlor transfers one hundred dollars to a trust and retains an income interest that equates to a value of forty dollars, then the settlor is considered the owner of the forty dollars.[19] Thus, a creditor may reach forty dollars under the RASST. On the other hand, if a creditor can show the settlor transferred assets in violation of fraudulent transfer law, the entire transfer may be voided. The RASST exists separate and apart from fraudulent transfer law, and consequently, both may provide a creditor with relief.[20]

A self-settled trust may exist notwithstanding the fact that the settlor did not actually receive the assets to transfer in trust. Thus, the RASST may be relevant in the context of guardianships, estate administration, marital agreements, etc.[21]

---

or assignments, oral or written, of goods, chattels, or things in action, made in trust for the use of the person making the same, are void as against the creditors, existing or subsequent, of such person.")

18. *Shoemaker v. Hastings*, 1881 WL 11585 (N.Y. Gen. Term. 1881).

19. *In re Brown*, 303 F.3d 1261, 1268–69 (11th Cir. 2002). ("Where the only interest a settlor has retained for herself under a trust is the right to income for life, it is solely this interest which her creditors can reach. *See* II Scott §156 ('Where the only interest which the settlor has created for himself under the trust is a right to the income for life or for some other period, it is this interest alone which his creditors can reach, unless the creation of the trust was a disposition in fraud of his creditors.') *** This result makes sense. Although the spendthrift provision of a trust is void as against a settlor-beneficiary's creditors, the trust itself remains valid.")

20. *See* Official Comment to Uniform Trust Code Section 505(a)(2). "This section does not address possible rights against a settlor who was insolvent at the time of the trust's creation or was rendered insolvent by the transfer of property to the trust. This subject is instead left to the State's law on fraudulent transfers. A transfer to the trust by an insolvent settlor might also constitute a voidable preference under federal bankruptcy law."

21. *See Calhoun v. Rawlins*, 93 Mass. App. Ct. 458, 465 (Mass. App. Ct. 2018) ("In *In re* Tosi, 383 B.R. 1, 4 (Bankr. D. Mass. 2008), the debtor's portion of his father's estate was placed into a discretionary trust. The debtor argued that the trust was not self-settled because the trust property passed directly from the executors to the trustees of the trust . Id. at 13. The court rejected the argument because the monies that funded the trust 'were monies that [the debtor] was legally entitled to receive and did receive from the settlement of his father's estate. In other words, there can be no dispute that the monies that funded [the trust] were attributable to the [d]ebtor's share of his father's estate.' Ibid.")

Colorado statute section 38-10-111[22] has been described as "one of several Colorado statutes which concern the avoidance of fraudulent conveyances and recovery of transferred property. This statute specifically focuses on the use of self-settled trusts."[23] This description is mostly accurate, however, nothing in Section 38-10-111 requires a finding of fraud; instead, Section 38-10-111 is merely Colorado's version of the RASST, without any provision protecting future creditors. In fact, Section 38-10-111 essentially prevents future creditors from obtaining relief as to assets transferred to a self-settled trust. In doing so, the section, "obviates the need to prove intent to defraud and is limited to then existing creditors."[24] This omission has led some to describe Colorado as being the first state to offer an asset protection trust, albeit limited to personal property.[25] Colorado did not alter its fraudulent transfer statute that would permit the creation of an asset protection trust, including a direction to ignore a trust agreement's terms as evidence of intent to hinder, so the effectiveness of this statute to avoid creditors is questionable at best.

# Corporate Clawback

Where distributions from a business entity are made at a time when the entity is experiencing financial difficulties, relief may be available to creditors under both the common law applicable to corporations, statutes dealing with corporations, as well as fraudulent transfer law (which is composed of both fraudulent transfer statutory law and common law.) It is important to determine whether the common law addresses a particular corporate action during corporate insolvency, such as the repurchase of stock from a shareholder.

> CBS has failed to show that there is an "irreconcilable repugnancy" between Sections 5 or 6 of the Fraudulent Transfer Act and the common law rule described in Reilly. The general purpose of the Fraudulent Transfer Act is "to protect a debtor's unsecured creditors from unfair reductions in the debtor's estate to which creditors usually look to security." *In re Randy*, 189 B.R. 425 (Bankr. N.D. Ill. 1995). The purpose of the common law rule is also to

22. Colo. Rev. Stat. §38-10-111.

23. *In re Alagna*, 107 B.R. 301, 313 (Bankr. D. Colo. 1989).

24. *Id.* (Emphasis added.)

25. Many courts have incorporated the RASST to include both real and personal property. *See Sandlin v. Robbins*, 62 Ala. 477, 484–86 (1878). ("**6 Section 2120 of the Code of 1876, and the statute of 3 Henry, 7, speak alone of goods, chattels and things in action. It is a common law doctrine, however, and is applicable alike to realty. There never was a time when a debtor could convey his property directly, or in secret trust, for his own benefit, or for the use of his family, and thereby defeat his creditors of their lawful demands.—Huggins v. Perrine, 30 Ala. 396.

In the present case, there is no secret trust. Both the mortgage to the son and the conveyance to the daughter, express on their face that they secure a valuable interest to the grantor. They are both fraudulent and void against the claim and title of appellants, if the debt on which the judgment was recovered was contracted before they were severally executed; and this, independent of any intent with which the conveyances were executed. There was, on this question, but a single inquiry for the jury, namely: Whether the debt, on which Temple recovered his judgment, was older than the conveyances? If it was, the law pronounces *486 them null and void, so far as that claim is concerned; and the jury should have been so instructed.")

> protect creditors, but it addresses the specific situation of when an insolvent corporation repurchases its stock from a shareholder. *See* Reilly, 201 N.E.2d at 298. "[I]t is not enough to justify the inference of abrogation from the simple fact that a subsequent statute covers some, or even all, of the questions covered by the common law." Sessions, 2012 IL 112906 ¶ 18. A party seeking to recover from a shareholder of a corporation who sold his stock to the corporation while it was insolvent could bring a claim under the Fraudulent Transfer Act and under the common law rule, as the Special Receiver does in this case.
>
> *4 The Court acknowledges that the common law rule is not frequently applied, and that since the Fraudulent Transfer Act was enacted, creditors usually bring claims against shareholders for illegal distributions under Sections 5 and 6 of the Fraudulent Transfer Act. *See, e.g.*, In re JOY Recovery Tech. Corp., 257 B.R. 253 (Bankr. N.D. Ill. 2001). However, a dearth of recent case law does not show that an "irreconcilable repugnancy" exists. The Court finds that the common law rule supplements the Fraudulent Transfer Act in a consistent manner.[26]

Similarly, the corporate statutory law might apply to a particular corporate action to achieve the same result as fraudulent transfer law, such as distributing corporate assets while insolvent. "Notably, although the statutes operate differently, DUFTA and Section 174 have a similar purpose—both are designed to protect creditors of a corporation from distributions of corporate funds viewed as inappropriate because they undermine the ability of the corporation to repay its debts. *** *See* 6 Del. C. §1304(a) (defining a fraudulent transfer under DUFTA as one where "the debtor made the transfer . . . with actual intent to hinder, delay, or defraud any creditor of the debtor"); 8 Del. C. §174(a) (holding directors liable "to [a corporation's] creditors in the event of its dissolution or insolvency, to the full amount of the dividend unlawfully paid")."[27]

# Federal Law

In some cases, federal law will provide additional remedies to creditors that do not exist under state fraudulent transfer law. For example, in bankruptcy law, the initial transferee of a fraudulent transfer might be strictly liable without any good faith defense. Further, while fraudulent transfer law may not void a transfer made in preference of one creditor over another, bankruptcy law so provides. "There is no rule against a failing debtor preferring one creditor over another, except where such preference is declared void by bankruptcy statute or other of similar nature."[28] The Internal Revenue Code may provide for additional time to seek recovery for a fraudulent transfer. The intersection between

---

26. Ferdose Al-Taie, Special Receiver, the Ticket Reserve, Inc., Plaintiff, v. CBS Corporation, Defendant., No. 3:17-CV-1106-M, 2019 WL 1532233, at *3–4 (N.D. Tex. Jan. 22, 2019).

27. *JPMorgan Chase Bank, N.A. v. Ballard*, No. CV 2018-0274-AGB, 2019 WL 3022338, at *10 (Del. Ch. July 11, 2019).

28. *Standard Acc. Ins. Co. v. Copper Hills Motor Hotels, Inc.*, 102 Ariz. 26, 28, 424 P.2d 154, 156 (1967).

fraudulent transfer law and federal law is discussed in more detail in chapter ten involving super creditors.

## Unjustment Enrichment

Where a transfer is made with actual fraud and particularly egregious, the court may turn to equity to fashion an appropriate remedy pursuant to the terms of the fraudulent transfer statute. It is not unusual to see unjust enrichment asserted in the alternative to relief under fraudulent transfer law.

> In the present case, unjust enrichment claims are not completely duplicative of the contracts and torts claims, as they are framed as an alternative to the fraudulent conveyance claims. *See* FAC ¶ 418 ("If this Court determines that [certain parts of the December 2015 and March 2016 transactions] are not voidable under New York law," the Receiver requests the Court to hold for the Receiver on the unjust enrichment claim.); ECF No. 169, at 25 n.23. Although not binding on this Court, various bankruptcy courts have refused to dismiss unjust enrichment claims on the basis that they were duplicative of fraudulent transfer claims, noting that "it is conceivable that the plaintiff could recover under one theory but not the other." *In re Operations N.Y. LLC*, 490 B.R. 84, 100 (Bankr. S.D.N.Y. 2013); *see also Silverman v. H.I.L. Assocs. Ltd.*, 387 B.R. 365, 412 (Bankr. E.D.N.Y. 2008) ("While there can be no doubt that the Trustee would not be entitled to duplicative relief, there similarly is no doubt that at the pleadings stage, a plaintiff is not required to elect a single theory upon which to proceed."). The Court chooses to follow this principle articulated by bankruptcy courts.
>
> *32 However, while the FAC adequately pleads how BCLIC, WNIC, and SHIP may have been enriched through the December 2015 and March 2016 conveyance transactions, the FAC fails to adequately allege facts as to how BAM Administrative benefited from the allegedly fraudulent transactions at issue. Therefore, the Court dismisses the unjust enrichment claim against BAM Administrative only.[29]

Notwithstanding the ability to seek relief under more than one theory, one must consider whether state fraudulent transfer law time bar prevents seeking fraudulent transfer relief.[30]

---

29. *In re Platinum-Beechwood Litigation (Cyganowski v. Beechwood Re Ltd.)*, 2019 WL 4924967, at pp. 31-32 (S.D.N.Y., Oct. 7, 2019)

30. *See Donell v. Keppers*, 835 F. Supp. 2d 871, 878–79 (S.D. Cal. 2011). ("As an initial matter, the Court notes that California courts are split as to whether an independent cause of action for unjust enrichment even exists. See *879 Manantan v. Nat'l City Mortg., 2011 WL 3267706, at *5–6, 2011 U.S. Dist. LEXIS 82668, at *14–15 (N.D.Cal. Jul. 28, 2011) (explaining the split and citing cases). Moreover, even assuming an independent causes of action exists, Plaintiff's cause of action would still be barred by California Civil Code §3439.09(c). Plaintiff is correct that "a suit under the UFTA is not the exclusive remedy by which fraudulent transfers may be attacked," and common law remedies remain available. Jhaveri v. Teitelbaum, 176 Cal. App.4th 740, 755, 98 Cal.Rptr.3d 268 (2009). However, in enacting §3439.09(c), "the Legislature clearly meant to provide an overarching, all-embracing maximum time period to attack a fraudulent transfer, no matter whether brought under UFTA or otherwise." Macedo v. Bosio, 86 Cal.App.4th 1044, 1051 n. 4, 104 Cal.

# Alter Ego

Under an alter ego analysis, a creditor may obtain fraudulent transfer like relief by showing the debtor never truly parted with the transferred property. Consequently, it is typical for a creditor to seek relief under both fraudulent transfer and alter ego arguments in the alternative.

> Considering the second possible interpretation of the complaint, it is possible that Plaintiff is seeking to collect the alleged fraudulently transferred assets directly from the transferees (i.e ., Defendants). At this stage, the viability of such a claim in this particular case is unclear because the transferors and the sued transferees are identical—according to the complaint, Defendants acted as both transferors and transferees in some transactions. In fact, as noted above, liability under corporate alter ego theory may be direct. *See* Fisher, 296 Fed.Appx. at 506; but see Belvedere, 617 N.E.2d at 1086. Therefore, if the judgment-debtors were merely Defendants' alter egos, then could be treated as the same entity. *Id.* In that circumstance, is unclear why a fraudulent transfer claim would need to be proven. Theoretically speaking, the money sought never left the entity comprised of Defendants and their alleged alter egos. The complaint alleges that Defendants received proceeds of a transfer that exceeded the amount of the 2007 judgment. *See* ECF Dkt. # 1 at ¶¶ 35–36. Therefore, if alter ego theory is in fact viable, it would appear that some type of claim seeking to collect directly from Defendants would be more appropriate than seeking to recover under a fraudulent transfer. However, the stand alone claims before this Court are for fraudulent transfer. Therefore, the undersigned will constrain the following analysis to the claims stated in the complaint.[31]

In the wealth transfer context, a settlor-debtor may have difficulty showing a trust agreement's provisions shield the trust assets from creditors as the settlor could be treated as the owner of the trust assets under an alter ego theory, obviating the necessity of proving fraudulent intent in transferring assets in trust. In one case, this had the effect of causing inclusion of the assets in the bankruptcy estate despite claimed ownership in a foreign entity. "Although there are limits to an extraterritorial application of the Bankruptcy Code (*see* Morrison v. Nat'l Australia Bank Ltd., 130 S. Ct. 2869 (2010) and Sec. Investor Prot. Corp. v. Bernard L. Madoff Inv. Sec. LLC, 2014 WL 2998557 (S.D.N.Y. July 6, 2014)), in [*In re Icenhower*], the fraudulent transfer was deemed to occur

---

Rptr.2d 1 (2001). "[T]he maximum elapsed time for a suit under either the UFTA or otherwise is seven years after the transfer." *Id.* (emphasis in original); accord. Roach, 369 F.Supp.2d at 1199. This conclusion is supported by the plain language of section 3439.09(c), which states that "a cause of action with respect to a fraudulent transfer . . . is extinguished." Cal. Civ.Code §3439.09(c) (emphasis added). Therefore, Plaintiff cannot attack a fraudulent transfer through an unjust enrichment claim without satisfying the requirements of section 3439.09(c). *See, e.g.*, Forum Ins., 62 Fed.Appx. at 152 (holding that plaintiff's civil conspiracy claim was barred by section 3439.09(c)); Roach, 369 F.Supp.2d at 1199 (holding that plaintiff's common law fraudulent transfer claim was barred by section 3439.09(c)).")

31. *Hitachi Med. Sys. Am., Inc. v. Branch*, No. 5:09-CV-1575, 2010 WL 3941824, at *9 (N.D. Ohio Sept. 14, 2010), *report and recommendation adopted*, No. 5:09-CV-01575, 2010 WL 3941912 (N.D. Ohio Oct. 7, 2010).

within the United States, the transferee was a U.S. citizen, and the application of the alter ego doctrine resulted in the interest in Mexican realty being part of the bankruptcy estate ab initio and thus, an unauthorized post-petition transfer."[32] As to whether alter ego can apply to a trust arrangement, see footnote sixteen of chapter seven.

Where business entities are used to effectuate a fraudulent transfer, alter ego may be used to show a transfer is made by an individual debtor who improperly controls the business entity. In other words, alter ego may be used to determine who has title at the time of a transfer, and a transfer by a debtor's alter ego may be considered a transfer by the debtor.

> The seventh and final question asks whether a transfer between alter egos or between the judgment debtor and an alter ego is a "transfer" under NUFTA. As an initial matter, NUFTA defines a "transfer" as "every mode, direct or indirect, absolute or conditional, voluntary or involuntary, of disposing of or parting with an asset or an interest in an asset, and includes payment of money, release, lease and creation of a lien or other encumbrance." NRS 112.150(12).
>
> *6 The Magliarditis assert that under NUFTA, a transfer must be from a debtor to a third person, not from a debtor to a debtor, relying on NRS 112.200(4) which states that "[a] transfer is not made until the debtor has acquired rights in the asset transferred." They reason that because the alter ego doctrine is merely an equitable remedy to satisfy an existing debt, it cannot be used to dictate who has title to an asset at the time of a transfer. Therefore, the Magliarditis argue, a transfer made between alter egos cannot be linked to the debtor—an equitable remedy like alter ego cannot decide title at the time of the transfer.
>
> However, jurisdictions that have found an alter ego may be a debtor for purposes of UFTA, likewise have found that transfers made to or between such alter egos are transfers under UFTA. For example, the Alabama Supreme Court held in Thompson Properties that a transfer of property made by a judgment debtor's alter ego was considered a transfer of the debtor. 839 So. 2d at 634. And "many states, including Georgia, have found that a 'transfer' may occur even if the debtor was not a party to, or did not carry out, the transfer." U.S. Capital Funding VI, 137 F. Supp. 3d at 1366; *see also* Sherry v. Ross, 846 F. Supp. 1424, 1428 (D. Haw. 1994) (stating that under Hawaii's UFTA, a fraudulent conveyance can occur even if the debtor is not a party to the conveyance); 37 C.J.S. Fraudulent Conveyances, §21. As we are compelled to conclude that an alter ego may be a "debtor" under UFTA, we are likewise compelled to conclude that transfers to or between alter egos can be "transfers" under UFTA.[33]

Unlike a fraudulent transfer, however, alter ego might not be viewed as an independent cause of action. "Ohio does not recognize alter ego theory or

---

32. *See* "In re Icenhower," LISI Asset Protection Planning Newsletter, No.255, August 5, 2014, citing *In re Icenhower*, 2014 WL 2978491 (9th Cir. July 3, 2014).

33. *Magliarditi v. TransFirst Grp., Inc.*, No. 73889, 2019 WL 5390470, at *5-6 (Nev. Oct. 21, 2019).

corporate veil piercing as independent causes of action. In contrast to New York, Ohio treats corporate veil piercing as equitable doctrine. *See Carter Jones Lumber Co. v. LTV Steel Co.*, 237 F.3d 745, 749 (6th Cir.2001)."[34]

## Tortious Interference with Contractual Relations

In some cases, a creditor may allege that one who helps a debtor engage in a fraudulent transfer has interfered with a contractual relationship between the creditor and debtor.[35]

34. *Hitachi Medical Systems America, Inc. v. Branch*, 2010 WL 3941824.

35. *In re* Bavelis, 571 B.R. 278 (Bankr. S.D. Ohio 2017).

CHAPTER 7

# Fraudulent Transfer Law and Wealth Transfer Planning

> "While it is not the policy of the law to hamper the transfer of property, or restrain, or in any manner interfere with the free and unlimited exercise of the rights of everyone to deal with his own as he pleases and in his own way, due regard being had to public rights and interests, yet the law will not permit transfers to be made in violation of the rights of creditors. A man must be just to his creditors before he is generous to those who are nearer to him by ties of relationship."[1]

Transfers made as part of a wealth transfer plan have been challenged on fraudulent transfer grounds, with varying results. Because a wealth transfer plan can be frustrated by a creditor, great care should be given to fully understanding the consequences of contemplated transactions.

> "Although planners place great emphasis on the structures that are used in asset protection planning, the method of transferring wealth to a structure is probably more important than the structure itself. If the transfer cannot be challenged as a fraudulent transfer or a preferential transfer, then it may be very difficult for the creditor to attack the structure. By contract, if a court deems a transfer to be fraudulent or preferential, then the assets may be backed out of a structure even if the structure itself is otherwise impenetrable. Worse, as we shall see, if the transfer is fraudulent or preferential, the debtor, along with his or her planner, risks charges of contempt, bankruptcy fraud, and civil conspiracy."[2]

The transfer of wealth can address numerous goals, which will be categorized herein to assist with fraudulent transfer analysis. Where the transfer of

1. John W. Smith, "The Equitable Remedies of Creditors in Relation to Fraudulent Conveyances, Transfers, Mortgages, Judgments, and Assignments," 1899.

2. Jay D. Adkisson and Christipher Riser, Asset Protection Concepts & Strategies for Protecting Your Wealth, 57, McGraw-Hill, 2004.

wealth is done with the stated goal of providing for the transferor's incapacity or death (which involves identifying who will manage assets and where the assets will go on such events), the planning is referred to as estate planning. Where the transfer of wealth is accomplished to minimize or eliminate tax liability, the planning is referred to as tax planning. Where the transfer of wealth incorporates the use of a business entity, the planning is referred to as business planning. Finally, where the goal is to transfer wealth into a particular ownership format (which may or may not be consistent with state public policy) to protect the wealth from the claims of creditors who would otherwise be able to reach the wealth, the planning is referred to as asset protection planning.

Each form of wealth transfer planning is susceptible to attack under fraudulent transfer law. However, asset protection planning faces the highest degree of exposure to avoidance in a fraudulent transfer context. A creditor may be able to more easily prove requisite intent to hinder creditors by showing a transaction was primarily motivated by creditor avoidance. This scenario is not much different than the IRS challenging a tax transaction by asserting the taxpayer was primarily motivated by tax avoidance. Like taxpayers asserting non-tax related motivations for entering a transaction the IRS challenged, debtors will often point to non-creditor motivated reasons for entering an asset protection transaction when challenged by a creditor.

## Estate planning

Often, estate planning goals motivate transfers of wealth. When estate planning is used to help the debtor lessen or eliminate the assets subject to guardianship or probate administration, the debtor often changes asset titles from sole name to a new ownership format. Where the new ownership format impacts a creditor's ability to reach the assets, such as transfers to an irrevocable trust, the debtor might be engaging in a fraudulent transfer, depending on the facts and circumstances. In contrast, where transfers are made to a revocable trust to help avoid probate and guardianship, unlike transfers to a spouse in a TBE (a creditor protected form of ownership), state law will provide that the assets in a revocable trust remain subject to the claims of creditors. In some cases, transfers will be motivated primarily by creditor issues, such as the transfer of assets in trust for the benefit of descendants. However, courts will often permit such transfers where the settlor of a trust places restrictions on a third-party beneficiary's interest for the beneficiary's creditor protection purposes. But as this chapter will show, estate planning is more than transferring assets in the traditional sense. In some cases, a debtor may refuse to accept ownership of an asset, which is known as a disclaimer of an asset. Here, the broad interpretation of transfer, as applied in the wealth transfer context, has assisted creditors attacking everything from the funding of trusts to the refusal to accept a gift.

Generally, where a debtor has a right to an asset that is subject to creditors' claims, the transfer of such asset or interest in such asset may be challenged as a fraudulent transfer. Thus, transfers out of a revocable trust to a third party, or relinquishment of certain rights in trust property, may be challengeable. Likewise, forfeiting an interest in property established through inheritance or via a power of appointment,[3] may also be challengeable, based on the facts and applicable law.

## *Transfers to revocable trusts*

Transfers to revocable trusts are generally not treated as fraudulent transfers because the transferred assets are available to creditors before and after the transfer. "If the settlor retains the right during his or her lifetime to revoke the trust, or retains an unrestricted right to amend it, the subject property will be reachable by the settlor's creditors, and later by the creditors of the settlor's estate, to the extent the property would be reachable were the settlor to own the property outright and free of trust."[4]

Creditors often seek to avoid transfers to trusts on two grounds, either a settlor is treated as the owner under the RASST and thus, the interest retained is subject to creditor claims, or the settlor made a fraudulent transfer, and all such transferred assets are subject to creditor claims, regardless of the degree of interest retained. This distinction follows through after death, and courts have found in favor of creditors on both grounds. The UTC also provides that transfers during life to a revocable trust remain subject to creditor claims after the death of the settlor.

> In establishing inter vivos trusts for Monea with part of the mutual funds which he had purchased, Leslie reserved an absolute power to revoke the trusts or to change the beneficiary and, therefore, he remained the "absolute owner of the estate conveyed, so far as the rights of creditors * * * are concerned" right up to the time of his death. (City Bank Farmers Trust Co. v. Cannon, 291 N.Y. 125, 133, 51 N.E.2d 674, 676, 157 A.L.R. 1424; *see* Real Property Law, s 139 (formerly s 145); Estates, Powers and Trusts Law, s 10—7.2 (eff. Sept. 1, 1967).) The City Bank case (291 N.Y. 125, 51 N.E.2d 674, 157 A.L.R. 1424, *supra*), like the case before us, involved securities which had been placed in a revocable trust. We declared that 'In such cases remaindermen have no vested interests until the retained powers of the settlor are terminated, usually by death' (p. 133, 151 N.E.2d p. 676). It follows that Monea was not given any interest in these trusts until Leslie's death and, to the extent that the trusts served to defeat Leslie's obligations to Alan, they

3. See Charles E. Rounds, Jr., & Charles E. Rounds III, Loring and Rounds: A Trustee's Handbook, Section 5.3.3.3 (2022 ed.) ("At common law, a nonsettlor holder of a general power of appointment, whether testamentary or inter vivos, could not be compelled by creditors or others to exercise it. This is a remnant of the pre-Restatement of Property distinction between personal rights and property rights. However, if the power is exercised, the property subject to the power may be fair game for the holder's creditors. It should be noted that in some states, statutes permit the creditors of the holder of a non-self-settled general inter vivos power of appointment to reach the property, even if the power is unexercised. The Restatement (Third) of Trusts takes this approach as well. In fact, it would afford even postmortem creditors of the holder of the power access to the subject property to the extent the power had not been exercised during the holder's lifetime. The UTC is generally in accord. Property subject to a nongeneral, i.e., limited/special, power of appointment, of course, can never be reached by the holder's creditors, whether or not the power is exercised, except to the extent required by rules of law relating to fraudulent conveyances.")

4. *See* Loring and Rounds, Section 5.3.3.1.

> constituted fraudulent conveyances which should be set aside to satisfy Alan's claims. (Debtor and Creditor Law, s 273; *see, e.g.*, Reff v. Kanterman, 18 A.D.2d 1104, 239 N.Y.S.2d 971; *affg*. 35 Misc.2d 1029, 1032, 231 N.Y.S.2d 720, 723; Matter of Baker's Estate, 48 Misc.2d 732, 734, 265 N.Y.S.2d 816, 817; *see also*, Scott, Trusts (2d ed., 1956), ss 58.5, 156, n. 12, s 330.12.)[5]

Local law should be considered as results may vary by state. For example, in Ohio, the RASST has been interpreted as not applying after the death of a debtor as to the assets in a revocable trust.[6] Importantly, however, the court held a creditor could seek relief under fraudulent transfer law.

> As we interpret the pertinent part of this section, giving the words employed their usual and ordinary sense, it means that the rights of creditors to reach the beneficial interest of the settlor-the interest he has retained for his own benefit including any returns or earnings from the trust property-and to force a revocation of the trust and subject the trust corpus to the payment of their claims, exists only during the lifetime of the settlor. As worded, the statute compels no *334 more than the exercise of a personal power reserved by the settlor, at the instance of his creditors. Obviously, such power, being personal, would terminate with his death.
>
> If it had been the intention of the General Assembly in amending Section 8617, General Code, to make a trust executed in accordance with its terms amenable to enforced revocation by creditors both before and after the settlor's demise, the amendment would not have qualified creditors' rights as it does, but would have concluded with the words 'and such trust shall be valid as to all persons except creditors.' In our opinion the statute is therefore inapplicable to creditors who do not act while the settlor is still alive.
>
> After the settlor's death, if the trust was in reality fraudulent as to creditors, a remedy would doubtless be available to the administrator or the creditors to subject the trust property to the satisfaction of the settlor's indebtedness. However, no fraud is asserted in the present case, nor is any discernible in the record before us.[7]

5. *Granwell v. Granwell*, 20 N.Y.2d 91, 95–96, 228 N.E.2d 779, 781–82 (1967).

6. The Ohio approach to revocable trusts is a minority approach. *See Matter of Estate of Nagel*, 580 N.W.2d 810, 812 (Iowa 1998). ("It must be conceded that Malcom and Lenore's powers to amend or revoke the trusts, or to direct payment from it, obviously died with them, and the remainder beneficiary's interests in the trust became vested. In one jurisdiction, at least, it has been held that when the settlor of a revocable living trust dies, the property is no longer subject to his debts. *See* Schofield v. Cleveland Trust Co., 135 Ohio St. 328, 21 N.E.2d 119, 122-23 (1939) (relying on interpretation of statute). We however think the better authority is to the contrary. *See* ITT Commercial Fin. Corp. v. Stockdale, 25 Mass.App.Ct. 986, 521 N.E.2d 417, 417-18 (1988); State St. Bank & Trust Co. v. Reiser, 7 Mass.App.Ct. 633, 389 N.E.2d 768, 771 (1979); In re Estate of Kovalyshyn, 136 N.J.Super. 40, 343 A.2d 852, 856-57 (N.J.Cty.Ct.Prob.Div.1975); Johnson v. Commercial Bank, 284 Or. 675, 588 P.2d 1096, 1099 (1978). The defendant trustee argues trusts' assets should not be reached because the contingent wrongful death claim is not a 'debt' required to be paid out of the trust. He points to the language of the trusts, 'any indebtedness owed by the trustor,' for support. (Emphasis added.) He insists the debt must have arisen during Malcom and Lenore's lifetime in order for the trusts' assets to be reached. We conclude that the case should not be reversed on such a basis. Even though the tort claim was not reduced to judgment before Malcom and Lenore's deaths, the facts precipitating it occurred during their lifetimes. The trial court was correct in holding the trusts' assets may be reached to satisfy the wrongful-death claim.")

7. *Schofield v. Cleveland Tr. Co.*, 135 Ohio St. 328, 332–35, 21 N.E.2d 119, 121–23 (1939).

Revocable trusts might present a slight advantage for non-settlor beneficiaries who ultimately file bankruptcy. This is because transfers to an *inter vivos* trust have been excluded from the definition of "bequest, devise, or inheritance" under Section 541(a)(5)(A) of the Bankruptcy Code, thereby creating incentive for individuals to pass wealth to their beneficiaries under an *inter vivos* trust versus outright or through a testamentary trust (i.e., a trust created pursuant to the terms of a will). This incentive is admittedly driven by a narrow fact pattern, where a beneficiary turned bankrupt debtor receives a distribution from a trust during the 180 days after filing bankruptcy.[8]

## *Modification of trust agreement*

A debtor may attempt to change terms of a trust agreement to hinder creditors, thereby rendering the modification voidable as a transfer. For example, a debtor may amend a revocable trust to provide the trust as irrevocable to claim lack of ownership. Such was the case in *In re Crawford*, where the bankruptcy court voided the modification (or amendment) of revocable trust.[9]

However, not all trust amendments will be fraudulent transfers. While the creditor in *Vickery v. Evelyn V. Trumble Living Tr.* successfully alleged injury in fact for purposes of establishing standing, the facts ultimately did not amount to a fraudulent transfer.

> The complaint alleges that Evelyn amended the trust instrument with the specific purpose and intent of defrauding Monica as a judgment creditor by diverting to Kerry the assets Merry Gayle would otherwise have received for the purpose of defeating Monica's efforts to collect her judgment; that Merry Gayle and Kerry participated in a common scheme to frustrate Monica's rights as a creditor; and that Monica's efforts to collect the judgment have been frustrated as a proximate result of defendants' actions. Thus, Monica has alleged that she was injured in fact by defendants' actions and that the injury was to her legally protected rights as a judgment creditor of Merry Gayle and Evelyn. *** We therefore conclude that the allegations in the complaint concerning the fraudulent transfer, fraudulent concealment, and civil conspiracy are sufficient to meet the "relatively easy" test for standing.[10]

In the marital planning context, a parent may amend his or her revocable trust to prevent assets from passing to a divorcing child. In this context, a creditor's focus is on the debtor/beneficiary's property interest in the parent's trust. "The beneficiary's equitable interest is an interest in property. However, it

---

8. *See In re Vetsch*, 620 B.R. 150, 157 (Bankr. W.D. Wash. 2020). ("The Court concludes that Debtor's interest in Survivor's Trust A was not acquired by bequest, devise, or inheritance. Therefore, 11 U.S.C. §541(a)(5)(A) does not operate to bring that property into the bankruptcy estate. This holding is consistent with the majority of courts that have reached this issue. *See Roth*, 289 B.R. at 167; *see also In re Ciano*, 433 B.R. 431, 436 (Bankr. N.D. Fla. 2010) (collecting cases holding a debtor's interest in any inter vivos trust is not within the reach of 11 U.S.C. §541(a)(5)(A)).")

9. *In re Crawford*, 172 B.R. 365 (M.D. Fla. 1994).

10. *Vickery v. Evelyn V. Trumble Living Tr.*, 277 P.3d 864, 867–68 (Colo. App. 2011).

is a type of interest that may, under certain circumstances, be inalienable or immune from attachment, or both."[11] Further, a direction by the divorcing child to dispose of his interest should not be a fraudulent transfer either, because the divorcing child has no interest.[12] The divorcing child takes on the status of a debtor with respect to the creditor spouse but does not transfer an asset because the divorcing child has only a mere expectancy interest in the parent's trust assets.

> The cases wife relies on are distinguishable in a critical way. Pursuant to statute and our jurisprudence, when a party to a divorce transfers property to a third person, a "nominee," with the intent of reducing the other party's share of marital property, that property will be considered part of the marital estate. See 15 V.S.A. §751(a) (establishing that "[a]ll property owned by either or both of the parties" is subject to equitable distribution and that "[t]itle to the property, whether in the names of either or, both parties, or a nominee, shall be immaterial"); *Nevitt v. Nevitt*, 155 Vt. 391, 400, 584 A.2d 1134, 1139 (1990). Wife relies partly on Nevitt, a case in which one party to a divorce put a third person's name on the deed of the marital home in an attempt to "avoid distribution of the property." 155 Vt. at 400, 584 A.2d at 1140. This Court affirmed the trial court's determination that the third person was a nominee and its decision to disregard the deed when distributing property and stated that we "will not condone such actions when taken with intent to deprive one's spouse of a fair portion of the marital assets." *Id.* Wife also cites Clayton v. Clayton, 153 Vt. 138, 569 A.2d 1077 (1989), a case in which the husband transferred his stock in a family business to his sister in anticipation of a divorce proceeding. This Court affirmed the trial court's decision to "disregard an agreement that would have conveyed marital assets in contemplation of divorce in return for little to no consideration," as this sort of agreement "has long been contrary to public policy and unenforceable as a fraudulent transfer." *Id.* at 142, 569 A.2d at 1079.
>
> ¶ 22. Nevitt and Clayton are inapposite to this case. Those cases involved the transfer of property owned by a party to the divorce. Here, husband did not own the trust assets when his father changed the trust beneficiary; he had only a future interest in the assets, contingent on remaining the beneficiary of the trust. See 14A V.S.A. §603(a) ("While a trust is revocable, rights of the beneficiaries are subject to the control of . . . the settlor.). And, as explained above, father had the authority to change the trust beneficiary, even if done purposefully to keep the trust assets out of the marital estate. The trust assets never belonged to husband; his interest was always subject to the whims of the settlors. The property was never part of the marital estate, and father's decision to bypass husband and identify the parties' son as the trust beneficiary did not improperly deprive wife of marital property in the way that the transfers at issue in Nevitt and Clayton did.[13]

---

11. Loring and Rounds, Section 5.3.

12. This should be contrasted with situations where a beneficiary/debtor's interest in a trust has vested. Depending upon applicable law, the direction to dispose of property in a fashion that hinders the beneficiary/debtor's creditors may be viewed as a transfer of an asset.

13. *Collins v. Collins*, 2017 VT 70, ¶¶ 21-22, 173 A.3d 345 (Vt. 2017).

## *Third-Party Trust Planning*

The cases featuring a creditor that challenges transfers for estate planning purposes often involve an irrevocable trust, either self-settled or for the benefit of others. Although there was a brief period of uncertainty as to whether a spendthrift trust would be effective for a beneficiary who did not contribute assets to the trust (a non-self-settled or "third-party" trust), that uncertainty was resolved by the Supreme Court in favor of such beneficiary in the late 1800s.

In 1866, the Supreme Court held the beneficiary of a trust created by his grandfather was not subject to the beneficiary's creditors, where the beneficiary's interest had not yet vested (i.e., subject to a condition precedent), or where the interest had divested in favor of a third party (i.e., a condition subsequent.)

> If the determination of this case depended upon the general principles of jurisprudence, the result must necessarily be in favor of the appellees. It is a settled rule of law that the beneficial interest of the *cestui que trust*, whatever it may be, is liable for the payment of his debts. It cannot be so fenced about by inhibitions and restrictions as to secure to it the inconsistent characteristics of right and enjoyment to the beneficiary and immunity from his creditors. A condition precedent that the provision shall not vest until his debts are paid, and a condition subsequent that it shall be divested and forfeited by his insolvency, with a limitation over to another person, are valid, and the law will give them full effect. Beyond this, protection from the claims of creditors is not allowed to go.[14]

In 1875, the Supreme Court addressed the public policy concern with respect to so-called third-party spendthrift trusts:

> Nor do we see any reason, in the recognized nature and tenure of property and its transfer by will, why a testator who gives, who gives without any pecuniary return, who gets nothing of property value from the donee, may not attach to that gift the incident of continued use, of uninterrupted benefit of the gift, during the life of the donee. Why a parent, or one who loves another, and wishes to use his own property in securing the object of his affection, as far as property can do it, from the ills of life, the vicissitudes of fortune, and even his own improvidence, or incapacity for self-protection, should not be permitted to do so, is not readily perceived.[15]

While the foregoing commentary from the Supreme Court is helpful for the creditor protection aspect of beneficial interest in third-party trusts, it should be noted that the foregoing is dictum. Further, instead of a traditional spendthrift clause in a third-party trust, *Nichols v. Eaton* involved a third-party trust with a cessor clause, whereupon the beneficiary's interest terminated in favor of a third party upon the occurrence of the beneficiary's insolvency or bankruptcy.

---

14. *Nichols v. Levy*, 72 U.S. 433 (1866).
15. *Nichols v. Eaton*, 91 U.S. 716, 727, 23 L. Ed. 254 (1875).

Whereas the use of a revocable trust might be marketed as a tool for minimizing estate tax and preserving assets for future generations in trust, with increasing lifetime estate and gift tax exemption amounts, the emphasis will be even more so on the creditor protection feature afforded to third-party dynasty trusts created under the terms of a revocable trust. This planning option continues to present a well accepted and viable form of creditor protection, with varying degrees of protection from creditors, based on the terms of the trust agreement (e.g., distribution standard, beneficiary powers, etc.) and the trust administration.

## Split-Interest Trusts

Some self-settled trusts are split-interest trusts, where the settlor retains an interest but also gives others (usually family members or charity) an interest. The retained interest is often an income or annuity interest for life or a term of years. The split-interest trust, like the self-settled trust, has been challenged successfully on both fraudulent transfer and the RASST grounds.

The primary difference between the traditional self-settled trust and a split-interest trust is the split-interest trust typically is geared toward a primary purpose of achieving tax savings and can take many forms, such as a grantor retained annuity trust, a charitable remainder trust, a qualified personal residence trust, etc. A qualified personal residence trust may be used to remove a highly appreciating residence from the gross estate of the settlor of such trust. Similarly, a grantor retained annuity trust also aims to remove any excess of value over the retained annuity out of the settlor's gross estate for federal estate tax purposes. Consistent with one of the unstated goals of asset protection planning, mixing the debtor's interest with third parties may appear as a roadblock for creditors.

Planners readily admit that the settlor's retained interest is subject to the claims of creditors. However, some argue that creditors are limited to the RASST, so only a portion of the transfer is subject to challenge. For federal tax law purposes, if the settlor dies during the term of the retained interest, either a portion or the full amount of the trust is included in the estate of the trust's settlor.

However, relief may also exist under the fraudulent transfer common law as explained above, or traditional fraudulent transfer law (i.e., the settlor made a transfer and triggered Section 4 or 5 of the UVTA.) Once the settlor's beneficial term is over, the trust ceases to be self-settled, and the RASST should not apply. However, fraudulent transfer law might still apply regardless of the date of challenge, subject only to statute of limitations or repose. Further, the facts and circumstances may reveal the true nature of the trust.

As should be obvious, merely citing a potential legitimate use for a split-interest trust will not be enough to overcome a fraudulent transfer challenge. In *Merch. Transaction Sys., Inc. v. Necela, Inc.*, the court found the transfer of a residence to be voidable because the creditor was able to prove numerous badges of fraud:

> As to the Scottsdale home, Mr. Campagna argues that the badges of fraud identified by this Court do not support an inference of actual intent because a QPRT, which is a legitimate estate planning device, necessarily requires that a home be transferred for no consideration, to a child, and that the settlor retain the right to possess the home for an agreed upon period of time. In so doing, he seems to assert that so long as an estate planning device is legitimate, it does not matter if it evidences badges of fraud. The Court does not agree. Were this proposition true, people seeking to fraudulently transfer their assets would be protected so long as the identifiable badges of fraud were inherent in the financial planning product utilized to affect that transaction. Such an outcome would clearly defeat the purpose of the AFTA and is against the weight of authority.[16]

The QPRT, like any other trust, may also be subject to alter ego or sham trust challenges.[17] Consequently, transactions involving QPRTS should be analyzed with respect to adherence to formalities as well as tax laws governing same:

> The Defendants argue that the elements of alter ego are not satisfied here because the QPRT was formed for legitimate estate planning purposes and was never used as a vehicle to conceal assets from creditors. The Trustee

16. *Merch. Transaction Sys., Inc. v. Necela, Inc.*, 2010 WL 382886, at *3 (D. Ariz. Jan. 29, 2010).

17. The application of alter ego as it applies to trusts varies by state. *See Bash v. Williams*, No. 5:16 CV 257, 2016 WL 1592445, at *3 (N.D. Ohio Apr. 20, 2016), where the court rejected the application of alter ego to Florida trusts, "the Trustee in this case does nothing to show that Florida trust law is commensurate with the laws of the states that recognize alter ego liability with regard to irrevocable trusts. Given Miller and the Henkel court's interpretation of Miller, the Court finds that the bankruptcy court correctly predicted that Florida law—as it currently stands—would not recognize alter ego liability with respect to irrevocable trusts." Notwithstanding this approach in Florida, the court noted, "nearly every court to have addressed the issue outside of Florida has concluded that alter ego liability should apply to trusts to the same it extent it applies to other legally created fictions." *See, Smith v. S.E.C.*, 432 Fed. Appx. 10 (2nd Cir. Aug. 8, 2011)("We assumed that New York courts would allow the veil of a trust to be pierced in situations where the complete domination of a trust has been shown" and the moving party can show fraud or another wrong was committed); In re Schwarzkopf, 626 F.3d 1032 (9th Cir. 2010)("It is well-settled [under California law] that a trust created for the purpose of defrauding creditors or other persons is illegal and may be disregarded."); *Vaughn v. Sexton*, 975 F.2d 498 (8th Cir. 1992)("the concept of personal liability for the obligations of an entity considered to be an alter ego of an individual is frequently employed in relation to corporations . . . [and] we see no reason why the alter ego concept should not have the same effect in the case of a trust."); *Acheff v. Lazare*, 2014 WL 894491 (D. New Mex. Jan. 29, 2014)("Under New Mexico law, the Delos Trust is Mr. Edelman's alter ego and the trust veil should be disregarded . . ."); *Dexia Credit Local v. Rogan*, 2008 WL 4543013 (N.D. Ill. Oct. 9, 2008)("To pierce the veil of the trusts, Dexia must show that they and Rogan have such unity of interest that their separate personalities no longer exist, and that there are circumstances such that continuing to recognize their separateness would sanction a fraud or injustice."); *In re Gillespie*, 269 B.R. 383 (Bankr. E.D. Ark. 2001) (although alter ego doctrine is most often applied to corporations, "it also applies to trusts."); *Bracken v. Early*, 40 S.W.3d 499 (2000)(Ct. App. Tenn. 2000)("The Trial Judge, in effect, found that defendant is the 'alter ego' of the trust, and we agree under all the circumstances the defendant is liable to the plaintiff for the monies received.") *William L. Comer Equity Trust v. United States*, 732 F.Supp. 755 (E.D. Mich. 1990)("[w]hile the Court uncovered no precedent analyzing the 'alter ego' theory of property ownership in the context of a trust, cases involving corporate entities provide appropriate guidance.").

asserts that "following the formation of the QPRT, the Debtor used the QPRT as his own personal vehicle to shield his assets from creditors." (Trustee's Memo of Law in Opposition at 2 *109 [Dkt. # 99] ). The Trustee alleges that the QPRT is the "mere instrumentality" of the Debtor and the trust should be pierced so that its sole asset, the Great Neck Residence, can be sold and the net proceeds distributed to the Debtor's unsecured creditors. *** The Court finds that the weight of the caselaw in the state of New York supports a ruling that estate planning trusts generally are susceptible to attack if used for a fraudulent purpose. However, as in *Vebeliunas*, the Court finds that the facts of this case do not rise to the level necessary to "pierce" the veil of the QPRT. *** While it is true the Debtor retained the use and enjoyment of the Great Neck Residence after it was transferred to the QPRT and continued to pay all expenses associated with the Great Neck Residence, those facts are consistent with the requirements of a valid QPRT.[18]

## *Power of Appointment Trusts*

With the mounting number of pro-creditor opinions thwarting debtors' attempts to curtail creditors using self-settled trusts, advisers have started moving away from the traditional self-settled trust in favor of non-traditional arrangements. The trend has been to rely on insiders to divert funds back to the transferor of wealth, without leaving much of a paper trail establishing rights to the transferred property.

The power of appointment trust (POA trust) is such an arrangement, providing the settlor with no documented beneficial interest since not designated as a beneficiary—but potentially all assets as an "appointee." Creditors should carefully examine a trust agreement and the facts and circumstances to determine potential arguments under fraudulent transfer law.

Because the settlor of a POA trust does not retain a documented right to the transferred property, the arrangement is not formally presented as a self-settled spendthrift trust. However, based on the circumstances, a creditor may attempt to argue that the arrangement is in substance a self-settled trust (or a "similar device") based on evidence of an implied agreement to provide for the settlor. Additionally, state law might provide that an appointee of a power of appointment does not have a beneficial interest.[19] Notwithstanding the terms of the trust agreement and state law's view of permissible appointees of a power of appointment, equitable concepts may still be used to recharacterize the transaction. For example, the circumstances may point to the settlor as the alter ego

18. *In re Yerushalmi*, 487 B.R. 98, 108–111 (Bankr. E.D.N.Y. 2012). (Emphasis added.)

19. *See, e.g.*, Fla. Stat. Section 736.0103(4). ("'Beneficiary' means a person who has a present or future beneficial interest in a trust, vested or contingent, or who holds a power of appointment over trust property in a capacity other than that of trustee. An interest as a permissible appointee of a power of appointment, held by a person in a capacity other than that of trustee, is not a beneficial interest for purposes of this subsection. Upon an irrevocable exercise of a power of appointment, the interest of a person in whose favor the appointment is made shall be considered a present or future beneficial interest in a trust in the same manner as if the interest had been included in the trust instrument.")

of the trust arrangement,[20] or a de facto beneficiary.[21] Finally, regardless of the potential arguments that can be made as to the nature of the trust arrangement, the transfer of assets to the trustee of the POA trust is still subject to fraudulent transfer law. Proving an implied agreement of retained possession or control may have adverse consequences for the settlor under the rule against self-settled trusts, as well as general applicability in an actual fraud analysis. Given the creditors' rights implications of an implied agreement, it should come as no surprise that an implied agreement may also have negative tax consequences.[22]

---

20. For a discussion on whether alter ego applies in the trust context, *see Bash v. Williams*, No. 5:16 CV 257, 2016 WL 1592445, at *3–4 (N.D. Ohio Apr. 20, 2016). ("[N]early every court to have addressed the issue outside of Florida has concluded that alter ego liability should apply to trusts to the same it extent it applies to other legally created fictions. See, Smith v. S.E.C., 432 Fed. Appx. 10 (2nd Cir. Aug. 8, 2011)("we assumed that New York courts would allow the veil of a trust to be pierced in situations where the complete domination of a trust has been shown" and the moving party can show fraud or another wrong was committed); In re Schwarzkopf, 626 F.3d 1032 (9th Cir. 2010)("It is well-settled [under California law] that a trust created for the purpose of defrauding creditors or other persons is illegal and may be disregarded."); Vaughn v. Sexton, 975 F.2d 498 (8th Cir. 1992)("the concept of personal liability for the obligations of an entity considered to be an alter ego of an individual is frequently employed in relation to corporations . . . [and] we see no reason why the alter ego concept should not have the same effect in the case of a trust."); Acheff v. Lazare, 2014 WL 894491 (D. New Mex. Jan. 29, 2014)("Under New Mexico law, the Delos Trust is Mr. Edelman's alter ego and the trust veil should be disregarded . . ."); Dexia Credit Local v. Rogan, 2008 WL 4543013 (N.D. Ill. Oct. 9, 2008)("To pierce the veil of the trusts, Dexia must show that they and Rogan have such unity of interest that their separate personalities no longer exist, and that there are circumstances such that continuing to recognize their separateness would sanction a fraud or injustice."); In re Gillespie, 269 B.R. 383 (Bankr. E.D. Ark. 2001) (although alter ego doctrine is most often applied to corporations, "it also applies to trusts."); Bracken v. Early, 40 S.W.3d 499 (2000)(Ct. App. Tenn. 2000)("The Trial Judge, in effect, found that defendant is the 'alter ego' of the trust, and we agree under all the circumstances the defendant is liable to the plaintiff for the monies received.") William L. Comer Equity Trust v. United States, 732 F.Supp. 755 (E.D. Mich. 1990)("[w]hile the Court uncovered no precedent analyzing the 'alter ego' theory of property ownership in the context of a trust, cases involving corporate entities provide appropriate guidance."). *4 Tax law is in accord. See, e.g. United States v. Lena, 2008 WL 2774375 (S.D. Fla. June 11, 2008)("Because the ultimate concern does not lie in the structure itself, but whether a person may hide behind a structure that is no more than the individual's alter ego, the Court finds there is no need to distinguish between a corporation and a trust."); United States v. Dornbrock, 2008 WL 769056 (S.D Fla. Jan. 17, 2008)("the alter ego doctrine focuses on whether the taxpayer is similar to or controls another individual, trust, business, or corporation"); United States v. Bahrs, 2006 WL 2507574 (N.D. Fla. Aug. 29, 2006)("there is an abundance of evidence to suggest that the trusts . . . were nothing more than shells set up to avoid both payment and collection of taxes").")

21. *See In re Porras*, 312 B.R. 81, 128 (Bankr. W.D. Tex. 2004). ([T]he Plaintiffs contend that Porras was, at least partially, the settlor of the Trust and should also be considered its de facto beneficiary so that, under Texas' Self-Settlor Rule, those assets that he contributed to the Trust should be subject to his creditors' claims. The Trust and Blakley respond that he is not the beneficiary and therefore the Rule is inapplicable. The Plaintiffs also assert that the Debtor had dominion and control over the Trust, such that its assets should be considered his. *** [T]he Plaintiffs have provided no authority whatsoever—and the court has found none—on what is required to establish a "de facto beneficiary" of a trust. ***Finally, even if the court were to find that Porras was the de facto beneficiary, it is also unclear that Blakley's interest in the 75% Portion should be displaced entirely. Where a self-settled trust also has beneficiaries other than the settlor, it has been held that it should not be declared void ab initio, because it may not be terminated without the consent of those other beneficiaries. See Fewell v. Republic National Bank of Dallas, 513 S.W.2d 596 (Tex.Civ.App.—Eastland 1974, writ ref'd n.r.e.).")

22. *See Est. of Thompson v. Comm'r*, 382 F.3d 367, 373 (3d Cir. 2004). ("The Tax Court found the family partnerships were validly formed and properly recognized for federal estate tax purposes. The court nevertheless sustained application of §2036(a)(1) to return decedent's transferred assets back to the estate. The Tax Court found an implied agreement existed at the time of transfer that decedent would retain lifetime enjoyment and economic benefit of the transferred assets.")

In some cases, the POA trust could be viewed as a reversion to the old secret trust case law; the act of giving sheep to a neighbor with the understanding that the debtor may use the sheep is not much different than giving assets to a trustee with the understanding that the assets will be appointed back to the debtor.

## *Self-Settled Spendthrift Trusts*

The intersection between fraudulent transfer law and transfers to self-settled spendthrift trusts is discussed in this chapter in the section "Asset Protection Planning."

## *Civil Law Foundations*

The foundation has been described as a mix between a corporation and a trust. From a creditor perspective, the foundation reflects the asset protection industry's continued departure from the use of formal asset protection trusts and onto more exotic arrangements where the debtor's retained beneficial interest is not exactly clear or documented. The evolution toward arrangements that provide secrecy and may hide the true nature of a transaction are sometimes consistent with the goal of frustrating creditors.

Although the foundation is the product of a civil law society, it found its way to the U.S., with the first domestic foundation statute enacted in New Hampshire in 2017. Because the self-settled trust has not enjoyed success in court (courts continually have declined to permit debtors to hardwire the law of foreign jurisdictions to defeat creditors where the debtor is domiciled), planners must consider alternatives. One trend has been to use a business entity as a substitute for a trust. This approach has its own risks, as the use of a business entity to shield personal property from personal creditors has not always worked.

The foundation might present another opportunity to shield assets without the perceived need to worry about self-settled trust rules. The new foundation legislation is an acknowledgment that some wish to use an entity but borrow from the trust concept.[23]

The foundation can appeal to those whose goal is to hinder creditors; if a creditor is not familiar with the entity holding the assets, it may cause the creditor to settle to save costs, depending on the amount at stake. Confining foundation disputes to a probate court might also be advantageous for debtors.

> While perhaps most appealing to international clients looking to onshore their wealth management structures to the United States, a foundation may

23. The first version enacted contained a reference to trust in the provision dealing with a beneficiary's creditors. ("15 New Hampshire Foundation Act; Rights of a Beneficiary's Creditors and Assignees. Amend the introductory paragraph of RSA 564-F:15-1503(d) to read as follows: (d) A beneficiary's creditor or assignee may not compel a beneficiary to exercise any right or power that, in any fiduciary or nonfiduciary capacity, the beneficiary has under the [terms of the trust] governing documents, including any of the following:").

> also be attractive to domestic clients because it combines elements of trusts and corporations. The Act borrows components from the New Hampshire Trust Code, Business Corporations Act, and Revised Limited Liability Company Act. The rights and duties of the founders, directors, and beneficiaries, for example, are based on established trust law, as is the process for modifying and reforming a foundation's governing documents. Likewise, the Act's establishment of the New Hampshire Circuit Court, Probate Division as the court of jurisdiction for disputes regarding foundations solidly grounds New Hampshire foundations in trust law. At the same time, the procedural rules governing the formation, registration, and dissolution of a foundation have their genesis in corporate law; as do the duties of good faith, loyalty, impartiality, and prudent judgment required of foundation directors. By combining trust and corporate principles in this unique way, foundations give clients the ability to establish a "best of both worlds" entity that many will find attractive.[24]

Notwithstanding the desire to create a self-settled trust alternative, a court might not see it that way. "Both the New Hampshire foundation and the Wyoming foundation are not trusts, at least not of the traditional variety, in that each is vested with legal personality. In other words, each is a legal entity that is separate and distinct from its founders, directors, protectors, and beneficiaries. That having been said, depending upon the particular facts and circumstances, one can imagine some court down the road in the exercise of its equitable powers deeming a particular domestic foundation a trust for certain purposes, as courts are wont to do when it comes to the statutory charitable corporation."[25]

The IRS, as a creditor, has encountered this arrangement when taxpayers use offshore civil law foundations or other vehicles for which no counterpart exists under U.S. law. In these situations, the IRS will look at the facts and circumstances and treat the entity as a U.S. corporation or trust to enforce the tax law. Presumably, creditors of debtors who utilize foundations may also rely on the common law in this regard.[26]

## *Transfers Pursuant to Power of Attorney*

A power of attorney is an essential document in an estate plan and may be used to effectuate the transfer of wealth for a debtor. In the fraudulent transfer context, an issue might arise as to whether an agent's transfer under the power

24. The New Hampshire Foundation Act: A Solid Foundation for Wealth Management on a Global Scale, International Journal (BNA), March 7, 2019.

25. Rounds and Loring, Section 9.9.15.

26. Creditors should review the facts and circumstances to determine whether any arrangement is akin to a secret trust. *See In re Saphire*, 139 F.2d 34, 35 (2d Cir. 1943) ("The appellant contends that the findings as to a secret trust in her favor are pure surmise and speculation. In cases of concealment of a retained interest in fraud of creditors it is seldom, if ever, that direct evidence of the retained interest is available. Usually, the proof must be circumstantial and must depend upon inferences reasonably to be drawn from the conduct of the parties during and after the transaction under attack. Their demeanor upon the witness stand is also an important factor of proof for appraisal by the referee or trial judge.")

of attorney is deemed to be a transfer by the debtor. In determining whether the acts of an agent are imputed to the principal-debtor, the courts have looked at the extent of a debtor's role (e.g., directed or participated) in the transactions, as well as whether the agent is the transferee.

A creditor may argue for application of principal and agent law to impute acts of an agent to the debtor-principal when arguing that the debtor transferred an asset. In the case of a fraudulent transfer, the creditor would argue the requisite transfer by the debtor transpired, even if the debtor did not technically transfer an asset. Looking to agency law to effectuate the purpose of the fraudulent transfer law is not only consistent with the UVTA direction to consider such law,[27] but also advances the goal of fraudulent transfer law.[28] If a debtor could avoid the application of fraudulent transfer law by simply recruiting an agent to make the fraudulent transfer, powers of attorney would create an absurd loophole.[29] Generally, courts have refused to let debtors achieve indirectly what they could not achieve directly.[30]

## *Change in Life Insurance Policy Ownership or Beneficiary Designation*

Whether changing a beneficiary designation amounts to a fraudulent transfer will depend on several factors. Where a non-debtor policy owner changes the beneficiary, and the beneficiary does not have an enforceable right in policy proceeds, there should be no fraudulent transfer. But where a debtor has a sufficient interest in the policy (generally as the policy owner) and acts to divert proceeds through change in designation or cash value (through transfer of policy ownership), the act might be successfully challenged as a fraudulent transfer. Whether a debtor has a sufficient interest in property to constitute a

27. See UVTA, Section 12, ("Supplementary Provisions.")

28. *Geriatrics, Inc. v. McGee*, 332 Conn. 1, 15-16 (Conn. 2019) ("The words of this court regarding our original fraudulent conveyance statute apply equally to CUFTA: 'As the statute was enacted for the suppression of fraud, the advancement of justice and the promotion of the public good, it should be liberally and beneficially construed to suppress the fraud, abridge the mischief, and enlarge the remedy. . . . [T]he common law . . . supplements the statute to the end that justice may be done.' (Citations omitted; internal quotation marks omitted.) Allen v. Rundle , 50 Conn. 9, 32 (1882). Given that the failure to apply the law of agency would create an easy end run around the act, and frustrate the ability of creditors to secure payment for debts owed to them, application of agency principles is manifestly consistent, not inconsistent, with the policies underlying the act. We cannot hypothesize a single adverse consequence that would arise from applying agency law under these circumstances.")

29. The dissenting judge in *Geriatrics, Inc. v. McGee*, 332 Conn. 1, 36 (Conn. 2019) argued the case law did not support the majority opinion. ("Indeed, a number of other courts have declined to find liability for transfers of a debtor's assets made by various third parties, including spouses; see, e.g., SPQR Venture, Inc. v. Robertson, 237 Ariz. 270, 273, 349 P.3d 1107 (App. 2015); subsidiary companies; see, e.g., Crystallex International Corp. v. Petroleos de Venezuela, S.A., 879 F.3d 79, 85–89 (3d Cir. 2018); and contractual parties; see, e.g., Ford–Torres v. Cascade Valley Telecom, Inc., 374 Fed. Appx. 698, 700 (9th Cir. 2010).")

30. In the context of whether a trust is self-settled, *see Calhoun v. Rawlins*, 93 Mass. App. Ct. 458, 464 (Mass. App. Ct. 2018) ("It would be anomalous indeed if a settlor could avoid the well-settled principle that one cannot avoid creditors through a self-settled trust by the simple expedient of identifying another person in the trust instrument as the settlor. Rather, in determining whether the trust was self-settled, we look to the facts surrounding the creation of the trust.")

transfer of an interest will depend on state law, where distinctions may be drawn between whether an interest has vested or is a mere expectancy. If a debtor does not own an asset outright, merely having a vested interest in the asset could be enough to qualify as a transfer of an interest.

The choice of law in a fraudulent transfer dispute may be a vital determination for either party as local law might define a debtor's interest. Notwithstanding the result under state law, federal law might demand a different result where a debtor has enough of an interest in an asset.

*In re Meza* illustrates how a court may look to whether a beneficial interest has vested, such that the beneficiary may own an asset to be transferred subject to fraudulent transfer law.

> As stated by the Arizona Supreme Court in McLennan, "Under insurance certificates of this nature, the beneficiary has no vested interest in the certificate until the death of the insured member. Up to such time the latter may change his designation of beneficiary at will." McLennan and Doss are unequivocal holdings that Arizona law provides the beneficiary, prior to the insured's death, has "no vested right which the law protects," and Arizona courts have not recognized any exceptions to those holdings. And Ninth Circuit law is clear that when state law recognizes no such vested right, bankruptcy law cannot find a property interest to exist, but only a mere expectancy.
>
> The Trustee argues that a named beneficiary's interest in a life insurance policy may have some value that the law protects once the insured knows of her impending death. In support of this argument, he cites two California cases. In Bryson, the California Court of Appeals upheld a fraudulent transfer to recover the death proceeds when the insured changed the beneficiary four months prior to committing suicide. The court reasoned that "the knowledge of impending death removed the element of contingency and gave the policy at the time of its transfer 'an actual pecuniary value closely approximating its face amount.'" And then Headon held that the rule of Bryson was not limited to changes of beneficiary made in contemplation of death, because that fact merely "increases the present value of the policy to something approaching its face value." Those California cases, as well as an Indiana case the Trustee cites, seem to eliminate the Code's requirement to find a transfer "of an interest of the debtor in property" as a necessary prerequisite to finding a fraudulent transfer, by stating the only "relevant inquiry is whether the debtor has put some asset beyond the reach of creditors which would have been available to them but for the conveyance."
>
> But while Bryson and Headen are undoubtedly correct that knowledge of impending value increases the market value of a term life policy, the existence of value alone is not determinative of whether state law protects a sufficient bundle of rights to *156 be deemed a property interest. While they may imply that California does recognize some vested right in the beneficiary, regardless of knowledge of impending death, that is clearly not the law in Arizona under Alarcon, McLennan and Doss. Without recognition of any vested right in the beneficiary, there is no possibility of a federal court concluding that a property interest exists under state law.

> The clear lack of any right in the beneficiary that is protected by law makes this situation entirely distinguishable from the protected right of a legatee, prior to a disclaimer, which some federal law may recognize as constituting a property right even if state law is to the contrary. And it is certainly the governing law in the Ninth Circuit, which has held, after Drye, that the "right to channel" by exercising the disclaimer under Arizona law, prior to either the fixing of a federal tax lien or the filing of a bankruptcy petition, "is not a 'transfer . . . of an interest of the debtor in property' for purposes of §548." Obviously the legatee's inheritance had a very definite, fixed value prior to the disclaimer, and yet that mere existence of value and lack of contingency was not sufficient for the Ninth Circuit to find that a property interest existed under Arizona law.
>
> This is also the clear holding of the Ninth Circuit in Harrell, where the seniority right to renew a professional basketball season ticket clearly had very substantial value. But because that seniority was not protected by state law it was a mere expectancy, regardless of its value, and not a sufficient bundle of rights to constitute a property interest that could become property of the estate. Under governing Arizona law, the beneficiary's interest is similarly not protected and therefore a mere expectancy, regardless of how valuable it might become upon knowledge of impending death.[31]

Where the debtor owns a policy, or owns an entity that owns a policy, such ownership interest may be enough to support a successful fraudulent transfer challenge. In addition to determining whether the change of beneficiary is a transfer of an asset, *In re Meza* also illustrates that it is necessary to determine whether the policy is exempt (and therefore, not an asset) in the first place.

In *United Bank v. Buckingham*, a family business defaulted on loans to United Bank, where the patriarch and his wife were also guarantors on loans to United Bank. Several life insurance policies insuring the life of the family patriarch (John Buckingham) were owned by the family business (SCS). More specifically, there were three categories of life insurance policies at issue: "(1) two policies from Northwestern Mutual (the JDB policies) that John had purchased and for which he paid the premiums; (2) four policies purchased by SCS from Northwestern Mutual (the split-dollar policies) under a split-dollar arrangement where John named the beneficiaries but SCS 'owned' the policies, paid the premiums, and upon John's death stood to recoup the premiums from the death benefits, with the remainder being paid to John's designated beneficiary; and (3) two policies from John Hancock (the John Hancock Policies) purchased and owned by SCS and operated under a similar split dollar arrangement, with SCS recouping the premiums upon John's death."

As John's health declined and SCS struggled to meet its loan obligations to United Bank, John's guardians changed the life insurance policy beneficiary designations from SCS to a life insurance trust to prevent SCS from receiving premiums paid under a split-dollar arrangement. United Bank objected to the change in beneficiary designation since the effect of doing so was to divert funds from SCS into the hands of the family via life insurance trusts. The expressed

31. *In re Meza*, 465 B.R. 152, 154–56 (Bankr. D. Ariz. 2012).

purpose for the change of beneficiary designation was not to hinder United Bank, but to provide care for John's wife. The guardian also accelerated the death benefit for some of the SCS-owned policies. Since accelerating the death benefit would have exposed the funds to SCS's creditors (i.e., United Bank), SCS sold the policies for a fraction of the policies' value[32] to another trust.

United Bank sought to void both the sale of the policies from SCS to the trust, and the change in beneficiaries on split-dollar polices. The U.S. District Court for the District of Maryland ruled in favor of the family, finding, in part, that the sale was for fair consideration and the change in beneficiary designation was not covered by the Maryland Uniform Fraudulent Conveyance Act. United Bank appealed to the Fourth Circuit, which overruled several findings and remanded to the District Court. The District Court had to determine whether the change of insurance beneficiary was valid regardless of whether the change was made with actual intent to hinder, delay, or defraud creditors, and if it was, whether that change should bear on the Court's interpretation of MUFCA. The District Court certified two questions to the Maryland Court of Appeals, one of which was whether a change of a beneficiary designation of a life insurance policy constituted a conveyance under the Maryland Uniform Fraudulent Conveyance Act.[33]

The Court of Appeals answered the question in the affirmative. "After conducting a plain language analysis of the definition of 'conveyance' provided for in CL§15-201(c) and reviewing the General Assembly's intent in enacting MUFCA as evidenced by the Act's legislative history, caselaw, and related statutory provisions, we hold that a change in life insurance beneficiary constitutes a conveyance under MUFCA."[34] The Buckingham's argued one cannot transfer an interest in a life insurance policy, and even if one could transfer an expectancy interest, the interest was exempt under Maryland law.

The Court of Appeals declined to utilize a restrictive interpretation of the definition of asset and transfer. "Thus, after a detailed review of the plain language of CL §15-201, we conclude that the use of the term 'includes' and the disjunctive nature of the language in CL §15-201(c) demonstrate the purpose of the General Assembly to provide illustrative examples of conveyances without any intent to limit the phrase 'transfer' to 'tangible or intangible property.' Therefore, the transfer of the right to receive insurance proceeds from one individual to another by altering the beneficiary designation on a life insurance policy falls within the definition of 'conveyance;' provided in CL §15-201(c)."

The Court of Appeals also cited the policy behind fraudulent transfer law as a guide behind statutory construction. In doing so, the court considered the impact of its decision on creditors' rights in general. "This Court has long

32. The sale price was $110,000, in contrast to the $709,000 of accelerated benefits. The family justified the sales price due to the fact that because the family business had stopped paying the premiums, the policies had a negative surrender value and were in danger of lapsing.

33. *See United Bank v. Buckingham*, 449 F.Supp.3d 521 (2020), where the question presented was, "Whether the Maryland Uniform Fraudulent Conveyances Act, see Md. Code Ann., Com. Law §§15-201 *et seq.*, which generally applies to conveyances made with the intent to hinder, delay, or defraud creditors, reaches a change in life insurance beneficiary, particularly in light of Md. Code Ann., Ins. §16-111(d)?"

34. *United Bank v. Buckingham*, 472 Md. 407, 412, 247 A.3d 336, 339 (2021).

recognized that the purpose of fraudulent conveyance law is to preserve the rights of creditors. In 1939, this Court concluded that the Maryland fraudulent conveyance statutes 'were designed to render null and void conveyances made for the purpose of hindering, delaying and defrauding creditors.' Kennard v. Elkton Banking & Trust Co., 176 Md. 499, 500 (1939). In 1973, this Court again reiterated that in enacting these statutes, the Legislature 'was not restricting the legal or equitable remedies already available to the creditor,' and the 'objective . . . [was]to enhance and not impair the remedies of the creditor.' Damazo v. Wahby, 269 Md. 252, 256–57 (1973). *** If this Court were to find that a transfer of the right to receive life insurance proceeds does not constitute a conveyance under MUFCA, then it would be difficult for the creditors of policy holders to have any remedy for the fraudulent change of a life insurance beneficiary."

Further, the life insurance policy's status as an asset turned on whether it was exempt in the first place. Once the court concluded a beneficiary designation could amount to a fraudulent transfer, the question of whether the policy was exempt was easy, given the terms of the exemption statute. Specifically, IN §16-111(d), which exempts the proceeds of life insurance, provides, "A change of beneficiary, assignment, or other transfer is valid except for transfer with actual intent to hinder, delay, or defraud creditors."

Although IN §16-111 does not provide a specific remedy where a designation change is fraudulent, the court found none was needed and it may look elsewhere for the appropriate remedy. "While we agree with the Buckinghams' assertion that perhaps no additional remedies are expressly created by this subsection, IN §16-111(d) nonetheless underscores the General Assembly's express rejection of the limitation on a creditor's remedies in the event of a fraudulent transfer of life insurance beneficiary. Therefore, it follows that for IN §16-111(d) to have any meaningful effect, a remedy for defrauded creditors must be available elsewhere under Maryland law." The court's approach may be especially instructive for creditors who seek to invalidate a protection under a statute that carves out fraudulent transfers but does not provide a particular remedy.[35]

## *Exemption Planning*

The use of state-sanctioned protections reflects public policy of the state, protecting an individual's use of certain assets that bring stability to the family or reflect a protected interest. Consequently, wages, life insurance and the family home are protected in varying degrees among the states. Where these investments are made in the ordinary course of life, courts have generally been hesitant to deny protection on fraudulent transfer grounds as the strong public

35. A common example is the fraudulent conversion of a state law corporation into a state law limited liability company that restricts a creditor's ability to reach business assets due to charging order provisions. State law might provide an exception to this charging order protection on fraudulent transfer grounds but not provide a particular remedy. The creditor should turn to the remedies available under applicable fraudulent transfer law.

policy supporting the stability of a family will outweigh the policy protecting creditors. For example, even when funds are expended by a debtor to pay the premiums on an insurance policy payable to his family, such transfers have been fairly protected:

> The law favors the making of reasonable provision by a man for his dependent family, and in *Johnson v. Alexander*, 125 Ind. 575, 25 N.E. 706, the Supreme Court of Indiana has said: "It is not a violation of the statute, and in fraud of creditors, for a debtor, though insolvent, to contribute and pay a reasonable amount for insurance for the benefit of his family." In *Pence v. Makepeace*, 65 Ind. 345, [1879 WL 5483 (1879)], it is held that only on the clearest proof of fraud, if at all, can the premiums paid by an insolvent debtor on a policy of insurance on his life for the benefit of his wife and children be revoked by his creditors, and in no event can any excess over the amount of the premium so paid be recovered.[36]

With respect to transfers for life insurance in the business setting, reasonably equivalent value might protect the transaction from fraudulent transfer attack.

> "The Court finds that no fact issue remains as to whether LivingWell received reasonably equivalent value for the payments to the insurance trust because the decision to provide liability protection to the board of directors and officers was subjective in nature. It could very well be that LivingWell's ability to attract officers and directors with the business acumen to serve on its board required the insurance trust. Moreover, the premiums paid were premiums saved by virtue of the fact that the funds remained available to LivingWell as an asset.
>
> Consequently, the Court denies the plaintiffs' motion for summary judgment on their fraudulent transfer claim as it pertains to the insurance trust and also closes the door on the question of the subjective reasonableness of that decision."[37]

However, courts will not hesitate to grant a creditor relief under fraudulent transfer law when the use of exemptions renders an individual insolvent or is done with the intent to hinder creditors. Here, the court does not view a debtor's actions as supporting the policy underlying the exemption (e.g., family stability) but instead views the debtor as attempting to "have his cake and eat it, too." In denying an exemption on these grounds, courts have taken the position that a debtor must be just to his creditors before his family.

If there was any question that public policy will not protect this "hoggish" motivation, Florida has a separate statute that prohibits the use of any exemption if created on fraudulent transfer grounds. Note, the result creditors desired under Florida's fraudulent conversion statute could also be obtained under Florida's fraudulent transfer statute. However, the fraudulent conversion

36. *In re First Fin. Associates, Inc.*, 371 B.R. 877, 894–95 (Bankr. N.D. Ind. 2007).

37. *Askanase v. Fatjo*, No. CIV.A.H-91-3140, 1996 WL 33373364, at *11 (S.D. Tex. Apr. 1, 1996).

statute sets forth Florida's clear message to debtors who attempt to abuse its generous exemptions.

While bankruptcy courts have also permitted the use of exemptions (either under the Bankruptcy Code or applicable state law) prior to bankruptcy, the theme continues to be permitting a fresh start instead of a head start, where being somewhat "piggish" is acceptable, but being "hoggish" results in "slaughter" (i.e., denial of exemption or discharge.)

> Bill Jay Bird (the Debtor) has found himself in a difficult situation: on one hand, he seeks the shelter and protection of the bankruptcy court from his creditors; but on the other, he wishes to manipulate the system in such a manner that he comes out on top instead of paying his creditors. His tactics go against the very bedrock of bankruptcy that seeks "to provide a 'fresh start' to individuals and to provide an equitable distribution to creditors."[38]

One should consider to the law of the appropriate Circuit when assessing whether pre-bankruptcy planning is subject to more scrutiny.

> Under relevant Seventh Circuit precedent, so-called exemption planning only rises to the level of fraudulent conduct if there is evidence that the debtor committed some act "extrinsic to the conversion" which hinders, delays, or defrauds creditors. . . . The fact that a debtor engages in exemption planning while faced with financial distress is not itself evidence of fraudulent conduct.
>
> After all, the use of exemptions is at least a legitimate form of asset protection, and debtors should only be penalized when they go beyond taking advantage of the exemption laws themselves. . . . [T]here is a difference between creating a smokescreen that makes it difficult for creditors to realize on their claims and merely attempting to take advantage of legally available exemptions.
>
> Woller, 483 B.R. at 901–02.[39]

*Kluck* is interesting in two regards. First, the *Kluck* court reasons that merely converting assets while under financial distress is not enough, by itself, to result in avoidance. The UVTA opposition expressed concern with Official Comments pertaining to the conversion of a corporation to an LLC while the clouds of financial distress gather. The Comment provides the conversion may be voidable but stops short of concluding the conversion is void. In a sense, the clouds of financial distress make conditions favorable for avoidance but fall short of labeling it as void. Second, the *Kluck* court contrasts creating smoke screens to intentionally hinder creditors with mere usage of state-sanctioned exemptions. The creation of hurdles often is the stated goal of asset protection planning, which unfortunately, if documented, puts the debtor-client in a bad position when arguing intent to hinder did not exist. In contrast, the use of state

38. *In re Bird*, No. 11-36001, 2017 WL 880864, at *1 (Bankr. S.D. Tex. Mar. 3, 2017).

39. *In re:* Lydell James Kluck & Margaret Marie Kluck, Debtors., No. 18-10019-7, 2019 WL 2495831, at *5–6 (Bankr. W.D. Wis. June 14, 2019)

exemptions, although having the effect of asset protection, is not by itself fraudulent.[40]

## Disclaimers

A disclaimer allows an individual to refuse property he or she would otherwise be entitled to receive. One might disclaim assets to prevent increasing his or her estate for federal estate tax purposes. On the other hand, one might disclaim property if he or she is concerned the property could be reached by creditors. It is the latter situation that is more likely to give rise to the potential application of fraudulent transfer law.

A creditor might argue that a debtor who has a vested interest in an asset and disclaims has effectively transferred the asset for fraudulent transfer law purposes. More specifically, the issue with a disclaimer is whether a court will equate the debtor's divestment of the debtor's vested, yet non-possessory, interest (or a portion of an interest) in an asset with a transfer of an asset for fraudulent transfer purposes. This scenario is not much different than a debtor who directs a trustee to withhold a mandatory distribution from a trust to avoid creditors. Although the debtor has a vested, albeit non-possessory, interest, the debtor's actions could arguably be viewed as a constructive transfer of an asset back to the trustee, or a sufficient interest to constitute a property right for federal law purposes, discussed in chapter ten. In these situations, it is important to consider whether state law addresses a creditor's rights as to the subject asset, including state law pertaining to the relation-back doctrine, and whether the application of federal law would trump any state law protection.

The case law is mixed as to whether a disclaimer constitutes a transfer for fraudulent transfer purposes. Some states might explicitly provide a disclaimer cannot be a fraudulent transfer,[41]while others, like Florida, might provide that an insolvent disclaimant is barred from disclaiming assets. Under the Florida Uniform Disclaimer of Property Interests Act, section 739.402 provides a disclaimer of an interest in property is barred if the disclaimant is insolvent when the disclaimer becomes irrevocable. A person is insolvent under 739.402 if the sum of a person's debts is greater than all of the person's assets at fair valuation and that the person is generally not paying his or her debts as they become

40. *See also, In re TOCFHBI, Inc.*, 413 B.R. 523, 540 (Bankr. N.D. Tex. 2009). ("Pre-bankruptcy planning and/or asset protection is a fact-intensive and unclear area of law. Courts that have struggled with it have written things like 'when a pig becomes a hog it is slaughtered,'" Swift v. Bank of San Antonio (In re Swift), 3 F.3d 929, 931 (5th Cir.1993) (quoting In re Zouhar, 10 B.R. 154, 157 (Bankr. D.N.M. 1981)), (hardly a bright-line test), indicating that there is a fine line debtors can cross whereupon there will be a price to be paid for exuberance. This court does not know in this case (particularly since it has not heard witnesses nor heard full evidence), if a jury would ultimately decide that there is a price to be paid for the pre-bankruptcy asset protection activities of the corporate-Debtor (and, if so, who all should be the "payees"). However, the court does perceive that this has become a very expensive fight—a fight that could ultimately easily exceed the $2.5 million of prepetition creditors' claims. *See, e.g.*, Maxwell v. KPMG LLP, 520 F.3d 713, 718 (7th Cir.2008) (Judge Posner warning that bankruptcy judges "must . . . be vigilant in policing the litigation judgment exercised by trustees in bankruptcy . . .").

41. *See, e.g.*, Cal. Prob. Code §283.

due.[42] Section 739.402 also provides that the term "assets" has the same meaning as that provided in Florida's Uniform Fraudulent Transfer Act.

As discussed in chapter ten, federal law might consider the mere ability to channel assets via disclaimer as sufficient to constitute a property interest under applicable federal law.[43] For federal tax law purposes, the IRS may argue a taxpayer engaged in a fraudulent transfer by disclaiming an asset, or transferred an asset that was subject to a federal tax lien.[44] This is true despite state law that might provide a disclaimant has no property rights in disclaimed assets under a relation-back doctrine.

In the bankruptcy context, a debtor's disclaimer can be challenged as a fraudulent transfer that can be avoided for the benefit of the bankruptcy estate, as well as serve as justification for a denial of discharge. "This finding that the renunciation was in fact a transfer, unaffected by the relation-back doctrine, fulfills one of the elements of §727(a)(2). Of the remaining elements mentioned above—(1) the debtors' actions took place within twelve months prior to the filing of their petition for bankruptcy relief; (2) the debtors took the actions with the intent to hinder, delay, or defraud their creditors; and (3) the debtors themselves took the actions—the only element not readily established by the uncontroverted facts in the record is the element of intent to hinder, delay, or defraud creditors."[45] Not all bankruptcy courts have found a disclaimer constitutes a fraudulent transfer.

---

42. Florida Statute Section 739.402(8). The definition of "insolvent" in Section 739.402 is somewhat narrower than the definition in Florida's Uniform Fraudulent Transfer Act. Specifically, Florida Statute Section 726 provides a disclaimant is insolvent "if the sum of the debtor's debts is greater than all of the debtor's assets at a fair valuation." However, the disclaimer statute also requires failure to pay debts as they come due.

43. United States of America, Plaintiff, v. Jim Henry Andrews, Jr., et al., Defendants. Additional Party Names: Katherine Andrews Francis, No. 1:09-CV-112 (HL), 2011 WL 13323634, at *2–6 (M.D. Ga. July 13, 2011). ("The renunciation statutes do not insulate a person from the FDCPA's reach. Persons who renounce property may never receive estate property, but under Georgia law, 'they were certainly entitled to receive the property until, through their own action, they gave up or renounced the property interest.' Georgia Dept. of Comm. Health v. Medders, 664 S.E.2d 832, 834 (Ga. Ct. App. 2008). It is not contested that Andrews had a valuable, transferable, legally protected right to his interest in his father's estate. The issue then is whether this right to receive or renounce is 'property' and therefore an 'asset' under the FDCPA. As already explained, this is an issue of federal law. In an analogous case involving federal tax liens on property, the Supreme Court found that the 'power to channel the estate's assets' means that an heir holds 'property' or a 'right to property' subject to the Government's tax liens. Drye v. United States, 528 U.S. 49, 61, 120 S. Ct. 474, 483, 145 L. Ed. 2d 466 (1999). To determine whether a person has property or a property interest courts consider "the breadth of the control the [taxpayer] could exercise over the property." Id. (citation omitted). Here, Andrews had 'power to channel the estate's assets' and could exercise control of the assets. He therefore had property or assets to transfer to Francis within the meaning of the FDCPA. The Court denies summary judgment on the FDCPA claim to the extent that Francis argues there was no transfer within the meaning of the FDCPA.")

44. *See Drye v. United States*, 528 U.S. 49, 60 (1999).

45. *In re White*, No. A13-4010, 2014 WL 555212, at *5 (Bankr. D. Neb. Feb. 12, 2014). ("While the Supreme Court in Drye said the Internal Revenue Code intentionally defines 'property' broadly, the Bankruptcy Code interprets the term broadly as well. Likewise, the distinction based on the fact that the tax lien had attached before the disclaimer was executed is not relevant because if there was a property interest to which the IRS's lien could attach, then there was also a property interest in Gerald White's estate that could be transferred by the disclaimer. Further, just as the tax lien had attached in Drye, the judgment liens here had attached before Craig White's disclaimer. The relation-back doctrine is simply a legal fiction created by state law. It has no applicability when trying to determine property of the bankruptcy estate.")

> This court agrees with the Ninth Circuit and finds Drye distinguishable. The court is aware of contrary decisions by its sister courts. E.g., *In re Kloubec*, 247 B.R. 246 (Bankr. N.D. Iowa 2000) (applying Drye to avoid a disclaimer under §548), aff'd on other grounds, 268 B.R. 173, 177 (N.D. Iowa 2001) (not addressing issue due to finding that debtor had waived right to disclaim by encumbering his interest in probate estate); *see* Nashville City Bank v. Peery (*In re* Peery), 40 B.R. 811 (Bankr. M.D. Tenn. 1984) (denying discharge based on fraudulent conveyance by way of renunciation of inheritance). However, in the absence of contrary authority from the Sixth Circuit, this court is not inclined to ignore the well-reasoned opinions from other appellate courts that properly defer to state law to define a debtor's interest in property in the bankruptcy context as directed by the Supreme Court in Butner.[46]

## *Probate Administration Issues*

The probate estate is somewhat analogous to the bankruptcy estate of a debtor, whereas instead of a bankruptcy trustee, the personal representative or executor has the duty to marshal assets, pay off decedent's debts and distribute the decedent's assets in accordance with the decedent's will or pursuant to state intestacy law.

Like the bankruptcy code's provision addressing fraudulent transfers, state law may protect creditors from a decedent's efforts to hinder creditors prior to death. This can occur by transfers prior to death or post-mortem transfers. In a post-mortem transfer situation, the personal representative of the estate must be cognizant of creditors' rights in the process of distributing assets or forgiving debts through a testamentary transfer. In a Florida case,[47] the court held the decedent could not, through his will, forgive a debt owed to him when his estate was not solvent. Similar to a bankruptcy setting, the personal representative should look to debts owed to the decedent as potential avenues of relief for the benefit of creditors of the decedent's estate. Similarly, there might be situations where transfers to an irrevocable trust might be subject to the claims of creditors after the settlor's death.[48]

In situations where probate estate funds are distributed to a beneficiary, the issue may arise as to whether the transfer is voidable by the federal government if estate taxes are not paid. In this case, federal statute might provide the government with relief against both the personal representative as well as the beneficiary/transferee. "First, Rose Saloom does not dispute that she distributed

46. *In re* Burke, 592 B.R. 834, 840 (Bankr. E.D. Tenn. 2018).

47. *Lauritsen v. Wallace*, 67 So. 3d 285 (Fla. Dist. Ct. App. 2011).

48. *See De Prins v. Michaeles*, 486 Mass. 41, 49, 154 N.E.3d 921, 928 (2020). ("Although we have found no case law that directly discusses the distinction between the reachability of the assets of a self-settled trust during the settlor's lifetime versus after his death (if one exists), it would be incongruent for a self-settled trust not to protect a settlor's assets from creditors while the settlor is alive but to have it protect the settlor's beneficiaries from the settlor's creditors after the settlor's death when, absent the self-settled trust, they would not be so protected. We therefore hold that a self-settled trust does not become protected from creditors on the settlor's death.")

all the property of the Richard Saloom Estate to herself. Additionally, Rose Saloom acknowledges the Richard Saloom Estate is insolvent. Finally, Rose Saloom had knowledge of her father's tax liabilities, which is demonstrated by her filing of a New Jersey inheritance tax return that listed 'indebtedness' for 'federal tax.' Despite her assertions, the United States has demonstrated that no genuine dispute of material fact exists as to the three elements. As such, Rose Saloom is liable under 31 U.S.C. §3713(b) for the Kelley Estate estate tax liability."[49] The federal government did not prevail on its fraudulent transfer theory, presumably because it relied on cases involving actual, fraud and the court determined the decedent did not have intent to defraud with respect to the transfer via inheritance.[50] The court also noted the estate assets remained within the reach of the United States via transferee liability under Internal Revenue Code Section 3713.

Another issue may be whether the personal representative of the probate estate must be joined in an action for relief against the beneficiary as transferee. Here a court might find a distinction between state fraudulent transfer law, which permits a judgment against subsequent transferees of *voidable* transfers, versus Section 550(a) of the Bankruptcy Code, which permits a judgment against subsequent transferees of *voided* transfers. In a trust administration context, a court may permit an action against a trust beneficiary under state fraudulent transfer law if the creditor can prove the initial transfer to the trustee was fraudulent.

Other issues that are relevant to this analysis include whether a party is necessary under Rule 19 of the Federal Rules of Civil Procedure. Generally, if a party is not necessary, the analysis is complete. If the party is necessary, the analysis turns to whether the joinder is feasible, and if not, whether the party is indispensable.[51] A fraudulent transfer action may be dismissed if a party is necessary, cannot be joined, and is indispensable.

Whether a party is indispensable may depend on the party's role and interest in the transferred asset. Generally, the debtor is indispensable if the fraudulent transfer action is brought prior to a judgment on the claim against the debtor. Further, the debtor may be indispensable if the debtor retained an interest in the transferred asset (e.g., as a trust beneficiary). There is a split of authority as

49. *United States v. Est. of Kelley*, No. 3:17-CV-965-BRM-DEA, 2020 WL 6194040, at *5 (D.N.J. Oct. 22, 2020).

50. *Id.* at *6 (D.N.J. Oct. 22, 2020). ("In the cases on which the United States relies, courts have entered summary judgment and enforced personal money judgment against transferees who were explicitly engaged in schemes to defraud creditors. For example, in *United States v. Patras*, the court entered a personal money judgment against a transferee where the transferor moved property that put that property beyond the reach of the United States. *United States v. Patras*, 909 F. Supp. 2d 400, 412 (D.N.J. 2012).")

51. *See Citizen Potawatomi Nation v. Norton*, 248 F.3d 993, 997 (10th Cir. 2001), stating the issue of whether a party is indispensable is "whether in equity and good conscience the action can continue in his absence." See also, *Zazzali v. Goldsmith (In re DBSI Inc.)*, No. 08-12687 (PJW), at *10 (Bankr. D. Idaho Apr. 11, 2013) citing *Confederated Tribes of Chehalis Indian Reservation v. Lujan*, 928 F.2d 1496, 1498 (9th Cir. 1991). ("An indispensable party is one who "not only [has] an interest in the controversy, but [has] an interest of such a nature that a final decree cannot be made without either affecting that interest, or leaving the controversy in such a condition that its final termination may be wholly inconsistent with equity and good conscience.")

to whether a debtor who did not retain an interest is an indispensable party.[52] The transferee who holds the asset should be indispensable since the transferee has an interest in the asset. Those that do not have a strong enough interest in the asset held (e.g., a straw person) may not be indispensable.

## Family Law Planning

Just as debtors attempt to rearrange assets to enjoy benefits to the exclusion of creditors, the same can be said for spouses who attempt to reorganize wealth with an eye toward divorce. While most states do not cater to this desire, some, like Nevada and South Dakota, have cut short the rights of divorcing spouses when it comes to assets in an asset protection trust. Proposed legislation that contains creditor-hindering aspects such as this might be introduced as legislation that merely updates or modernizes current law. This innocuous description helps to avoid raising a red flag that might draw negative attention and opposition from the creditors' rights bar during the legislative process.

> The latest salvo in the trust wars is now ready for signing and top estate planners throughout the nation are already betting on how it will shift the industry landscape.
>
> At first glance, SD House Bill 1056 amounts to 6,800 words of boilerplate under the innocuous title, "An Act To Revise Various Trust and Trust Company Provisions."
>
> But buried in the text is a little bombshell that's got email boxes around the asset protection community lighting up from Delaware to Nevada and beyond.
>
> "This keeps South Dakota ahead of the curve and provides the changes to keep South Dakota the top place in the nation to situs trusts or form trust companies," says Sioux Falls attorney Terry Prendergast.
>
> A tiny gap just closed
>
> Now that Governor Dennis Daugaard has signed the bill into law, SD 1056 will formally eliminate divorcing spouses' right to assets that have already gone into South Dakota domestic asset protection trusts starting on July 1.
>
> The list of creditor exceptions in the state now includes the ex-spouse and kids only to the extent to which the trust creator already owes them money –

52. *See* Geriatrics, Inc. v. McGee, 332 Conn. 1, 19 n.18 (Conn. 2019). ("In the case of a debtor who has retained no legal interest in the property conveyed, there is a conflict of authority as to whether that person is a necessary party defendant to an action to set aside a fraudulent conveyance. In some jurisdictions, apparently on the theory that having parted with all interest in the property the grantor can no longer be affected by any decree pertaining to the property, the debtor is not a necessary party to the action although the debtor may be a proper party. Under other authority, the debtor, as the originator of the fraudulent conduct complained of, and as the person directly involved in the fraud in the first instance, is a necessary party to the action.")

> otherwise, the special carve-out that once gave them the power to make future claims is gone.
>
> In effect, unless there's already an outstanding alimony, child support or property division issue on the table, a trust administrated out of South Dakota is now as secure from an ex-spouse as anyone else.
>
> * * *
>
> Don't confuse the sizzle with the steak
>
> Ultimately, the impact of South Dakota's move may be theoretical at best for most clients, but that's exactly the kind of fine distinction that separates truly high-end asset protection lawyers— and the jurisdictions they favor—from the rest.
>
> For the everyday run of wealthy family looking to protect their assets from most creditors as fast as possible, more basic considerations come first, like the length of time that assets have to "season" in trust before being protected.
>
> On that basis, Nevada and South Dakota are neck and neck with a two-year window between when the check clears and when the protection kicks in.[53]

All the usual badges of fraud that can deprive a traditional creditor of its rights might be present as to an unsuspecting spouse in divorce. Attorney-advisers who represent both spouses must consider carefully state ethical rules pertaining to joint representation. If the attorney represents only one spouse, the "injured" spouse might sue the attorney for what the injured spouse views as improper.

> In the factual allegations of her complaint, the former wife alleges that after the final judgment of dissolution was entered, the former husband engaged in a scheme with attorney Michael Presley to protect the former husband's assets. She alleges that the former husband resigned as trustee of the family trusts and that the new trustees "began drastically reducing, at least on the surface, the amount of distributions made" to the former husband. She also alleges that the former husband transferred his two-thirds interest in his real property, the Banyan House, to one of the trusts in an attempt to avoid his alimony obligation and that the home was sold, with the proceeds remaining with the trust. She further avers that a family partnership was set up by the former husband "to fraudulently transfer assets of" the former husband "to intentionally defraud [the former wife] of her right to receive alimony" and that the assets in the partnership were transferred back to the former husband's new wife for the benefit of the former husband. The former wife further alleges that under the asset protection scheme devised by the former husband and his attorney, the former husband receives no direct distributions from the trusts but the trusts continue to pay for his living expenses. In the complaint, the former wife alleges counts of fraudulent transfer against the former husband, the trustees, and Michael Presley individually, and these

53. Scott Martin, "Trust Wars: Experts Say New Law Makes South Dakota Asset Protection Trusts Top Choice," The Trust Advisor, available on https://www.thewealthadvisor.com/article/trust-wars-experts-say-new-law-makes-south-dakota-asset-protection-trusts-top-choice.

counts relate to the transfer of the Banyan House. The former wife also alleges a count for equitable lien against the proceeds from the Banyan House and injunctive relief regarding the proceeds.[54]

## *Trusts or Entities Created During Marriage*

Sometimes an innocent wealth transfer engagement can have fraudulent transfer consequences in a divorce proceeding. Given the frequent use of family trusts formed under asset protection trust statutes, the intersection is an important concern for family lawyers, both before and after marriage.[55] Often, a spouse is presented with a family trust planning opportunity, potentially unaware that, hidden deep within boilerplate language, the spouse vanishes as a beneficiary of the trust upon the occurrence of certain events, one of which includes separation or divorce.[56] In reviewing such agreements (sometimes too late as a self-settled trust often serves as a substitute for a marital agreement), family lawyers must be fully aware of the rights of their client in the event of separation, divorce or otherwise.[57]

For fraudulent transfer purposes, it is critical to identify whether a creditor exists while planning with family assets as a transaction might subsequently be challenged by one spouse as voidable. For example, the Supreme Court of West Virginia has held that merely holding a right to an elective share, based on the facts, should not transform a spouse into a creditor.[58] Further, even if a spouse could qualify as a creditor, the nature of the planning might negate a finding of fraud. In *Gibson v. Gibson*, the Supreme Court of Georgia ruled that a husband's transfers of approximately $2.3 million to an irrevocable trust during marriage were not fraudulent transfers and thus, not part of the marital estate subject to

---

54. *Inglis v. Casselberry*, 200 So. 3d 206, 211 (Fla. Dist. Ct. App. 2016).

55. An asset protection trust is often marketed as part of pre-marital planning that can supplement or obviate the need for a premarital agreement. A marital agreement is often reviewed by an independent lawyer who has the best interests of the client at stake. This might not be the case with asset protection trusts used in the marital planning context.

56. Sometimes referred to as a "floating spouse" or "vanishing spouse" clause. *See* Kearney v. Kearney 129 So. 3d 381. ("The financial statement included money in an irrevocable offshore grantor asset protection trust (the RSK trust) of which the husband and wife are beneficiaries. By its terms, the RSK Trust removed the wife as a beneficiary when she filed for dissolution of marriage.")

57. A third party, often referred to as a "Protector," who might not be subject to a fiduciary duty to the beneficiaries, might be given the power under the trust agreement to exclude a beneficiary based on certain events or circumstances.

58. *See Rosier v. Rosier*, 227 W. Va. 88, 101, 705 S.E.2d 595, 608 (2010). Notwithstanding the court ruling that it would be inappropriate to consider an elective share right as creating a claim to support creditor status for a spouse, the court entertained the idea if the "debtor" spouse was rendered insolvent. ("IT WOULD BE AN INAppropriate stretch, however, to take the notion of this unexercised elective share as being a 'claim' within the definition of the Act to warrant declaring transactions fraudulent. Even if this Court were to declare that this was a legitimate claim to create a debtor-creditor relationship between Mrs. Rosier and Stearl Rosier, within the definition of the Act, there is still the issue of whether the transfer rendered Stearl Rosier insolvent, or whether he was insolvent at the time of the transfer. *** Therefore, because Mrs. Rosier cannot be deemed a creditor under the Act, and also because Stearl Rosier was not insolvent as a result of making the conveyance at issue, this Court determines that the conveyance of the 139–acre farm to Robert Lee Rosier by Stearl Rosier was not a fraudulent conveyance under the Uniform Fraudulent Transfers Act.")

division. This was so even though the spouse claimed she was not fully aware of the transfers and was defined as a vanishing spouse. The court focused on the fact that the husband was not a beneficiary of the trust:

> The trial court determined after a lengthy bench trial that Husband's transfers of property to the Trusts were not fraudulent. The trial court properly cited OCGA §18-2-74 (b), which provided a non-exclusive list of factors, or "badges of fraud" that might be considered in determining the existence of actual intent to defraud under the former UFTA. The trial court made factual findings to the effect that several of these factors weighed against concluding that Husband intended to defraud Wife, finding that Husband did not actively conceal the transfers from Wife, did not retain possession or control of the assets transferred, did not transfer substantially all of his assets or become insolvent after the transfers, and did not abscond. There is evidence to support these findings, and they are sufficient to support the trial court's ultimate conclusion that the creation and funding of the Trusts was not fraudulent.[59]

Although communication might be lacking between couples who eventually divorce, communication about estate planning prior to divorce might save the estate plan from fraudulent transfer attack.

> *In re* Marriage of Frederick, 218 Ill. App. 3d 533 (1991), on which John relies, is inapposite. In that case, this court, relying on the supreme court's analysis in Johnson, recognized that even an "ostensibly valid" trust may actually be a "sham transaction" to defraud a spouse's marital rights. *Id.* at 536. The husband in Frederick convinced his wife to sign a letter agreeing that property they had just put into a revocable trust would not be marital property. *Id.* at 538-39. The husband misrepresented "the true nature of the letter" to the wife, telling her that it was to protect the trust for the children so that neither one of them could challenge the trust in a divorce. *Id.* at 535, 538-39. In fact, however, the husband, as trustee, could revoke, terminate, or modify the trust at any time. *Id.* at 536. In addition, the husband hid from the wife that he had already consulted a divorce attorney when the trust was created, and he asked her to sign the letter. *Id.* at 537-39. In that case, the court found that the husband had an intent to defraud the wife and that the transfer of land into a trust was "illusory and created to defeat [the wife's] marital rights to the property in a dissolution proceeding." *Id.* at 539.
>
> ¶ 57 There are no similar facts in this case. Ellen told John she wanted to file for divorce approximately a year before the estate planning began, Ellen did not possess any powers that were unknown to John, and Ellen did not misrepresent the terms of the trusts.[60]

Tax planning may drive the desire to move assets into trusts or entities such as family limited partnerships (FLP). In one case, the stated desire was to fund

59. *Gibson v. Gibson*, No. S17F0593, 2017 WL 2417057, at *5 (Ga. June 5, 2017).
60. *Reidy v. Reidy*, 2021 Ill. App. 200733, 16 (Ill. App. Ct. 2021).

an FLP to protect assets from a former spouse in the event of a divorce.[61] While the goal behind documenting such intent might be to fend off an attack from the IRS challenging the FLP's economic substance, this documentation could be used as evidence to "hinder, delay or defraud any creditor" in a fraudulent transfer action.

In *Vanderlugt v. Vanderlugt*,[62] the court had to determine whether assets held in an irrevocable life insurance trust (ILIT) were divisible as community property where neither spouse was a trustee or beneficiary. Like the court in *Gibson*, the wife's status as a beneficiary disappeared upon divorce.[63] The *Vanderlugt* court found the funds were not subject to division because there was no evidence of an improper purpose or fraudulent transfer. The potentially fraudulent transfers to the ILIT, which permitted payment of the policy premium, were treated by both spouses as gifts on their tax return. "The parties regarded the community funds used to pay the life insurance premiums as gifts and treated them as such for tax purposes. No argument has been made that Husband set up the Trust for an improper or fraudulent purpose, or that he made any fraudulent transfers to the Trust for the purpose of safeguarding assets from division in the divorce." Consequently, spousal consent to gift-splitting on a gift tax return may be used to show a legitimate non-fraudulent transfer motivated purpose.

Where both spouses have engaged in planning to divide their estates through the use of APTs (one for each spouse), a Nevada court held that the transfers will be respected and are not part of the marital estate. *Klabacka v. Nelson* illustrates how the spouse was an active participant in the division of community property as well as the potential for successfully creating and using an APT in certain circumstances.[64]

Estate planners need to consider the impact that creating an irrevocable trust can have, not only for tax and estate disposition purposes, but also for potential fraudulent transfer purposes where a spouse may be removed as a

---

61. *See Keller v. United States*, No. CIV.A. V-02-62, 2009 WL 2601611, at *19 (S.D. Tex. Aug. 20, 2009), aff'd, 697 F.3d 238 (5th Cir. 2012), and aff'd, 697 F.3d 238 (5th Cir. 2012) ("Mrs. Williams' transfer of the Community Property Bonds to the Partnership was a bona fide sale. First, the lengthy discussions that went into creating the Partnership Agreement, which Mrs. Williams signed, provide sufficient objective evidence that the Partnership transaction was 'real, actual, genuine, and not feigned.' Kimbell, 371 F.3d at 263. Second, the primary purpose underlying the Partnership's formation was to protect family assets from depletion by ex-spouses through divorce proceedings. This was accomplished by creating an entity that, by altering the legal relationship between Mrs. Williams and her heirs, could facilitate the administration of significant family assets. In other words, the creation and funding of the Partnership was undertaken for a legitimate business purpose and not the mere 'recycling' of wealth.")

62. Pete Vanderlugt, Petitioner-Appellant, v. Kristina Vanderlugt, n/k/a Kristina Cervantes, Respondent-Appellee., No. A-1-CA-35260, 2018 WL 4275373 (N.M. Ct. App. Sept. 5, 2018).

63. *Id.* ("Wife is also not a beneficiary or a trustee and has no property interest in the Trust because she lost her beneficiary status upon divorce.")

64. *See Klabacka v. Nelson*, 133 Nev. 164, 178, 394 P.3d 940, 951 (2017). ("We conclude Nevada SSSTs are protected against the court-ordered child-support or spousal-support obligations of the settlor/beneficiary that are not known at the time the trust is created. Here, Eric's child- and spousal-support obligations were not known at the time the trust was created. Accordingly, the district court abused its discretion in ordering Eric's Trust to pay Eric's child- and spousal-support arrears. We further conclude the child- and spousal-support exception articulated in section 59 of the Third Restatement of Trusts is inconsistent with Nevada's statutory framework and the legislative history of NRS Chapter 166, and we expressly reject that exception here.")

beneficiary. Generally, a transfer by one spouse to a third party, such as a trustee of a trust, should be respected if both parties are aware of the transfer and one spouse is not treated differently than the other spouse.[65] However, anything short of this scenario is fair game for potential avoidance in a divorce action. Even if a court determines that a spouse does not attain creditor status for purposes of voiding pre-divorce transfers, a divorce courts sits in equity and may fashion a fair result if the transfer was done to deprive the other spouse an interest in marital property.[66] The effect of wealth transfer on marital property rights also underscores the importance of securing independent counsel to review and approve transactions that might be unfair to one spouse.

## *Marital Settlement Agreements & Sham Divorces*

Fraudulent transfer issues might arise in the context of marital settlement agreements (MSA) as such agreements have been held by numerous courts[67] to be subject to fraudulent transfer law. Such was the case for the California Supreme Court, where it ruled that spouses may not use an MSA to defraud creditors. "In view of this overall policy of protecting creditors, it is unlikely that the Legislature intended to grant married couples a one-time-only opportunity to defraud creditors by including the fraudulent transfer in an MSA."[68]

While the true motivation behind a requested divorce might not be apparent to some advisors, *In re Wolf* provided a fairly simple formula for MSA avoidance (and denial of discharge). "Start with an unfortunate, unsophisticated—yet untruthful—debtor. Add the transfer of the debtor's properties to his wife, while facing a large judgment. Divide by a rushed uncontested divorce. Multiply by a bankruptcy filing where there is an attempted cover-up. The net result: the properties are recoverable as fraudulent transfers and the debtor's discharge is denied."[69]

---

65. It is essential to review the powers granted to another individual and whether such powers may be exercised for the benefit of one spouse to the detriment of the other spouse.

66. *See Thames v. Thames*, 191 Mich. App. 299, 302, 477 N.W.2d 496, 499 (1991). ("Generally, a court has no authority to adjudicate the rights of third parties in divorce actions. Id., at p. 146, 443 N.W.2d 464. An exception to the general rule exists when it is claimed that a third party has conspired with one spouse to deprive the other spouse of an interest in the marital estate. Id. See also anno: Propriety of consideration of, and disposition as to, third persons' property claims in divorce litigation, 63 ALR3d 373. The court, therefore, has authority to find that assets were fraudulently transferred to a third party to deprive a spouse of an interest in marital property. It follows that another exception exists for situations like the one before us. One spouse cannot deprive the other of an interest in the marital estate by transferring marital property into a trust for the benefit of a third party.")

67. *See Mejia v. Reed,* 31 Cal. 4th 657, 664, 74 P.3d 166, 170–71 (2003). ("[M]ost decisions of other states construing parallel provisions of the UFTA hold that it does apply to marital property transfers, including those in connection with divorce. (*See, e.g., Scholes v. Lehmann* (7th Cir.1995) 56 F.3d 750, 758–759 [applying Ill. law]; *Kardynalski v. Fisher* (1985) 135 Ill.App.3d 643, 90 Ill.Dec. 410, 482 N.E.2d 117, 121–122; *Dowell v. Dennis* (Okla.Ct.App.2000) 998 P.2d 206, 209, 212–213; *Greeninger v. Cromwell* (1996) 140 Or.App. 241, 915 P.2d 479, 482; *see also Federal Deposit Ins. Co. v. Malin* (2d Cir.1986) 802 F.2d 12, 18 [under New York law, UFTA **171 applies but ex-wife was good faith purchaser for value]; but see Britt v. Damson (9th Cir.1964) 334 F.2d 896, 901 [Wash. law]; *Witbart v. Witbart* (1983) 204 Mont. 446, 666 P.2d 1217, 1219.)")

68. *Mejia v. Reed,* 31 Cal. 4th 657, 668, 74 P.3d 166, 173 (2003).

69. *In re Wolf,* No. 15-31477-HCM, 2016 WL 4940198, at *1 (Bankr. W.D. Tex. Sept. 15, 2016). ("There are several irregular and peculiar circumstances surrounding the Divorce Proceeding and entry of the Divorce

Collusion between spouses may sometimes require a severe sacrifice to protect assets from creditors; numerous cases involve a married couple's strategic decision to divide up assets in divorce as an attempt to prevent creditors from reaching the same assets. In a sense, this is no different than a secret trust, only the spouses involve the courts to achieve this result.

> In this action, Plaintiffs allege that Defendants Rick and Lisa Rizzolo engaged in fraudulent transfers of their assets in an attempt to shield them from Plaintiffs' claim. Plaintiffs allege that shortly after the Henrys filed the underlying suit in October 2001, Rick and Lisa Rizzolo formed a "so-called 'family trust'" to which they transferred their assets. Second Amended Complaint (# 200), ¶ 17. Plaintiffs further allege that the Rizzolos entered into a sham 2005 divorce decree which awarded Lisa Rizzolo "nearly every listed community asset" except for the Crazy Horse Too, which Defendants knew would be subject to forfeiture to the Government. *Id.*, ¶ 19. Rick Rizzolo also allegedly agreed to pay Lisa Rizzolo $5 million in alimony, secured by his interest in the Crazy Horse Too, with the knowledge that he would default on this obligation and thereby further diminish the assets that would be available to pay damages to the Henrys. *Id.*, ¶¶ 21–22. Plaintiffs also allege that Rick Rizzolo "engaged in numerous cash transactions involving millions of dollars in the form of 'loans,' gambling 'debts' and other third-party transactions, all of which were designed to further obscure and conceal the nature, extent, and location of his assets." *Id.*, ¶ 23. Defendants deny these allegations and assert that the Crazy Horse Too business was worth substantially more than the property received by Lisa Rizzolo in the divorce. Defendants also argue that proceeds from a forfeiture sale of the Crazy Horse Too would have been sufficient to pay the Henrys' settlement, but for the Government's failure to preserve its business licenses.[70]

## *Creation of Marital Property*

Because certain forms of marital property provide some degree of protection from creditors, the transfer of assets into a marital unit is often challenged on fraudulent transfer grounds. One example involves the creation of TBE property; such property is protected from the claims of the creditors of one spouse, so long as the couple maintains marriage. But the creation of TBE property typically requires satisfying certain unities before attaining TBE status.

---

Decree in the year 2014. First, Abie effectively 'sandbagged' in the Divorce Proceeding—Abie did not appear at the Divorce Proceeding and voluntarily waived notice and participation in the proceeding on June 19, 2014 (about one month after the Starr Judgment was rendered against Abie). In substance, Abie let Rema take whatever assets Rema wanted in the divorce. This also appears to be a 'rush' divorce pushed by Rema. The divorce petition was filed by Rema against Abie immediately after the Starr Judgment was entered. The Divorce Decree was submitted for entry by the court on August 20, 2014 (soon after the statutorily required waiting period). The divorce was so rushed that the Divorce Decree (signed by Rema but not Abie) contains inaccurate and garbled legal descriptions. The Divorce Decree and the docket in the Divorce Proceeding state that the Divorce Decree was an 'Agreed Judgment,' yet only Rema signed the Divorce Decree.")

70. *Henry v. Rizzolo*, No. 2:08-CV-00635-PMP, 2010 WL 3385448, at *1 (D. Nev. Aug. 24, 2010).

Thus, if a debtor claims property as TBE and immune from a creditor's claim, the creditor must determine whether all unities were present at the time of the TBE creation. Once property attains TBE status, further transfer of such property can be made without triggering fraudulent transfer law. In a sense, TBE status can wash an asset so it can be transferred subsequently in a fashion that would make collection much more difficult, perhaps into an LLC (limiting a creditor to a charging order), to the trustee of an asset protection trust,[71] to a foreign trustee, etc. Some states have made it easier to establish TBE status, especially regarding real estate, often relaxing the creation requirements and expanding the types of property eligible for this status. Lobbyists for the creditors' rights industry should be mindful of any proposed expansion of TBE status that could result in the inconspicuous depletion of available assets.[72]

## Business Planning

Typical business planning transactions often can trigger fraudulent transfer law. Evidence of intent with respect to transactions involving an entity can be gleaned from direct evidence,[73] but, like transactions involving individuals, is often gleaned from facts and circumstances. Resorting to the use of a business entity to hinder or delay creditors may result in avoidance under fraudulent transfer law.

In 1932, the Supreme Court decided a case involving a Pennsylvania lumber dealer who was unable to pay his debts as they came due and whose creditors were seeking payment. The dealer believed he could retain assets if a receiver was appointed. However, Pennsylvania did not permit the appointment of a receiver for a business conducted by an individual as distinguished from one conducted by a corporation. Consequently, the Pennsylvania dealer formed a Delaware corporation, then transferred all his assets in exchange for all the stock. The new corporation also assumed all the dealer's debts. The dealer then sued in conjunction with a creditor against the new corporation.

---

71. Delaware enacted a statutory tenancy by entireties trust, which attempts to preserve the TBE status of property in another state while held in trust by a Delaware trustee.

72. A proposal was made to enact a Florida statute that would have eliminated the unities of time and title as to transfers from one spouse to both spouses as tenants by the entireties. This proposal was ultimately rejected.

73. *Fish v. East*, 114 F.2d 177, 182 (10th Cir. 1940). ("The court found that an additional object of making that lease and organizing the Placers Company to receive the grant or demise as lessee was 'to hinder and delay creditors' of the Mines Company, direct evidence of such fact being found in the minutes of the meeting of the board of directors of the bankrupt held November 2, 1932, at which a resolution was adopted to the effect that the stock of the Placers Company should be issued to Edward Cunningham, Erland F. Fish, and John A. Traylor, as trustees for the Mines Company, and the president of the Placers Company, stating that one of the reasons for this arrangement was that it was desired to have the stock 'out of the name of Mines Company, so it could not be attached.' In re Holbrook Shoe & Leather Co., D.C., 165 F. 973; In re Looschen Piano Case Co., D.C., 261 F. 93; Shapiro v. Wilgus, 287 U.S. 348, 53 S.Ct. 142, 77 L.Ed. 355, 85 A.L.R. 128.")

Justice Cardozo noted the transfer to the corporation was fraudulent as well as the resulting receivership because it was part and parcel of a scheme whereby the form of a judicial remedy was to supply a protective cover for a fraudulent design. "A conveyance is illegal if made with an intent to defraud the creditors of the grantor, but equally it is illegal if made with an intent to hinder and delay them. Many an embarrassed debtor holds the genuine belief that, if suits can be staved off for a season, he will weather a financial storm, and pay his debts in full. *Means v. Dowd*, 128 U.S. 273, 281, 9 S.Ct. 65, 32 L.Ed. 429. The belief even though well founded, does not clothe him with a privilege to build up obstructions that will hold his creditors at bay."[74]

## *Limited liability companies*

Because the asset protection trust is laced with evidence of intent to hinder creditors ab initio, the use of a limited liability company is tempting because it enjoys a disguise as a valid business entity unrelated to the owner's personal creditor issues. However, if a creditor can show a debtor fraudulently transferred assets to an LLC (e.g., through a contribution of capital), the transfer to the LLC may be voided, just as a fraudulent transfer to a trustee of a trust may be voided.[75] To the surprise of some planners, a contribution of capital in exchange for membership interests does not necessarily equate to "reasonably equivalent value."[76]

The limited liability company, and its charging order protection preventing creditors from reaching a member's distribution until the LLC makes a distribution, is expressly permitted by most state laws. In a minority of states, an LLC need not have more than one member but still provide charging order protection. With an LLC, a veil of protection is created so that a business owner's individual assets are protected from the claims of creditors of the business (inside creditors).[77] This protection helps promote entrepreneurial spirit and is long recognized by the courts. "After all, there is nothing fraudulent or against

74. *Shapiro v. Wilgus*, 287 U.S. 348, 354, 53 S. Ct. 142, 144, 77 L. Ed. 355 (1932).

75. *See SE Prop. Holdings, LLC v. McElheney*, No. 5:12CV164-MW/EMT, 2016 WL 7494300, at *11 (N.D. Fla. May 7, 2016). ("For Crestmark, it appears at this point that there is nothing to garnish—there is no debt owed to McElheney individually by the LLC. But SE Property may be able to garnish assets of Crest-mark if it can show that McElheney transferred those assets to Crestmark fraudulently.")

76. *See, e.g., Interpool Ltd. v. Patterson*, 890 F. Supp. 259, 265-66 (S.D.N.Y. 1995) ("The contribution by Cuneo of all or substantially all of his non-exempt assets to RMC in exchange for general and limited partnership interests in an entity of which he and his wife are the sole partners, even disregarding the subsequent transfer of the limited partnership interest that the Court already has set aside, left him substantially judgment proof. A judgment creditor can do no more than levy upon Cuneo's interest in the partnership, which is defined by statute as his right to receive distributions, the amount and timing of which would remain in control of Cuneo and his wife, from the entity. Thus, the judgment creditor would be entitled to sell at auction the right to receive such sums as Cuneo and his wife might choose to distribute to the successful purchaser. This makes the transfer constructively fraudulent as to Interpool irrespective of the law applied.")

77. *See generally*, Thomas O. Wells & Jordi Guso, *Asset Protection Proofing Your Limited Partnership or LLC for the Bankruptcy of A Partner or Member*, Fla. B.J., January 2007, at 34. ("An FLP has two types of creditors — inside creditors and outside creditors. Inside creditor claims arise from alleged actions or omissions of the FLP. Inside creditors may levy against the assets of an FLP, but generally cannot levy against the individual assets of limited partners or members of the FLP. Outside creditor claims arise from alleged

public policy in limiting one's liability by the appropriate use of corporate insulation."[78] But where the LLC is used as a trust substitute to protect assets from a member's personal creditors, the member's concern is not creditors of the business, but rather, the debtor's personal creditors (outside creditors.)

## LLCs as Trust Substitutes

Conceptually, the LLC is developing into a variant of the self-settled trust, where the rights of members and creditors are handled primarily by statutes, which in turn, permit the parties to do as they please under an operating agreement. This contrasts with centuries of developed case law and modern statutes adopting the case law as it applies to the use of trusts. With trust law, certain safeguards developed over time to protect creditors, the most obvious being the centuries old rule against self-settled trusts, which essentially provides one cannot use a trust to have his cake and eat it, too. The LLC and the law of contract, coupled with the benefit of not having to account to beneficiaries, are options for some to sidestep centuries of trust law and its protections for creditors and beneficiaries alike.

Today, some may attempt to enjoy the benefits of a self-settled trust in the form of an LLC. Managers can make decisions instead of trustees. The tax treatment can be replicated as well. A self-settled trust is usually treated as a so-called grantor trust in tax parlance, meaning the settlor pays the income tax on trust income. The LLC achieves the same result where it has a single member. This is because the default classification of a single-member LLC, for federal tax purposes, is to treat the LLC as disregarded (meaning all the tax consequences flow through to the member.)

The concept of a charging order has roots in trust law. At its core, a charging order is a lien on a debtor's interest where a creditor has to wait for distributions to be made from a third party to the debtor before seizing the distributed property.[79] In the trust setting, generally a court does not refer to this lien as a "charging order" but instead enters an order permitting a creditor to attach present and future mandatory distributions due to a trust beneficiary. If the trust is discretionary, a court may enter an order permitting garnishment of distributions when made in the discretion of a trustee.[80]

---

actions or omissions by a debtor partner of the FLP. This article's focus is on the rights of outside creditors to the debtor partner's interest in the FLP.")

78. *See Miller v. Honda Motor Co.*, 779 F.2d 769, 773 (1st Cir. 1985).

79. *See* Loring and Rounds, Section 5.3.3.3(a). ("A creditor is then left with little recourse other than perhaps to attempt to obtain a judicial charging order that, if granted, might snare any discretionary distributions actually made to the beneficiary." citing *Hamilton v. Drogo*, 241 N.Y. 401, 401, 150 N.E. 496 (1926) ("By the enactment of section 684 of the Civil Practice Act, providing that an execution may issue against a certain proportion of income from trust funds due and owing, or thereafter to become due and owing to a judgment debtor, it was the intention of the Legislature to extend the scope and effect of an execution as it had theretofore existed. There is no requirement that the income be due at the time the order is made and the execution served. It is enough either that it will become due in the future from the trustee to the cestui que trust, or that it may become so due. If ever the day of payment arrives the lien of the execution attaches.")

80. Historically, a beneficiary has a "reachable" interest in a trust when the interest has vested. This may occur when an event occurs such as the death of a lifetime beneficiary where the debtor-beneficiary receives the trust corpus outright, or when a trustee has decided to make a distribution in favor of the debtor-

> According to section 736.0504(2), a former spouse may not compel a distribution that is subject to the trustee's discretion or attach or otherwise reach the interest, if any, which the beneficiary may have. The section does not expressly prohibit a former spouse from obtaining a writ of garnishment against discretionary disbursements made by a trustee exercising its discretion. As a result, it makes no difference that the instant trusts are discretionary. Casselberry is not seeking an order compelling a distribution that is subject to the trustee's discretion or attaching the beneficiary's interest. Instead, she obtained an order granting writs of garnishment against discretionary disbursements made by a trustee exercising its discretion.[81]

Where the trust is self-settled, generally, a creditor may reach the maximum amount that could be distributed to the settlor. Where a debtor does not contribute assets to a trustee but is merely a discretionary beneficiary of the trust (referred to as a third-party trust), the beneficiary's interest generally is protected from creditors, at least until distributions are made.[82]

Contrast with the LLC, which essentially takes a best of both worlds approach; the debtor-member may contribute assets to the LLC much like the debtor would a self-settled trust, however, the debtor-member is essentially treated as a beneficiary of a third-party trust because the LLC charging order statutes permit a creditor to reach distributions only if made by the LLC.[83] If the LLC was treated like the self-settled trust, a creditor could, like a creditor of a beneficiary of a self-settled trust, take the maximum amount distributable to the member. With an LLC, this would mean foreclosing on the member's interest, voting the member's interest, etc.

But the LLC is not a trust; the LLC is a business entity. The charging order for purposes of trust law was meant to ensure a beneficiary could not thwart a creditor by enjoying the benefits of a trust despite an obligation to creditors. For LLCs (and partnerships), the charging order is justified on the grounds that a creditor should not step into the debtor's shoes as a member of the LLC. Instead, the creditor may receive the same economic benefits the debtor member enjoyed. The goal with the LLC charging order is to prevent the

---

beneficiary. An interest may vest in a debtor-beneficiary but be non-possessory; in this situation, a creditor may reach the property unless state law provides otherwise. (*See* Ariz. Rev. Stat. Ann. §14-10506. "Whether or not a trust contains a spendthrift provision, a creditor or assignee of a beneficiary may reach a mandatory distribution of income or principal if the trustee has not made the distribution to the beneficiary within a reasonable period after the mandated distribution date *unless the terms of the trust expressly authorize the trustee to delay the distribution to protect the beneficiary's interest in the distribution.*")

81. *Berlinger v. Casselberry*, 133 So. 3d 961, 965–66 (Fla. Dist. Ct. App. 2013).

82. *See, e.g., Hamilton v. Drogo*, 241 N.Y. 401, 150 N.E. 496 (1926). ("In the present case no income may ever become due to the judgment debtor. We may not interfere with the discretion which the testatrix has vested in the trustee any more than her son may do so. Its judgment is final. But at least annually this judgment must be exercised. And if it is exercised in favor of the duke then there is due him the whole or such part of the income as the trustee may allot to him. After such allotment he may compel its payment. At least for some appreciable time, however brief, the award must precede the delivery of the income he is to receive and during that time the lien of the execution attaches.")

83. Transfers to an LLC are subject to avoidance under fraudulent transfer law. Florida's charging order statute also expressly refers to fraudulent transfer relief. *See* Florida Statute Section 605.0503(7)(b). ("This section does not limit any of the following: *** The principles of law and equity which affect fraudulent transfers.")

creditor from interrupting other members of the LLC in conducting LLC business. But if there is no business other than dodging creditors, the public policy supporting the charging order weakens.

The law in some jurisdictions is written in a way that makes it difficult to disregard public policy. Like choice of law disputes in the trust context, debtors also attempt to hardwire the governing law of an operating agreement to force creditors to play by the rules of debtor-friendly states or countries.

In sum, the LLC is increasingly being used as a quasi-trust with the goal of protecting a member's assets from the member's personal creditors. Consequently, creditors who engage in discovery will look for evidence of the LLC serving as a personal use vehicle. This may lead to a court viewing the LLC as an alter ego or sham, permitting the creditor to reach the assets. Not only can general creditors rely on personal use evidence to reach assets, but the lack of a true business purpose can have negative consequences for federal tax law purposes.

## *Capital Contributions*

In some cases, the contribution of an asset to a business entity is not meant to assist with business operations but instead intended to help the owner insulate the transferred asset from the claims of the owner's creditors. Fraudulent transfer law provides a creditor with an opportunity to challenge the transfer of assets to a business entity.

In *Firmani v. Firmani*, the court reviewed debtor's argument that the transfers to an LLC were made not to hinder a creditor, but for estate planning purposes. The court did not buy the excuse and found the transfer to the LLC to be fraudulent under an actual fraud analysis.

> Defendants failed to present any substantial evidence to counter the strong inference of fraudulent intent established by these badges of fraud. Firmani submitted a certification which asserted that he established the Family Partnership and conveyed the Haddonfield property to this entity for "estate planning purposes." However, we are unable to discern from Firmani's certification how the transaction could have served any estate planning purposes, except by increasing the total amount of his estate by the $25,000 he seeks to avoid paying plaintiff and by the amounts of the judgments that certain casinos have against him. In any event, N.J.S.A. 25:2–25(a) does not require that an intent to hinder, delay, or defraud a creditor be the exclusive motivation behind a transfer in order for the transfer to be deemed fraudulent.[84]

If more than one person transfers assets to an LLC, but only one person is a debtor, such that his transfer is voidable by a creditor, it should not matter if the transaction involved a non-debtor; one cannot insulate a fraudulent transfer by

84. *Firmani v. Firmani*, 332 N.J. Super. 118, 123, 752 A.2d 854, 857–58 (App. Div. 2000).

arguing the avoidance would complicate matters or affect another person's interest. Such was the case in *First Citizens Bank & Trust Co., Inc. v. Park at Durbin Creek, LLC*, where the debtor transferred his 50 percent interest in real property, together with the other 50 percent owner (Whiteman), to PDC, LLC. It should be noted that debtor offered evidence of his intent, which included legitimate business planning, to no avail.[85] Despite the complications of unwinding a transfer to an LLC where some members do not have fraudulent intent, the court ruled in favor of the creditor:

> Accordingly, we find the conveyances of Whiteman's 50 percent interest and Clifton's 50 percent interest to PDC were each distinct transfers that Whiteman and Clifton merely chose to accomplish in a single deed. The fact they utilized one instrument to transfer their separate interests does not negate the distinct ownership interest each person possessed in the Property. As mutually exclusive conveyances, we also find that the invalidity of one does not necessarily invalidate the other. To that end, Whiteman's intent in transferring her share of the Property to PDC is irrelevant to the circuit court's finding of fraudulent intent as to Clifton. Clifton's proportional interest is subject to the claims of his creditors, and he cannot legitimize the fraudulent transfer of his interest by lumping it together with Whiteman's presumably valid transfer of her interest. Regardless of the parties' choice of instrument to convey the Property, we find the circuit court properly set aside the conveyance pursuant to the Statute of Elizabeth.[86]

The transfer of assets to an LLC may be viewed as a badge of fraud where the debtor removed assets by transferring to an LLC to enjoy charging order protection.[87] The Official Comments to the UVTA also

85. *See First Citizens Bank & Trust Co., Inc. v. Park at Durbin Creek, LLC*, 419 S.C. 333, 342, 797 S.E.2d 409, 414 (Ct. App. 2017), *reh'g denied* (Mar. 16, 2017). ("At trial, Clifton asserted he transferred the Property to PDC at the insistence of Whiteman. Clifton testified that Whiteman was 'hammering' him every day to place the Property into an LLC based on her fear of the liability associated with the Property being used for recreational hunting. Renee Gilreath, Clifton's daughter, also testified they transferred the Property to PDC based on Whiteman's liability concerns as well as for legitimate business purposes.")

86. *First Citizens Bank & Trust Co., Inc. v. Park at Durbin Creek, LLC*, 419 S.C. 333, 344, 797 S.E.2d 409, 415 (Ct. App. 2017), reh'g denied (Mar. 16, 2017). (Emphasis added.)

87. *Firmani v. Firmani*, 332 N.J. Super. 118, 122–23, 752 A.2d 854, 857 (App. Div. 2000). (Firmani's conveyance of the Haddonfield property to the Family Partnership manifested at least five of the "badges of fraud: set forth in N.J.S.A. 25:2–26. Defendant was the sole general partner and primary limited partner of the Family Partnership prior to the conveyance, and therefore the conveyance was made to an insider. N.J.S.A. 25:2–26(a); see Gilchinsky, *supra*, 159 N.J. at 478–79, 732 A.2d 482. By continuing to use the Haddonfield property as a residence and place of business, and as the sole general partner with a total ninety-five percent interest in the Family Partnership, defendant clearly retained possession or control of the property after the conveyance. N.J.S.A. 25:2–26(b). Firmani does not dispute that he was aware that the $25,000 had become due to plaintiff, and therefore he knew or should have known that absent voluntary payment, an enforcement action *123 probably would be brought. N.J.S.A. 25:2–26(d). By putting plaintiff in a position where she could only recover the money owed through the Limited Partnership charging process, defendant "remove . . . assets." N.J.S.A. 25:2–26(g); see Gilchinsky, *supra*, 159 N.J. at 479, 732 A.2d 482 ("[I]n transferring assets from New York to New Jersey [where more debtor-protective IRA laws exist], defendant effectively prevented them from being attached by [her creditor].").

address the intersection between charging order protection and fraudulent transfer law.[88]

In *Interpool*, the debtor, Cuneo, transferred non-exempt assets to an LLC (RMC). The RMC interests were then transferred to a trust (RAC). The court examined the transfers under both New York and Florida fraudulent transfer law, finding their holding would have been the same, regardless of the applicable law because there was no conflict between the state laws. As is typical in wealth transfer transactions challenged under fraudulent transfer law, the debtor argued he was motivated by non-creditor reasons. This did not persuade the court to find in the debtor's favor.

> Cuneo was deposed in March 1995 in connection with the proceedings to enforce the judgment. His explanation for the challenged transfers was unilluminating. He was unable, or chose not, to explain how he and his wife determined what property to transfer into RMC and RAC or why the transfers were made other than to say that he "picked stuff that [he] thought had a worth to it" and that he did so on the advice of counsel for "estate planning" reasons. He testified that he did what [Attorney] suggested and that he "assume[d] that it had to do with tax purposes if [he] die[d]." But he did not articulate any specific reasons why he believed the transfers to be advantageous.[89]

As to whether the membership interests received in exchange for non-exempt assets constituted reasonably equivalent value, the court did not focus on the LLC's value, and thus, the potential value of the LLC interests Cuneo received in exchange for his assets. Instead, the court focused on a creditor's rights to the property that was transferred. In other words, the court examined a creditor's rights before and after the transaction in determining the value of the debtor's asset from the creditor's perspective.

> The contribution by Cuneo of all or substantially all of his non-exempt assets to RMC in exchange for general and limited *266 partnership interests in an entity of which he and his wife are the sole partners, even disregarding the subsequent transfer of the limited partnership interest that the Court already has set aside, left him substantially judgment proof. A judgment creditor can do no more than levy upon Cuneo's interest in the partnership, which is defined by statute as his right to receive distributions, the amount and timing of which would remain in control of Cuneo and his wife, from the entity. Thus, the judgment creditor would be entitled to sell at auction the right to receive such sums as Cuneo and his wife might choose to distribute to the successful purchaser. This makes the transfer constructively fraudulent as to Interpool irrespective of the law applied.

---

88. See Comment 8 to UVTA Section 4. ("Likewise, it is voidable for a debtor intentionally to hinder creditors by transferring assets to a wholly-owned corporation or other organization, as may be the case if the equity interest in the organization is more difficult to realize upon than the assets (either because the equity interest is less liquid, or because the applicable procedural rules are more demanding). See, e.g., Addison v. Tessier, 335 P.2d 554, 557 (N.M. 1959); First Nat'l Bank. v. F. C. Trebein Co., 52 N.E. 834, 837-38 (Ohio 1898); Anno., 85 A.L.R. 133 (1933).")

89. *Interpool Ltd. v. Patterson*, 890 F. Supp. 259, 263 (S.D.N.Y. 1995).

*Interpool* can be contrasted with *United States v. Holland*, where the debtor transferred assets to a limited liability company but remained the sole member. The transfer of assets to a single-member LLC, where the governing law does not provide single-member charging order protection, is akin to the transfer of assets to a revocable trust.

> The US contests this characterization, contending that, when compared to the prospect of garnishing the Royalty Assets, the 1998 Transaction left Holland's creditors with "the far less appealing recourse of seizing [Holland's] partnership interest (which is subject to major partnership-level debts)." (Doc. 310, p. 7). In this connection, the US asserts that "a conveyance is not an exchange for equivalent value when it makes the debtor 'execution proof.'" (Id.). In support, the US cites Interpool Ltd. v. Patterson, 890 F.Supp. 259 (S.D.N.Y. 1995), in which a debtor-husband transferred assets to a partnership jointly owned by his wife, and Dunn v. Minnema, 323 Mich. 687, 36 N.W.2d 182, 184 (1949), in which a debtor-husband "invest [ed] of $9,600 of his personal assets in property to which he and his wife held title by the entireties."
>
> Under the particular facts of this case, the transfer to EHLP did not make Holland "execution proof" because, unlike the debtors at issue in Interpool and Dunn, Holland was the sole owner of the assignee entity, EHLP. Accordingly, seizing Holland's partnership shares would, apparently, enable a creditor to reach the Royalty Assets. The US is correct that, under this scenario, the Royalty Assets would be subject to "partnership-level debts." However, because Holland received the benefit of such partnership-level debts in the form of the Note proceeds, this factor is of no avail to the US. If Holland had simply left the Note proceeds in his bank account, his creditors would have been no worse off—they could garnish the cash and recover the remaining value of the Royalty Assets upon repayment of the Notes.
>
> In view of these factors, the 1998 Transaction and 2005 Transaction did not significantly hinder Holland's creditors. Accordingly, the transfer did not result in the type of "wrong" that would support a finding that (i) that EHLP held title to the Royalty Assets as Holland's nominee, (ii) that Holland fraudulently conveyed the Royalty Assets to EHLP, or (iii) that EHLP is the alter ego of Holland. Because the US demonstrates no basis for attaching property held by EHLP, the Court must deny its motion for summary judgment.[90]

*United States v. Holland* illustrates why some states have enacted statutes providing charging order protection for a single-member limited liability company. The LLC becomes a quasi-exemption debtors may use to avoid paying their personal creditors. Like the asset protection trust, the single-member LLC offering charging order protection presents public policy issues relevant to fraudulent transfer law and choice of law for debtors attempting to import protections into their own state against their personal creditors.

90. *United States v. Holland*, No. 213CV10082MOBMKM, 2017 WL 4676607, at *5 (E.D. Mich. Sept. 12, 2017).

Although avoiding a transfer to a business entity has an impact on the business and its owners, this is of no consequence if the transfer is fraudulent. As previously addressed, some have argued that it is unfair to other business entity owners if a creditor may void a transfer to the business entity by a debtor. This argument has also been used in the trust context, where some maintain it is not fair to void a transfer to a trust if the debtor created rights in third parties (via beneficial interest.) Like the choice of law in a trust agreement, or avoidance of a transfer to a self-settled trust, a creditor who has been injured and seeks relief under fraudulent transfer law is not always held subject to rules created in advance by a debtor. Stated differently, a debtor cannot transfer assets to an entity or trustee, muddy the ownership rights to such property by creating rights in third parties (often insiders), and then expect these third-party interests will automatically defeat a creditor.

If business entities are utilized to effectuate a fraudulent transfer, there is a risk that the court will disregard the business entity. This could have the effect of rendering the individual who controls the business entity liable as transferee. For example, *In re Pace* featured an attorney who helped his client (the debtor) transfer assets to an LLC controlled by the attorney. This was done to avoid the debtor's creditors. The court held the LLC was the initial transferee, and further found that the attorney, due to his participation, was jointly liable and might have been considered the person for whose benefit the transfer was made.[91] As discussed in the civil liability section of this book, lawyers must be careful as to their degree of involvement in fraudulent transfers.

## *Distributions to Pay Business Owner Taxes*

In some cases, a company's distributions to its owners to satisfy the owners' tax obligations associated with their respective ownership interests has been attacked as fraudulent transfers. Several cases support an entity making these payments where it was bargained for by the company owners and the creditors are not worse off. "Trustee relies heavily on SGK Ventures, which summarily concludes that a tax distribution is equivalent to a corporate dividend and can never be for reasonably equivalent value. SGK is not persuasive. It did not involve a conversion from a C-Corp to an LLC or a subchapter S election premised on the payment to members/shareholders of funds to pay any pass-through tax liability, nor did it discuss such a scenario. And, the scant analysis provided is conclusory.

As in Northlake and Kenrob, the tax distributions are inextricably linked to the LLC conversion that spawned them, and under the totality of the

91. *In re Pace, 456 B.R. 253,* 278 (Bankr. W.D. Tex. 2011). ("The court's previous findings and conclusion that Hensley [the attorney] did not act in good faith in connection with the transfer of the condo underscores the conclusion here that Hensley used CFM to help Pace [the debtor] carry out a fraudulent transfer. That evidence is sufficient to justify piercing the corporate veil and to thus recover the condo from both Hensley and CFM under the theory of joint and several liability. *See Resource Dev. Int'l, LLC,* 487 F.3d at 303 (affirming district court's conclusion that defendant shareholder had 'utilized his control over defendant corporation' to perpetuate the debtor's fraudulent conduct where defendant had agreed with debtor to pay debtor's legal fees in exchange for a wire transfer to defendant's corporation, and holding defendant and defendant's corporation jointly and severally liable under section 550).")

circumstances, it is fair to regard the entire arrangement as a single, cohesive transaction that had a net-zero impact on F-Squared's finances. As discussed by the Kenrob court, 'Where is no requirement that the consideration be contemporaneous,' and the tax avoidance granted by the conversion constituted a continuing benefit to F-Squared. Ignoring the benefit of the tax avoidance would not return F-Squared's creditors to their rightful position under the fraudulent conveyance statute; rather, it would provide them a windfall at the expense of the shareholders who agreed to take on F-Squared's tax liability only if the Tax Distributions were made."[92]

## Distribution From Entity in Repayment of Owner Loan

Entity transferees, often owners of the entity, might argue a distribution from an entity is merely a repayment of a preexisting debt, to avoid having the distribution challenged on fraudulent transfer grounds. However, creditors will often thwart this attempt by pointing to evidence supporting a lack of loan treatment.

> Plaintiff asserts that Debtor's records reflect that Debtor treated the Advances as contributions, regardless of using the term "loan" on certain documents. They were recorded on the books as loans because, as Defendant testified, the doctors were prohibited by law from adding to their membership units. (Trial Tr., vol. 1, 73; Trial Tr., vol. 2, 12). Plaintiff stresses that Ms. Feighner testified that in her thirty years of experience as a controller, every loan transaction required a corresponding amortization schedule with interest. If interest was not paid it would be accrued. However, Debtor did not maintain an amortization schedule for any loans. (Trial Tr., vol. 1, 225). Moreover, according to Ms. Feighner when a payment was made, the person instructing that a payment be made would not identify the loan to which the payment should be applied. (Trial Tr., vol. 1, 225). Finally, Plaintiff claims that the Loan Summary lists certain capital contributions that were paid for "Class E Stock" as "loans" because Ms. Feighner was instructed by an unnamed attorney to "just treat it as a loan." (Trial Tr., vol. 1, 244-246).[93]

## Entity conversions

Business owners might decide to convert a corporation to an LLC to obtain charging order protection against the owners' creditors. The conversion could be avoided under fraudulent transfer law, regardless of the impact the avoidance has on non-debtor members.

The conversion of a state law corporation to a state law limited liability company can be done on a tax-free basis for a few prudent business reasons.

---

92. *Jalbert v. McClelland (In re F-Squared Inv. Mgmt. LLC)*, No. 15-11469 (Bankr. D. Del. Aug. 10, 2021).

93. Matter of Oakland Physicians Med. Ctr., L.L.C., No. 15-51011, 2019 WL 442296, at *6 (Bankr. E.D. Mich. Feb. 1, 2019).

This conversion may also bring with it the added benefit of providing creditor protection under certain state laws where the sole and exclusive remedy for a creditor is a charging order. The Official Comments recognize how business entities can be abused in the creditors' rights context (as with any other type of planning), and have identified the transfer of assets to an entity under certain conditions as a potentially fraudulent transfer. However, recognizing there is no bright line and the legitimate use of business entities, the Official Comments also provide that merely transferring an asset to an affiliated corporation or insider is not, without more, a fraudulent transfer.[94]

## *Sale of business*

The sale of a business can also be scrutinized by creditors in various contexts, such as an improper allocation of purchase price, leveraged buyout, or an attempt to evade creditors using a successor entity. Where the parties to a transaction are related, there will be heightened scrutiny afforded to the transfer of assets in an otherwise innocuous setting.

### Allocation of Purchase Price

The allocation of a purchase price to assets may not be respected for creditors' rights purposes, notwithstanding a desired result for income tax purposes. In *Hinrichsen, Inc. v. Messersmith Ventures, LLC*, Risk Assessment and Management, Inc. (debtor) entered into a purchase agreement with Henrichsen (creditor) to acquire 90 percent of creditor's insurance business for $108,870. Debtor subsequently defaulted on the purchase agreement, and creditor obtained a judgment against debtor. Debtor subsequently sold a customer list used as part of an insurance business to Messersmith Ventures, which was owned by the same individual that owned debtor. The purchase price for the customer list was $250. The district court determined that creditor had the burden to prove the customer list was worth more than $250, and because the creditor did not offer "adequate and sufficient evidence to establish the value" of the customer list, the district court entered judgment in favor of creditor in the amount of $250.

On appeal, the Supreme Court of Nebraska noted the relief sought under fraudulent transfer law was equitable in nature.[95] Because the purchase price

94. *See* Official Comment 6 to Section 4 of the UVTA. ("The fact that a transfer has been made to a relative or to an affiliated corporation has not been regarded as a badge of fraud sufficient to warrant avoidance when unaccompanied by any other evidence of intent to hinder, delay, or defraud creditors."

95. *Janice M. Hinrichsen, Inc. v. Messersmith Ventures, L.L.C.*, 296 Neb. 712, 716–17 (2017). ("An action under the UFTA is equitable in nature, *Reed v. Reed*, 277 Neb. 391, 763 N.W.2d 686 (2009), and an appeal of a district court's determination that transfers of assets were in violation of the UFTA is equitable in nature. *Eli's, Inc. v. Lemen*, 256 Neb. 515, 591 N.W.2d 543 (1999).")

was over $100,000, and given the nature of the business being sold, it was error to assign only $250 to a customer list.

> Having reviewed the record, we recognize that JMH did not establish the specific value of the assets RAM transferred to Messersmith Ventures in October 2013. However, it was not required to do so to support its contention that the $250 was not a reasonably equivalent value compared to the assets received. The evidence shows that in January 2011, JMH sold 90 percent of its assets to RAM for $108,870; that in July 2012, the district court entered judgment in favor of JMH and against RAM in case No. C112-88 in the amount of $98,606.94; and that in October 2013, RAM transferred its customer lists and agency contracts to Messersmith Ventures for $250.
>
> * * *
>
> The record supports JMH's assertion that the $108,870 which RAM paid JMH in 2011 included 90 percent of the book of insurance business and good will of the Platte Valley Insurance Agency, as well as furniture, fixtures, and equipment. The purchase included the carrier and customer contracts, and as JHM notes, "RAM utilized these contracts and was paid commissions of $83,311 in 2012 . . . and $47,220.00 in 2013." Brief for appellant at 12. It is reasonable to infer from such evidence that the assets RAM transferred to Messersmith Ventures in October 2013 were basically the book of insurance business that RAM purchased from JMH in January 2011 at a price in excess of $100,000. It is further reasonable to infer that the worth of such assets in October 2013 was considerably closer to the $98,606.94 judgment, rather than the $250 that Messersmith Ventures paid to RAM.[96]

In obtaining relief, a creditor should be entitled to what is fair; in this case, the assignment of a low value to the customer list, and the corresponding judgment in creditor's favor of only $250 was not fair, not only given the purchase price, but also given the goal and flexibility of creditor remedies under fraudulent transfer law.

> Section 36-708 of the UFTA is entitled "Remedies of creditors," and §36-709 of the UFTA is entitled "Defenses, liability, and protection of transferee." Both sections relate to remedies. Subsection (a) of §36-708 sets forth remedies including, inter alia, avoidance of the transfer, attachment against the asset transferred, and "any other relief the circumstances may require." The district court's award of a monetary judgment set at the amount of $250 appears to be either "other relief" under §36-708(a)(3)(iii) or relief in the form of avoidance of the transfer, which pursuant to §36-709(b) may be accomplished by a "judgment for the value of the asset transferred." However, as we discussed above, the evidence in this case indicates that the value of the asset transferred was significantly more than the $250 that Messersmith Ventures paid to RAM.
>
> * * *

96. *Janice M. Hinrichsen, Inc. v. Messersmith Ventures, L.L.C.*, 296 Neb. 712, 720–21 (2017).

> Given the fraudulent transfer and the equities involved, the court in this case should order, pursuant to §36-708(b), that JMH may levy execution on the assets or the proceeds of the assets that RAM transferred to Messersmith Ventures. This remedy allows JMH to levy execution on the assets transferred to Messersmith Ventures or their continuing proceeds in order to satisfy JMH's judgment against RAM. This remedy is more equitable than the specific monetary judgment awarded by the district court because it allows JMH to execute on the assets or the proceeds of such assets in the hands of Messersmith Ventures to the extent of their productive value and JMH's judgment against RAM, rather than limiting JMH's recovery to $250.[97]

## Substance Over Form

Generally, courts will not disturb otherwise legitimate business transactions unless evidence is provided that supports avoidance of a transaction.

> While the transaction might be characterized in several ways—a sale of assets, or a dissolution and reincorporation, for example—Plaintiffs urge the Court to apply the "modern view" to "collapse" the transaction and test the substance of the transaction against fraudulent transfer law.
>
> This the Court has done, but Plaintiffs' suspicions about the transfer are unsupported by facts. First, the Plaintiffs have not pointed to, nor has this Court found, examples of similar transactions which have been attacked as fraudulent. There is nothing inherently wrong with a corporation exiting certain businesses and thereby returning value to its shareholders. It is the shareholders, after all, who own the company. Such transactions should not be presumptively suspect. Moreover, Defendants argue that only "leveraged" transactions are subject to fraudulent transfer scrutiny. Whether this is always true is not before the Court; however, absent such leverage, and the accompanying deleterious effects on the transferor corporation, it is difficult to see fraud here. In re Vadnais, 100 B.R. 127 (Bkrtcy.D.Mass.1989) cited by Plaintiffs to illustrate the reach of the doctrine, is essentially a leveraged transaction—the corporation became indebted to the close shareholders in return for their ownership interests and non-compete agreements.
>
> Even if the Court scrutinizes the Pepsi transaction closely, Plaintiffs offer no basis for finding that it was made without an exchange of adequate consideration. Put another way, Plaintiff's theory automatically makes suspect any unleveraged intercorporate transfer involving a bona fide purchaser and a concomitant distribution to shareholders. The Court cannot discern any way in which an "innocent" corporation could get out of a business and return equity to shareholders without arousing this kind of suspicion. Thus, the Court is very skeptical that the Pepsi sale could be viewed as having been effected without adequate consideration.

97. *Id.* at 723-724. (Emphasis added.)

> Moreover, Plaintiffs offer no evidence that the new MEI was insufficiently capitalized or unable to pay its debts. As Plaintiffs acknowledge, MEI paid debts after the sale and raised money for new ventures.[98]

## Leveraged Buyouts

When the UFTA was adopted in 1984, controversy arose over whether the new law applied to the leveraged buyout (LBO), a relatively modern business transaction. Some argued that because an LBO was a legitimate business transaction, it should not be disturbed by ancient fraudulent transfer law. Courts have since concluded an LBO may be voided by a creditor. *Official Comm. of Unsecured Creditors of Great Lakes Quick Lube LP v. Theisen* provides a succinct summary of how fraudulent transfer law applies to this relatively modern business transaction.

> [A leveraged buyout (LBO)] is the acquisition of a target company financed by debt that is secured by the assets of the target company and paid with the target's future cash flows. . . . The acquirer then uses these funds to buy the target from the target's current shareholders, often at a large premium, and the acquirer becomes the new owner.
>
> The transaction leaves the target with a highly leveraged (or debt-heavy) capital structure, often close to a ninety percent debt-to-equity ratio. . . . The transaction, then, may be harmful to the existing, unsecured creditors of the target, who gained nothing from the transaction but saw the value of their debt decrease as the risk associated with that debt increased.
>
> The existing creditors face a real loss if the LBO is a failure and the highly leveraged target does in fact go into bankruptcy. In that case, the former shareholders lose nothing—they have already sold their interest in the company. But the unsecured creditors have to stand in line behind the secured lender in order to get their money. Since the lender has a lien on all of the target's assets, there will be few (if any) unsecured assets left for the unsecured creditors to share.
>
> The transaction looks a lot worse if the target was close to bankruptcy at the time of the LBO. . . . The failed LBO . . . allows the shareholders to cash out in full—at a premium, no less—at the time of the acquisition, while the creditors get paid—if they get paid at all—months after the acquisition when the company finally enters bankruptcy.[99]

## Successor Liability

Similarly, where the target business assets are moved from the target company (the transferor company) to an acquiring company (the transferee company),

98. *Brogren v. Pohlad*, 960 F. Supp. 1401, 1404–05 (D. Minn. 1997).

99. Official Comm. of Unsecured Creditors of Great Lakes Quick Lube LP v. Theisen, 2018 WI App 70, 384 Wis. 2d 580, 588, 920 N.W.2d 356, 360, *review granted*, 2019 WI 49, 386 Wis. 2d 522, 927 N.W.2d 907.

and those in control of the target are also in control of the acquiring company, creditors of the target might scrutinize the sale under fraudulent transfer law. In these situations, it is common for creditors to also seek relief under the common law successor liability doctrine. Generally, a transferee company is not liable for the debts of the transferor company. There are circumstances where non-liability will not apply (i.e., the transferee company will be liable for prior debts), and this tends to occur where (1) the transferee company expressly or impliedly agrees to assume such debts; (2) the transaction amounts to a consolidation or merger of the corporations; (3) the purchasing corporation is merely a continuation of the selling corporation; and (4) the transaction is entered into fraudulently to escape liability for the seller's debts.[100]

Some jurisdictions may be more willing to apply the successor liability doctrine over others but in any event the inquiry is fact specific.[101]

## Related Party Sales and Loan Transactions

Notes often are used as part of the wealth transfer process. For example, sales to defective grantor trusts are a popular way to remove the value of an asset from an individual's estate for transfer tax purposes but permit the individual to pay the income tax associated with the asset(s), thereby permitting the transferred assets to appreciate income tax free. But in other cases, a debtor experiencing financial difficulties might attempt to argue a loan exists, often with a related party, and attempt to move assets on account of such loan.

In either case, the transferred asset may be the subject of a fraudulent transfer. Aside from the actual fraud issue, with respect to a new loan, a creditor may assert constructive fraud since the note received was not reasonably equivalent value in exchange for the transferred asset. In situations where an old loan appears, creditors will look to the history of the loan to see whether it in fact, exists.

Aside from the circumstances surrounding the loan transaction, the note itself is often the target of great scrutiny. Creditors often argue a promissory note does not constitute reasonably equivalent value because value is determined from the viewpoint of the creditor. Courts will look at the facts and circumstances to determine whether a note is reasonably equivalent value. For example, a slow payout over time is a relevant factor.[102] A list of loan factors has developed over time, where certain factors may cause a loan to be more sus-

100. *See* Wells Fargo Vendor Fin. Servs., LLC v. Nationwide Learning, LLC, 56 Kan. App. 2d 259, 429 P.3d 221 (2018).

101. *Id.* ("From these cases, we understand that application of the equitable doctrine of successor liability is fact-specific, and that the *267 underlying goal is to determine whether justice between the real parties to the transaction requires imposition of successor liability.")

102. *See* Attebury Grain, LLC, a limited liability company, Plaintiff, v. Grayn Company, a corporation; Vicente Cortez, an individual, Defendants., No. 215CV05258RPJWX, 2016 WL 10933017, at *4–5 (C.D. Cal. May 3, 2016). ("It is uncontroverted that the transfer of assets from Superior to Defendants did not involve payment of the reasonably equivalent value of the assets. Defendants instead funded these transfer largely through intra-family loans of which no evidence suggests will ever need to be paid.")

ceptible to fraudulent transfer attack (for example, delayed payments, low interest rate, no security, related parties, and so on.)

> The 2012 Note provided that it was interest free and only due upon the sale of Potala Village. (Vecchio Decl. ¶ 4, Ex. I.) In Dexia Credit Local v. Rogan, No. 02 C 8288, 2008 WL 4855416, at *8 (N.D. Ill. Nov. 10, 2008), the court examined whether a loan remarkably similar to the 2012 Note provided reasonably equivalent value for purposes of Illinois's UFTA. The court initially examined transfers made in exchange for services and found that they tended to show reasonably equivalent value. *Id.* at *7. Turning to a $305,000.00 transfer, the court stated:
>
> The Court cannot say the same regarding the $305,000[.00] that Cuppy caused the RPP Finance Trust to transfer to Dynamic. Cuppy's characterization of this loan is somewhat suspect, but even if the characterization is accurate, it was an interest-free loan for an indefinite term, made by and to the person who had control of the trust's assets at his apparent whim, without any documentation of an obligation to repay. Nor was there any apparent benefit to the trust or its beneficiaries from making the "loan."
>
> Like the loan in Dexia Credit Local, the 2012 Note was interest-free and for an indefinite term with the triggering event—the sale of Potala Village—entirely in the hands of the borrower, Potala Village. Further, the 2012 Note was executed by Mr. Dargey as both the transferor—Darey Enterprises—and the transferee—Potala Village. (See Vecchio Decl. ¶ 4, Ex. I at PVE_0003.) As a result, similar to the court in Drexia Credit Local, this court also concludes that the 2012 Note provided no apparent benefit to Dargey Enterprises, and Mr. Dargey executed the 2012 Note to assist in concealing his actual intent to defraud PAFM and the immigrant investors of the transfers at issue here. Thus, the court concludes that the 2012 Note does not create an issue of fact precluding summary judgment on Mr. Granssmueck's UFTA claim.[103]

Similarly in *Morales*, the court found a lack of reasonably equivalent value, which also supported an actual fraud argument.

> Under the circumstances of this case and considering the relationship between the transferring parties, a bare deed coupled with property maintenance and the assignment of rents, which totaled less than $20,000, did not provide the Defaulting Defendants with a sufficient economic benefit to support a finding of reasonably equivalent value. To the contrary, all of the circumstances surrounding the Transfer suggest that it occurred for no other reason than to avoid Ms. Morales's payment obligation to Plaintiff. see Donell, 533 F.3d at 777. No reasonable juror could find otherwise. see Schempp, 18 P.3d at 765 (the reasonable equivalence standard implies a rule of reasonableness in light of the particular circumstances).[104]

---

103. *See* Michael A. Grassmueck, Plaintiff, v. Potala Village, LLC, Defendant., No. C17-0236JLR, 2018 WL 2984831, at *10 (W.D. Wash. June 14, 2018).

104. *Fifth Third Bank v. Morales*, No. 16-CV-01302-CMA-STV, 2017 WL 6492108, at *4–5 (D. Colo. Dec. 19, 2017).

Old loans that surface upon financial distress are nothing new, and creditors should review the transaction carefully to determine whether transfers pursuant to such loan are fraudulent. A debtor who intends to advance this argument in support of moving assets should carefully consider whether the loan was bona fide. This would entail reviewing whether loan payments have been made, whether such loan was properly reported for income tax purposes (or in contrast, was reported as a gift for transfer tax purposes.) Florida Statute Section 726.201, enacted in 1823 and entitled "Fraudulent loans void," provides an example of how loans were scrutinized long ago for creditors' rights purposes.

> When any loan of goods and chattels shall be pretended to have been made to any person with whom or those claiming under her or him, possession shall have remained for the space of 2 years without demand and pursued by due process of law on the part of the pretended lender, or where any reservation or limitation shall be pretended to have been made of a use or property by way of condition, reversion, remainder or otherwise in goods and chattels, and the possession thereof shall have remained in another as aforesaid, the same shall be taken, as to the creditors and purchasers of the persons aforesaid so remaining in possession, to be fraudulent within this chapter, and the absolute property shall be with the possession, unless such loan, reservation or limitation of use or property were declared by will or deed in writing proved and recorded.

On top of the circumstances that would support a fraudulent loan, UVTA Section 5(b) also provides that an insolvent debtor's payment to an insider on account of an antecedent debt is voidable.[105]

> A transfer made by a debtor is voidable as to a creditor whose claim arose before the transfer was made if the transfer was made to an insider for an antecedent debt, the debtor was insolvent at that time, and the insider had reasonable cause to believe that the debtor was insolvent.

## Tax Planning

Perhaps no other creditor has witnessed as much ingenuity in avoiding an obligation as has the tax collector. Consequently, the tax law has developed several legal doctrines that permit the IRS to look through the formalities to identify the substance of a transaction. These "anti-avoidance" doctrines have been used to deny taxpayers their ability to hinder the IRS's attempt to collect a tax debt. Given the powerful effect of anti-avoidance doctrine to recast a transaction, it is no surprise that some who openly market aggressive techniques

105. UVTA Section 9(c) provides that a claim for relief with respect to such a transfer is extinguished not later than one year after the transfer was made.

must provide disclaimers to the effect that all bets are off if the arrangement is challenged by a taxing authority.

In many cases, transfers of wealth are made pursuant to tax planning in an effort to reduce tax otherwise due to taxing authorities. Some of these transactions have overlap with transactions undertaken to avoid creditors in general. "For example, small farmers in ancient Rome would transfer their lands to larger landowners to avoid tax while continuing to live and work on the land."[106] Like asset protection planning, transfers often are made in abusive tax planning scenarios that attempt to move assets out of reach just enough to claim lack of legal ownership but not far enough to deny the transferor the benefit of the transferred assets.

> After a bench trial, the district court in South Capital entered a $622,226 judgment against Regina Planes and found that the Planeses — to defeat tax collection — had "intentionally" engineered the following "fraudulent" scheme:
>
> By managing the [the Planeses'] businesses while retaining no ownership interest in them, Mr. Planes ensured that he would be the person assessed with trust fund recovery penalties. However, by placing the assets in Mrs. Planes's name, the couple also ensured that Mr. Planes lacked funds to satisfy the penalties. This structure has allowed the couple to accrue substantial liabilities that have been virtually impossible to collect.
>
> (South Capital, Doc. 139 at 6)
>
> In this action, the United States sues (Doc. 1) to disregard the corporateness of entities on which William and Regina Planes allegedly rely to thwart tax collection. A temporary restraining order (Doc. 6) prohibits the Planeses — and anyone acting on behalf or in concert with the Planeses — from transferring the entities' assets. Two hours after an IRS agent served Regina Planes with the temporary restraining order, William Planes transferred $160,000 — 99 percent of the entities' money—to a third party. A contempt hearing followed.[107]

Not all tax planning is abusive, and certainly some types of planning have been condoned by the IRS even though the primary motivation for such planning is tax avoidance (e.g., tax credits, tax-free reorganizations, etc.) Like tax planning, some transfers challenged under fraudulent transfer law have been upheld, despite the presence of creditor avoidance motivations. In the bankruptcy setting, some pre-bankruptcy transactions have been upheld even though motivated by creditors.[108]

---

106. Jared H. Binstock, "Transactions of Interest: Are They 'Interesting' Enough to Warrant the New Obligations?" 61 Tax Law. 949, 967 (2008). (Citing Charles Adams, For Good and Evil: The Impact of Taxes on the Course of Civilization 121 (1999).

107. United States, Plaintiff, v. William Planes, et al., Defendants. Additional Party Names: Regina Planes, S. Capital Constr., Inc., No. 8:18-CV-2726-T-23TGW, 2019 WL 3024895, at *1 (M.D. Fla. July 11, 2019).

108. Congress closed certain loopholes with amendments to the Bankruptcy Code in 2005. *See In re Wrobel*, 2015 WL 643839. ("Before those amendments, 'bankruptcy planning' in New York (but not in some other states) relied upon this statement in the Legislative History to the 1978 Bankruptcy Reform Act: 'As

The IRS may assert its status as a creditor under fraudulent transfer law, and such, has the benefit of both federal and state law in avoiding transfers. Unlike a typical creditor, however, the IRS's status as a federal agency brings additional powers, discussed in chapter ten.

Transfers made to avoid the payment of taxes can be voided under traditional fraudulent transfer law. Like general creditor debtor law, federal tax law has evolved to deal with certain transactions that involve badges of fraud and are more susceptible to jeopardizing the rights of the federal government, such as transfers between related parties. Many state revenue laws piggyback the same concepts and provisions within the Internal Revenue Code.

## Federal Tax Liens

In cases where taxpayers move assets to third parties to avoid ownership for purposes of tax liens, the federal government has also applied a badges of fraud analysis under a nominee theory, very similar to the fraudulent transfer badges of fraud analysis. The federal government may seek to void a transfer of such property, or it may seek to impose a lien on the property, thereby obviating the fraudulent transfer analysis and treating the property as being owned by the debtor/taxpayer. Of course, if this theory applies to a fact pattern involving a self-settled trust, it is also likely the assets held by the trustee would not escape inclusion in the gross estate of the settlor, thereby subjecting the assets to estate taxation.

> A nominee is someone who holds legal title for the benefit of another person — in this context, a taxpayer. *See United States v. Swan*, 467 F.3d 655, 658 (7th Cir. 2006). Because the nominee does not hold a valid ownership interest in the property, a creditor of the property's true owner can recover against it—even though the true owner is not the legal title holder. *See id.* ("Suppose a person who wants to evade taxes parks his property with a friend or family member. That would be a fraudulent conveyance, and so the person to whom the property was conveyed would be deemed the taxpayer's 'nominee' and forced to cough it up."). Because "Illinois courts have never articulated a detailed standard for what constitutes a nominee," federal courts apply federal law in the analysis. *United States v. Szaflarski*, 614 Fed. App'x. 836, 838 (7th Cir. 2015) (non-precedential disposition). Courts "consider several factors in determining whether a titleholder is actually serving as a nominee for the benefit of another. *Id.* The factors include:

under current law, the debtor will be permitted to convert nonexempt property into exempt property before filing a bankruptcy petition. See Hearings, pt. 3, at 1355–58. The practice is not fraudulent as to creditors, and permits the debtor to make full use of the exemptions to which he is entitled under the law. (H. Rept. No. 95-595 to accompany H.R. 8200, 95th Cong., 1st Sess. (1977) pp. 360–363.)' *** Clearly Congress had changed its mind after 30-odd years of notoriety cases (e.g. In re Bowie Kuhn) and possible enticements by some states to get very wealthy persons accused of tort or of crime to move there and shelter their wealth in an unlimited homestead exemption.")

> (1) whether there is a close personal relationship between the nominee and the transferor; (2) the nominee paid little or no consideration for the property; (3) the parties placed the property in the name of the nominee in anticipation of collection activity; (4) the parties did not record the conveyance; and (5) the transferor continues to exercise dominion and control over the property. *Id.* at 838-839; *see also* Stone v. United States, 2014 WL 1289788, at *10-11 (N.D. Ill. March 31, 2014) (applying the same five factors).[109]

# Asset Protection Planning

With asset protection planning, clients will often move personal assets into trust and business entities, and otherwise change ownership title, all of which can provide beneficial estate, business, and tax planning results. Where motivated by a desire to avoid future creditors, all such planning can also be considered asset protection planning. This type of planning is most at risk for avoidance under fraudulent transfer law, because the primary goal is to safeguard assets from the claims of creditors.

> In the instant matter, Nagel alleges Lawson and Westen enlisted Westen's brothers, attorneys Derek and Peter Westen, to help them design and implement an "asset protection plan" when it became apparent the arbitrator would rule in Nagel's favor. The plan had three components. First, they converted respondent Westen Family Group, LLC (WFG), of which Lawson and Westen held a 20.7 percent membership interest, from a California LLC into a Nevada LLC. Second, they placed a portion of the Brentwood sale proceeds into an annuity. Third, they bought a house in Texas and improved it with the balance of their sale proceeds. Nagel further alleges Lawson and Westen promptly moved to Texas upon receiving the arbitrator's preliminary award so they could invoke the state's unlimited homestead exemption to shield the new house and annuity from creditors.[110]

## *Asset Protection Trusts*

While there are many forms of asset protection planning, one of the most popular examples is the use of an asset protection trust. Traditionally, an asset protection trust is a self-settled spendthrift trust formed under the law of a jurisdiction that reverses the long-standing rule against self-settled spendthrift trusts and modifies its fraudulent transfer law. If the trust is governed by the laws of a state within the U.S., the trust is referred to as a "domestic asset protection trust" (DAPT), whereas a trust governed by the law of a foreign

109. See United States of America, Plaintiff, v. Terry James Maier & Denise Lynn Maier, Defendants., No. 17 C 08433, 2019 WL 1399983, at *8–9 (N.D. Ill. Mar. 28, 2019).

110. *Nagel v. Westen*, 59 Cal.App.5th 740, 744-45 (Cal. Ct. App. 2021).

jurisdiction is referred to as a "foreign asset protection trust" (FAPT). With this trust, a settlor may transfer assets to a trustee and retain an interest in the assets as a beneficiary. This retained interest is enjoyed by the settlor to the exclusion of the settlor's creditors. Although most asset protection trusts clearly document whether the settlor is also a beneficiary, situations may require a creditor look beyond the terms of the trust agreement.[111]

While third-party spendthrift trusts experienced a period of uncertainty in the United States, their validity was blessed by the Supreme Court in *Nichols v. Eaton*, and eventually withstood attack in both state and federal courts. However, the self-settled spendthrift trust has not enjoyed the same degree of success. Whereas the third-party spendthrift trust was (eventually) deemed not to violate public policy, the self-settled trust has been squarely rejected for centuries as a violation of public policy.[112]

Thirty-eight years after *Nichols v. Eaton*, and the same year the Sixteenth Amendment was ratified, the U.S. Supreme Court reiterated the effectiveness of third-party trusts and distinguished such trusts from self-settled trusts.

> The foundation of the English doctrine in both classes of cases is an assumption that there is some settled principle of public policy which subjects all property in which one has a beneficial ownership to the claims of creditors and forbids restraint upon alienation. That this theory of public policy is not of universal application, at least, in this country, is manifest from the numerous exemption statutes existing which protect to a limited extent the

---

111. *Hernandez v. Shove* (*In re* Shove), No. 17-31052, at *34 (Bankr. D. Mass. May 10, 2021) ("In determining which person or entity is properly considered the 'settlor' of a trust, a court should look to the 'reality' of the situation, as '[t]he person who provides the consideration for a trust is the settlor even if another person or entity nominally creates the trust.' Lassman v. Tosi (In re Tosi), 383 B.R. 1,13 (quoting Brooks v. Interfirst Bank, Fort Worth (In re Brooks), 844 F.2d 258, 263 (5th Cir.1988)). While the EJM Trust agreement names Gold Dome as the 'Grantor(s)/Settlor(s)' and Shove as the beneficiary, Shove paid for the property and had it placed into the EJM Trust via deed from Gold Dome. Inasmuch as Shove provided the consideration for the property transferred to the EJM Trust, the Court finds that Shove is likely more properly characterized as both the settlor as well as the original beneficiary, and the EJM Trust would likely be found to be a self-settled trust.")

112. The common law rule against self-settled trusts finds its origin dating back to 1487 and has been adopted by the States. *See Arizona Bank v. Morris*, 6 Ariz. App. 566, 569, 435 P.2d 73, 76 (1967), modified, 7 Ariz. App. 107, 436 P.2d 499 (1968). ("While the issues presented in this case are novel in Arizona, it was considered under the common law as early as 1487 in England under 3 Henry VII, Chapter 4, wherein the English statute provided that: 'All deeds of gift of goods and chattels, made or to be made in trust to the use of that person or persons that made the same deed of gift, be void and of none effect.' By virtue of A.R.S. s 1-201, the common law is adopted in this jurisdiction. The clear import of 3 Hen. VII, Ch. 4, is that any trust settled for the benefit of the settlor is invalid notwithstanding the lack of fraudulent intent on the part of the settlor. It is equally clear that under A.R.S. s 1-201, 3 Hen. VII, Ch. 4 is part of the adopted common law of this state, and as such, it is further reason why the decision below should be upheld."); *see also*, *In re Lewiston*, 532 B.R. 36, 46 (Bankr. E.D. Mich. 2015). ("Because the MTC does not state that it abrogates the common law in Michigan regarding the enforceability of a spendthrift provision in a self-settled trust, well established principles of statutory construction in Michigan compel the Court to conclude that the common law prohibition against self-settled spendthrift trusts, as articulated in *Fornell*, retains its vitality. The Court declines Richard's invitation to hold that the MTC by implication abrogates the common law in Michigan. Instead, the Court holds that the MTC neither authorizes self-settled spendthrift trusts nor abrogates Michigan common law public policy regarding self-settled spendthrift trusts. The public policy against self-settled spendthrift trusts, articulated by the Michigan Supreme Court in *Fornell, Johannes and Hertsberg*, remains intact and continues to limit the purposes for which a trust can be created in Michigan.")

acquisitions of a debtor from the claims of his creditors and restrain his power of alienation in the interest of his family. Neither do we for a moment question the rule that one may not by his own act preserve to himself the enjoyment of property in such manner that it shall not be subject to the claims of creditors or placed beyond his own power of alienation.[113]

## Self-Settled Trusts in History

Transfers of property by a debtor, whether memorialized in writing or not, have always been subject to creditor avoidance.[114] This holds especially true for those who hold such property for the use or benefit of the debtor; this type of arrangement has historically been either void or voidable as contrary to public policy providing that individuals may not tie up property for their benefit but to the exclusion of creditors.

The concept of permitting unlimited protection of wealth, has, until relatively recent time, long been rejected.

> Our laws have specified what property of a debtor the creditor shall not take from him. Any attempt of the debtor to set apart a fund for his own support must be fraudulent and void. If he may take to his own use $2,000 a year, why not $5,000? And if for four years, why not for ten, or even twenty, as in the case of *Murray v. Riggs*? To state such a proposition, is a sufficient refutation of it. It offends the moral sense; it shocks the conscience and produces an exclamation. It is directly against the statute and cannot stand before it.[115]

In 1908, Dewitt C. Moore authored a treatise entitled "Fraudulent Conveyances" where he emphasized that transfers (in trust for one's benefit) were void as to all creditors, not just existing creditors, under the common law of fraudulent transfers:

> It is well established as a general rule that a debtor cannot settle his estate in trust for his own use or benefit, so as to free it from liability for his debts, and such a conveyance or transfer by a debtor is fraudulent and void as against his creditors, whether prior or subsequent, and the property may be subjected by them to the payment of their debts.[116]

---

113. *Shelton v. King*, 229 U.S. 90, 97, 33 S. Ct. 686, 688, 57 L. Ed. 1086 (1913). (Emphasis added.)

114. *See Smith v. Parker*, 41 Me. 452, 456 (1856). ("By the 5th c. of the statute of Eliz. 'every feoffment, gift, grant, alienation, bargain and conveyance of lands, tenements and hereditaments, goods and chattels, or any of them,' by writing or otherwise, 'that had been or afterwards should be' had or made to or for any intent or purpose, 'to delay, hinder or defraud creditors, or others, of their just and lawful actions, suits, debts, accounts,' &c., is declared to be 'clearly and utterly void, frustrate and of no effect; any pretence, color, feigned consideration, expressing of use, or any other matter or thing to the contrary notwithstanding.' Under this statute, voluntary conveyances, made without consideration by persons who are insolvent, may on that very account be deemed fraudulent, even as against subsequent creditors, and when made, by persons whether insolvent or not, for the purpose of defrauding such creditors, are to be declared void as against them. Howe v. Ward, 4 Maine, 195.")

115. *Mackie v. Cairns*, 1825 WL 1865 (N.Y. 1825).

116. Dewitt C. Moore, *Fraudulent Conveyances* (1908), 417--418. (Emphasis added.)

The Uniform Trust Code identifies the RASST as a restriction on the use of self-settled trusts, and also acknowledges the simultaneous application of fraudulent transfer law:

> Subsection (a)(2), which is based on Restatement (Third) of Trusts Section 58(2) and cmt. e (Tentative Draft No. 2, approved 1999), and Restatement (Second) of Trusts Section 156 (1959), follows traditional doctrine in providing that a settlor who is also a beneficiary may not use the trust as a shield against the settlor's creditors. The drafters of the Uniform Trust Code concluded that traditional doctrine reflects sound policy. Consequently, the drafters rejected the approach taken in states like Alaska and Delaware, both of which allow a settlor to retain a beneficial interest immune from creditor claims. *See* Henry J. Lischer, Jr., Domestic Asset Protection Trusts: Pallbearers to Liability, 35 Real Prop. Prob. & Tr. J. 479 (2000); John E. Sullivan, III, Gutting the Rule Against Self-Settled Trusts: How the Delaware Trust Law Competes with Offshore Trusts, 23 Del. J. Corp. L. 423 (1998). Under the Code, whether the trust contains a spendthrift provision or not, a creditor of the settlor may reach the maximum amount that the trustee could have paid to the settlor-beneficiary. If the trustee has discretion to distribute the entire income and principal to the settlor, the effect of this subsection is to place the settlor's creditors in the same position as if the trust had not been created. For the definition of "settlor," see Section 103(1415).
>
> This section does not address possible rights against a settlor who was insolvent at the time of the trust's creation or was rendered insolvent by the transfer of property to the trust. This subject is instead left to the State's law on fraudulent transfers. A transfer to the trust by an insolvent settlor might also constitute a voidable preference under federal bankruptcy law.[117]

Although some may argue the RASST preempts the application of fraudulent transfer law, it is clear the UTC contemplates the dual application of both theories of recovery. However, the UTC comment fails to address the application of fraudulent transfer law in its entirety, instead focusing on Section 5(a) claims involving insolvency.

As discussed in chapter six, the RASST and fraudulent transfer law represent separate avenues of relief for creditors with respect to transfers in trust, and such avenues have coexisted separately for centuries.

> Bump on Fraud. Con. 2d ed. 208, speaking of the Stat. 3, Hen. 7, ch. 4, which in substance constitutes §2120, Code of 1876, says, "It is not directed against trusts made with fraudulent intent, but against trusts themselves. There is not one word about intent, or object, or purpose, or excluding, injuring, or delaying creditors. The effect of the trust is not a subject for consideration. Its mere existence avoids the transfer and destroys the title as against creditors existing or subsequent.[118]

117. §505. Creditor's Claim Against Settlor., Unif. Trust Code §505.
118. *Sandlin v. Robbins*, 62 Ala. 477, 484–85 (1878).

Similarly, in his 1911 treatise on Fraudulent Conveyances, Herman Melville notes that the Statute of 13 Elizabeth was "perhaps a broad codification of the earlier statutes [referring to the statutes enacted under King Edward and King Henry]" and that the Statute of 13 Elizabeth "dropped the specific declaration of these [earlier] statutes for the general words under consideration. That it was not intended to change the law was soon afterwards, in the same reign, shown by a famous decision of the Star Chamber."[119] Despite the adoption of the earlier statutes by the states, Melville notes the application of the earlier statutes versus the Statute of 13 Elizabeth was not "the subject of much judicial consideration; most of the questions arising upon the broader legislation [Statute of 13 Elizabeth] against alienations with 'intent to hinder, delay, or defraud creditors.'"

Melville's reasoning in 1911 holds true today. In *Rush v. Sessions*, the Illinois Supreme Court found the RASST coexisted with fraudulent transfer statute, because the RASST addressed a particular circumstance (retained interest in a transfer in trust) versus the broad application of fraudulent transfer law.

> We find defendants' contention unpersuasive. The common law and the statute are supplementary, not contradictory. Both laws have a general purpose of protecting creditors. But the common law focuses on the additional matter of the interest retained by the settlor of a specific kind of trust, and not simply the fraudulent transfer of an asset or the fraudulent incurring of a debt, as does the statute. Additionally, the Act and the common law rule each operate in some circumstances where the other does not, thus negating any inference that the common law rule would render the Act superfluous. The Act is effective, but the common law rule is not, in a much larger sphere, which includes both situations that do not involve trusts and in connection with transfers into trusts that are not for the settlor's benefit because they permit distributions only to other persons.[120]

As a result of APT statutes, some states have essentially recreated modern-day sanctuaries like Westminster Abbey, only today's debtor does not have to travel to a sanctuary to enjoy protection from creditors. Thus, to say the APT can exist in harmony with traditional fraudulent transfer law ignores centuries of history and is also why modern-day sanctuaries must modify their fraudulent transfer law (e.g., require intent must be directed at a specific creditor,[121]

---

119. *See* Melville Madison Bigelow, The Law of Fraudulent Conveyances, 240 (rev. ed.1911) (1890).

120. *Rush Univ. Med. Ctr. v. Sessions*, 2012 IL 112906, ¶ 22, 980 N.E.2d 45, 52

121. *See* Title 12 Delaware Statute §3572(a) Avoidance of qualified dispositions. ("Notwithstanding any other provision of this Code, no action of any kind, including, without limitation, an action to enforce a judgment entered by a court or other body having adjudicative authority, shall be brought at law or in equity for an attachment or other provisional remedy against property that is the subject of a qualified disposition or for avoidance of a qualified disposition unless such action shall be brought pursuant to the provisions of §1304 or §1305 of Title 6 and, in the case of a creditor whose claim arose after a qualified disposition, unless the qualified disposition was made with actual intent to defraud such creditor. The Court of Chancery shall have exclusive jurisdiction over any action brought with respect to a qualified disposition.") (Emphasis added.) *See also*, Alaska Statute Section 34.40.110(b). (" If a trust contains a transfer restriction allowed under (a) of this section, the transfer restriction prevents a creditor existing when the trust is created or a person who

prohibit a court from using the trust agreement as evidence of intent to hinder creditors, prohibit claims against those who assist with the creation of the trust, etc.)

While the RASST[122] requires no finding of fraudulent intent, such is not the case with fraudulent transfer statutory law, which generally requires a finding of intent to hinder, delay, or defraud in the absence of any presumptions. In *Rush v. Sessions*, the defendants argued that the RASST, which would subject assets held in trust to creditors, was abrogated by the Illinois Uniform Fraudulent Transfer Act. However, because fraudulent transfer law and the RASST are two separate avenues of relief, the Illinois Supreme Court correctly held that it was improper to find the fraudulent transfer act displaced the RASST.

Given the separate avenues for relief, it is not unusual (and often a necessary exercise) for a creditor to examine both the fraudulent transfer common and statutory law. Such was the case for the Supreme Court of Minnesota, when it went as far back as 1868 to determine that a longer statute of limitations existed due to the nature of the fraudulent transfer. "Here, by contrast, the parties do not dispute that fraudulent-transfer claims based on an actual intent to hinder, delay, or defraud creditors existed at common law as early as 1868, and likely earlier. *** In short, for the limited purpose of determining the applicable statute of limitations, we conclude that a claim against a transferee that receives an actually fraudulent transfer under MUFTA is for 'relief on the ground of fraud,' just as it was for a transferee that received a fraudulent transfer at the time of *McMillan* and *Duxbury*."[123]

Just as a court can examine fraudulent transfer common law for purposes of applicable statutes of limitation (if not adopted by the state), it can also examine the fraudulent transfer common law with respect to self-settled trusts since the fraudulent transfer statutory law expressly supplements the common law.

In his treatise on fraudulent conveyances, Frederick Wait noted, with the exception of statutory exemptions, it would violate public policy to otherwise permit a debtor to enjoy property to the exclusion of creditors. "Aside from statutory exemptions trivial in amount, the idea of the existence of rights of property of any kind in a debtor, which cannot be reached by creditors and applied toward the satisfaction of debts, is abhorrent to modern convictions of justice toward the creditor class. The personal liberty of the debtor being no longer in danger, there exists no controlling check upon his recklessness and

---

subsequently becomes a creditor from satisfying a claim out of the beneficiary's interest in the trust, unless the creditor is a creditor of the settlor and (1) the creditor establishes by clear and convincing evidence that the settlor's transfer of property in trust was made with the intent to defraud that creditor . . .") (Emphasis added.)

122. The Rule Against Self-Settled Trusts has also been referred to as the "common law trust rule." *See, e.g., Rush Univ. Med. Ctr. v. Sessions*, 2012 IL 112906, ¶ 25, 980 N.E.2d 45, 54. ("Given the longstanding coexistence of the common law trust rule and the statutory provisions against fraudulent conveyances that have remained essentially consistent in terms of the relevant language, we do not believe that the legislature intended to abrogate the common law rule by implication when it enacted the Uniform Fraudulent Transfer Act.")

123. *See Finn v. All. Bank*, 860 N.W.2d 638, 658 (Minn. 2015).

improvidence. This is the source of the strong tendency, manifested in the courts, to strengthen, enlarge and perfect the creditors' remedies and recourses against the property and interests of the debtor class."[124]

Wait identified two main purposes manifested in modern law in extending relief to creditors. The first main purpose was to "enforce the creditors' equitable lien upon the debtor's property considered as a trust fund," and the second was to "inflict a species of negative punishment upon the debtor by depriving him of the personal comforts and enjoyments which result from the possession and use of property or accumulated wealth. There can be no spectacle more revolting to the mass of mankind, and especially in a community such as ours, than that of a bankrupt or insolvent reveling in luxury. It is opposed to a wise public policy that a man 'should have an estate to live on, but not an estate to pay his debts with,' or that he should possess 'the benefits of wealth without the responsibilities.'"

Thus, for public policy reasons, self-settled trusts were not popular, as they simply did not work, whether it be due to the rule against self-settled trusts or under fraudulent transfer law. Of course, debtors would push the limits, even in the 1800s, to retain a benefit to the exclusion of creditors. This sometimes occurred in the context of assignments for the benefit of creditors, where assets would be transferred into a trust for creditors. Debtors sometimes provided that, after satisfying debts to creditors, trust assets would be used for the benefit of the debtor and his family.

> An assignment for the benefit of creditors may undoubtedly contain a clause so plainly indicative of the fraudulent intent pointed out by the statute, or recognized by the policy of the law, 'as to carry its death-wound upon its face.' An instance of this might be a gratuitous provision out of the assigned property for the insolvent assignor or his family. The New York cases clearly establish the rule that where the assignment shows upon its face that it must necessarily have the effect of hindering and defrauding the creditors of the assignor, it is conclusive evidence of a fraudulent intent, and may be avoided. The actual motive and belief of the debtor in such cases is immaterial. <u>Where it is apparent from the face of the instrument itself that is a conveyance to the use of the assignor, it is the duty of the court trying the cause to tell the jury as a matter of law that the conveyance is fraudulent as against creditors.</u>[125]

In *McIlvaine v. Smith*, the Supreme Court of Missouri addressed the public policy concern with benefitting from property held in trust to the exclusion of creditors:

> Here is an attempt of a man, apparently, to tie up his own property under a trust in such manner that himself, as owner, may be enabled to enjoy the income and set his creditors at defiance. This is a thing which the law does not allow. A man cannot own property or money and not own it at the same time. Whatever might be said of the justice or honesty of the thing in point of

124. Frederick S. Wait, *Fraudulent Conveyances and Creditors' Bills*, 483 (1889).
125. *Id.* at p. 423. (Emphasis added.)

> morals, it is enough that such an arrangement is in contravention of the rules of law and equity. He cannot be permitted to have the beneficial enjoyment of an income of this nature, beyond the reach of his honest debts.[126]

In *Twyne's Case*, the arrangement, not reduced to a formal written agreement, was referred to as a secret trust and was considered a badge of fraud. A variation on this arrangement is where the terms of holding such property are reduced to writing, creating what is known as an express trust. The badges of fraud in the UFTA do not explicitly refer to use of a trust, as the badges enumerated account for such a device, whether express or secret.

> Had this deed been made without any trust expressed upon its face, still there would have been a resulting trust in favor of Frederic J. Thomas, which, if made to defraud creditors, it cannot be doubted, would be void as to subsequent creditors as well as to those existing at the time. No sufficient reason is perceived why the expression of a trust upon the face of a voluntary conveyance should change the rule.[127]

Today, most self-settled spendthrift trusts are reduced to writing with a governing law provision that points to a jurisdiction that permits individuals to have their cake and eat it, too. However, since these arrangements have failed in court where the debtor resides in a jurisdiction that does not permit self-settled spendthrift trusts, the trust arrangements are sometimes drafted in a manner that cloaks the settlor/debtor's retained interest, or are abandoned in favor of foreign structures or new structures that have not been tested in U.S. courts.

As discussed elsewhere, equitable ownership may be muddied by omitting the settlor's name from the trust agreement as a beneficiary. Instead of a settlor being named as a beneficiary, the settlor might be listed as an appointee. Notwithstanding the settlor's omission as a beneficiary of the trust, a creditor can still apply fraudulent transfer law to a transaction where a debtor transfers property to a third party, regardless of the nature of the settlor's retained rights. The arrangement might be nothing more than a secret trust which has been viewed as a badge of fraud under fraudulent transfer common law.

## Enforceability of Weakened Fraudulent Transfer Law

An individual who forms an APT in an APT jurisdiction state but is domiciled in a non-APT state, essentially is attempting to force a result (recognition of self-settled trust) that often violates important public policy of the non-APT state. The DAPT state caters to this desire; its statute might provide that any fraudulent transfer controversies involving transfers to an APT governed by its (weakened) fraudulent transfer law are handled exclusively in the DAPT state.

A creditor may find support for applying the non-DAPT state fraudulent transfer law. In *Bertran*, the Alaska Supreme Court held that such an exclusive

126. *McIlvaine v. Smith*, 42 Mo. 45, 58 (1867).
127. *Smith v. Parker*, 41 Me. 452, 456 (1856).

forum statute was an unconstitutional violation of full faith and credit. Because a fraudulent transfer was a transitory action (as opposed to a local action), Alaska could not make itself the exclusive jurisdiction to hear such matters. The Alaska Supreme Court acknowledged Alaska's legislative intent, but dismissed it as well. This opinion has raised serious concerns about the effectiveness of DAPTs when used by non-DAPT settlors, forcing many to conclude that only foreign APTs remain as viable asset protection trusts.

In addition to the potential rejection of a state's exclusive forum clause, DAPTs encounter issues with the full faith and credit clause as it applies to the recognition of sister state judgments. Consequently, if the non-DAPT state court enters judgment in favor of creditor on a fraudulent transfer claim, the DAPT state must respect the fraudulent transfer judgment. "Regarding judgments, however, the full faith and credit obligation is exacting. A final judgment in one State... qualifies for recognition throughout the land.... [I]n other words, the judgment of the rendering State gains nationwide force."[128]

## Adviser Immunity

To entice advisers in non-APT states to sell APTs, the APT state law may provide that any adviser who assists may be entitled to some protection for his or her participation in the creation of the APT. Like the weakened fraudulent transfer law, the adviser immunity statute also creates problematic choice of law and public policy issues. Some may question whether the APT state may force its policy upon the creditors and courts of the non-APT state. Further, some states permit adviser liability for assisting with fraudulent transfers, explained in more detail in chapter nine. Because certain aspects of fraudulent transfer law implicate tort or tort like actions, a state that wishes to absolve a party from tort liability will have an uphill battle attempting to force this view on other states.

## Relevant Case Law

In some states, the common law provides that transfers to self-settled trusts are so offensive, that the transfers are presumed to be fraudulent. Unless overridden by statute, this common law remains in existence, in harmony with fraudulent transfer statutory law and the RASST. If a jurisdiction follows this presumption voidable per se approach, a creditor may cite such case law, assuming it has not been overruled by other law, in addition to proving actual fraud under fraudulent transfer statutory law.

Creditors and debtors alike should keep in mind that the fraudulent transfer common law has not been repealed and continues in force. "Much of the pre-UFTA case law remains applicable on the issues related to fraudulent transfers, including the application of the badges of fraud, and often is cited

128. *Baker v. GMC*, 522 U.S. 222, 233, 118 S.Ct. 657, 139 L.Ed.2d 580 (1998).

without distinction between pre-UFTA and UFTA circumstances."[129] The fact that the case law is relatively old should not impact a creditor's ability to cite it as authority in attacking a self-settled trust arrangement. Professor Kettering elaborated on this point. "In short, the proposition that a transfer to a self-settled spendthrift trust is repugnant to fraudulent transfer law is, quite literally, black-letter law. If the proposition genuinely comes as a surprise to anyone today, that can only be because it has been so firmly settled for more than a century that it ceased to be a subject of discussion. The relevant cases have not been overruled. So far as the present author is aware, the cases are unanimous. The Article [in opposition to the UVTA] cites no case that has ever held that a transfer to a self-settled spendthrift trust is exempt from the basic rule of fraudulent transfer law."[130]

In *Citizens Bank*, the Supreme Court of Tennessee focused on the nature of a trust agreement that features the settlor's retention of an interest (i.e., a self-settled spendthrift trust.) The court found it offensive that an individual could take property, which could have been used to satisfy creditor claims, and transfer the property in trust, to protect the property from creditors. The design itself was enough for the court to conclude it was meant to hinder or delay creditors.

> From the nature of the deed of trust in question we are of opinion that its legal effect amounts to nothing more than a scheme to hinder and delay creditors in the collection of their debts. No other proof of the scheme is required than the terms of the instrument itself. The defendant was already possessed of an estate in the property of his own right, holding the legal title and the beneficial use, and the only benefit which he could acquire by the conveyance to his brother in trust for himself would be to hinder and delay creditors in the collection of their debts. He cannot own the property and not own it at the same time. Whatever might be said of the justice or honesty of the arrangement in point of morals, it is enough that such conveyance contravenes a sound public policy announced in *Menkin v. Brinkley*, *supra*, and is therefore void. Being void, it may be reached by the bill in this case, upon an allegation that the conveyance is fraudulent, and was made for the purpose of hindering and delaying creditors, without any further proof of the fraudulent arrangement than the instrument itself. Its inevitable effect is to hinder and delay creditors, and the maker must be conclusively presumed to have so intended.[131]

About a half-century earlier, another court ruled a self-settled trust violated public policy as to all creditors of the debtor.

> This deed conveys all the property of the grantor, without any exception whatever, upon the trusts declared by her previous will and codicils, and thereby (according to the construction of that deed by this court in 6 Md. Rep., 235) passed the whole property immediately and irrevocably to the

---

129. In re Seitz, 400 B.R. 707, 713 n.8 (Bankr. E.D. Mo. 2008).

130. Kenneth C. Kettering, "The Comments to the Uniform Voidable Transactions Act Relating to Self-Settled Spendthrift Trusts Are Correct," Tax Management Estates, Gifts, and Trusts Journal, Vol. 42, 5, p. 267, 09/14/2017.

131. *Citizens' Nat. Bank v. Watkins*, 126 Tenn. 453, 150 S.W. 96, 97 (1912). (Emphasis added.)

> trustees, upon the trusts, as if recited in the deed. By this deed, therefore, it appears that Mrs. Chase placed all her property beyond the reach of her creditors, except the rents and profits of her reserved life-estate, she being then about or quite ninety years old, and one-half of such rents as might arise after her decease, from a ground rent of $43.50, and from the leasing thereafter by the trustees of an unimproved and unleased piece of ground called "Newington," containing about seven acres, which latter, by her will, is made applicable, and only after her decease, to any balance of money due and owing from her at her death, on account of her grandson William Chase Barney. This deed is in law fraudulent and void, as to the then creditors of Mrs. Chase, not only because it did not leave open to them an ample and unembarrassed sufficiency of property to pay their debts in any mode, but also because it threw them for the *219 payments of their debts, during her life, upon the mere rents and profits of her property, and that only to be reached against and not under the trusts, and after her death left no property applicable to the payment of any of them, except only the half of the rent of $43.50, and of "Newington," when leased, and that only to pay such of them as fall within the special trusts above stated. And being thus fraudulent and void as to prior creditors, it was properly vacated and set aside for the benefit of all creditors, subsequent as well as prior. It was also void as to subsequent as well as prior creditors, because it was made in contemplation of future indebtedness by Mrs. Chase, and to protect her property against such future indebtedness, and that too by means of a deed, whose trusts, after her decease, being declared by her will, were necessarily kept secret from such creditors, and her purposes as to them and their debts kept concealed from them until her death. These positions are fully sustained by the authorities. 3 Md. Rep., 11, 37, 40, Green vs. Trieber. 1 Md. Rep., 470, Waters vs. Dashiell. 8 Md. Rep., 426, 427, Malcolm vs. Hodges. 3 Md. Rep., 52, Sangston vs. Gaither. 5 Gill, 449, Worthington & Anderson vs. Shipley. 1 Md. Ch. Dec., 507, Atkinson vs. Phillips. 2 Md. Ch. Dec., 455, Sewell vs. Baxter & wife. 3 Md. Ch. Dec., 105, Bullett vs. Worthington. 2 Younge & Coll., 172, 177, Ede vs. Knowles. 1 Conn., 525, Salmon vs. Bennett. 9 Smedes & Mar., 394, Arthur vs. Commercial & Rail Road Bank of Vicksburg. 13 How., 98, Parish vs. Murphree. 4 Cond. Eng. Ch. Rep., 265, Richardson vs. Smallwood. 2 Bland, 35, Kipp vs. Hanna. 10 Paige, 210, Brownell vs. Curtis, et al. 6 Barb., 91, Browning vs. Hart. 1 Amer. Lead. Cases, 55 to 73, (3rd Ed.) 1 Story's Eq., secs. 361 and notes, 354, 355. 1 McCord's Ch. Rep., 518, Iley vs. Niswanger.[132]

Note that the court in *Williams v. Banks* addressed concealment as evidence of fraudulent intent. For this reason, some might set up a self-settled trust and publish notice of the trust's creation to help negate a badge of fraud (in addition to statute of limitation reasons).

---

132. *Williams v. Banks*, 11 Md. 198, 218–19 (1857).

## Rule Against Self-Settled Trusts and Fraudulent Transfer Law

As discussed elsewhere herein, both the rule against self-settled trust (RASST) and fraudulent transfer remedies have been applied to ignore or avoid transfers made by settlors to a trust for the settlor's benefit. The distinction makes sense from a policy perspective; where a transfer subject to RASST does not require any showing of fraud (either constructive or actual), a fraudulent transfer involves a transfer in violation of the norms of creditors' rights. Professor Gray noted the potential for confusion between these two separate avenues of relief for creditors:

> "A conveyance, valid as against existing creditors, can be avoided by subsequent creditors only when made with intent to defraud them. *Kane v. Roberts*, 40 Md. 590. Here, the transaction was admitted to be in good faith; but nevertheless the ample powers reserved were held conclusive evidence of actual fraud. This is, perhaps, going beyond the existing authorities; but the decision, although possibly judicial legislation, is not unlikely to meet with approval. But another, and, it seems, an untenable position was also taken. If the deed had been upheld, only the life estate would have been liable for the debts of S., who was yet practically owner of the property and therefore the case was declared to fall within the rule which forbids a man, while retaining the benefits of ownership, to place his property beyond the reach of his creditors. *In re Pearson*, 3 Ch. D. 807; *Brown v. McGill*, 39 Atl. Rep. 613 (Md.) This reasoning confuses conveyances in fraud of creditors and provisions in restraint of alienation. Gray, Restraints on Alienation, 2d ed., §91. In the one case the whole deed is void, but only as regards creditors; in the other, the unlawful provisions are invalid as against all the world, but the remainder of the deed is unimpeachable."[133]

Dewitt C. Moore also identified the distinction between the RASST and fraudulent transfer law, finding the RASST did not require any inquiry into intent, as opposed to fraudulent transfers:

> The statute of Henry VII, enacted in 1487, against trusts in personal property for the use of the persons creating them, re-enacted in New York in 1787, and in many other jurisdictions with immaterial differences in phraseology, applies, however, only to conveyances primarily and wholly for the use of the grantor, and not to instruments made in good faith for the actual and real use of the grantee and where the reservations to the grantor are incidental and partial. ***The simple inquiry is whether the property belongs to the debtor, not upon a theory of fraud and against the terms of his conveyance, but upon a theory of equitable title reserved to himself by the very conveyance which transfers the legal and nominal title to another. *** While these statutes are in terms limited to goods and chattels, the principle upon which they rest is a part of the common law, and in some jurisdictions it is applied to transfer of realty as well as personal, and a transfer of real or

133. Property - Conveyances in Fraud of Creditors - Powers, 12 Harv. L. Rev. 279, 283 (1898-1899).

personal property by a debtor to a third party to be held in trust for his use and benefit is held to be void as to existing and subsequent creditors."[134]

A preliminary issue for creditors is how to approach the retained interest in a trust; seek avoidance of the use retained by the settlor (treat the assets as owned by the settlor), or avoid the entire transfer under fraudulent transfer law. Obviously, nothing prevents seeking relief on both grounds.

Based on the foregoing, if a state's fraudulent transfer common law provides that a transfer to a self-settled trust is presumptively fraudulent, such common law should be examined along with the fraudulent transfer statutory law, as well as the RASST and other law unless expressly repealed by the legislature or modified by court decision.

## Self-Settled Trusts: Various Badges of Fraud

In the wealth transfer context, creditors may point to the form of transaction (i.e., purchase of a life insurance policy or transfers to an asset protection trust) to help establish intent, in addition to various other badges of fraud (such as timing, receipt of reasonably equivalent value, etc.) Where no creditor issues are present, and an individual utilizes state exemption law (such as life insurance or a homestead), it may be difficult for a creditor to prove intent to hinder, delay, or defraud as the insurance policy or homestead is often supported by state public policy and is simultaneously a prudent financial decision for many. The same may be said for transfers to a business entity, again, where there are no circling clouds of financial distress.

Unlike life insurance, which has been justified on public policy grounds by providing liquidity and stability to a family after an insured's death, the asset protection trust is primarily meant to protect the settlor's assets from future creditors. The trust agreement reflects multiple badges of fraud, making it easier for a creditor to prove intent to hinder, delay, or defraud. Courts, too, are now familiar with asset protection trusts, and such a view may not necessarily be helpful for the debtor.[135] The Supreme Court of Wyoming considered the location and type of trust in determining whether actual fraud was present. "The trial court found that the family trust was an asset protection trust. A special expert was appointed by the court to review the family trust and present testimony. The special expert intimated that because the family trust was located in the Commonwealth of the Bahamas the family trust would be considered an

134. Dewitt C. Moore, *Fraudulent Conveyances* (1908), p. 419–420. (Emphasis added.)

135. *Breitenstine v. Breitenstine* 2003 WY 16, 62 P. 3d 587, 593 (Wyo. 2003). ("We have not previously addressed OAPTs but other courts have. Generally, OAPTs are trusts established in a foreign jurisdiction to protect assets from creditors without requiring the settlor to lose control over the assets. *See S.E.C. v. Brennan*, 230 F.3d 65 (2nd Cir.2000); *FTC v. Affordable Media, LLC*, 179 F.3d 1228 (9th Cir.1999). Because it is outside the scope of this opinion to discuss the merits of OAPTs, we decline to do so. However, the characteristics of and the motives for establishing such trusts are known to us. While such trusts may have benefits in asset protection, the use of such trusts to avoid alimony, child support, and a fair division of marital property upon divorce is reprehensible to us.")

offshore asset protection trust (OAPT). We agree. We would note that many badges of fraud can be found in the very form of the family trust."[136]

The asset protection trust has not fared well when tested by creditors in court. Professor Jeffrey Pennell addressed this track record at the Heckerling Institute in 2014 before covering the *Huber* case. "Huber is one of seven cases in the last eighteen months all dealing with domestic asset protection trusts. All seven cases say 'these things do not work.' They say it for a variety of different reasons. Just at the noon hour an asset protection maven said, 'oh, the only cases that have reached judgment are the bad fact cases.' I frankly don't know whether there are good fact cases that have determined that these things work. And indeed, my sense is that what is happening is courts are finding reasons to say, 'these things don't work.' The reasons vary one case to another. In some cases they say that there's an alter ego argument, others it's a nominee argument, in some cases it's a fraudulent transfer."

136. *Id.* at 593.

CHAPTER 8

# Estate, Business or Tax Planning Excuse

For creditors seeking relief under fraudulent transfer law, the facts and circumstances may require looking beyond any of the debtor's stated purposes for entering a transaction. Where a creditor argues a fraudulent transfer occurred due to insolvency or lack of reasonably equivalent value, a debtor's self-serving statement as to the motivation of the transaction is generally ignored. Where a creditor argues the transaction was done with the actual intent to hinder, delay, or defraud creditors, the debtor's excuse is relevant. A court may determine that the intent to hinder can be sufficient to permit avoidance even if accompanied by non-fraudulent transfer motives.[1] This result is problematic for asset protection advisers who insist that intent to hinder, delay, or defraud must be the primary or driving force behind a transaction for a creditor to seek relief.

In *Citibank N.A. v. Bombshell Taxi LLC*, the court gave little weight to the debtor's excuse, and in doing so, asked whether the transfer made sense. "The more plausible interpretation is that Friedman's companies are in default, his rationale for transferring assets to his family members for alleged 'tax and estate planning' purposes is a poor effort to cover fraudulent transfers, and Citibank is entitled to payment."[2]

Many tout asset protection planning as a mechanism to take assets off the table and force a settlement with creditors. However, the mere documentation of transferring assets to force a lower settlement amount can be used as evidence

1. *See Jones v. Mackey Price Thompson & Ostler*, 2020 UT 25, P 43, 469 ¶ 3d 879, 889, reh'g denied (July 13, 2020). ("We first conclude that a 'mixed motive' is sufficient to establish an 'actual intent' to hinder, delay, or defraud under the Fraudulent Transfer Act. *** We begin by clarifying the governing legal standard on a question that has been decided in other states but never in Utah. The question is whether 'actual intent' to hinder, delay, or defraud requires proof that such intent was the sole or primary purpose of the defendant, or whether proof of a "mixed motive" is sufficient. We conclude that there is no requirement that the intent to hinder, delay, or defraud be the sole or even primary motive of the defendant. This follows from the text of the statute, which requires proof only that a defendant act "with actual intent" to hinder, delay, or defraud.") UTAH CODE §25-6-5(1)(a) (2016). It would add an unstated qualifier to require that a defendant acting "with actual intent" act solely or primarily with that actual intent. And such an addition is foreclosed by our canons of interpretation.

2. *See Citibank N.A. v. Bombshell Taxi LLC*, No. 15 CIV. 5067 (BMC), 2017 WL 3054832, at *4 (E.D.N.Y. July 19, 2017).

of intent to hinder creditors. "Specifically, Bankruptcy Court commented that, 'the arrangement certainly suggests that Mr. Baird wanted to gain over Izzo Golf a negotiating advantage, or, in fraudulent transfer law parlance, Mr. Baird wanted to hinder or delay Izzo Golf by depleting Old King Par of all of its assets and, in particular, its cash.'"[3]

Planners must consider how courts will liberally construe terms in favor of creditors under fraudulent transfer law. For example, the term "claim" has been interpreted to provide relief where a loan default has not yet occurred. It is common lore in the asset protection world that so long as a debtor-client is making payments to creditors, the client's lenders may not challenge any transfers. This may provide the client with an opportunity to continuously transfer wealth piecemeal over time to a self-settled trust (or into an exempt form.) If the client subsequently experiences financially difficulty, the lenders may decide to challenge the prior transfers. But the lenders do not need to helplessly watch a guarantor's assets be depleted over time. They may monitor the guarantor's financial health on a regular basis, but more importantly, the lender may challenge transfers before the borrower defaults.

> "[debtors do] . . . not dispute that [p]laintiffs have a right to payment, but they essentially argue that [p]laintiffs cannot take steps under the UFTA to protect [their] right[s to payment] unless [Debtor] has 'missed a payment' or 'breached an obligation'—regardless of whether the corporation currently may be rendering itself insolvent through insider transfers so that it will ultimately be unable to repurchase the notes at full value when they become due. Reaching this conclusion would require the Court to disregard the plain language of the UFTA that expressly encompasses claims that are unmatured and contingent."[4]

Not surprisingly, a debtor's excuse for transferring assets will be consistent with the benefit sought. For example, an individual seeking tax benefits will point to asset protection as the motivation behind the creation of an entity, as opposed to the tax benefits.[5] An individual seeking asset protection benefits will point to tax benefits associated with the transer instead of the asset protection benefits.

With respect to documenting "asset protection" as the motivation for a transfer, consideration should be given to the test for actual fraud, which provides a creditor may avoid a transfer if the transfer was intended to hinder, delay, or defraud any creditor of the debtor. While an asset protection excuse

3. Izzo Golf Inc., f/k/a Dancorp Investors, Inc., Plaintiff v. King Par Corporation, B&P Baird Holdings, Inc., KP Acquisition Company, King Par LLC, William J. Baird, Pamela Baird, "John Doe" 1-10, "Mary Roe" 1-10 & XYZ Corporation 1-10, Defendants, No. 10-CV-6507 CJS, 2018 WL 2739396, at *4 (W.D.N.Y. June 7, 2018).

4. *Akanthos Capital Mgmt., LLC v. CompuCredit Hldgs. Corp.*, 770 F. Supp. 2d 1315, 1329–30 (N.D. Ga. 2011), rev'd on other grounds, 677 F.3d 1286 (11th Cir. 2012).

5. *See Estate of Turner v. Commissioner*, 102 T.C.M. (CCH) 214 (T.C. 2011), *supplemented sub nom. Turner v. Commissioner*, 138 T.C. 306 (2012) (agreeing that asset protection may be a legitimate reason for forming a family limited partnership, but concluding that there was no credible argument that the company at issue was formed for that reason); *c.f., Breitenstine v. Breitenstine*, 2003 WY 16, ¶ 21, 62 P.3d 587, 593 (Wyo. 2003) ("While there are surely some legitimate reasons for establishing OAPTs, such as estate planning or tax planning, the exclusive intent to hinder creditors is not such a legitimate reason.")

might help in a valuation discount dispute with the IRS, documenting such intent could aid other creditors seeking to avoid transfers to a business entity. This might occur where one creditor points to the taxpayer's intent to hinder other creditors by transferring assets to the business entity, thereby establishing the debtor's intent to hinder *any* creditor.[6] This is not to say a client's intent should not be documented, however, if a client does not express intent to avoid creditors, an adviser should carefully consider creating a paper trail not supported by reality. This is true especially where such documentation can be used against a client.

In many cases, debtors deny making transfers for creditor-motivated purposes, but instead, assert just about anything one can imagine showing the transfer was not motivated by the creditor seeking to enforce its claim. In at least one case, the debtor claimed the Affordable Care Act motivated a fraudulent transfer,[7] and in another case, transfers were motivated by religion.[8] In the wealth transfer context, it is stated often that transfers were done for estate planning purposes, with no intent to hinder or delay creditors. However, notwithstanding the purported goal behind wealth transfer planning transactions, a court may determine whether circumstantial evidence supports the debtor's argument that she lacked intent to hinder, delay, or defraud.

Where a stated intent is to avoid estate tax, a court will review whether the debtor's assets were sufficient to trigger an estate tax in the first place.[9] In *In re*

---

6. Non-taxing authority creditors may also benefit from the IRS' presence as a golden creditor in the bankruptcy setting. The fraudulent transfer statute does not permit a debtor to "pick-and-choose" which creditors the debtor intends to hinder.

7. *See Hazeltine Gates, LLC v. Hoffman*, 2015 WL 4877086 (Minn.Dist.Ct.), 13. ("Hoffmann and Tompach insisted that Metro Oral's sale of its assets and inventory to Minnesota Oral had nothing to do with Metro Oral's liability to Hazeltine Gates. They offered a number of explanations, including the departure of Curtis and his ability to act as a buffer between Hoffmann and Tompach, the economy, the Affordable Care Act, Metro Oral's status as a C-corporation, and the fact that Minnesota Oral would no longer require its officers, Hoffmann and Tompach, to be subject to written employment agreements containing non-compete clauses. The Court finds, however, that none of these reasons provide a legitimate basis for Hoffman and Tompach, as Metro Oral, to sell Metro Oral's assets to themselves as Minnesota Oral. All of the purported benefits of this sale could have been achieved without the resulting sale; the only benefit gained through structuring the transaction as Hoffman and Tompach did was to be relieved of Metro Oral's debt to Hazeltine. Minnesota Oral had the same owners as Metro Oral; the sale of the assets and inventory would not affect how Hoffmann and Tompach would deal with each other as of November 1, 2010.")

8. *See In re Witt*, 231 B.R. 92, 95–97 (Bankr. N.D. Okla. 1999). Some protection does exist for transfers to charity under Federal and State law. ("On June 19, 1998, the Liberty Act was passed by Congress. The Liberty Act severely restricts the ability of a bankruptcy trustee to avoid pre-petition transfers by debtors to charitable institutions, including but not limited to religious entities through certain amendments to §544 and §548 of the Bankruptcy Code.3 Under the terms of the Liberty Act, a bankruptcy trustee may not avoid a transfer by a debtor to a charitable institution if the transfer does not exceed fifteen per cent (15%) of the debtor's gross annual income in the year the contribution was made. A contribution which exceeds fifteen per cent (15%) of the debtor's gross annual income in the year the contribution was made may not be avoided if it was consistent with debtor's prior charitable contribution practices. Any transfer made with the actual intent to hinder, delay or defraud a creditor of the debtor remains subject to avoidance. The amendments to §§544 and 548 apply "to any case brought under an applicable provision of title 11, United States Code, that is pending or commenced on or after the date of the enactment of this Act." Liberty Act, §5.")

9. In other words, in order to assert the estate planning excuse for estate tax reasons, one should first have an "taxable estate." Notwithstanding the current asset value, one should inquire as to the *expected* value of the transferred assets. If it can be shown that planning was done to remove assets that could greatly appreciate in

*Hypnotic Taxi LLC*, the court found various factors, including the timing of the transfers, hard to believe:

> Zimmerman similarly testified that Freidman came to him for estate planning and asset protection. (November 30 Tr., ECF 66, p.34, ln. 6–10.) This consultation led to the creation of four separate trusts, the Kelly Funding Trust and the Birkin Funding Trust, both located in the Cook Islands, the Evelyn Funding Trust, located in Belize, and the Lindy Funding Trust, located in Nevis. *** Freidman asserts that he undertook these transfers simply for estate planning purposes, a proposition that strains credulity. From the perspective of an inquiry into the presence of the badges of fraud, it is difficult to imagine a more arresting chronology. These transfers occurred against the background of a suit by Citibank to recover in excess of $40 million dollars, and a confession of judgment entered by Capital One, which resulted in a judgment of almost $8.5 million dollars. It is impossible to conclude that the timing of the transfers is merely coincidence.[10]

In *JPMorgan Chase Bank v. Winget*, the court declined to accept an estate planning excuse:

> As Winget frames the request, he seeks "to explore through discovery whether Chase, as contingent trustee, was privy to information relating to Mr. Winget's purpose behind forming, maintaining and managing the assets within the Trust." (Doc. 695 at p. 3.) Winget says that this information is "relevant to the central question here," which he claims is "[w]hether [he] managed the assets within the Trust with the exclusive intent of estate planning or, as Chase alleges, with the 'actual intent to defraud Chase.'" (*Id.* at 3–4).Winget's request turns fraudulent transfer law on its head. Under the Act, a transfer that occurs after the creditor's claim arose is fraudulent when the transfer was made for less than reasonably equivalent value and renders the transferring party insolvent. M.C.L. §566.35(1). This is known as a constructive fraudulent conveyance. Alternatively, a transfer violates the Act if made with "actual intent to hinder, delay, or defraud any creditor of the debtor." M.C.L. §566.34(1)(a). This is known as an actual fraudulent conveyance. Chase has plead that Winget violated both provisions of the Act. (*See* Doc 688 ¶¶ 26–37.). Putting aside that the issue of "intent" is only pertinent to Chase's actual fraudulent transfer claim, the relevant intent is whether Winget revoked the Trust for purposes of hindering or delaying the Trust's creditors. Winget's intent in forming, maintaining, and managing the property prior to the relevant transfer, which is the purported focus of his discovery, is not relevant. Any information that Winget seeks through his 30(b)(6) deposition notice about what Chase may or may not have known about the original purposes of the Winget Trust is simply not relevant to Chase's claims and defenses.[11]

---

value, a legitimate issue might be raised (depending on all the facts and circumstances) that could support the debtor's intent to minimize transfer taxes.

10. *In re Hypnotic Taxi LLC*, 543 B.R. 365, 379 (Bankr. E.D.N.Y. 2016). (Emphasis added.)

11. *JPMorgan Chase Bank v. Winget*, No. 08-13845, 2016 WL 7242136, at *4 (E.D. Mich. Dec. 15, 2016). (Emphasis added.)

Many transactions are designed to provide numerous wealth transfer benefits. For example, some have utilized an incomplete non-grantor trust (ING) to provide income tax savings. This was common for those domiciled in New York until the New York Department of Revenue discovered the loophole and legislation was enacted preventing the use of such trusts, often in Delaware (DINGs), to avoid state income tax. In these cases, the APT jurisdiction provides legislation that would enable those domiciled in a state that imposes income tax to avoid such tax by forming an ING in the APT jurisdiction (i.e., a DING or an ING in Nevada.) While utilizing the law of the APT jurisdiction, the ING is often created to simultaneously take advantage of the APT state's law permitting self-settled spendthrift trusts. Consequently, a debtor may fund a trust and attempt to assert either income tax or creditor protection justifications, depending upon the identity of the challenging creditor.

If a debtor made a transfer to avoid creditors, which is typically inferred when a self-settled trust is used in an asset protection trust haven, it may be that a court accepts the estate planning excuse but simply disregards it. That was the case in *In re Huber*.

> In the instant case, the Debtor failed to submit his own declaration regarding his intent, let alone the declarations of other witnesses, such as Mr. Snow and Kevin Huber, who would be the witnesses most likely to testify as to the Debtor's intent in creating the Trust and transferring his assets. Moreover, while the Debtor's deposition testimony states that he created the Trust for estate planning purposes, it does not directly address or deny the evidence submitted by the Trustee establishing that the Debtor wanted to protect his assets in light of his increasingly bleak financial situation. The Court finds that the Debtor's desire to provide for his children and grandchildren through estate planning by protecting his assets that they would otherwise stand to inherit, is not *816 mutually exclusive of the desire to shield his assets from creditors. Accordingly, estate planning alone does not create an issue of fact as to intent. *See* Adeeb, 787 F.2d at 1343 (where the court held that if a debtor intended to hinder or delay a creditor, he had "the intent penalized by [section 727(a)(2)(A)] notwithstanding any other motivation he may have had for the transfer."). Furthermore, as previously indicated, the Debtor's deposition testimony regarding Mr. Terhune's goal to transfer his assets into his own spendthrift trust establishes that he knew the purpose of a spendthrift trust.
>
> Accordingly, viewing the evidence in the light most favorable to the Debtor, the Trustee has established that there is no genuine dispute as to any material fact, and the Trustee is entitled to summary judgment as a matter of law on its UFTA claim based on actual fraudulent intent.[12]

Interestingly, a debtor was successful claiming his transfers to an offshore trust (shortly before judgment) were not done with the intent to hinder, delay, or defraud the creditor bank. The debtor's excuse for transferring assets offshore were his beliefs as to whether an ex-wife would pursue him sometime in the

12. *In re Huber*, 493 B.R. 798, 815–16 (Bankr. W.D. Wash. 2013).

future, and the fact that the debtor's mother had Alzheimer's disease.[13] Further, the debtor admitted he was sending money offshore to hinder creditors other than the bank. These reasons, the court found, appeared to justify the rationale for sending money to the Cook Islands.

> Also on November 17, 2011, Ora Fiduciary Unlimited, the company that set up Bellinger's Cook Islands Trust, sent Bellinger an Estate Planning Questionnaire for him to complete in order to establish the Trust. [DE 377-13, p. 1]. Bellinger's testimony, which this Court found to be credible, established that he created the Trust for multiple reasons: (1) the unusual nature of Bellinger's Marital Settlement Agreement with his ex-wife, which he thought she may violate and seek more money from him; (2) end-of-life medical expenses that he anticipated because of his mother's recent passing from Alzheimer's disease; (3) exposure to risk from new and uncertain business ventures in commercial property; and (4) a desire to secure his retirement.
>
> * * *
>
> The Court has considered all of the badges of fraud alleged by BB&T. BB&T has proven several badges of fraud, and therefore BB&T has established a prima facie case of actual fraud and has raised a rebuttable presumption that the transaction is void. Despite BB&T having established several badges of fraud, the Court finds that Bellinger sufficiently rebutted the rebuttable presumption. Bellinger credibly testified as to his reasons for creating the Trust in 2011. With regard to the creation and funding of the Trust, the undersigned found Bellinger's demeanor and testimony to be candid and truthful. First, Bellinger had a marital settlement agreement [DE 377-12] with his ex-wife, which he believed she may violate and seek more money from Bellinger in the future because of its unique terms. Second, Bellinger's mother passed away from Alzheimer's disease, and he witnessed how her medical expenses drained all of her financial assets. He was reasonably concerned that he, too, may ultimately suffer from Alzheimer's disease, which could negatively impact his assets. Third, Bellinger was considering getting into the commercial real estate development business, which was apparently volatile, and he wanted to protect his assets from any future creditors' claims. Fourth, Bellinger wanted to secure funds for his support after his retirement. For all of these reasons, Bellinger attested that he created the Trust. Taking into account all the evidence and the totality of the circumstances that surrounded the 2011 creation of the Trust and the 2012 conveyance of Bellinger's assets to the Trust, the undersigned concludes Bellinger set forth legitimate reasons for creating the Trust. *See In re Bifani*, 580 Fed. Appx. 740, 745 (11th Cir. 2014). The Court finds that Bellinger created the Trust in 2011 and transferred the assets to the Trust in 2012 in good faith, without any intent to defraud BB&T. A careful review of all the evidence and the totality of the circumstances supports a finding that the

13. Query whether sending money across the globe makes sense if the fear is susceptibility to developing Alzheimer's disease.

> transfer of approximately $1.7 million in assets by Bellinger to the Trust in 2012 was not a fraudulent transfer.[14]

Although the court did not find a fraudulent transfer (for various technical reasons), the debtor's girlfriend was a beneficiary of the trust and used trust distributions to benefit the debtor. Although the debtor did not technically transfer assets to his girlfriend, the court determined that a transfer did take place. Unfortunately for the girlfriend, given the broad scope of the term "transfer," she instantly became a transferee and therefore liable under the fraudulent transfer law.

14. *Branch Banking v. Hamilton Greens, LLC*, 2016 WL 3365270, at 10 (S.D. Fla. Jan. 13, 2016), report and recommendation adopted in part, rejected in part sub nom., 2016 WL 3251165 (S.D. Fla. June, 2016).

CHAPTER 9

# Fraudulent Transfer Law Issues for Planners

> "Without an award of punitive damages or attorneys' fees, there would be no deterrence to a debtor weighing whether to make a fraudulent transfer. This is because the debtor would only lose the same asset he would have lost if he had not made a fraudulent transfer."[1]

Given the potential for wealth transfer planning that can result in more harm than good, planners—especially those who market the protection of assets—must understand the reach of fraudulent transfer law, so as to (1) identify a conflict between wealth transfer planning and fraudulent transfer law; (2) prevent client's plan from being unwound by creditors; (3) avoid the imposition of penalties for planning that violates fraudulent transfer law; and (4) avoid negative adviser-related consequences, such as reputational harm as well as ethical, civil, and criminal liability.

The following Venn diagram illustrates how one may view the intersection between the transfer of wealth in the form of a gift and the actual and constructive fraud prongs under fraudulent transfer law:

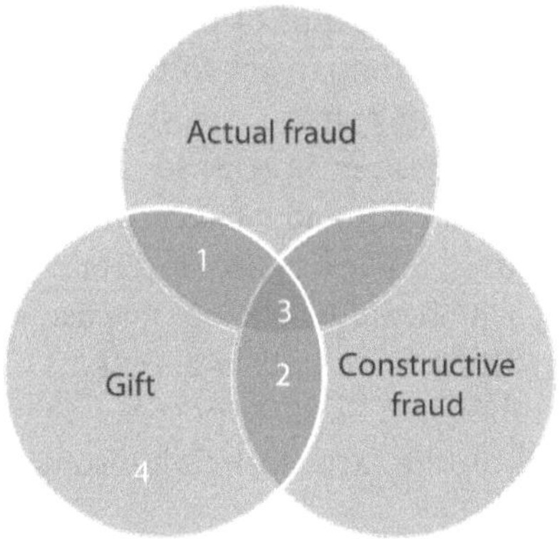


1. *SE Prop. Holdings, LLC v. Judkins*, 2019 WL 177981, at *10 (S.D. Ala. Jan. 11, 2019).

For a creditor looking to avoid a transfer of wealth, and an individual attempting to make a transfer of wealth, it is important to understand how the transaction may be challenged under both actual and constructive fraud prongs. The Venn diagram illustrates how a common wealth transfer transaction, a gift, may fall subject to avoidance under Sections 4 and 5(a) of the UVTA. A gift is commonly viewed as a transfer made with detached and disinterested generosity where the donor parts with an asset without receiving value in exchange. In Zone 1, the gift may be challenged by a creditor if the creditor can prove the gift was made with the intent to hinder, delay, or defraud any creditor of the debtor. Where a gift is made years before any issues with creditors, it might be difficult for a creditor to prove the gift was done with intent to hinder creditors. If the gift implicates one of three financial conditions, the gift may fall within Zone 2 and be challenged under the constructive fraud rules. Zone 3 reflects a transfer that satisfies both actual and constructive fraud prongs of a fraudulent transfer analysis.

Many planners focus on Zone 2 and ignore Zones 1 and 3, with the thought being that if a debtor makes a transfer and is not rendered insolvent, a creditor may not void the transfer. By adopting this erroneous reasoning, the wealth planner focuses solely on Section 5(a) and ignores a constructive fraud analysis under Section 4(a)(2) and an actual fraud analysis under 4(a)(1).

A transaction may fall subject to one or both prongs depending on the facts and circumstances. However, where transactions involve the debtor's receipt of reasonably equivalent value, none of the financial condition tests under constructive fraud will apply; in this situation, the transaction may be subject to avoidance under an actual fraud analysis. If the transferee acted in good faith and gave reasonably equivalent value, the transferee has an absolute defense under the fraudulent transfer statutory law, with an exception for the initial transferee under the bankruptcy code.

To illustrate, consider a debtor's contribution of cash to a limited liability company in exchange for a membership interest. This transfer (what might be considered a contribution of capital to the LLC) might be done with the intent to hinder, delay, or defraud any creditor of the debtor. If the requisite intent is present, a creditor may successfully attack the transfer of assets to the LLC. A creditor may also argue that the receipt of the LLC membership interest is not reasonably equivalent value in comparison to the cash contributed to the LLC, thereby triggering application of constructive fraud analysis. A gift to a family member outright and free of trust, or in trust for the benefit of family members, should, by definition, automatically fall subject to a constructive fraud analysis requiring the creditor establish the existence of certain financial conditions. The gift to family members, whether outright or in trust, may also be challenged under the actual fraud analysis. With both transactions (contribution to the LLC and gift to family members), it is also possible that neither amount to a fraudulent transfer based on the facts and circumstances.

# Due Diligence

A preliminary consideration to wealth transfer planning should entail a review of the client's occupation, financial condition, and motivation for seeking planning. All these factors are relevant to understanding how proposed planning could impact a creditor's rights. If a transaction is voided the planning goals might be thwarted.[2] But an avoided transaction could mean more than just putting the debtor back to the starting point. A wealth transfer transaction constituting actual fraud under fraudulent transfer law could result in a subsequent denial of discharge in bankruptcy. It could mean exposure to the transferee involved in the transaction, such as a friend or family member. The attorney could face exposure for the attorney's role in hindering creditors, both from plaintiffs in a civil suit as well as the state bar pursuant to an investigation based on an ethical complaint. If the planning is thwarted, the adviser may be at risk for a malpractice lawsuit, thereby triggering the determination of whether insurance covers assisting with a fraudulent transfer. For all the foregoing reasons, advisers should engage in due diligence before facilitating wealth transfers.

If a client is subject to regulatory oversight, care must be taken in handling the transfer of assets. This is because any of the client's wealth that can be traced to violations of regulatory provisions (reporting violations, ill-gotten gains, etc.) could potentially be clawed back or disgorged. In cases where a client is currently under investigation, the attorney must review applicable law regarding disgorgement of attorney fees.

It is no surprise that transactions made pursuant to wealth transfer planning can be voided under fraudulent transfer law if the client was insolvent or rendered insolvent because of such planning.[3] State asset protection statutes may include provisions to entice planners to utilize that state asset protection versus competing jurisdictions. In addition to providing for the protection of planners who assist with the creation of the asset protection trust, the provisions may require a solvency affidavit prior to a client funding the trust. The affidavit requirement helps turn the asset protection trust formation and funding process more cookie cutter from a due diligence perspective and requires less concern for hindering creditors. This has led to the common practice of having the client execute a solvency affidavit prior to engaging in any transfers (including any non-asset protection trust transactions) pursuant to an engagement explicitly for asset protection planning.

However, one should not be lulled into thinking that transactions a solvent debtor enters will defeat a fraudulent transfer challenge. The rationale behind the affidavit is, if the client is not rendered insolvent because of a proposed

2. If a transfer is made to minimize federal taxation, the status of the transaction vis-à-vis creditors might result in negative tax consequences. If a transfer is made for creditor protection but constitutes a fraudulent transfer, the result might put the client in a position far worse than before the engagement.

3. *See Michael v. Moore*, 157 N.C. 462, 73 S.E. 104, 105 (1911). ("It is a principle of the common law, as old as the law itself, and upon which the preservation of all property depends, that, except so far as the same may be exempt by positive law, the whole of every man's property shall be devoted to the payment of his debts. He cannot gratuitously give away any part of it; the law meaning that he shall be just to his creditors before he is generous to his family.")

transaction, a creditor may not claim the transaction is voidable. This approach completely ignores the fact that fraudulent transfer law extends beyond mere numbers; the adviser must understand the facts and circumstances surrounding the client's wealth and any transactions involving such wealth. Although some asset protection trust statutes attempt to shorten the period for which a creditor must bring a claim for relief, the period still exists, and it is questionable whether one state can force its weakened laws on creditors in another state.

## Documenting the File

Because the fraudulent transfer common law adopts the concept of substance over form, modern-day planning techniques that reflect an intent to hinder or delay creditors could be avoided by examining substance, regardless of how sophisticated the planning structure.

Unlike other forms of planning that provide creditor protection, such as the purchase of an annuity or life insurance policy, the use of a trust agreement essentially spells out the settlor's intent. Thus, the same document that purports to protect assets often creates an evidence trail that can be used to reach such assets. Realizing this problem, and as discussed elsewhere in this book, the law of asset protection states will often prohibit the use of the trust agreement as evidence of intent to hinder creditors. Like the prohibition against holding advisers liable, this might work in the asset protection trust jurisdiction, but is unlikely to prevent a court in another jurisdiction from upholding its state's important public policy.

Should a trust be designed to permit someone other than the settlor (e.g., a "protector") transfer or direct the transfer of trust assets when a claim arises against the settlor be any different than the settlor making such a transfer? Similarly, where fraudulent intent is present, should the debtor who transfers assets to a self-settled trust and leaves distribution decisions in favor of the debtor to a third-party trustee be treated any differently than a debtor who transfers assets to a third party who may subsequently exercise a power of appointment in favor of the debtor? The ability to collude and thus, defeat creditors, exists with either a trustee or the powerholder.[4] As discussed elsewhere herein, there has been a shift from using hyper-technical agreements establishing when a settlor may receive property to vague arrangements that make it more difficult to prove an implied agreement. However, it is precisely this type of arrangement that was considered a badge of fraud (i.e., a secret trust) centuries ago. The documentation of a client's file may very well support an inference that a client had intent to hinder, delay, or defraud creditors.

---

4. *See In re Strasser*, 303 B.R. 841, 847 (Bankr. D. Ariz. 2004), citing Plaintiff's opening brief at 7, dkt. 51 ("The term 'future creditors' in this context is nothing more than a euphemism for preferring yourself to your creditors. All that debtor did was move $62,000+ out of reach of her actual creditors, and then use it later whenever and wherever she needed, including thousands each month for new credit card shopping, clothes, groceries, private school tuition etc. These ongoing expenses were not 'creditors' future or otherwise, at the time of the transfer. Taking $62,000 and parking it with her father for her own use in the future, and then claiming 'no harm no foul, I used it on my future creditors' defies logic.")

Although asset protection is not by itself impermissible (all states expressly provide by statute the ability to shelter assets from creditors), a debtor's stated goal of asset protection as justification for transferring wealth does not appear to help the debtor in a fraudulent transfer action as to the transferred wealth. Advisors who offer such planning will often charge a premium for the documents they prepare; this is not necessarily because the planning is too sophisticated for the typical planner, rather, it is because the advisor must consider numerous ancillary issues. Given the number of cases involving lawyers who assist with fraudulent transfers, the adviser may require higher fees to deal with extensive due diligence to avoid various forms of liability and negative public relations exposure, such as potential ethical discipline.

In one case, a court found asset protection to be synonymous with fraudulent transfer, "[m]oreover, it is unclear from the evidence presented whether Thomas Woolsey or [Trust 1] actually purchased the Inglewood property in 2009, and thus, whether a fraudulent conveyance (or any other asset protection scheme) actually occurred."[5]

In *Cutuli*, e-mail between debtors and their counsel was used as evidence of intent to hinder, delay, or defraud. This was so because of the stated desire to obtain information on a Wyoming LLC and asset protection. In addition to the emails, the bankruptcy trustee also pointed to the law firm's website, where the lawyers offered asset protection services. Taken together, the emails, the timing of the assistance and the law firm's website were all reasons cited by the trustee supporting discovery of attorney-client communications.

Consequently, use of terms and phrases synonymous with hindering creditors (i.e., asset protection, wealth preservation, creating roadblocks, ring-fencing, bullet-proof protection, etc.) might be used by a creditor to help prove actual intent to hinder, delay, or defraud. The phrases are not helpful for purposes of establishing a client's intent not to hinder creditors, and in rare cases, the use of the phrases may also impact the integrity of the attorney-client privilege.

> The Trustee conducted searches of electronic and documentary information relating to possible asset protection mechanisms employed by Debtor.
>
> 8. Based upon those searches the Trustee's counsel identified email communications between the Debtor, her husband Greg Cutuli, and The Andersen Firm.
>
> *2 9. The electronic communications apparently included emails between the Debtor, Greg Cutuli, and The Andersen Firm attorney, Matt Harrod, purporting to relate to "offshore info" and "information on the WY LLC in regards [sic] to asset protection . . . " [ECF 866-1 at ¶ 5; 866-2]. Other emails request a "description regarding the protections offered by the [sic] Wyoming LLC that we are about to enter into" and state "I would like to

5. *Video Tech Services, Inc., Plaintiff & Appellant, v. Edward Abdalla et al., Defendants & Respondents.*, No. B266891, 2017 WL 1180413, at *5 (Cal. Ct. App. Mar. 30, 2017). (Emphasis added.)

discuss it [sic] with our accountant and one of Kathy's attorneys." [ECF 866-3 at p. 6 of 15].

10. One email attachment describes the "benefits of the Wyoming Close Limited Liability Company," including a discussion of the limitations that structure imposes on creditor's rights and specifically the limited efficacy of charging orders issued against Wyoming LLCs. [ECF 866-2 at p. 7 of 15]. Another attachment states: "Asset Protection: It is difficult for a member's creditor to reach the assets of the LLC. Under Wyoming law, the creditor of a member can only reach distributions made to the member, but the creditor cannot force the LLC to make such distributions." [ECF 866-2 at p. 1 of 15; and 12 of 15].

11. The Trustee contends The Andersen Firm holds itself out as a law firm providing estate planning and asset protection services to its clients. [ECF 866-1 at ¶ 6; *see also* http://www.theandersenfirm.com/asset-protection-planning.htm], that the email communications between the Debtor, Greg Cutuli, and The Andersen Firm occurred during the same time period that Greg Cutuli and the Debtor were allegedly engaged in a "conspiracy to defraud creditors" and, therefore, the Trustee should be allowed to obtain discovery from The Andersen Firm to determine whether assets rightfully belonging to the estate were transferred in an effort to defraud the creditors of the estate. [ECF 865-2 at 2–23; 865-2 at 23; 865-3 at 1–5; 865-4 at 1–10].[6]

Ironically, the marketing of the asset protection trust, complete with colorful pamphlets depicting well-guarded castles, vaults, and merchandise marketing a particular domicile distributed by asset protection trust companies, can be detrimental in certain circumstances. This is especially true in bankruptcy court, where the goal is to distribute assets for creditors and give a debtor a "fresh start, not a head start."[7] It goes without saying that a particular technique should not be advertised as being immune from fraudulent transfer attack.

The Defendants do not dispute that the transfer of the $142,742 to the LNDP & G Ultra Trust was a fraudulent transfer under Section 548(a)(1)(A) and (B) of the Bankruptcy Code. 11 U.S.C. §548(a)(1)(A)-(B). In this, they are well advised. The Ultra Trust and related documents are vague, confusing, verbose, and internally inconsistent.

They plainly were designed for the purpose of protecting assets from creditors. Pl. Exs. 3 ("Financial Instrument avoids creditor claims of fraudulent conveyance"), & 5 ("For Asset Protection purposes"). The Defendants properly concede that the Trustee has met her burden of putting on a prima facie case under Sections 548 and 550 of the Bankruptcy Code. Rather, the Defendants argue that the property at issue, the $142,742, was never property of the Debtor's estate and always was held in trust for the Debtor's mother, Ms. Stutesman.[8]

6. *In re Cutuli*, No. 11-35256-BKC-AJC, 2013 WL 5236711, at *1–2 (Bankr. S.D. Fla. Sept. 16, 2013).

7. *See In re Erskine: Debtor Attempts to Exclude Assets Held in "Tennessee Asset Protection Trust,"* LISI Asset Protection Newsletter #324 (June 14, 2016).

8. *In re Woodworth*, No. 11-11051-BFK, 2013 WL 753509, at *4 (Bankr. E.D. Va. Feb. 27, 2013). (Emphasis added.)

Avoiding the use of these creditor-thwarting terms may also enable asset protection trust legislation to successfully pass through a state's legislature. Often, these debtor-friendly statutes are described as mere trust code updates or modernizations without raising the eyebrows of various interest groups, such as the creditors' rights bar, family law bar, state bankers association, plaintiffs' attorneys, etc.

A planner confronted with a client who does not express a desire to hinder creditors should document the client's non-creditor motivated reasons for making transfers, such as illness. *In re Jackson* illustrates how documenting estate planning goals can help negate a finding of actual fraud. In this case, the adviser properly documented the motivations for engaging in wealth transfer planning; the debtor husband had an upcoming hip surgery and had not updated his estate plan for at least twenty years. Estate planning counsel recommended the debtor husband and defendant wife (defendant wife was transferee as trustee of trusts created) "equalize" their estates to create two trusts, to hold the assets of the husband and wife, and to "obtain the maximum benefit of the marital deduction for federal estate tax planning purposes." Estate planning counsel also created an estate planning questionnaire, which was later used as evidence of the husband's solvency for purposes of negating both actual fraud and constructive fraud.

> The Court finds the transfers of the Subject Parcels were for a legitimate purpose: estate planning. *See In re White*, 130 B.R. 979, 989 (Bankr.D. Mont.1991) (finding estate planning in the face of medical advice constitutes sufficient consideration to avoid being labeled as a badge of fraud). The estate plan was the result of the advice of specialized legal counsel contacted for that purpose. The timing was dictated by the Debtor's medical condition and the lengthy interval since the last estate planning. The Plaintiff presented no evidence that the nature of the controversy or the level of the dispute between Citizens Bank and the Debtor over his obligations under the Note was materially different immediately before the transfers than at any time during the preceding six years. Finally, the estate plan executed by the Debtor and the Defendant, in form and substance, was consistent with estate plans routinely followed by persons whose combined assets exceed the amount of property sheltered from federal estate taxation by the Unified Gift and Estate Tax Credit. Such plans are recommended by legal advisers and are entered into by spouses to reduce the potential for federal estate taxes to shrink their combined estates and to avoid the publicity and expense of probate. The Plaintiff presented no evidence which leads the Court to conclude the actual intent of the Debtor and the Defendant, in executing their estate plan, was motivated by any different considerations. The Court further finds these legitimate purposes outweigh any of the indicia that suggest fraudulent intent. Accordingly, the Court finds the Plaintiff has failed to establish by a preponderance of the evidence, let alone clear and convincing evidence, that the Debtor transferred the Subject Parcels to the Defendant with actual intent to defraud creditors under section 4(I) of UFTA.[9]

9. *In re Jackson*, 318 B.R. 5, 17–18 (Bankr. D.N.H. 2004), subsequently aff'd, 459 F.3d 117 (1st Cir. 2006).

Documentation evidencing non-creditor avoidance motivations may be helpful in defending a client facing a denial of discharge in bankruptcy.[10] Documenting a client's file to support a client's intent is nothing new to many wealth transfer planners. In the tax planning arena, many planners utilize the family limited partnership to obtain valuation discounts on the transfer of assets for federal tax purposes. The IRS challenged these arrangements under anti-avoidance law theories, arguing that the partnership was used for the sole purpose of obtaining a tax benefit, without any real economic or business purpose. This prompted planners to cite asset protection as the motivation for the use of such partnerships.

## Consequences of Actual Fraud

Recent decisions illustrate various forms of evidence that may be used to show a client's intent to hinder or delay creditors. The evidence can range from the lawyer's time entries,[11] to the lawyer's expertise,[12] to mere conversations without the purchase of any legal services.[13] It is important to consider whether assisting a client engage in a transaction that exhibits actual intent to hinder, delay, or defraud because actual fraud can trigger a whole host of unfortunate consequences for the debtor and those involved.

---

10. *In re Burzee*, 402 B.R. 8, 17 (Bankr. M.D. Fla. 2008). ("The Plaintiff has not established its Section 727(a)(2)(A) allegations. The Rogel and Nancy Street Property transfers were not made with the intent to hinder, delay, or defraud the Plaintiff. The Rogel transfers were made to put the Debtor's grandmother back to her original position. The Nancy Street Property transfer was made at Zika's request for estate planning purposes. The Debtor did not conceal any assets. She did not undervalue her assets. Information relating to her USAA Rollover Account was unintentionally and inadvertently omitted from her original schedules and statements.")

11. *See Sardis v. Frankel*, 113 A.D.3d 135, 138, 978 N.Y.S.2d 135, 138 (2014). ("Proskauer's attorney time records for November 2008 describe a conversation of November 7 'with Sofia and Michael re: asset protection plan,' followed two days later by a conversation 'with Michael Frankel re: asset protection planning.' The various items under consideration included the 'sale/transfer of N.Y. condos,' 'homestead waiver issues,' the 'option of filing claim in bankruptcy court to obtain indemnification for arbitration award' and 'efforts to identify insurance coverage or indemnification for arbitration award.' *** Any flaw in the motion court's reasoning notwithstanding, the record fails to support defendants' contention that the conveyance was made pursuant to a previous agreement rather than as part of an asset protection plan contrived to insulate property from the claims of judgment creditors.")

12. *See Carmelle v. Coletti*, No. G049266, 2014 WL 4354069, at *6 (Cal. Ct. App. Sept. 3, 2014). ("Finally, although Coletti could have been far more diplomatic in his approach, Carmelle's expertise in asset protection and her alleged efforts to escape detection for prior fraudulent asset protection activity was relevant to a claim under the UFTA.")

13. *See In re: Joseph Ellison, Debtor. JP Morgan Chase Bank, N.A., JP Morgan Securities, LLC, Plaintiffs, vs. Joseph Ellison, Defendant.*, No. 2:14-BK-24463-RK, 2016 WL 5349715, at *6 (Bankr. C.D. Cal. Sept. 23, 2016). ("As indicated by Defendant's testimony that prior to filing his bankruptcy petition, he met with an asset protection firm, and one of his goals in doing so, was to potentially protect his assets from potential creditors, Trial Testimony of Joseph Ellison, November 19, 2015 at 10:58-10:59 a.m., and while he changed his mind about using the asset protection firm, the evidence of his consideration, meeting and paying the asset protection firm supports a finding that Defendant intended to hinder or delay his nonpreferred creditors.")

## *Attorney-client privilege*

Although communications are protected by the attorney-client privilege, an exception exists for communications related to fraud. This exception has extended to a fraudulent transfer and is commonly applied in situations involving actual fraud:

> Moreover, Federal Rule of Civil Procedure 26 is clear: when a party makes a claim of privilege, it must "describe the nature of the documents, communications, or tangible things not produced or disclosed—and do so in a manner that, without revealing information itself privileged or protected, will enable other parties to assess the claim." Fed. R. Civ. P. 26(b)(5)(A); *see also, e.g., Smith v. ComputerTraining.com, Inc.*, 2014 WL 4231175, at *3 (E.D. Mich. Aug. 27, 2014) ("A privilege log must contain the basis for withholding discovery of the document and sufficient detail beyond conclusory allegations to demonstrate the fulfillment of the legal requirements for application of the privilege.") A privilege log is also necessary to allow Chase to assess whether Winget is improperly claiming privilege over documents that do not contain legal advice or amount to work product. Further, a log will help Chase to determine whether the crime-fraud exception to any claim of privilege applies. While Winget argues Chase is seeking a "fishing expedition" because "Chase has no evidence that the crime/fraud exception applies," Chase has justified its right to make the inquiry. Among other things, Winget has acknowledged that Larry Winget "paid the Trust nothing for the assets transferred out of the Trust" which is a marker of a fraudulent conveyance. *See Estate of Page v. Slagh*, 2007 WL 1385957, at *2 (W.D. Mich. May 8, 2007) (invoking the crime-fraud exception because "the timing and effect of the [allegedly fraudulent] transfers at issue in this case raise a reasonable suspicion that the transfers were undertaken in violation of the MUFTA"). Moreover, Winget has asserted that documents related to the revocation of the Trust are subject to privilege or work product protection, indicating that attorneys played a role in that revocation. Thus, Winget's assertion that Chase has put forward no basis to suggest the crime-fraud exception may apply is incorrect.[14]

## *Jurisdictional Issues*

The presence of actual fraud can also help a creditor establish jurisdiction over parties that otherwise might not exist. Here, a court may examine the circumstances surrounding the transferee's knowledge, as well as any who assist the debtor in thwarting a creditor. Actual fraud, especially where there is direct evidence and the timing is near judgment, is more likely to be viewed as especially offensive to courts as a violation of public policy. This conduct, when

14. JPMorgan Chase Bank, N.A., Plaintiff/Counter-Defendant, v. Larry J. Winget & the Larry J. Winget Living Trust, Defendants/Counter-Plaintiffs., No. 08-13845, 2017 WL 2868538, at *12 (E.D. Mich. July 5, 2017).

considering the facts and circumstances, might rise to the level of what a court finds to be a legal wrong. In the context of tort law, as described more fully below, establishing the facts in this fashion may support a theory of secondary liability for a fraudulent transfer. It follows that a fraudulent transfer that constitutes a legal wrong would also help the plaintiff establish both standing and jurisdiction. Consequently, the case law supports a creditor establishing personal jurisdiction over an out-of-state party to a fraudulent transfer under the tortious activity prong of a state's long-arm statute. The court in *Welsh v. Martinez* addressed the issue as it applied to potential jurisdiction over a transferee who resided outside the forum state hearing the fraudulent transfer matter:

> In support of the plaintiff's argument that acceptance of fraudulently transferred monies constitutes "tortious conduct within the state," the plaintiff principally relies on one Superior Court decision and several decisions by the New York Appellate Division, Second Department. The court has carefully examined that collection of cases and finds them either inapposite and/or unpersuasive.4 In Chrysler Credit Corp. v. Berman, No. 0057971, 1992 WL 165723 (Conn.Super. June 25, 1992), the trial court found §52-59b(a)(2) satisfied, but the decision does not make clear why. In Ed Moore Advertising Agency, Inc. v. I.H.R., Inc., 494 N.Y.S.2d 400, 400-02 (App. Div.2d Dept. 1985), and Neilson v. Sal Martorano, Inc., 319 N.Y.S.2d 480, 482 (App.Div.2d Dept. 1971), there was at least some evidence in the record that the defendant movant had knowledge of a collusive or conspiratorial purpose underlying the allegedly fraudulent transaction. In Liberty Co. v. Boyle, 708 N.Y.S.2d 122, 124-25 (App.Div.2d Dept. 2000), the court makes no mention of personal jurisdiction. Finally, the court is not persuaded by Weitz v. Weitz, 926 N.Y.S.2d 305 (App.Div.2d Dept. 2011), because the decision does not provide a recitation of the allegations in the complaint or evidence submitted.
>
> Here, there is no evidence that Marilyn engaged in any relevant conduct other than when she was in Texas (and perhaps New Jersey) or that she had any knowledge of the judgment against her son. While the plaintiff spends considerable time arguing that Marilyn's conduct in Texas was tortious, the plaintiff has not satisfied her burden to demonstrate the applicability of the long-arm provision requiring a showing of "tortious conduct within the state." Accordingly, the court concludes that §52-59b(a)(2) does not apply.[15]

In *Team Express Distributing LLC v. Junction Solutions, Inc., et. al.*, the court found "mere passive acceptance" of a fraudulent transfer was insufficient to establish personal jurisdiction.

> Defendants dispute that their alleged involvement in an alleged fraudulent transfer scheme subjects them to personal jurisdiction in this lawsuit. The due process clause requires that a court exercise personal jurisdiction over a nonresident defendant only if the defendant has "certain minimum contacts

15. *Welsh v. Martinez*, 2017 WL 4106323, at *4 (Conn. Super. Ct. Aug. 7, 2017).

with [the forum state] such that the maintenance of the suit does not offend traditional notions of fair play and substantial justice." Int'l Energy Ventures Mgmt., L.L.C. v. United Energy Grp., Ltd., 818 F.3d 193, 212 (5th Cir. 2016) (*quoting* Int'l Shoe Co. v. Washington, 326 U.S. 310, 316 (1945)). According to the MK Entities, defendants "engaged in one transaction, negotiated and agreed to outside of Texas, regarding its investment in a Colorado company with assets that also were outside of Texas, between out of state parties." (Docket no. 97, p. 7). A tortious act committed outside the forum state that has consequences or effects within the forum will establish minimum contacts if the tortious conduct is purposefully or expressly aimed at the forum state. Dontos, 582 Fed.App'x at 344–45. *See* Mullins v. TestAmerica, Inc., 564 F.3d 386, 400 (5th Cir. 2009)(citing Calder v. Jones, 465 U.S. 783, 789–90 (1984)).

As the Individual Defendants note, in a fraudulent transfer case, there is no personal jurisdiction over non-residents where the plaintiff does not plead that the alleged tortfeasor acted with an intent to single out the plaintiff as a debtor. *See* Dontos, 582 Fed.Appx. at 347. ("[T]o allege a prima facie case of specific personal jurisdiction based on TUFTA liability, the Plaintiffs must allege more than mere passive acceptance of a fraudulent asset transfer that harmed a creditor in the forum state; they must also allege some purposeful conduct directed at a creditor in the forum state.")(citing Mullins, 564 F.3d at 400); Heavy Duty Productions, LLC v. Bandwdth, LLC, A-14-CV-974-LY, 2015 WL 2374461, at *7-9 (W.D.Tex. May 12, 2015), supplemented, A-14-CV-974-LY, 2015 WL 3936180 (W.D.Tex. June 26, 2015).[16]

In *Gilmore Bank v. AsiaTrust New Zealand Limited*, a California court held a Cook Islands trustee was subject to personal jurisdiction based on the trustee's actions directed to California. The debtor employed a foreign asset protection trust to protect assets.

We conclude it is unnecessary to apply the effects test here. Instead, we apply several other purposeful availment formulas, any one of which is sufficient to meet the first requirement for specific jurisdiction. The undisputed facts show AsiaTrust (1) created continuing obligations between itself and California residents, (2) purposefully directed (and continues to direct) its activities toward California residents, and (3) purposefully derived (and continues to derive) benefits from its activities in California. AsiaTrust conducted due diligence on California resident Sonia, the trustee of Cindy's Retirement Trust. AsiaTrust sent promotional materials to Sonia and otherwise marketed to her the advantages of forming a New Zealand trust. AsiaTrust drafted the trust contract, negotiated the contractual terms with California residents Sonia and Berardo, and amended the contract. Sonia signed the amended contract, witnessed by Berardo, in California. AsiaTrust communicated by e-mail and telephone with Sonia and Berardo in California. AsiaTrust has invoiced Sonia in California for fees owed to AsiaTrust.

16. Team Express Distributing LLC, Plaintiff, v. Junction Solutions, Inc., et al., Defendants., No. SA-15-CA-00994-DAE, 2016 WL 11552404, at *2 (W.D. Tex. Sept. 7, 2016).

> AsiaTrust has received funds **536 from Cindy's Retirement Trust in California and from a Swiss annuity that insures California resident Cindy. AsiaTrust has followed Berardo's instructions concerning the ownership of the Swiss annuity. AsiaTrust has wire transferred funds to Cindy's Retirement Trust's bank account in California in accordance with Sonia's instructions. Essentially, AsiaTrust has received compensation for accepting, investing, managing, disbursing, and shielding the assets of Cindy, a California judgment debtor, in a scheme that contemplates an ongoing contractual relationship for Cindy's lifetime.
>
> * * *
>
> Here, the New Zealand Trust is the instrumentality by which the Dalrymple defendants have transferred Cindy's assets out of plaintiffs' reach, and which enables Cindy to continue to enjoy a substantial income from her transferred assets. Although Cindy's assets are central to plaintiffs' lawsuit against her, half of her assets reside in an irrevocable trust or Swiss annuity in AsiaTrust's possession or under its control. This is a sufficient nexus to fairly subject AsiaTrust to California's jurisdiction.[17]

Although foreign asset protection trusts are touted for their creditor protection due to the lack of jurisdiction over a foreign trustee, query whether that result occurs where the trust company offers its business to residents of a particular state. Where a transfer is made with actual fraud, it is also possible that the foreign trustee is not acting as a mere passive recipient. Here, it is also important to see whether the fraudulent transfer facts and circumstances would satisfy another cause of action that might establish personal jurisdiction, such as a business tort or tortious interference with a contract.

## *Denial of Discharge*

While negligent planning advice can certainly be a cause for the attorney's concern, if the planning involved actual fraud under the fraudulent transfer law, the client might be denied a discharge of debt in bankruptcy.[18] Under Bankruptcy Code Section 523(a)(2)(A), "[a] discharge under [Chapters 7, 11, 12, or 13] of this title does not discharge an individual debtor from any debt . . . for money, property, services, or an extension, renewal, or refinancing of credit, to the extent obtained by . . . false pretenses, a false representation, or actual fraud."

Given the Supreme Court's broad interpretation of "actual fraud" in *Husky Int'l Elecs., Inc. v. Ritz*,[19] neglecting to discuss denial of discharge as a potential

---

17. *Gilmore Bank v. AsiaTrust New Zealand Limited*, 223 Cal.App.4th 1558 (2014).

18. Aggressive planning may be considered in the context of a payment plan under a Chapter 13 proceeding as well. *See* In re Wrobel, —B.R.—(2015), 2015 WL 643839. ("Simply committing all of one's non-exempt assets and meeting the 'projected disposable income' test, does not compel a ruling that a plan is 'feasible.' Identically, it does not compel a ruling that a plan meets the 'good faith' test of 11 U.S.C. §1325(a)(3).")

19. *Husky Int'l Elecs., Inc. v. Ritz*, 136 S. Ct. 1581, 1586, 194 L. Ed. 2d 655 (2016). *See also, Havoco of Am., Ltd. v. Hill*, 197 F.3d 1135, 1143 (11th Cir. 1999), *certified question answered*, 790 So. 2d 1018 (Fla. 2001), opinion after certified question answered, 255 F.3d 1321 (11th Cir. 2001). ("Adding to the confusion in this area is the conclusion of some courts that, although a debtor's fraudulent conversion of non-exempt assets

consequence could add fuel to a malpractice argument (effectively creating a worst-case scenario; denial of discharge for the debtor and a claim against the attorney.) Importantly, the court noted the principles of the Statute of 13 Elizabeth are reflected in fraudulent transfer statutory law. "The degree to which this statute remains embedded in laws related to fraud today clarifies that the common-law term 'actual fraud' is broad enough to incorporate a fraudulent conveyance." The Court also observed, "the common law also indicates that fraudulent conveyances, although a 'fraud,' do not require a misrepresentation from a debtor to a creditor. As a basic point, fraudulent conveyances are not an inducement-based fraud. Fraudulent conveyances typically involve 'a transfer to a close relative, a secret transfer, a transfer of title without transfer of possession, or grossly inadequate consideration."[20] In some cases, a debtor may argue that following an attorney's advice should prevent a court from denying discharge.

> Both the Bankruptcy Court and the BAP overlooked the fact that Ellison did rely on the advice of his bankruptcy counsel when he made the pre-petition payments to his lenders. Ellison undertook the pre-bankruptcy planning at the advice of his former bankruptcy counsel David Hagen, a certified bankruptcy specialist. [Tab 15; Tr. 24].
>
> *19 Q. Okay. And the decision to make that - to make the six-month prepayment, did you consult with anyone to make that - to make the five-month prepayments?
>
> A. I was consulting with my current counsel about the entire bankruptcy proceeding, yes.
>
> [Tab 15; Tr. 24]. Generally, a debtor who acts in reliance on the advice of his attorney lacks the intent required to deny him a discharge of his debts." First Beverly Bank v. Adeeb (*In re* Adeeb), 787 F.2d 1339, 1343 (9th Cir. 1986) (citing Hultman v. Tevis, 82 F.2d 940, 941 (9th Cir. 1936). However, the debtor's reliance must be in good faith. *Id.* See Hultman, 82 F.2d at 941. Ellison was not aware that there was anything improper by making those payments, and his desire to protect his family and to make sure that they had a roof over their heads should not be equated with an intent to hinder or delay a creditor.[21]

Considering the risk associated with asset protection in particular, some attorneys specifically decline to provide such service in engagement letters. Although some may believe refusal to provide asset protection violates ethical obligations, such risk appears unsubstantiated considering the broad scope of fraudulent

---

into a homestead does not provide a basis for denying him the homestead exemption, the debtor's fraudulent transfer may serve as the predicate for denying the discharge. *See, e.g. Marine Midland Bank, N.A. v. Mollon*, 160 B.R. 860 (M.D.Fla.1993) (denying discharge under 11 U.S.C. §727(a)(2)(A) when the "[d]ebtor who clearly by law is entitled to convert nonexempt assets to exempt assets did so in this case with a fraudulent intent"); *In re Hendricks*, 237 B.R. at 826; *In re Young*, 235 B.R. at 671.")

20. *Husky Int'l Elecs., Inc. v. Ritz*, 136 S. Ct. 1581, 1587, 194 L. Ed. 2d 655 (2016). It is important to note how the Supreme Court focused heavily on fraudulent transfer common law.

21. *In re*: Joseph Ellison, Debtor, Joseph Ellison, Appellant, v. JPMorgan Chase Bank, N.A.; JP Morgan Securities, LLC, Appellees., 2018 WL 1676283 (C.A.9), 18–19.

transfer law (especially with respect to self-settled trusts),[22] as well as the fact that a disclaimer in an engagement letter properly advises the client of the scope of engagement. Consequently, a happy medium appears to exist when an attorney considers state-sanctioned exemption laws (e.g., the proper use of insurance, annuities, homestead, etc.) of the state of the client's domicile as part of an overall estate planning approach, or business entities for a client's business operations.

## *Disregarding Trust Relationship/Terms*

In some situations, a creditor may pierce the corporate veil to hold the business owner liable for the debts of the business. This typically requires a show of control and an attempt to achieve some wrong or fraud. In some cases, a court may consider a fraudulent transfer made with actual fraud to qualify for the essential wrong or fraud that would result in ignoring the trust provisions protecting assets from a debtor/beneficiary's creditors.

> "New York law requires the party seeking to pierce a corporate veil to make a two-part showing: (i) that the owner exercised complete domination over the corporation with respect to the transaction at issue; and (ii) that such domination was used to commit a fraud or wrong that injured the party seeking to pierce the veil." Am. Fuel Corp., 122 F.3d at 134. "Liability therefore may be predicated either upon a showing of fraud or upon complete control by the dominating corporation that leads to a wrong against third parties." Wm. Passalacqua Builders, 933 F.2d at 138 (citing cases).
>
> In Babitt v. Vebeliunas (In re Vebeliunas), 332 F.3d 85 (2d Cir. 2003), the Second Circuit assumed that New York courts would pierce trusts under similar circumstances and has noted that New York appellate courts have pierced trusts where "the respective parties used trusts to conceal assets or engaged in fraudulent conveyances to shield funds from adverse judgments." Vebeliunas, 332 F.3d at 90 (*discussing* Posner v. S. Paul Posner 1976 Irrevocable Family Trust, 688 N.Y.S.2d 548 (N.Y. App. Div. 1999), Goldberg v. Goldberg, 568 N.Y.S.2d 394 (N.Y. App. Div. 1991), and Pappas v. Freund, 660 N.Y.S.2d 302 (N.Y. Sup. Ct. 1997)). The standard for piercing a trust is similar to piercing the corporate veil: the claimant "must establish that (1) the owner of the Trust exercised such control that the Trust has become a mere instrumentality of the owner; (2) the owner used this control to commit a fraud or 'other wrong;' and (3) the fraud or wrong resulted in injury or loss." Smith v. SEC, 432 Fed.Appx. 10, 13 (2d Cir. 2011) (*quoting* Vebeliunas, 332 F.3d at 91–92.)[23]

In *Hypnotic Taxi*, the debtor removed himself as a discretionary beneficiary, presumably hoping to thwart creditors. The mere act of removing himself as the beneficiary did not go unnoticed by the court, which disregarded the

22. With respect to a client who resides in a non-DAPT state, the provision of services for a DAPT without a disclaimer of viability can result in just the opposite.

23. *In re Hypnotic Taxi*, 2017 WL 4464876.

action and found the debtor's retained interest as a discretionary beneficiary enough to constitute control. When combined with evidence of a fraudulent transfer, the court permitted veil piercing, which obviated the necessity of obtaining personal jurisdiction over the trustees.

> The evidence establishes that Freidman controls the Trusts. The Trusts are structured so that Freidman reserves the right to continue to use the Properties owned by the Real Estate Entities. The trust deeds of all of the Trusts provide that:
>
> > The Trustees, with the written consent of the Protector, shall have power to permit a Discretionary Beneficiary to occupy, use or enjoy personally any movable or immovable property which may, for the time being, be comprised in the Trust Fund upon any terms and conditions which the Trustees may think fit.
>
> (Ex. A, Birkin Trust at 24–25, ¶ 17; Kelly Trust at 23, ¶ 17; Evelyn Trust at 23, ¶ 17; Lindy Trust at 23, ¶ 17.) The third and seventh schedules of all of the Trusts designated Freidman as both the Protector and a Discretionary Beneficiary. (Ex. A, Evelyn Trust at 64 (Third Schedule), 68 (Seventh Schedule); Birkin Trust at 66 (Third Schedule), 70 (Seventh Schedule); Kelly Trust at 65 (Third Schedule), 69 (Seventh Schedule); Lindy Trust at 64 (Third Schedule), 68 (Seventh Schedule).) There are no beneficiaries other than discretionary beneficiaries. Furthermore, the Protector is empowered to remove and replace the Trustees at any time. (Ex. A, Birkin Trust at 35–36, ¶ 35(d); Kelly Trust at 34–35, ¶ 35(d); Evelyn Trust at 34, ¶ 35(d); Lindy Trust at 34, ¶ 35(d).) Freidman's attempt to remove himself from those schedules effective March 1, 2016, after the issuance of Amended TRO on November 16, 2015, violated the prohibition "to make or suffer any sale, assignment, or transfer, or any interference with, any property in which Freidman has an interest not in the ordinary course of such person's business or personal affairs." (TRO, ECF No. 6; Am. TRO, ECF No. 29 (incorporating terms of TRO).) It therefore may be disregarded in the context of this proceeding.

Given the adverse results associated with actual fraud, the planner should review the client's financial situation carefully, as well as the facts and circumstances, including careful consideration to the badges of fraud. That is, if a client is in poor health, but also faces a looming judgment, the badges of fraud can be used to negate any estate planning excuse.[24]

---

24. Of course, this assumes the creditor properly makes a claim for the transfer in light of the badges of fraud. *See Branch Banking v. Hamilton Greens, LLC*, No. 11-80507-CIV, 2016 WL 3365270, at *3 (S.D. Fla. Jan. 13, 2016), report and recommendation adopted in part, rejected in part sub nom. Branch Banking & Trust Co. v. Hamilton Greens, LLC, No. 1180507CIVMARRAMATTH, 2016 WL 3251165 (S.D. Fla. June 14, 2016). ("the Court need not consider Plaintiff's objections to the Magistrate's conclusions regarding Bellinger's creation of, and transfer of funds to, the Trust. Even if these objections were meritorious and the transfer to the Trust was fraudulent, the outcome would be the same because, as the Magistrate noted, Plaintiff's complaint is devoid of any request for relief as to this transfer. (DE 394 at 14–15) (noting that "BB&T's Complaint does not sufficiently seek any relief as to the initial creation of the Trust in 2011 and the transfer of assets to the Trust in 2012"). Indeed, the Trust, the recipient of the alleged fraudulent transfer, is not even a party in this suit. Tellingly, Plaintiff fails to address this threshold issue in its objections.")

## Solvency Affidavits

A solvency affidavit is sometimes used in conjunction with contributions to an asset protection trust or for a disclaimer (where, for example, solvency is required for an effective disclaimer under state law.) The attorney must realize the self-serving nature of the affidavit and consider how a fraudulent transfer might arise despite a statement of solvency before and after a proposed transfer.[25]

## Attorney Civil Liability as Transferee

*In re Harwell* illustrates how an attorney (or law firm) may be held liable as a transferee for assisting a client who was attempting to shelter assets from a creditor. Harwell moved to Florida, filed bankruptcy, and transferred funds to his Florida attorney's trust account after a judgment was entered in another state. The creditor domesticated the judgment in Florida and attempted to garnish the trust account to satisfy the judgment. However, there was a defect in the domestication order, and in the time it took to correct the defect, the law firm assisted with transfers of funds to various individuals, excluding, of course, the creditor. The assumption must have been that because the funds were held in a trust account, a fiduciary duty existed, and the law firm could not be held liable as the law firm did not have control over the funds.

Counsel for the bankruptcy trustee did not relent, appealing the lower court decision to the Eleventh Circuit, where, for the first time, it was determined the conduit defense was available only where the transferee has control and acts in good faith. In other words, claiming lack of control was only part of the defense; one must also act in good faith. On remand, the lower court had no choice but to find the law firm liable given the attorney's role in the planning. The parties eventually settled.

Consequently, attorneys should be mindful of the circumstances surrounding the use of a trust account for a client in financial distress. The bankruptcy judge in *Harwell*, on remand after the 11th Circuit required an attorney act in good faith, advised that if an attorney suspects he received funds in a trust account via fraudulent transfer, the attorney should return the funds.

---

25. *See In re Erskine: Debtor Attempts to Exclude Assets Held in "Tennessee Asset Protection Trust,"* LISI Asset Protection Newsletter #324 (June 14, 2016) ("What the court did not examine (or did not find, based on what was submitted) in *Niroomand* were other facts and circumstances, aside from the debtor's solvency, that can show actual fraud. Relying on solvency as the sole factor in determining whether a transfer is voidable has its appeal; the test is perceived to be mechanical and straightforward. Solvency is relevant to both actual and constructive fraud claims (solvency being an element under an UVTA Section 5(a) constructive fraud claim), and under UVTA Section 4(b) as indirect evidence of actual intent (a.k.a. 'badges of fraud.') But while solvency might foreclose an UVTA Section 5(a) claim, it will not rule out an UVTA Section 4 claim. The court in *Erskine* implied that even if the debtor executed an affidavit, such a document would not obviate the necessity of analyzing other facts and circumstances.")

"Accordingly, I will—in summary, I will find that an attorney finding himself, getting objective facts that put him on notice that a client is in the process of fraudulently conveying assets, needs to immediately cease participating and take actions to return the money to the client and cease participating and assisting the client in the steps that the client is undertaking to fraudulently transfer assets out of the reach of the creditor."[26]

Not only can the improper use of an attorney's trust account result in attorney liability as a transferee, but the use of the trust account might trigger a denial of discharge for the client.[27] As discussed elsewhere, improper conduct may result in disciplinary action and allegations of malpractice (which could give rise to a bankruptcy estate asset.)

## Attorney Liability for Assisting with Wrongful Conduct

Advisers should understand how certain jurisdictions view those who assist others with fraudulent transfers. A jurisdiction might treat a fraudulent transfer as a tort in certain situations. This could result in liability for the client where it might not be expected (e.g., transfers from a business entity to an owner)[28] and it could mean liability for those who assist with the commission of the tort. If a court views a fraudulent transfer as a tort or tort-like, assisting with a fraudulent transfer could result in secondary liability for the attorney. Although one of the

---

26. Transcript of Oral Argument on Remanded Matters at 30, *In re Harwell*, No. 05-41744-ABC, (Bankr. M.D. Fla. Nov. 20, 2012).

27. *See In re Wise*, 590 B.R. 401, 440 (Bankr. E.D. Mich. 2018). ("Given the terms of that Revised Fee Agreement, the $250,000 was 'an additional retainer' and thus, was subject to an attorney's lien to secure payment of attorney fees that Olivia incurred with the Rebeck law firm. And while Olivia could request and direct that disbursements be made from the funds, the disbursements were limited to 'the following uses: Periodic billing by Attorney for representation, payment of tax liability-currently unknown amount, and as directed by client, in writing.' Therefore, while Olivia did retain some control of, and some interest in, the $250,000, it was limited by and subject to the terms of the Revised Fee Agreement. This was quite different from the sole and unfettered control and ownership of the funds that Olivia had before the transfer, when the funds were in the credit union account owned solely by Olivia. Olivia's transfer of the $250,000 in Proceeds to the Rebeck law firm not only was a 'transfer,' but also was an act by which Olivia 'concealed' the funds, within the meaning of §727(a)(2)(A). As discussed in Part III.B.1.a of this Opinion, concealment includes 'placing . . . assets beyond the reach of creditors;' 'placing title to property in others' names and retaining beneficial interest.' This is what Olivia did when she transferred the $250,000 to the Rebeck law firm's trust account.")

28. *See Walker v. Anderson*, 232 S.W.3d 899, 918 (Tex. App. 2007). ("However, it is the general rule in Texas that a corporation's employee is personally liable for tortious acts which he directs or participates in during his employment. *See Leyendecker & Assocs., Inc. v. Wechter*, 683 S.W.2d 369, 375 (Tex.1984); *Kingston v. Helm*, 82 S.W.3d 755, 758 (Tex.App.Corpus Christi 2002, pet. denied). Also, a corporate officer who knowingly participates in tortious or fraudulent acts may be held individually liable to third persons even though he performed the act as an agent of the corporation. *See Kingston*, 82 S.W.3d at 759. It is not necessary to pierce the corporate veil to impose personal liability, if it is shown that the corporate officer knowingly participated in the wrongdoing. *See id.* The fraudulent transfer of assets is a tort. *See* Tex. Bus. & Com.Code Ann. §24.005; *In re Texas Am. Express, Inc.*, 190 S.W.3d 720, 725 (Tex.App.Dallas 2005, orig. proceeding).") (Emphasis added.)

goals with the UVTA was to remove the perception that a fraudulent transfer involved common law fraud, the Official Comments make it clear that no change was intended with respect to how a state views the circumstances surrounding a fraudulent transfer.

Where a court finds a fraudulent transfer to be a tort or tort-like, an attorney could be held liable for aiding and abetting or conspiring to commit a fraudulent transfer. "Based on the above analysis, the Court finds that Plaintiffs can bring a claim against Batson as an attorney for his clients that allegedly fraudulently transferred their assets to avoid paying their creditors, even though he was neither the debtor nor the transferee of Stratford Operator's assets."[29] Although each case stands on its own, and the courts have varied on this issue, generally, a court will not hesitate to find an attorney liable for assisting with a fraudulent transfer where the attorney does so with the intent of helping a client avoid a particular creditor.

Justification for secondary liability in some situations makes sense when considering the Statute of 13 Elizabeth considered a fraudulent transfer to be a crime, and in light of various state statutes that also penalize fraudulent transfer scenarios. Historically, there was uncertainty as to whether a person who assists with a fraudulent transfer could be held liable, with case law holding in some cases that a lien was required for third-party liability. A trend appeared to develop in the 1800s where courts would be willing to find such liability, leading to what has been referred to as the "modern era of aider and abettor/conspiracy liability:"

> Pennsylvania was the first, holding in 1837 that those who assisted a fraudulent transferor in violating the Statute of Elizabeth were liable for conspiracy (a ruling refreshed in a more recent decision). Arkansas followed in 1883, Ohio in 1913 and Idaho in 1941. In 1964, Illinois produced the first decision, *Celano v. Frederick*, to hold attorneys liable for assisting in a fraudulent transfer. Celano had obtained a judgment against Frederick and a post-judgment order directing Frederick to turn over all payments on a lawsuit Frederick had instituted against a third party referred to as the Geocaris group. A fluke in the Illinois rules of procedure put the order in question and Frederick and his attorneys arranged to settle the Geocaris lawsuit and to hide the funds from Celano. Celano sued Frederick's attorneys, and the appellate court ruled that "One may not use his license to practice law as a shield to protect himself from the consequences of his participation in an unlawful or illegal conspiracy."
>
> The modern era of aider and abettor/conspiracy liability for assisting a fraudulent transfer began in 1976 with the Wisconsin Supreme Court's decision in *Dalton v. Meister*.[30]

---

29. *RehabCare Grp. E., Inc. v. Stratford Health Care Properties, LLC*, No. 14-0886-CV-W-FJG, 2016 WL 11469771, at *6–7 (W.D. Mo. Feb. 8, 2016).

30. Thomas Moers Mayer, *Will the Lawyers Pay? Counsels Ethical, Civil and Criminal Exposure for Creating Asset Protection Trusts*, TSWB26 ALI-CLE 33 (May 4, 2015).

Conversely, other courts have concluded that a fraudulent transfer is not a tort. In *Sheehan v. Saoud*, the Fourth Circuit identified cases where a fraudulent transfer was[31] and was not[32] considered a tort.

In *Sheehan*, the Fourth Circuit did not rule out the possibility that such a cause of action existed, however, declined to do so:

> Further, while very few have addressed the issue, some circuit courts have recognized a cause of action for civil conspiracy based on a violation of the Uniform Fraudulent Transfer Act. *See, e.g.*, **155 CNH Capital Am. LLC v. Hunt Tractor, Inc.*, 568 Fed.Appx. 461, 473 (6th Cir. 2014), as amended (July 2, 2014) (recognizing that Kentucky law allows recovery from a transferee or transferor for civil conspiracy to commit a fraudulent conveyance, but denying relief because defendant was neither the transferee nor the transferor); *Chepstow Ltd. v. Hunt*, 381 F.3d 1077, 1090 (11th Cir. 2004) (recognizing a cause of action for civil conspiracy based on the UFTA under Georgia law against non-transferee defendants); *Forum Ins. Co. v. Comparet*, 62 Fed. Appx. 151, 153 (9th Cir. 2003) ("California allows for a cause of action for conspiracy to commit fraudulent transfers and allows a plaintiff to recover legal damages on such a cause of action."). However, in these cases, the

---

31. *Sheehan v. Saoud*, 650 F. App'x 143, 154 (4th Cir. 2016). ("a handful of courts from other jurisdictions have recognized violations of the Uniform Fraudulent Transfer Act as torts. *See, e.g.*, *Alliant Tax Credit Fund 31-A, Ltd. v. Murphy*, 2011 WL 3156339, at *8 (N.D. Ga. July 26, 2011) ("Although Plaintiffs' claim for civil conspiracy does not furnish an independent cause of action on which to hold Defendants liable, it can be used to establish some of Defendants' liability for fraudulent transfers under the UFTA."); *Valvanis v. Milgroom*, 529 F.Supp.2d 1190, 1203 (D. Haw. 2007) ("[T]he underlying actionable tort for the conspiracy claim is the fraudulent transfer of the Hawaii Property [under the HUFTA]."); *Gutierrez v. Givens*, 1 F.Supp.2d 1077, 1087 (S.D. Cal. 1998) ("The Court finds that a triable issue of fact exists as to whether Colonial may be found liable for a civil conspiracy to violate the UFTA."); *In re Advanced Telecomm. Network, Inc.*, 2013 WL 414654, at *3 (Bankr. M.D. Fla. Feb. 4, 2013) ("The Amended Complaint properly pleads civil conspiracy against the Defendants to the extent it alleges they knowingly agreed and aided the Allens in violating the UFTA's constructive fraudulent transfer provisions."); *In re Penn Packing Co.*, 42 B.R. 502, 505 (Bankr. E.D. Pa. 1984) (Pennsylvania's fraudulent conveyance act claim a tort for purposes of choosing Pennsylvania statute of limitations); *Banco Popular N. Am. v. Gandi*, 184 N.J. 161, 876 A.2d 253, 263 (2005) (recognizing a claim for civil conspiracy for aiding and abetting a fraudulent transfer under the UFTA); *Double Oak Const., LLC v. Cornerstone Dev. Int'l, LLC*, 97 P.3d 140, 146 (Colo. App. 2003) ("[W]e conclude that a transfer in violation of CUFTA is a legal wrong which will support a conspiracy claim."); *McElhanon v. Hing*, 151 Ariz. 386, 728 P.2d 256, 263 (Ariz. Ct. App. 1985) aff'd in part, vacated in part, 151 Ariz. 403, 728 P.2d 273 (1986) ("[U]pon passage of the Uniform Fraudulent Conveyances Act, a conveyance to defraud a general creditor became a legal wrong, properly the subject of a suit for civil conspiracy.").")

32. *Sheehan v. Saoud*, 650 F. App'x 143, 154 (4th Cir. 2016). ("courts from varying jurisdictions have refused to recognize violations of the Uniform Fraudulent Transfer Act as torts. *See, e.g.*, *United States v. Neidorf*, 522 F.2d 916, 917–18 (9th Cir. 1975); *Desmond v. Moffie*, 375 F.2d 742, 743 (1st Cir. 1967) (finding fraudulent conveyance claim under Massachusetts Uniform Fraudulent Conveyance Act to be a contract rather than tort action for purposes of applying appropriate statute of limitations); *S. Prawer*, 829 F.Supp. at 456 (finding fraudulent conveyance claim not to be a tort claim for purposes of the Federal Tort Claims Act); *Branch v. Fed. Deposit Ins. Corp.*, 825 F.Supp. 384 (D. Mass. 1993) (finding fraudulent conveyance claim not to be a tort claim for purposes of the Federal Tort Claims Act); *Fed. Deposit Ins. Corp. v. Martinez Almodovar*, 671 F.Supp. 851, 871 (D.P.R. 1987) (finding fraudulent conveyance claim not to be a tort for purposes of choosing appropriate statute of limitations); In re Fedders N. Am., Inc., 405 B.R. 527, 549 (Bankr. D. Del. 2009) ("Likewise, the authorities are also clear that there is no such thing as liability for . . . conspiracy to commit a fraudulent transfer as a matter of federal law under the Code."); *Freeman v. First Union Nat'l Bank*, 865 So.2d 1272, 1277 (Fla. 2004) ("We simply can see no language in FUFTA that suggests an intent to create an independent tort for damages.").)"

circuit courts applied the law as already decided by state courts recognizing such civil conspiracy claims.

* * *

[T]he Court is reticent to expand the bounds of West Virginia policy by recognizing a civil conspiracy claim for violation of the WVUFTA for the first time. "Absent a strong countervailing federal interest, the federal court . . . should not elbow its way into this controversy to render what may be an uncertain and ephemeral interpretation of state law." *Time Warner Entm't-Advance/Newhouse P'ship v. Carteret-Craven Elec. Membership Corp.*, 506 F.3d 304, 314 (4th Cir. 2007) (quoting *Mitcheson v. Harris*, 955 F.2d 235, 238 (4th Cir. 1992)). Therefore, the Court declines to make such a policy determination to recognize that a violation of the WVUFTA sounds in tort.[33]

In *Holder v. Howe*, a California court also concluded that the California UFTA did not provide a remedy for aiding and abetting, but acknowledged prior California cases that found liability for a conspirator:

The UFTA gives no remedy against a non-transferor or non-transferee. Therefore, the conduct of a non-transferor or non-transferee, separately considered, cannot constitute a breach of duty to the injured creditor, and thus cannot support a cause of action for aiding and abetting a fraudulent transfer. Holder relies on *Qwest Communications Corp. v. Weisz* (S.D.Cal. 2003) 278 F.Supp.2d 1188, 1192, *Filip v. Bucurenciu, supra*, 129 Cal.App.4th at pages 837-838, and *In re Acequia, Inc.* (9th Cir. 1994) 34 F.3d 800, for the proposition that California recognizes aiding and abetting liability for fraudulent transfer. But those cases address claims for civil conspiracy, not aiding and abetting. (*E.g., Filip v. Bucurenciu, supra*, 129 Cal.App.4th at p. 838.) The claims are distinct. (*See Neilson v. Union Bank of California, N.A.* (C.D.Cal. 2003) 290 F.Supp.2d 1101, 1134 [unlike conspirator, aider and abettor does not adopt tort of the primary violator as his own].) "There simply is no language in [the UFTA] that suggests the creation of a distinct cause of action for aiding-abetting claims against non-transferees." (*Freeman v. First Union Nat'l Bank* (Fla. 2004) 865 So.2d 1272, 1276-1277.) Accordingly, the judgment as to Maynard Howe and Linton for aiding and abetting fraudulent transfer must be reversed.[34]

*In re Kohner* featured the viability of a cause of action existing under Arizona fraudulent transfer common law for conspiring to commit a fraudulent transfer. This area (secondary liability) of the fraudulent transfer common law is especially important for wealth transfer planners (especially asset protection planners.) Although a cause of action for seeking fraudulent transfer relief would be handled by the Arizona Uniform Fraudulent Transfer Act (AUFTA), to the extent a secondary liability claim existed outside of Arizona's predecessor

33. *Sheehan v. Saoud*, 650 F. App'x 143, 154–55 (4th Cir. 2016).

34. *Holder v. Howe*, No. B260967, 2016 WL 7229833, at *8 (Cal. Ct. App. Dec. 14, 2016).

fraudulent transfer act, the Arizona Uniform Fraudulent Conveyance Act, it would continue to exist outside the AUFTA upon its adoption.

In *Kohner*, the defendant law firm argued that because a prior decision finding secondary liability involved the AUFCA, secondary liability would no longer be recognized under the AUFTA. But under Arizona fraudulent transfer common law, a "conspiracy to commit a fraudulent transfer is a cause of action that exists independently and apart from the Uniform Fraudulent Conveyance Act." Because the cause of action existed outside the Arizona UFCA, it would also exist outside the Arizona UFTA. The court in *Kohner* concluded "that a cause of action for conspiring to commit a fraudulent transfer is still recognized in Arizona and exists independent of the UFTA, thereby surviving its adoption." Although it is true that the only party liable for a fraudulent transfer is the transferee (or person for whose benefit the transfer was made), per the terms of the fraudulent transfer statute, the statute does not address secondary forms of liability which may exist under the common law.

The Florida Supreme Court held aiding and abetting a fraudulent transfer was not a viable cause of action, but the court punted on the issue of conspiracy. In *Yaralli v. American Reprographics Company, LLC*,[35] the Florida 4th District Court of Appeals held that while constructive fraud did not amount to an underlying tort or wrong sufficient to support conspiracy, the case should not be dismissed based on the potential for a valid conspiracy claim:

> Accordingly, we reverse the entry of summary final judgment as to Count VII. *See* Lab. Corp. of Am. v. Prof'l Recovery Network, 813 So. 2d 266, 271 (Fla. 5th DCA 2002) ("'Ordinarily, the issue of fraud is not a proper subject of a summary judgment. Fraud is a subtle thing, requiring a full explanation of the facts and circumstances of the alleged wrong to determine if they collectively constitute a fraud.'" (*quoting* Rosen v. Zoberg, 680 So. 2d 1050, 1052 (Fla. 3d DCA 1996))). As it relates to Count IX, because a cause of action for civil conspiracy "requires an actionable underlying tort or wrong," and because we find summary judgment was improperly granted as to Count VII (the underlying wrong), we reverse the entry of summary judgment as to Count IX as well. Raimi v. Furlong, 702 So. 2d 1273, 1284 (Fla. 3d DCA 1997).

In *Qwest Commc'ns Corp. v. Weisz*, a California court held that a cause of action for secondary liability is provided for pursuant to the terms of the fraudulent transfer statute, specifically, under the catch-all provision found in Section 7 of the UVTA, providing a court may award whatever form of relief "the circumstancces shall require."[36]

The distinction between aiding and abetting and conspiracy is important because some courts have delineated secondary liability between aiding and abetting, which involves substantial assistance to effectuate a fraudulent trans-

35. 165 So. 3d 785.

36. *See Qwest Commc'ns Corp. v. Weisz*, 278 F. Supp. 2d 1188, 1192 (S.D. Cal. 2003). ("Even if this Court's interpretation of the UFTA is incorrect and direct application of the statute is limited solely to debtors and transferees, it does not follow that a non-transferee cannot engage in a conspiracy to violate the UFTA.")

fer, and conspiracy, which involves an agreement to effectuate a fraudulent transfer.[37] Although the Florida Supreme Court, in *Freeman v. First Union Nat. Bank*, held that a lawyer is not liable to a creditor under an *aiding and abetting* theory of secondary liability, footnote 4 in the decision provided: "We caution that our answer to the certified question in this case is confined to the context of FUFTA. We do not address whether relief is available under any other theory of liability or cause of action. *See, e.g., Bankfirst v. UBS Paine Webber, Inc.*, 842 So.2d 155, 157 (Fla. 5th DCA 2003) (Harris, Senior Judge, dissenting) (stating that the non-transferee defendants 'devised and implemented a plan by which the debtor was able to transfer his money' and opining, 'I believe BankFirst stated a cause of action for civil conspiracy')."

Several years after *Freeman*, the southern federal district court of Florida noted the distinction between aiding and abetting and conspiracy and refused to dismiss a claim for conspiracy to commit a fraudulent transfer:

> The individual defendants also argue that Count II is defective because Florida law does not support a cause of action for civil conspiracy to commit a fraudulent transfer. I disagree. Although the Florida Supreme Court made clear in Freeman that FUFTA did not support a cause of action for aiding and abetting a fraudulent transfer, in dicta it left open the possibility that Florida common law might support a cause of action for conspiring to effect a fraudulent transfer. *See id.* at 1275 n.4 (citing *Bankfirst v. UBS Paine Webber, Inc.*, 842 So. 2d 155, 157 (Fla. 5th DCA 2003) (Harris, S.J., *dissenting*) ("I believe [the plaintiff] stated a cause of action for civil conspiracy" against non-transferee defendants who "devised and implemented a plan by which the debtor was able to transfer his money.")
>
> It is therefore unsettled whether Florida common law supports a civil conspiracy claim seeking damages from defendants who aided and abetted a fraudulent transfer. In *Chepstow Limited v. Hunt*, 381 F.3d 1077, 1090 (11th Cir. 2004), the Eleventh Circuit addressed this issue under Georgia law, and found that—although the state's fraudulent transfer statute did not provide a cause of action against non-transferee defendants—the plaintiff stated a claim for civil conspiracy against those who assisted the debtor in fraudulently hindering the collection of its outstanding debts. Lantech is correct that Florida requires an underlying actionable tort or wrong to support a civil conspiracy claim. *See Palmer v. Gotta Have It Golf Collectibles, Inc.*, 106 F. Supp. 2d 1289, 1303–04 (S.D. Fla. 2000) (citing *Liappas v. Augoustis*, 47 So. 2d 582, 582 (Fla. 1950)) ("Florida law is well established that an actionable conspiracy requires an underlying actionable tort or wrong."). But the alleged fraudulent transfers at issue in this case certainly constitute an actionable wrong. The fact that the Florida legislature did not incorporate into FUFTA an independent cause of action against those who assist debtors in fraudulently evading their creditors should not be equated with the abrogation of all common law claims that would otherwise exist against the

37. *See Chepstow Limited v. Hunt*, 381 F.3d 1077 (11th Cir. 2004). ("We conclude that the district court did not err in dismissing Chepstow's claim against Horizon based upon aiding and abetting liability as a non-transferee. However, . . . Horizon may still be liable to Chepstow as a participant in the alleged conspiracy to assist Hunt in fraudulently transferring assets to the transferee defendants.")

> debtors' co-conspirators. *See Bankfirst*, 842 So. 2d at 156–57 (Harris, S.J., *dissenting*) (noting that such an interpretation would effectively immunize a wide range of tortious conduct). I therefore find that Florida law does not preclude Canon's civil conspiracy claim against the individual defendants.[38]

*Canon Latin America* illustrates that courts are not confined to the text of the fraudulent transfer statute but will look to the fraudulent transfer common law as well. However, some courts may feel constrained to actions expressly listed and not look to the common law to afford creditors relief. Such was the case in *In re Glick*, where the bankruptcy court for the northern district of Illinois interpreted the UFTA 11 clause to eradicate all principles of law and equity that are not expressly stated within the UFTA:

> Finally, Paloian cited section 11 of the IUFTA, saying it "supplement[ed] applicable aider-abettor state law." Paloian, 397 B.R. at 897-98. That section provides: "Unless displaced by the provisions of this Act, the principles of law and equity . . . supplement its provisions." 740 ILCS 160/11 (2014). The difficulty in relying on section 11 as a basis for applying aiding and abetting liability principles is that another section of the IUFTA has displaced them. Section 8 specifies the remedies a creditor "may obtain" in "an action for relief against a transfer or obligation under this Act." 740 ILCS 160/8 (2014). An award of damages against an aider-and-abettor is not one of them.[39]

Thus, although Section 11 provides that the common law supplements the UFTA, the court seemingly interpreted this clause as eradicating the common law since a list of remedies was provided in the UFTA. This was so even though the remedies list expressly provides that a court may provide any other relief, i. e., the list was not to be interpreted as exhaustive.

It is also not clear whether the bankruptcy trustee clearly made this distinction. Section 11, by itself, does not provide for secondary liability; the section merely permits the application of other law outside of the IUFTA. In other words, simply because the remedies available under the IUFTA (in Section 8) do not include secondary liability, does not mean such an action would not apply under law outside of the IUFTA (or potentially under the IUFTA, if the courts take a view like the one taken in *Qwest Commc'ns Corp. v. Weisz* by adopting an expansive view of the catch-all provision under UVTA Section 7.)

The *Glick* holding conflicted with *Firstar Bank*,[40] where the bankruptcy court for the northern district of Illinois held that fraudulent conveyance is sufficient to constitute fraud for purposes of secondary liability. Although the court in *Glick* determined *Firstar Bank* "contained no analysis," *Firstar Bank* did in fact equate a fraudulent conveyance with fraud that would be sufficient to

38. *Canon Latin America, Inc., v. Lantech* (C.R.), S.A., 2009 WL 10664392, at *4 (S.D. Fla. Apr. 29, 2009). (Emphasis added.)

39. *In re Glick*, 2017 WL 2473312, at *33 (Bankr. N.D. Ill. June 8, 2017).

40. *In re Glick*, 2017 WL 2473312 (Bankr. N.D. Ill. June 8, 2017).

support secondary liability under the fraudulent transfer common law.[41] Had the court in *Glick* been presented with a conspiracy cause of action, or the numerous cases holding secondary liability exists under the fraudulent transfer common law, it might have decided differently. Instead, the court observed that "[o]verwhelmingly, courts have concluded that parties cannot be liable for a fraudulent transfer if all they have done is participate in it."[42] To an extent, this is true; the real question is the degree of involvement, which is typically much higher where the adviser orchestrates the transaction, thereby being more likely to have conspired to commit the fraudulent transfer.

In New Jersey, it was once thought that a separate cause of action existed for creditor fraud,[43] however, that theory was rejected. Instead, and unfortunately for those who design fraudulent transfers, New Jersey courts will still find liability for those who assist under the fraudulent transfer common law.[44] In a somewhat related matter, creditor fraud exists as a crime on the books of many states, and should be examined carefully by both debtors and advisers before taking aggressive actions under the false assumption that "all a creditor can do is avoid the transfer."[45]

## Racketeering Influenced and Corrupt Organizations Act (RICO) Actions

An adviser who assists a client evade creditors may be subject to exposure under the Racketeering Influenced and Corrupt Organizations (RICO) Act. In *Kruse v. Repp*,[46] the attorney defendants (along with bank officers) who were associated with a client's fraudulent transfer of assets (after the client was involved in a car accident) could not dismiss a RICO action against them. "The Racketeering Influenced and Corrupt Organizations Act renders it unlawful 'for any person employed by or associated with any enterprise engaged in, or the activities of which affect, interstate or foreign commerce, to conduct or participate, directly

41. *See Firstar Bank, N.A. v. Faul*, No. 00 C 4061, 2001 WL 1636430, at *6 (N.D. Ill. Dec. 20, 2001). ("However, as noted above, Illinois law permits a cause of action for fraud against any party who participates in a fraud, *see Citizen Savings & Loan*, 214 N.E.2d at 616, and we see no reason not to extend this rule to fraudulent conveyances. Moreover, if Firstar amends Count III such that it complies with the particularity requirement of Rule 9(b), the fraud claim against Faul would constitute a claim sufficient to make him a debtor under UFTA.")

42. *In re Glick* at 33.

43. *See Morganroth & Morganroth v. Norris, McLaughlin & Marcus, P.C.*, 331 F.3d 406, 414 (3d Cir. 2003). "We hold that when a complaint alleges that an attorney has knowingly and intentionally participated in a client's unlawful conduct to hinder, delay, and/or fraudulently obstruct the enforcement of a judgment of a court, the plaintiff has stated a claim under New Jersey law for creditor fraud against the attorney. This is so even if the complaint does not allege any misrepresentation by the attorney to the judgment creditor and does not allege that the creditor detrimentally relied on such misrepresentation."

44. *See Cevdet Aksut Ve Ogullari Koll. Sti v. Cavusoglu*, No. CIV. 14-3362 WJM, 2015 WL 4318131, at *2 (D.N.J. July 14, 2015). ("We hold that there is no cause of action for creditor fraud in this jurisdiction but that the attorney may be liable for conspiracy to violate the Uniform Fraudulent Transfer Act (UFTA), N.J.S.A. 25:2-20 to -34, for his participation in the transfer.")

45. See Chapter six, where several states provide for criminal penalties.

46. *Kruse by and through Kruse v. Repp*, 543 F. Supp. 3d 654 (2021); 2021 WL 2451230.

or indirectly, in the conduct of such enterprise's affairs through a pattern of racketeering activity.' 18 U.S.C. §1962(c). The remedial purpose of the statute is broad, *see United States v. Turkette*, 452 U.S. 576, 589, 101 S.Ct. 2524, 69 L. Ed.2d 246 (1981), and provides civil recourse to '[a]ny person injured in [her] business or property by reason of' the enterprise's racketeering activities, 18 U.S.C. §1964(c). Those who conspire to violate RICO also fall within the statute's purview. 18 U.S.C. §1962(d)."

In *Kruse*, the court considered the RICO elements in the context of the attorney's (Repp's) actions. In determining whether the defendant's motion for summary judgment would stand, the court considered the attorney's own material regarding asset protection (when analyzing whether the attorney participated in the conduct of the enterprise's affairs). In *Kruse,* the first attorney (Weller) helped the debtor make cash gifts in addition to the formation of a revocable trust. The second attorney, Repp, assisted with the transfer of debtor's assets to an LLC. The court found it odd that Repp agreed that Weller's actions were inappropriate, but Repp's were not. "In essence, Repp agreed Weller's previous efforts were inappropriate. All of his advice that followed was consistent with the expertise in asset protection that Repp, not Weller, possessed. *See generally* David M. Repp, Asset Protection (For the Rich and Not) In Iowa, 56 Drake L. Rev. 105, 106–08, 106 n.5 (2007). *** But '[f]or whatever reason, ultimately transferring the [assets] to the LLC and away from creditors did not strike [Weller] or his counsel as just as eyebrow-raising.' [ECF No. 53-2 at 104]."

# Attorney immunity defense

An attorney may argue that helping a client hinder future creditors is ethically required because a lawyer must be a zealous advocate for his client. However, ethical opinions confirm this is not the case if the attorney assists a client engage in a fraudulent transfer, with the possibility of disciplinary action increasing the closer an attorney's assistance is to judgment. Outside of ethical concerns, discussed in more detail in this chapter, an attorney may argue for immunity from civil liability by raising an attorney-immunity defense. The problem with this approach, like the analysis associated with ethical discipline, is the attorney's conduct may fall outside the scope of permissible conduct.[47] Put

47. *See* Rose Turner and Stephanie Moore, Appellants v. Linda Williams, Andrew Ross, and Steven A. Sinkin, Appellees, No. 01-17-00494-CV, 2019 WL 922057, at *7–8 (Tex. App. Feb. 26, 2019). ("Because immunity focuses on the type of conduct, it may apply even to unsound or unmeritorious conduct. See Easton, 2012 WL 1650024, at *8. '[A]n attorney's conduct, even if frivolous or without merit, is not independently actionable if the conduct is part of the discharge of the lawyer's duties in representing his or her client.' Alpert, 178 S.W.3d at 406. 'The filing of pleadings and motions—even if they are unmeritorious or frivolous—and the rendition of legal advice cannot form the factual basis of a fraud claim against an attorney when the acts are performed within the context of discharging duties to a client.' Easton, 2012 WL 1650024, at *8. Although attorney immunity is broad, it is not absolute. See id. Attorney immunity will not shield 'independently fraudulent activities,' Alpert, 178 S.W.3d at 406, such as 'knowingly assisting a client in evading a judgment through a fraudulent transfer.' Essex Crane, 371 S.W.3d at 382. In a case involving fraud,

differently, if the attorney's conduct is not permitted, the attorney may not assert an immunity defense for such conduct. In *Youngkin v. Hines*, the Texas Supreme Court identified assistance with post-judgment fraudulent transfers as conduct that would not qualify for the attorney-immunity defense.

> This is not to say that an attorney could not be held liable to his own client for misconduct similar to that alleged by Hines or be reprimanded for ethics violations. But to be held liable to the opposing party is a wholly different matter. This is also not to say that attorneys are insulated from all liability to nonclients for all wrongdoing in the name of a client. Though attorney immunity is broad, it is not limitless. In *Cantey Hanger*, we identified several nonexhaustive examples of conduct that may fall outside the reach of the attorney-immunity defense—participation in a fraudulent business scheme with a client, knowingly helping a client with a fraudulent transfer to avoid paying a judgment, theft of goods or services on a client's behalf, and assaulting opposing counsel during trial. *Id.* at 482-83. Thus, while we recognize that some fraudulent conduct, even if done on behalf of a client, may be actionable, Hines does not allege any such behavior.[48]

Attorney immunity is especially controversial as it applies to the actions of attorneys who hold themselves out as asset protection planners. Here, the attorney charges a premium to "firewall" or "ring-fence" a client's assets out of creditor reach. Judges have not been particularly fond of fact patterns where law firms cross a line by assisting debtors move assets to avoid creditor claims.[49]

## Attorney Fees

If assisting a client move assets results in avoidance under fraudulent transfer law, the client may be faced with paying for the creditor's attorney fees. This possibility must be discussed before engaging in some forms of wealth transfer planning; the worst-case scenario would involve a client's transaction being unwound and, essentially, having to pay the creditor to unwind the transaction. This is not the worst-case scenario, as all of the above can occur, plus the

---

the plaintiff must prove that the attorney 'agreed to the injury to be accomplished, not merely the conduct ultimately resulting in injury.' *Id.* (citing Chu v. Hong, 249 S.W.3d 441, 446–47 (Tex. 2008)). Other situations in which attorney immunity may not apply include fraudulent concealment (when the attorney has a duty to speak), negligent misrepresentation, and when the law specifically provides for punishment of an attorney. *See* McCamish, Martin, Brown & Loeffler v. F.E. Appling Interests, 991 S.W.2d 787, 791 (Tex. 1999) (negligent misrepresentation); Bradt v. West, 892 S.W.2d 56, 72 (Tex. App.—Houston [1st Dist.] 1994, *writ denied*) (sanctions); Hennigan v. Harris Cty., 593 S.W.2d 380, 384–85 (Tex. App.—Waco 1979, *writ ref'd n.r.e.*) (fraudulent concealment when there is a duty to speak).")

48. *Youngkin v. Hines*, 546 S.W.3d 675, 682-83 (Tex. 2018). (Emphasis added.)

49. *See In re Harwell*, 414 B.R. 770, 787 (M.D. Fla. 2009), *rev'd*, 628 F.3d 1312 (11th Cir. 2010). ("In saying that, this Court does not hold that such an action for civil conspiracy exists for aiding a fraudulent transfer. It is not required to reach that issue since there were no 'wrongs' committed by the lawyer in this case. This issue is best left for another day, but, at the least, a warning bell has sounded for parties involved in 'asset preservation.'")

attorney can wind up answering to the creditor as well as the state bar, discussed in this chapter.

Courts may be more inclined to award attorney fees in situations where the fraudulent transfer was especially egregious and an obvious attempt to make things more difficult for creditors. In this situation, awarding attorney fees helps to not only restore the creditor for expending fees to unwind a transfer, but also provide a deterrent effect to support public policy and prevent waste of judicial resources.

> In the view of this Court, attorneys' fees are necessary in this case both to make the defrauded creditors whole, and to deter conduct of the character present here. Undoing the fraudulent conveyances is not enough.
>
> The creation of a second mortgage has had serious implications for Vaniman, and has substantially diminished the assets available to creditors by the costs to the estate which it has created. Any possibility of rehabilitating Vaniman under Chapter 11 required that it be left in possession of its real estate, which James Martin and Pirrone opposed when they initiated the present proceeding seeking relief from stay so they could enforce the mortgage which this Court has now found was created in fraud of creditors. It is true that Roslyn Savings Bank, which held a first mortgage on Vaniman's realty, was seeking similar relief, but the fair market value of the Vaniman real estate was so far in excess of Roslyn's claim that the debtor, if it faced Roslyn alone, and if its financial situation had not been so grave, might well have been permitted to stay in possession of its real estate had the outstanding second mortgage not reduced its equity to zero. When Vaniman's Chapter 11 petition was converted to Chapter 7, James Martin and Pirrone continued to press to remove Vaniman's real estate from the bankruptcy court and strenuously opposed its sale, predicating their opposition on the mortgage they had created on September 4, 1979, forcing the trustee into extended litigation to establish his right to do no more than liquidate Vaniman's assets.
>
> This proceeding itself has been time consuming, involving discovery and pretrial conferences, as well as a protracted trial. None of this would have been necessary but for the wrongful creation of a purported security interest in Vaniman's real estate. Simply avoiding the fraudulent conveyances, declaring the mortgage invalid, and requiring James Martin and Pirrone to restore the life insurance policies to Vaniman will not act as a deterrent, since anyone similarly tempted will calculate correctly that they have nothing to lose by similar misconduct if the worst that can happen is that they be required to restore what was improperly taken. Furthermore, the creditors of Vaniman should not be penalized for the wrongdoing of James Martin and Pirrone. Martin and Pirrone, not Vaniman's creditors, should bear the cost of the extensive litigation which they have forced on the trustee in bankruptcy.
>
> Accordingly, an appropriate application should be submitted to this court to determine the amount of attorneys' fees to be awarded.[50]

50. *In re Vaniman Intern., Inc.*, 22 B.R. 166, 194-95 (Bankr. E.D.N.Y. 1982).

In some cases, attorney fees associated with a fraudulent transfer might be settled by statute. For instance, the Texas Uniform Fraudulent Transfer Act provides, "[i]n any proceeding under this chapter, the court may award costs and reasonable attorney's fees as are equitable and just."[51] Although not expressly permitted under the uniform acts, a claim brought under fraudulent transfer statutory law will not prevent a creditor to seek attorney fees permitted under other law, including the fraudulent transfer common law. "We see no reason why a plaintiff in a fraudulent transfer case who would have had a claim for attorney fees under the third-party litigation exception before UFTA was enacted should now be denied attorney fees. UFTA does not expressly address attorney fees. Instead, it expressly grants courts the authority to employ a full array of remedial measures insofar as they are warranted under the particular facts of the case."[52]

Not all courts have gone so far to award attorney fees, taking the position that fees are not available unless the parties agreed in advance via contract or state law provides otherwise.

> There is no provision in FUFTA that explicitly provides for an award of attorneys' fees. See Fla. Stat. §726.101, et seq. Undeterred, Pasternak attempts to shoehorn an attorneys' fee remedy into the statute's "catch-all" provision, which permits a creditor to obtain a money judgment or "any other relief the circumstances may require." Fla. Stat. §§726.108(1)(c)(3), 726.109(2). Pasternack, however, does not cite any authority to support this interpretation of FUFTA, and the case law on the matter is decidedly to the contrary. Euro RSCG Direct Response, LLC v. Green Bullion Fin. Servs., 872 F. Supp. 2d 1353, 1364 (S.D. Fla. 2012) (striking attorney fee demand because FUFTA does not contain a fee provision); *In re* Empresa Naviera Santa USA, Inc., 235 B.R. 130, 133 (Bankr. S.D. Fla. 1999) (finding no statutory basis for attorneys' fees under FUFTA); Janvey v. Suarez, 978 F. Supp. 2d 685, 709 (N. D. Tex. 2013) (discussing differences between Texas Uniform Fraudulent Transfer Act and FUFTA, and noting that under Texas law, a court may award prevailing party attorneys' fees, but that the parties agree there is no such provision under FUFTA); Nat'l Union Fire Ins. Co. of Pittsburgh Pennsylvania v. Garber, 288 F. App'x 319, 320 (9th Cir. 2008) (finding the California Uniform Fraudulent Transfer Act—which is worded similarly to FUFTA—does not provide for an award of attorney fees); but see Samsara Mem'l Tr. v. Kelly, Remmel & Zimmerman, 2014 ME 107, ¶ 49, 102 A.3d 757, 774, *as corrected* (Nov. 13, 2014) (finding attorneys' fees authorized under Maine Uniform Fraudulent Transfer Act based on its legislative history and a unique provision that damages are recoverable up to twice the value of the transferred asset).

51. Tex. Bus. & Com. Code Ann. §24.013 (West).

52. *See Macris & Assocs., Inc. v. Neways, Inc.*, 2002 UT App 406, ¶ 17, 60 P.3d 1176, 1180.

> *3 In light of this authority and the absence of any express attorneys' fee provision in FUFTA, I find that Pasternak does not demonstrate a valid statutory basis for her attorneys' fees request.[53]

Consequently, creditors should consider whether attorney fee provisions should be included in contracts, and debtors and their counsel should carefully review contracts to determine whether a transaction could result in the award of attorney fees.

> The language of the Mortgage provides that in a suit to foreclose the Mortgage or to enforce any other remedy of the Lender under the Mortgage or Note, the Lender is entitled to recover attorney's fees and costs. This lawsuit for fraudulent transfer is not a foreclosure action or a remedy under the terms of the Mortgage or Note. The language of the Mortgage also provides that expenses such as attorney's fees and costs associated with the protection of the Collateral or maintenance of the lien of the Mortgage or the enforcement of the Lender's rights under the Mortgage are recoverable. The Defendants have not alleged that Tract II was used a collateral for the Mortgage and Promissory Note on Tract I, and therefore the instant lawsuit is not related to the protections or maintenance of the Collateral for the Mortgage and Note. The Mortgage also provides that attorney's fees associated with any lawsuit which affects the Mortgage, Note or Collateral are recoverable. However, the instant action has no bearing on the Mortgage, Note, or Collateral.
>
> The Court finds that provisions of the Mortgage and Note that pertain to Tract I do not provide for attorney's fees in the instant action. This type of action was not listed in the provisions for attorney's fees in the Mortgage and Note, and a plain reading of the Mortgage and Note do not allow for a recovery of the attorney's fees and costs in this action.[54]

# Ethics issues

ABA Model Rule 1.2(d) provides that a lawyer shall not counsel a client to engage, or assist a client, in conduct that the lawyer knows is criminal or fraudulent. However, a lawyer may discuss the legal consequences of any proposed course of conduct with a client and may counsel or assist a client to make a good faith effort to determine the validity, scope, meaning, or application of the law. One might readily assume that a fraudulent transfer is not a crime, so the attorney should never be worried about engaging or assisting with conduct that is criminal. However, several states have criminalized fraudulent transfers

53. Alla Pasternack, Ex'x of the Estate of Leon Frenkel, Plaintiff, v. Bruce K. Klein, individually, & in all other employee, owner, member, corporate & agent capacities as regards his various business entities, & Ozean Partners, LLC, Defendants., No. 8:16-CV-482-T-33CPT, 2019 WL 5111974, at *2–3 (M.D. Fla. Aug. 26, 2019).

54. *Commerce First Fin., LLC v. Summerlin Bass, LLC*, No. 2:10-CV-290-FTM-36, 2011 WL 7316326, at *3 (M.D. Fla. Sept. 13, 2011), *report and recommendation adopted*, No. 2:10-CV-00290-FTM-36, 2011 WL 4902988 (M.D. Fla. Oct. 14, 2011).

to some degree.[55] Here, the attorney must understand what jurisdictions are involved before assuming away this issue. When reviewing these criminal statutes, the adviser should determine whether the offense applies to all creditors or just judgment creditors.[56]

Even if the action giving rise to a fraudulent transfer does not amount to a criminal offense, a court may view a fraudulent transfer as activity for which an attorney's assistance can result in ethical discipline.

> We conclude assisting a client with a fraudulent transaction can in the appropriate circumstances constitute a "fraud" under our disciplinary rules. *See id.* *42 Courts in other jurisdictions have similarly concluded that lawyers can run afoul of disciplinary rules by facilitating fraudulent conveyances or fraudulently conveying property themselves. *See, e.g.*, In re Morris, No. 11–O–13518, 2013 WL 6598701, at *1 (Cal.Bar Ct. Dec. 4, 2013) (unpublished opinion) (finding lawyer violated rule prohibiting moral turpitude, dishonesty, and corruption by assisting a client in creating promissory notes and recording deeds of trust to delay a creditor's collection of its judgment); Fla. Bar v. Rood, 620 So.2d 1252, 1255 (Fla.1993) (finding rule violation when lawyer fraudulently transferred property to his father); Att'y Grievance Comm'n v. Culver, 381 Md. 241, 849 A.2d 423, 444 (2004) (sanctioning lawyer for, among other things, advising client "how she could avoid repaying" creditors); Dayton Bar Ass'n v. Marzocco, 79 Ohio St.3d 186, 680 N.E.2d 970, 971 (1997) (disbarring lawyer based in part on lawyer's "apparent attempt to transfer property to evade the effect of a judgment"); *In re* Conduct of Hockett, 303 Or. 150, 734 P.2d 877, 883–84 (1987) (suspending lawyer for violating rules prohibiting misrepresentation and illegal conduct when lawyer helped client unlawfully convey property to avoid the claims of creditors).[57]

However, a court may examine the attorney's knowledge of the facts in determining whether the attorney violated an ethical rule, as well as whether the

---

55. *See, e.g.*, Cal. Penal Code §154. ("Every debtor who fraudulently removes his or her property or effects out of this state, or who fraudulently sells, conveys, assigns or conceals his or her property with intent to defraud, hinder or delay his or her creditors of their rights, claims, or demands, is punishable by imprisonment in the county jail not exceeding one year, or by fine not exceeding one thousand dollars ($1,000), or by both that fine and imprisonment."); Ohio Rev. Code §2913.45 ("(A) No person, with purpose to defraud one or more of the person's creditors, shall do any of the following: (1) Remove, conceal, destroy, encumber, convey, or otherwise deal with any of the person's property; *** Whoever violates this section is guilty of defrauding creditors. Except as otherwise provided in this division, defrauding creditors is a misdemeanor of the first degree. If the value of the property involved is one thousand dollars or more and is less than seven thousand five hundred dollars, defrauding creditors is a felony of the fifth degree. If the value of the property involved is seven thousand five hundred dollars or more and is less than one hundred fifty thousand dollars, defrauding creditors is a felony of the fourth degree. If the value of the property involved is one hundred fifty thousand dollars or more, defrauding creditors is a felony of the third degree.")

56. *See* Ariz. Rev. Stat. §13-2205, applicable to judgment creditors. "A. A person commits defrauding judgment creditors if such person secretes, assigns, conveys or otherwise disposes of his property with the intent to defraud a judgment creditor or to prevent that property from being subjected to payment of a judgment. B. Defrauding judgment creditors is a class 6 felony."

57. *Iowa Supreme Ct. Att'y Disciplinary Bd. v. Ouderkirk*, 845 N.W.2d 31, 41–42 (Iowa 2014).

attorney was engaged in some form of self-dealing.[58] In *Iowa Supreme Ct. Att'y Disciplinary Bd. v. Ouderkirk*, an attorney assisted a client engage in transfers after the client was charged with murder.[59] The Iowa Supreme Court stated that if a lawyer knows a transfer is fraudulent but nonetheless assists with the client's transfer, the lawyer cannot claim that the lawyer was acting as a mere scrivener. The Court further noted that "[i]t should go without saying that a lawyer cannot avoid disciplinary sanctions simply because a particular unethical practice is commonplace among lawyers."[60] The Iowa Supreme Court ultimately found the Iowa disciplinary board did not prove by a preponderance of the evidence that the lawyer knowingly helped his client fraudulently convey property, or that it was obvious.[61]

Based on a review of the disciplinary cases, the most dangerous fact patterns for lawyers are those where a claim already exists. Obviously, this is not to say that a claim must exist at the time of a transaction to trigger application of the fraudulent transfer law, but for purposes of ethical discipline, the existence of a claim appears to create a heightened degree of risk, with the degree of risk increasing as the client moves closer to a judgment and post-judgment.

Canons 1 and 2 of the Code of Judicial Conduct are also relevant for judges who participate in a fraudulent transfer. In a disciplinary action, the Supreme Court of New Hampshire had to determine whether a judge, who helped her husband facing potential legal problems, assisted with a fraudulent transfer. If so, the court had to determine whether such conduct required discipline. The judge asserted that the transfers from her husband (to the judge as trustee of a

---

58. *Id.* at 44. (Most of the cases cited by the Board, however, involve lawyers who were self-dealing. *See* People v. Koller, 873 P.2d 761, 762, 763 (Colo.1994) (per curiam) (suspending lawyer who fraudulently conveyed his property to his wife); People v. Bennett, 843 P.2d 1385, 1385–86 (Colo.1993) (per curiam) (disbarring attorney who fraudulently conveyed his property to his wife and his wife's parents); Rood, 620 So.2d at 1254–55 (disbarring lawyer who transferred his property to his father to hinder creditors); In re Diller, 308 A.D.2d 14, 763 N.Y.S.2d 827, 829–30 (2003) (per curiam) (suspending lawyer who helped her husband fraudulently convey property). In the remaining cases, the lawyers were found to have knowingly facilitated fraudulent conveyances. See Bd. of Overseers of the Bar v. Murphy, 570 A.2d 1212, 1213 (Me.1990) (per curiam) (finding rule violation when lawyer "actively promot[ed] a fraudulent conveyance"); In re Orlow, 197 N.J. 507, 964 A.2d 303, 303 (2009) (suspending lawyer based on disciplinary review board's conclusion that the respondent assisted a client to conceal his assets from creditors); Mahoning Cnty. Bar Ass'n v. Sinclair, 105 Ohio St.3d 65, 822 N.E.2d 360, 364–65 (2004) (per curiam) (suspending lawyer who drafted deed despite "kn [owing] of tax judgments against [client] and that [he] was trying to hide assets from creditors"). In contrast, the Missouri Supreme Court dismissed an ethical complaint after finding the prosecuting body failed to prove by a preponderance of the evidence that the lawyers knew of their clients' fraudulent intentions. In re Mirabile, 975 S.W.2d 936, 941 (Mo.1998) (dismissing ethical complaint when attorneys testified "they believed [their clients'] separation was real" and was not an attempt to fraudulently avoid husband's prior child support obligations).)

59. *Id.* at 33. ("The Lyon estate brought collection actions challenging the asset transfers as fraudulent conveyances. The district court ruled in favor of the estate and found the transactions with which Ouderkirk assisted to be "part of a complex shell game." The court found the Heemstras transferred assets in an "intentional, harsh and cruel effort to put truth in Rodney Heemstra's arrogant claim that Ronda Lyon would never see a dime of his money." The court unwound a number of the asset transfers *and awarded actual and punitive damages* against the Heemstras.") (*Emphasis added.*)

60. *Id.* at 44.

61. *Id.* at 51. ("We conclude the Board has failed to prove by a convincing preponderance of the evidence that Ouderkirk violated Iowa Code of Professional Responsibility DR 7–102(A)(1), DR 1–102(A)(4)DR 1–102 (A)(4), DR 7–102(A)(7)DR 7–102(A)(7), or DR 1–102(A)(5)DR 1–102(A)(5).")

trust for the judge's benefit) took place before there were any claims pending or seriously contemplated. The judge also claimed the trust was created only as "end of the year estate planning, plain and simple."[62] Notwithstanding the justifications offered by the judge, the Supreme Court of New Hampshire concluded she violated the Code of Judicial Conduct:

> Judge Coffey has stipulated that she "[a]ided Mr. Coffey in protecting his assets from the reach of creditors." Therefore, the only question is whether the transfers were made "[w]ith actual intent to hinder, delay, or defraud any creditor," as those terms are used under the Fraudulent Transfer Act. RSA 545-A:4, I(a) (emphasis added). In resolving this issue, we note first that Judge Coffey admitted to the JCC prosecutor that she and Mr. Coffey decided to transfer all of the property into her sole name because, at least in part, they were concerned about "some crazy client coming out of the woodwork and suing [Mr. Coffey]." Judge Coffey acknowledged that making these transfers with such a consideration in mind could be construed as "an effort to fraudulently convey something to put it out of the reach of some creditor down the road." <u>Arguably, these admissions alone are sufficient to find "actual intent," as all that is required under the statute is an intent to hinder, delay, or defraud any creditor, not necessarily the one who is ultimately defrauded.</u> RSA 545-A:4, I(a).
>
> * * *
>
> In light of these facts, as well as Judge Coffey's admission of some intent to defraud potential future creditors and her concession in her brief that the PCC proceedings had caused her concern for her family's "emotional and financial security," we conclude that the record sufficiently demonstrates that Judge Coffey was complicit in a fraudulent transfer. *See Estes v. Titus*, 273 Mich.App. 356, 731 N.W.2d 119, 130-34 (2006) (finding that a judgment creditor had a valid claim under the Uniform Fraudulent Transfer Act where the judgment debtor had, prior to conclusion of the underlying case, entered into a consent divorce that transferred all of his assets to his former wife, thus making him insolvent), appeal granted, 478 Mich. 864, 731 N.W.2d 423 (2007). <u>By participating in the fraudulent conveyances, Judge Coffey contravened the public policies embodied in RSA</u> 545-A:4, *see Matter of Seaman*, 133 N.J. 67, 627 A.2d 106, 122 (1993) (holding that a judge's infringement of an important public policy is grounds for aggravation); Sup.Ct. R. 38, Canon 2 ("A judge shall respect . . . the law"), and, at minimum, created an appearance of impropriety. *See* Sup.Ct. R. 38.[63]

# Malpractice Issues

An attorney must determine whether his or her contemplated actions will trigger fraudulent transfer issues, and this determination should be made, ideally, at the engagement stage or prior to assistance with a new matter for an

62. *See In re Coffey's Case*, 157 N.H. 156, 167, 949 A.2d 102, 111 (2008).
63. *In re Coffey's Case*, 157 N.H. 156, 179, 949 A.2d 102, 120 (2008). (Emphasis added.)

existing client. According to the Attorneys' Liability Assurance Society (a risk retention group for law firms), some of the claims filed involved what ALAS characterized as unworthy clients. "The leading causes of claims against ALAS firms are unworthy clients, mistakes, and conflicts of interest. Claims in the T&E practice reflect the same issues. Analyzing the 900-plus claims, we see that many T&E claims involve unworthy clients - such as a settlor client who fraudulently transferred assets into trusts . . . "[64]

Of particular concern to those who provide asset protection or wealth preservation, is when to draw the line and how to effectively provide such protection or preservation service to a prospective client. For lawyers in larger firms, this type of engagement might require input from general counsel as the engagement, by its very nature, creates heightened exposure to the firm. This is so because the attorney undertakes planning that is specifically aimed at making things difficult for creditors. In some cases, the planning may directly conflict with fraudulent transfer law, which is meant to provide remedies to creditors who are hindered because of this planning.

There are common situations where an attorney faces increased exposure for assisting with a fraudulent transfer. These transactions include planning for a client who (a) hinders present creditors, including creditors for which the client has previously made a personal guarantee or (b) hinders certain future creditors, such as a spouse, child, or governmental agency. For this reason, the attorney must exercise extreme due care when assisting a client who articulates a concern over a particular event or individual.

In *Schwartz v. Bloch*, the attorney advised the client to transfer business interests to the client's father before the client was married, in lieu of a pre-nuptial agreement. Unfortunately for the client, a dispute arose between the client and his father, prompting the client to sue the attorney:

> In 2004, plaintiff consulted Bloch and his firm for asset protection advice in light of his forthcoming marriage to his current wife. Bloch discussed with plaintiff the possibility of obtaining a prenuptial agreement and fully disclosing all assets prior to executing such an agreement. Plaintiff informed Bloch, however, that a prenuptial agreement was not a viable option. Bloch then advised plaintiff that the most effective alternative would be for plaintiff to assign his interests in family businesses to other members of his family so as not to own those assets during the marriage. Plaintiff followed this advice, and on September 23, 2004, he assigned his interests in the following six entities to his father.[65]

A client seeking asset protection might not be forthcoming as to the client's financial situation, which could lead to problems not only as to third-party creditors, but also in a suit for malpractice against the lawyer.[66]

---

64. Rady J. Curato, "Trust and Estate Practice: Avoiding Trouble," ALAS Loss Prevention Journal, Volume XXV, Number 1, (Winter 2014.) (Emphasis Added.)

65. *Schwartz v. Bloch*, 88 So. 3d 1068, 1069 (Fla. Dist. Ct. App. 2012).

66. *See Butler v. King; Dunham; & Culp Elliott & Carpenter*, 2019 WL 4440307 (D.S.C. Sept. 17, 2019). ("Regarding the actual drafting of the premarital contract at issue, Defendants raise that Butler misguided them on her true financial status at the time she sought their counsel related to asset protection . . . ")

In *Korotki v. Hiller & Arban, LLC*,[67] the client, Abraham Korotki, a real estate developer, encountered disputes with various third-party builders and developers, as well as a dispute over a letter of credit with Wilmington Trust Company, personally guaranteed by the client. Various lawyers were retained, including the Schwartz defendants, serving primarily as litigation counsel but also performing "transactional services including effectuating the conversions of certain entities into limited liability companies and preparing by-laws, corporate minutes, and deeds."[68] Korotki also sought the advice of Hiller, "who allegedly 'held himself out to the public as a bankruptcy specialist.'"[69] Approximately a year later, and as a result of all the litigation, Korotki was advised by the Schwartz defendants and Hiller defendants to retain Offit Kurman, P.A. to represent Korotki and his entities in "creating and implementing an 'asset protection plan.'"[70] Hiller and Schwartz received copies of the asset protection plan, which provided:

> a. On December 1, 2008, STL was created and 100 shares of STL's common stock were issued to Reserves;
>
> b. On December 2, 2008, Reserves transferred the STL stock to Mr. Korotki;
>
> c. On December 3, 2008, Reserves deeded 69 lots to STL (the 69 Lots); and
>
> d. On January16, 2009, Mr. Korotki's stock in STL was transferred to Saleena. . . .
>
> e. Additionally, all other real property owned by Mr. Korotki, as well as all of his personal property, were transferred to Saleena . . . at or about the time of the stock transfer to her, and Mr. Korotki directed his attorneys in writing to "pay over, distribute and convey any and all monies received on my behalf and those of the above corporations [Resort] [and Management] to Saleena. . . ."[71]

The client was advised that he should file for relief under Chapter 11 of the bankruptcy code, even though because of the asset protection plan, the client was "judgment proof."[72] Accordingly, the client filed a Joint Plan of

---

67. *See Abraham Korotki, Saleena Korotki, Reserves Development, LLC, STL Development LLC, ST2K, LLC, The Reserves Resort, SPA & Country Club, LLC, & The Reserves Management, LLC, Plaintiffs, v. Hiller & Arban, LLC, Adam Hiller, ESQ., Brian Arban, ESQ., Schwartz & Schwartz, Attorneys at Law, P.A., & Steven Schwartz, ESQ., Defendants.*, No. CVN15C07164CCLDWCC, 2017 WL 2303522, at *2 (Del. Super. Ct. May 23, 2017).

68. *Id.*

69. *Id.*

70. *Id.*

71. *Korotki v. Hiller & Arban, LLC*, 2017 WL 2303522, at *2 (Del. Super. Ct. May 23, 2017).

72. *Id. at* 3. ("In a 'series of telephonic meetings that took place in Philadelphia and elsewhere throughout the latter part of 2012,'" Defendants allegedly advised Mr. Korotki that both he and Resort should file for bankruptcy relief under Chapter 11 of the United States Bankruptcy Code. Defendants purportedly assured Mr. Korotki that pursuing this course of action would allow him and Resort to remain "debtors-in-possession" and thereby "retain possession and control of their assets, business, and property" and "continue to prosecute their pending state court litigations." Defendants apparently rendered such advice "even though as a result of the Asset Protection Plan that the Offit [Kurman attorneys] had implemented, Mr. Korotki was 'judgment proof.'")

Reorganization (Reorganization Plan) and Disclosure Statement. However, according to the client, the Disclosure Statement "conceded that a Chapter 7 liquidation was the only realistic alternative to the Reorganization Plan (which was *per se* non-confirmable) and further conceded, prophetically, that a Chapter 7 Trustee would 'settle quickly, even for nominal values, without realizing the true value of the . . . Claims.'"[73] Further, the client faced the possibility of losing certain properties to the bankruptcy estate if the bankruptcy trustee pursued a fraudulent transfer action. Consequently, the client was allegedly left with no choice but to accept the bankruptcy trustee's proposed settlement whereby:

> "(i) they released all claims they had, and the right to collect" on those claims, and "(ii) the lots that they owned, including but not limited to the 90 lots owned by STL and ST2K, would be sold as part of a sale, from which Plaintiffs would be entitled to a fractional payment of the proceeds "instead of the [ ] actual value."[74]

The client then filed a malpractice lawsuit in July 2015 against the lawyers involved.[75] The allegations included, "advising Mr. Korotki to file a personal bankruptcy, despite the fact that his Asset Protection Plan essentially rendered him 'judgment proof' from creditors," "'[m]istiming the filing of the Chapter 11 . . . Petitions and thereby exposing the transfers made pursuant to the Asset Protection Plan to the Chapter 7 Trustee's avoidance powers;'" and "'[c]reating and proposing" a plan of reorganization that was "ill-conceived, non-confirmable as a matter of law, and destined for total failure.'" The Hiller and Schwartz defendants filed motions for summary judgment, alleging, among other items, that summary judgment was warranted under the doctrines of unclean hands and *in pari delicto* because of the client's conduct. Regarding the fraudulent transfer issues, "Hiller Defendants also contend Korotki's Asset Protection Plan was in violation of Delaware's fraudulent transfer laws, thereby further supporting this Court's application of *in pari delicto*."[76]

Although the court believed the client's conduct was "concerning" and "his credibility is and will be a continuing issue," such conduct was not sufficient to warrant application of unclean hands or *in pari delicto* doctrines. The court noted, "many of the acts Defendants point to as justifying the imposition of *in pari delicto* are ones which were performed with their advice and counsel."[77] The court permitted the claims of malpractice against the lawyers and their firms.[78]

---

73. *Id. at* 3.

74. *Id.* at 4.

75. The client pursued a separate claim against the Pennsylvania law firm.

76. *Id.* at 12.

77. *Id.*

78. *Id.* at 17. ("The conclusion rendered by this Opinion is that Plaintiffs' claims of malpractice against Mr. Hiller and Mr. Schwartz and their law firms may proceed. However, the issue of the damages they suffered by the alleged improper advice will be limited to the development property losses that resulted from the bankruptcy proceeding. If the jury believes Plaintiffs' experts, the losses are not an insignificant amount. The claim for damages based on the potential value of pending litigation, however, is simply too speculative and must be foreclosed along with the claims against Mr. Arban.")

## Insurance Coverage

How a court views a lawyer's assistance in hindering creditors is important, not only with respect to civil, criminal, or ethical issues for the lawyer, but also as to whether the actions are covered by the lawyer's insurance policy. Coverage issues can arise in various contexts, depending on the lawyer's involvement and potential liability. If the lawyer or law firm is viewed as a transferee of transferred funds, and if a policy potentially covers such liability, a court may view subsequent lawyer liability (as transferee) as akin to uninsurable disgorgement versus insurable loss under the terms of a policy.

An attorney may also be asked to opine on the coverage issues involved with a wealth transfer plan, at least with respect to distributions that could be challenged involving business transactions.[79] In situations involving a trust account, complex issues may arise involving possession of the funds for purposes of coverage versus control of funds for purposes of pleading an equitable conduit defense.

Where the lawyer is being sued for conspiracy or aiding and abetting a fraudulent transfer carried out with actual intent to hinder, delay, or defraud, either under fraudulent transfer common law or fraudulent transfer statutory law, one may argue that the lawyer's liability for such action may result in denial of coverage.[80] This may be due to an exclusion in a professional liability policy for dishonest or criminal acts. Whereas assisting (e.g., via conspiracy) with a fraudulent transfer that is characterized as being done by the client with actual intent to hinder, delay, or defraud any creditor, could be viewed as excluded,

---

79. *See Twin City Fire Ins. Co. v. Oceaneering Int'l, Inc.*, No. CV H-16-666, 2017 WL 2999269, at *6–7 (S. D. Tex. Feb. 28, 2017), report and recommendation adopted, No. CV H-16-666, 2017 WL 1160514 (S.D. Tex. Mar. 29, 2017). ("The Fifth Circuit answered a similar question under Texas law in *In re* TransTexas Gas Corp., 597 F.3d at 298, which provides binding authority for this court's analysis. That case addressed a bankruptcy judgment against the company's prior chief executive officer to whom the company paid a severance package after his resignation. *Id.* at 302–03. The parties had entered into an employment agreement that allowed severance payments if the officer was terminated—$3,000,000 if terminated without cause and $1,500,000 if terminated for cause—but no severance if he voluntarily resigned. *Id.* at 302. Nevertheless, when the officer resigned, the company's board decided to invoke the severance provision of the contract and paid the officer $2,270,794.90. *Id.* In bankruptcy court, the severance payments were held to be fraudulent transfers, and the officer was ordered to repay the severance money he had received, plus attorneys' fees and costs. *Id.* at 303. *7 The insurance company that issued a D&O liability policy filed a declaratory judgment action regarding insurance coverage for the disgorgement of the officer's severance compensation. *See* Nat'l Union Fire Ins. Co. of Pittsburgh, Pa. v. U.S. Bank, Nat'l Assoc., Civil Action No. 4:07-CV-1958, 2008 WL 2405975, at *1 (S.D. Tex. June 11, 2008) (*applying Texas law*) (unpublished). The coverage issue was the same as here, whether amounts in restitution/disgorgement were damages covered under the policy. *See id.* at *4. The definition of loss in the policy under consideration explicitly did not include "matters which may be deemed uninsurable under the law pursuant to which this policy shall be construed." *Id.* at *2. The district court decided the issue on summary judgment, holding that the insureds did not carry their burden of establishing coverage under the policy. *See id.* at *5. In reaching this conclusion, the district court relied on Nortex Oil & Gas Corp. v. Harbor Insurance Co., 456 S.W.2d 489 (Tex. Civ. App.—Dallas 1970, no writ), and Level 3 Communications, Inc. v. Federal Insurance Co., 272 F.3d 908 (7th Cir. 2001). *See* Nat'l Union Fire Ins. Co. of Pittsburgh, Pa., 2008 WL 2405975, at * *4-5.")

80. Care should be taken by both insured and insurer in reviewing applicable coverages and exclusions, including whether a wrongful act must have been committed knowingly.

query whether constructive fraud would yield the same result. This distinction should be considered in light of the terms of the underlying insurance policy.[81] Although it is commonly asserted that a lawyer's actions in assisting with a fraudulent transfer are not covered by professional liability insurance, consider whether this result changes based on varying forms of underlying intent.

> It is appropriate to distinguish between the two types of fraud based on intent for several reasons. One reason is that the ordinary dictionary meaning and the legal dictionary meaning of fraud manifest the idea that fraud carries with it wrongful intent. And, the exclusion on the professional liability policy uses the words "dishonest," "criminal," and "malicious" in describing acts or omissions that will not be covered; these words connote intentional conduct and incorporate intent into their legal definitions. So, it follows that the word "fraudulent," used as it is in connection with these words, should also be interpreted as a term requiring and encompassing intent. Finally, liability insurance is not generally meant to apply to intentional acts of the insured. It is in keeping with this idea that a professional liability policy would exclude coverage for fraudulent acts that include wrongful intent, but would apply coverage for other acts of fraud.
>
> The bottom line is that, absent a clear definition in the policy, the common meaning of fraudulent act in a professional liability policy should apply only to actual fraud. This would allow the policy to cover acts or omissions of the insured attorney wherein he or she did not have the requisite intent to deceive the client.[82]

Further, consideration should be given to whether applicable law may be construed to hold a fraudulent transfer as criminal in nature (and thus, whether there is an exclusion to coverage.) As discussed elsewhere, in situations involving choice of law, the characterization of tort-like activity may have unforeseen consequences resulting in the application of another jurisdiction's law.

---

81. See *Fraudulent Acts Covered by Professional Liability Insurance?* FC&S Legal, June 24, 2008. ("A legal example of this distinction can be found in the case of *Brooks, Tarlton, Gilbert, etc. v. U.S. Fire Insurance Company*, 832 F2d 1358 (C.A. 5 1987). The U.S. court of appeals in this case held that the basis of the complaint in the lawsuit was a breach of fiduciary duty owed by the lawyers, and that this involved constructive fraud where a lawyer's intent or state of mind was immaterial. The court went on to state specifically that the insurance policy exclusion did not refer to constructive fraud, but to actual fraud only, which would include an element of wrongful intent. The court said that actual fraud involves dishonesty of purpose or intent to deceive whereas the benchmark of constructive fraud is the existence of a fiduciary relationship; it is the existence of the relationship, apart from any state of mind of the attorney, that casts doubt on a transaction between the attorney and the client.")

82. *Id.*

CHAPTER **10**

# Super Creditors

Although all creditors have access to remedies under the fraudulent transfer law, some creditors have additional tools that make attacking fraudulent transfers easier. Such is the case with what are referred to as "super creditors." This category of creditors includes governmental agencies (such as the Securities and Exchange Commission, Federal Trade Commission, Internal Revenue Service, and state law equivalents), bankruptcy trustees, receivers, as well as spouses and children in family law controversies. In some cases, super creditors will have access to an interest that otherwise would not be accessible for other creditors.

> Despite the TBE presumption established in Beal Bank, the trial court mistakenly allowed Wells Fargo, a creditor to only Mr. Gibson, to seek execution on TBE assets by claiming an authority reserved exclusively to the IRS. *See* Sinnreich, 391 F.3d at 1298. Hundley's analysis began with the observation that "[a]s a matter of Federal law, the right to a refund resulting from loss-carryback of prepetition losses constitutes property of the estate. Accordingly, any interest that the husband in this case may have in the joint refund is properly in the trustee's possession." 944 N.E.2d at 130 (*citations omitted*). Wells Fargo is not the IRS and lacks the IRS's special authority under the Internal Revenue Code. To allow otherwise would be to countenance the evisceration of the protections afforded TBE property discussed in Uttermohlen. Thus, Hundley is inapposite.[1]

Where federal law conflicts with state law, federal law will govern, which may sometimes result in disregarding state fraudulent transfer law in favor of similar federal provisions. In bankruptcy, bankruptcy courts may disregard state restrictions in finding fraudulent transfers, and may also apply choice of law that accomplishes federal law purposes. Other times, the federal common law might be applied.

1. *Gibson v. Wells Fargo Bank, N.A.*, 255 So. 3d 944, 951 (Fla. Dist. Ct. App. 2018), *reh'g denied* (Oct. 16, 2018), *review denied*, No. SC18-1913, 2019 WL 1924900 (Fla. Apr. 30, 2019). (Emphasis added.)

> "The Supremacy Clause of the Constitution provides that any state law conflicting with federal law is preempted by the federal law and is without effect." Nathan Kimmel, Inc. v. DowElanco, 275 F.3d 1199, 1203 (9th Cir. 2002) (citing U.S. Const. art. VI, cl. 2). Where a statute contains an express preemption clause, we "focus on the plain wording of the clause, which necessarily contains the best evidence of Congress' preemptive intent." Chamber of Commerce of U.S. v. Whiting, 563 U.S. 582, 594, 131 S.Ct. 1968, 179 L.Ed.2d 1031 (2011) (*quoting* CSX Transp., Inc. v. Easterwood, 507 U.S. 658, 664, 113 S.Ct. 1732, 123 L.Ed.2d 387 (1993)) (*internal quotation marks omitted*).[2]

# FDCPA

The FDCPA contains its own fraudulent transfer statute.[3] In *United States Small Bus. Admin. v. Bensal*,[4] an individual domiciled in California executed a disclaimer, which deflected away property he would have otherwise received from his father's estate. The individual lost at trial and on appeal, asked the Ninth Circuit to apply California law, which provided that a disclaimer was not a fraudulent transfer. The Ninth Circuit held in favor of the federal government, finding the individual had the power to disclaim and thus, held the "reins" to the property sufficient to permit application of Federal law. Citing the *Drye* case cited herein, the Ninth Circuit declined to apply state law where federal law was meant to apply.

# Internal Revenue Service

Fraudulent transfers of wealth can arise in numerous contexts with the IRS. One example is where a taxpayer with a tax liability transfers assets to avoid paying the tax liability. A taxpayer might also use a complex structure to avoid general (non-taxing authority) creditors, but in the process, engage in tax abuse or fail to report income. This concern appears on the IRS "Dirty Dozen" list, an

---

2. *United States Small Bus. Admin. v. Bensal*, 853 F.3d 992, 997–98 (9th Cir. 2017).

3. The FDCPA fraudulent transfer provision allows the federal government to void a fraudulent transfer by a debtor owing a debt to the United States. Pursuant to 28 U.S.C. §§3301–3308. *See also, United States Small Bus. Admin. v. Bensal*, 853 F.3d 992, 996–97 (9th Cir. 2017). ("Specifically, the FDCPA provides that a transfer made or obligation incurred by a debtor is fraudulent as to a debt to the United States which arises before the transfer is made or the obligation is incurred if—

> (1)(A) the debtor makes the transfer or incurs the obligation without receiving a reasonably equivalent value in exchange for the transfer or obligation; and
> (B) the debtor is insolvent at that time or the debtor becomes insolvent as a result of the transfer or obligation[.]

28 U.S.C. §3304(a).")

4. *United States Small Bus. Admin. v. Bensal*, 853 F.3d 992 (9th Cir. 2017).

annual list warning taxpayers of certain tax traps to avoid. "Abusive trust arrangements often use multiple layers of trusts as well as offshore shell corporations and entities that are disregarded for U.S. tax purposes to attempt to hide the true ownership of assets and income or to disguise the substance of transactions. Although these schemes give the appearance of separating responsibility and control from the benefits of ownership, such as through the use of purported mortgages or rental agreements, false invoices, fees for services never performed, purchase and sale agreements and distributions, the taxpayer in fact continues to control the structures and directs any benefits received from them."[5]

A wealth transfer structure designed to cloak true ownership for general creditor purposes might also have the same effect as to the IRS. The presence of fraudulent intent for fraudulent transfer purposes might be relevant in the context of civil tax penalties as well as criminal violations. Like general creditors who point to badges of fraud to show actual intent to hinder, delay, or defraud, the IRS points to its own badges of fraud in the context of civil fraud penalties pursuant to Internal Revenue Code Section 6663. In this situation, direct evidence of fraudulent intent typically is not available, so the IRS will point to various badges of fraud— some of which may overlap with badges of fraud under fraudulent transfer law. "Courts routinely consider whether the following 'badges of fraud' are present: (1) understating income, (2) maintaining inadequate records, (3) failing to file tax returns, (4) giving implausible or inconsistent explanations of behavior, (5) concealing assets, (6) failing to cooperate with tax authorities, (7) engaging in illegal activities, (8) attempting to conceal illegal activities, (9) dealing in cash, and (10) failing to make estimated payments. *See, e.g.*, Spies v. United States, 317 U.S. 492, 499 (1943); Bradford v. Commissioner, 796 F.2d at 307; Recklitis v. Commissioner, 91 T.C. 874, 910 (1988); *see also* McGraw v. Commissioner, 384 F.3d 965, 971 (8th Cir. 2004) (citing Spies, 317 U.S. at 499, and Bradford v. Commissioner, 796 F.2d at 307–308), *aff'g* Butler v. Commissioner, T.C. Memo [*35] 2002-314. This list is nonexclusive, and no single factor is dispositive, although the combination of several factors may constitute persuasive evidence of fraud. Petzoldt v. Commissioner, 92 T.C. at 700."[6]

Further, either class of creditors may use evidence of intent directed toward any creditor when attempting to void the transaction or seek other relief. The IRS may also use evidence of intent to hinder, delay, or defraud to show a wealth transfer structure involves a sham trust or lacks economic substance, which may be relevant to a whole host of tax issues, including, for example, rejecting proposed valuation discounts or inclusion of the transferred assets into the taxpayer's estate. If assets are fraudulently transferred and subject to the claims of creditors, such assets could be included in a debtor's taxable estate. Of

---

5. Press Release, IRS, Abusive Tax Shelters, Trusts, Conservation Easements Make IRS' 2019 "Dirty Dozen" List of Tax Scams to Avoid (March 19, 2019) (on file with the Internal Revenue Service).

6. Benavides & Co., P.C. v. Commissioner of Internal Revenue, T.C. Memo 2019-115 (2019).

course, the IRS may also argue the nature of the structure violates the public policy of a debtor's domicile (e.g., a self-settled trust), which can also have negative consequences for the taxpayer. In *Rensin*, a bankruptcy court held that a self-settled trust governed by the law of Belize would be interpreted under Florida law. Because the trust agreement violated Florida public policy, the trust agreement would be interpreted in accordance with Florida law.[7] Consequently, the IRS may choose to assert any such trusts are not completed gifts and/or are not excluded from a settlor's estate.[8]

Similar to important public policy providing children and spouses with super powers, compliance with federal tax laws is an important policy as it supports the federal government. Not only can the IRS refer certain cases for criminal investigation and potential prosecution, but it can act proactively as to certain transactions that it believes are abusive by categorizing certain transactions as reportable transactions. Unlike general creditors, the IRS can take proactive measures against those who promote transactions that the IRS finds abusive, and impose severe penalties on those who engage in certain transactions.[9] In contrast, general creditors may seek penalties and injunctions, but this is primarily through seeking equitable relief, which is within the discretion of a court. Further, a general creditor who is a lender may attempt to use contractual terms that require a debtor report certain transactions as part of a loan or guarantee. Notwithstanding a general creditor's attempts to achieve a deterrent effect, which may include seeking punitive damages under the fraudulent transfer common law, the severe penalties outlined in the Internal Revenue Code, together with established case law interpreting such provisions, provides a significant deterrent effect on those who may attempt to engage in tax abuse that might transpire along with a fraudulent transfer.

## *IRS As a Transferee*

The IRS may also be a transferee of a fraudulent transfer that may result in IRS liability to the taxpayer/debtor's creditors. Generally, a debtor's payment of taxes to the IRS should not result in transferee liability for the IRS because the IRS, as an agency of the federal government, enjoys immunity. However, this immunity does not exist where the federal government provides an exception. A common example of this situation is in the bankruptcy context, under Section 544.

---

7. *In re: Joseph K. Rensin, Debtor. Nicole Testa Mehdipour, Chapter 7 Tr., Plaintiff, v. Joseph K. Rensin*, Defendant., No. 17-11834-EPK, 2019 WL 2004000, at *7 (Bankr. S.D. Fla. May 6, 2019). ("The Joren Trust falls squarely within this category of trusts. To permit Mr. Rensin to rely on the law of Belize, to enforce an asset protection trust designed to offend his creditors, is contrary to Florida public policy. The Court will not apply Belize law but will apply the law of Florida to all aspects of the Joren Trust. *See* Goldberg v. Lawrence (In re Lawrence), 227 B.R. 907, 917-18 (Bankr. S.D. Fla. 1998).")

8. Where creditors can reach the trust assets, such assets are included in the settlor's estate for estate tax purposes. *See Paxton v. Commissioner*, 86 T.C. 785 (1986).

9. This includes the potential for obtaining injunctions and imposing penalties on those who fall within the definition of "promoter," "tax preparer," and "material advisor."

> It is undisputed that Debtor does not have a tax liability to the IRS. In its fraudulent transfer action under §544(b)(1), the Trustee is simply seeking to recover money that Debtor should have used to pay her own creditors. In abrogating governmental immunity for suits brought under §544, Congress's clear intention was that the fraudulently transferred property must be recovered for the benefit of Debtor's creditors, regardless of the status of the recipient of the fraudulent transfer. In light of the clear language of §106(a), the Court finds the IRS's argument that it should be protected from defending fraudulent transfer suits on the merits unpersuasive.[10]

Consequently, if a bankruptcy trustee can satisfy the actual creditor requirement, the IRS may be liable as a transferee under Section 106. "Here, the United States concedes that Salazar fulfills the actual creditor requirement, except that sovereign immunity would bar any suit she could bring against the United States under the UUFTA. But '[s]overeign immunity is the very defense that is abrogated by §106(a)(1).' Because the Trustee, standing in Salazar's shoes, need not defeat the defense of sovereign immunity, he has satisfied the actual creditor requirement of §544(b)."[11]

## *IRS as Creditor*

The IRS may seek to satisfy a tax obligation of a debtor taxpayer by avoiding transfers made by the taxpayer to others. This can be accomplished by use of both state and federal law. "In Count I of the underlying action, the government sought recovery of the refund under both the Minnesota Fraudulent Transfer Act, Minn.Stat. §513.44, and the Federal Debt Collection Procedure Act, 28 U.S. C. §3301 *et seq.*"[12] The IRS may avoid a transfer pursuant to Internal Revenue Code Section 6901, which, in turn looks to applicable state law for purposes of determining whether a transfer is voidable by creditors.

> Section 6901 does not independently impose tax liability upon a transferee but merely provides a procedure through which the IRS may collect unpaid taxes—owed by a transferor of assets—from the transferee who received those assets. Commissioner v. Stern, 357 U.S. 39, 42, 78 S.Ct. 1047, 2 L.Ed.2d 1126 (1958) (addressing section 311 of the Internal Revenue Code of 1939, the predecessor of today's section 6901). Thus an independent basis for liability must be available, and this basis is generally found [*26] under applicable State law or equity principles. Sec. 6901(a)(1)(A); Ginsberg v. Commissioner, 305 F.2d 664, 667 (2d Cir.1962), *aff'g* 35 T.C. 1148, 1961 WL 1326 (1961).
>
> 3 Accordingly, three requirements must be met for the Commissioner to assess transferee liability against a party under section 6901:(1) the party

10. *Matter of Hatchett,* No. 17-45163-MBM, 2018 WL 1882914, at *5 (Bankr. E.D. Mich. Apr. 18, 2018).
11. In re: All Resort Group, Inc., Debtor. David L. Miller, as Chapter 7 Tr. of the Bankr. Estate of All Resort Grp., Inc., Plaintiff, v. United States of America, Defendant., No. AP 18-2089, 2020 WL 1943204, at *3-12 (Bankr. D. Utah Mar. 31, 2020).
12. *U.S. v. Bame,* 721 F.3d 1025, 1028 (8th Cir. 2013).

> must be subject to liability under applicable State law or equity principles; (2) the party must be a transferee under section 6901 pursuant to Federal tax law principles; and (3) the transferor must be liable for the unpaid tax. Swords Trust v. Commissioner, 142 T.C. 317, 336, 2014 WL 2218977 (2014); see Cullifer v. Commissioner, T.C. Memo.2014–208, at *42. The Commissioner bears the burden of proving that a party is liable as a transferee of the taxpayer's property but not of proving that the taxpayer is liable for the tax. *See* Secs. 6902(a), 7454(c); Rule 142(d).[13]

Not only may the IRS take advantage of the applicable statute of limitations/repose under applicable state fraudulent transfer law, but the IRS also has the benefit of a lengthened statute under federal law.

> As a preliminary matter, the Gurule Defendants argue that the United States' claim is barred by the statute of limitations under the Utah Fraudulent Transfer Act (UFTA). This argument is without merit. As a sovereign, the United States is subject to a limitations period only when Congress has expressly created one. It is well-established that a state statute of limitations cannot cut off the rights of the United States. The Tenth Circuit has specifically held that state statutes of limitation do not apply in "a proceeding in court to collect a tax" because the government is "acting in its sovereign capacity in an effort to enforce rights ultimately grounded on federal law[.]" In this case, where the United States is seeking to collect delinquent taxes, the applicable statute of limitations is the ten-year period pursuant to 26 U.S.C. §6502(a). Therefore, the Gurule Defendants' request for judgement as a matter of law under Rule 12(b) is denied.[14]

The IRS also has the benefit of a well-developed body of law regarding substance over form, such that the IRS may challenge the substance of a transaction to bolster the likelihood of success under a fraudulent transfer claim.

# Securities and Exchange Commission

Wealth transfer planning for clients subject to securities regulatory bodies should consider the impact of securities laws as it pertains to a client's wealth transfer. Securities laws might require disgorgement of funds, which would generally pierce any wealth transfer structure. "To allow the nominal defendants

13. *Shockley v. C.I.R.*, 109 T.C.M. (CCH) 1579 (T.C. 2015), *supplemented sub nom. Shockley v. Comm'r of Internal Revenue*, 111 T.C.M. (CCH) 1038 (T.C. 2016).

14. United States of America, Plaintiff, v. T.J. Enterprises & Acoustical, Inc.; Gurule Properties Incorporated d/b/a Gurule Properties, Inc.; Linda Gurule a/k/a Linda Lee Roach; RDLC Management; State of Utah, Tax Commission; State of Utah, Department of Workforce Services; Salt Lake County, Utah; Workers Compensation Fund of Utah; Certified Reprographics, Inc.; Chekline, Inc. d/b/a Check Max; New Hampshire Insurance Company, a member company of American International Group, Inc.; & Savage Scaffold & Equipment, Inc., Defendants., No. 2:15-CV-00065-DN, 2019 WL 2327614, at *13 (D. Utah May 31, 2019).

to keep the illegal proceeds would give potential violators a blueprint for pursuing 'estate planning' through securities fraud. Corporate managers could create the 'custodial stock,' falsify their company's financial results, and then sell the 'custodial stock' at prices that are inflated by the fraudulent results. Thus, the violator's chosen beneficiaries would unlawfully profit from the violator's having duped innocent market participants into 'investing' in his company. The Court cannot condone such an inequitable result in this case."[15]

The SEC may generally pursue assets notwithstanding state or foreign law protections. "The SEC explains that in the days preceding the jury trial, and the months before the entry of the Final Judgment, Mr. Solow and his wife liquidated joint securities accounts, and transferred the proceeds to an account in Mrs. Solow's name. Thereafter, Mrs. Solow traveled to Switzerland to deposit cash and jewelry in safe deposit accounts. In addition, after the jury's verdict, and less than 60 days prior to the entry of the Final Judgment, Mr. Solow executed a $5.26 million mortgage on his homestead property for the purpose of funding a Cook Islands asset protection trust in his wife's name. The SEC alleges that this enabled him to transfer $5.49 million of his individual net worth to his wife, in addition to the transfer of two real estate parcels whose combined value is over $3 million."[16]

# Bankruptcy Court

Several issues arise in bankruptcy court that a debtor should consider before transferring wealth if bankruptcy is contemplated. These issues range from a court's disregard of state law protections to the denial of the debtor's discharge. Many of these disastrous results turn on whether the debtor made a fraudulent transfer with the actual intent to hinder, delay, or defraud creditors. Transactions involving self-settled trusts, or similar devices, may also be subject to avoidance under Bankruptcy Code 541(c)(2) or 548(e).[17]

## *Strong-arm Provision*

A bankruptcy trustee may use Section 544 to use applicable non-bankruptcy law. This is often the state fraudulent transfer statute, which is commonly four years as opposed to two years under Section 548. One must also consider the aforementioned six-year statute of limitation under the FDCPA and ten-year

15. *S.E.C. v. Antar*, 831 F. Supp. 380, 401 (D.N.J. 1993).

16. *S.E.C. v. Solow*, before number 682 F. Supp. 2d 1312 (2010).

17. *See In re* Erskine: Debtor Attempts to Exclude Assets Held in "Tennessee Asset Protection Trust," LISI Asset Protection Newsletter #324 (June 14, 2016). ("If the Trust was a TAPT, the Trust assets, held by a valid and enforceable TAPT, would be eligible for exclusion from the bankruptcy estate under Section 541(c)(2). But even if the TAPT provided an applicable restriction under Tennessee law, that wasn't the end of the story. Among other hurdles, the TAPT would then need to clear the 10 year claw back rule under Section 548(e).")

statute of limitation under the Internal Revenue Code are also applicable non-bankruptcy law such that those statues may be used via 548.[18]

## Bankruptcy Estate Claim for Malpractice

Given the potential for malpractice associated with asset protection advice and bankruptcy (discussed in chapter nine), a bankruptcy trustee may consider a claim for malpractice as an asset of the client's bankruptcy estate. Such was the case in *In re Niroomand*, where a foreign trust was created shortly before the debtor filed for bankruptcy. If the facts surrounding a fraudulent transfer are particularly egregious, such that the assisting attorney should have known not to assist, a bankruptcy trustee may pursue a legal malpractice claim against the attorney.[19] Such advice (and attorney-client privilege) may be obtained by the trustee of the bankruptcy estate.

## Extended Statute of Limitations

A bankruptcy court will typically enforce the statute of limitations applicable to a fraudulent transfer claim, either by reference to the applicable state statute (if the trustee uses the strong-arm provision) or the Code's provision in Section 548. However, a court will extend the limitations period due to fraud or extraordinary circumstances beyond the trustee's control. This equitable tolling will act to prevent harm to the bankruptcy estate where the trustee is unaware of the fraud or extraordinary circumstances. An example of this approach occurred in *International Administrative Services*, where the debtor engaged in a purge-and-plunder scheme involving the transfer of wealth with creditors looming.[20] While obscuring assets is part and parcel with some forms of aggressive asset protection, it may certainly backfire if discovered.

---

18. For more on this topic, *see* John F. Rabe, Jr., "Golden Creditors, Copper Rules: An Analysis of Avoidance Actions Under Section 544(b) of the Bankruptcy Code in Cases Where a Federal Creditor Holds a Claim," Brooklyn Law Review (2017) Volume 82 Issue 4, wherein the author concludes that these statutes are available to a bankruptcy trustee. ("This note will argue that the expansive nature of the plain text of Section 544(b) creates a powerful presumption in favor of treating the FDCPA and IRC as applicable law and that the evidence typically used to discourage courts from treating Section 544(b) as such is insufficient to overcome this presumption.")

19. *In re Niroomand*, 493 F. App'x 11, 12 (11th Cir. 2012). ("The Trustee brought the underlying adversary proceeding against the defendants seeking to recover the attorneys' fees and costs as fraudulent transfers under 11 U.S.C. §548. The Trustee's theory of fraud was that the Debtor was insolvent at the time of these transfers. The Trustee also asserted damage claims for legal malpractice and unjust enrichment against the defendants.")

20. *In re* International Administrative Serv. Inc., 408 F.3d 689, 696 (11th Cir. 2005) ("Tedder moved to Florida in order to implement the IAS/Givens asset protection plan. First, assets were transferred to various Tedder-owned foreign and domestic entities. Tedder then recycled the assets through a tangled and complex web of multi-step international transactions. In total, Tedder transferred assets more than one hundred times among twenty-three different entities. Between January 1992 and 1996, Givens removed a treasure chest in excess of $50 million from IAS's coffers; putting it out of the direct reach of IAS's creditors. On June 20, 1996, IAS filed a voluntary Chapter 11 bankruptcy petition, no doubt due in part to Givens and Tedder's purge and plunder scheme.")

CHAPTER 11

# Wealth Transfer Planning Issues for Creditors

"The inn that shelters for the night is not the journey's end. The law, like the traveler, must be ready for the morrow. It must have a principle of growth."[1]

Given the complexity of today's planning transactions, creditors need to be mindful of the various ways planning can be used to remove available assets from a creditor's reach. Just as planners are vigorous in protecting a client's assets, the creditor, too, must be vigilant in protecting its assets. Creditors must fully analyze the wealth transfer plan to avoid missing critical claims for relief. At the same time, creditors should understand the full scope of fraudulent transfer law, not only as reflected in the applicable statutes, but also under the common law.

Realizing the prospect of profitability in "immunizing" a client's assets, the planning bar has recently become more aggressive introducting legislation that is meant to dilute a creditor's efforts in protecting rights. For example, in the past several years, several states have enacted self-settled spendthrift trust legislation. These laws, often marketed as trust code updates, reverse centuries of common law finding the use of such trusts as contrary to public policy and expressly weaken fraudulent transfer law.

This trend has appeared primarily in states that do not have the larger economies, and where perhaps the creditors' rights and plaintiffs' bar is not as strong. In effect, the legislation has been successful in lower GDP states whose creditors' rights bar is asleep at the wheel. Under DAPT legislation, guarantors may gradually transfer non-exempt funds into a DAPT while simultaneously providing vague notice to lenders of same, discussed below. Over time, a substantial amount can be built up in the DAPT, available to the guarantor but to the exclusion of lenders if the borrower defaults. When the creditor attempts to prove actual fraud, the DAPT statute prevents a court from considering the

1. Cardozo, The Growth of the Law 20 (1924).

terms of the trust agreement and potentially immunizes certain parties who profited off the transaction.

However, the risk of passing these laws is minimized in states with a more active creditors' rights bar. Or, in the case of Georgia, a governor (who was formerly a judge) spotted issues with a proposed bill enacting asset protection trust legislation. The real threat was not passage of an incredibly weak Georgia asset protection trust statute; the real threat was passage of a statute that attempts to destroy the public policy argument against self-settled spendthrift trusts. The threat to lenders in such states is not that the borrowers or guarantors will form self-settled trusts in those states, the real threat to lenders is that borrowers or guarantors will transfer funds out of the state or country to more debtor friendly domiciles. Debtors will then rely on the law of those jurisdictions to argue the foreign asset protection trust is consistent with public policy of the borrower's or guarantor's domicile. The foreign asset protection trust may provide severely weakened rights for lenders, and the choice of law protection might tilt in favor of the debtor's chosen domicile because no violation of public policy exists.

# Discovery Issues

In fraudulent transfer litigation, creditors must understand the nuances of estate planning that directly impact creditors' rights. For example, given the tendency of debtors to mix their assets with third parties, creditors will not only need copies of estate planning documents to identify how this occurs, but also communications surrounding the transaction to establish intent.

> The Trustee seeks documents responsive to his Document Request Nos. 68, 30 and 66 to John Dunne, among which the following categories of documents have not been produced:
>
> 1. Documents and communications concerning any trust established for John Dunne's benefit, directly or indirectly, by the Debtor or Killilea.[2]

By understanding the nature of a transfer, when it occurred, and how such a transfer fares considering both actual and constructive fraud categories, the creditor has a better chance at formulating a successful fraudulent transfer argument.

A debtor may argue the creditor may not obtain estate planning communications based on privilege. In this situation, the creditor will want to show the capacity in which communications were made or received.

> As previously noted, the SGB 2007 Trust was ordered to produce a wide variety of documents, including the Trustee's e-mail (Dkts. 19, 53, Case No. 2:17-cv-00528) and in January 2018, the Trustee completed the ordered

2. *Richard M. Coan, Truste, et al. v. Sean Dunne, et al.* Additional Party Names: Barclay Beattie & Brown LLC, Gayle Killilea, Heagney, Lennon & Slane, LLP, John J. Slane, Jr., Molly Blossom LLC, Mountbrook USA, LLC, Thomas J. Heagney, WAHL, LLC, No. 3: 15 CV 50 (JAM), 2018 WL 6616820, at *10 (D. Conn. Dec. 18, 2018).

> production. LVB seeks to discover fraudulent transactions, self-settled assets, and abuse of the trust since January 2018 and therefore, seeks communications that have occurred since that production. The Trustee refuses to make such production because he claims such emails since the filing of this lawsuit are privileged.
>
> Mr. Dean has continued to operate as the Trustee of the SGB 2007 Trust, and therefore, LVB is entitled to all non-privileged emails he sent in that capacity since January 2018 to supplement what was previously produced.[3]

Regarding foreign trustees, it may be especially important for a creditor to request the production of any onboarding or due diligence documents. These documents may show trustee knowledge of an attempt to hinder creditors, which could be relevant to obtaining jurisdiction over the foreign trustee. Generally, because these documents and communications involve a non-lawyer, such evidence may not be subject to attorney-client privilege.

Creditors should critically examine details surrounding transactions that purport to occur on a certain date. Backdating documents is not outside the realm of possibility and creditors have various means of verifying whether events took place. A request for production might reveal tax reporting inconsistent with the debtor's description of a transaction. A subtle clue in one case involved the expiration date for a notary who notarized documents.

> According to the Amended Complaint, Defendants falsely asserted that: (1) the "Family Agreement" sets forth that Defendant Soni Holdings, LLC was a "place holder" for the purchase of the Newark Property; and (2) the "Family Agreement" was notarized on August 26, 2011 by Defendant Weanona Hugie, a Notary Public. Am. Compl. ¶ 55. Although Defendant Weanona Hugie claims to have notarized all of the signatures on the "Family Agreement" on August 26, 2011, Plaintiff states that Hugie's notary stamp on the document "sets forth that her commission expires on November 21, 2020, clearly demonstrating that the document is fraudulent and backdated, because notaries public in New Jersey only hold their respective offices for the term of five (5) years." *Id.* ¶ 58. Therefore, Defendant Hugie would have "renewed her notary license five (5) years prior to November 21, 2020, which would have been on or about November 21, 2015, which was four (4) years after the date which she purportedly notarized the bogus 'Family Agreement.'" *Id.* According to Plaintiff, it is clear that Defendants rushed to fabricate the "Family Agreement" which is backdated to August 26, 2011, but in their haste to do so failed to realize that Hugie's notary stamp proves that Defendants had recently fabricated the document. *Id.* ¶ 59. The Amended Complaint asserts that this was done by the Defendants in an attempt to intentionally mislead and to commit a fraud on the United States District Court, as well as on the Plaintiff. *Id.* Plaintiff states that in January and

3. LVB-Ogden Marketing, LLC, Plaintiff, v. David S. Bingham, Sharon Bingham, Christopher Bingham, Cherish Bingham, Kelly Bingham, Bingo Investments, LLC, CCRB Enterprises, LLC, SKBB Enterprises, LLC, Park Place Motors, Ltd., Hytech Power, Inc., Henry Dean, in his individual capacity & as Tr. for the Sharon Graham Bingham 2007 Trust, & BGH Holdings, LLC, Defendants., No. 2:18-CV-00243-TSZ, 2019 WL 142031, at *6 (W.D. Wash. Jan. 9, 2019).

February 2019, Defendants transmitted the false and fraudulent "Family Agreement" as well as the false and fraudulent "Sale Agreement" through the mails and/or the wires across State lines. *Id.* ¶ 63. Plaintiff alleges that in February 2019, Defendant Hugie committed a further unlawful act by submitting more false and fraudulent statements in an affidavit under oath claiming that she notarized the signatures of the Defendants on the alleged "Family Agreement" in 2011, but then affixed her stamp in 2019. *Id.* ¶ 64.[4]

## Pro-debtor Legislation

Recall the terms of some state statutes where the fraudulent transfer laws have been modified to the detriment of creditors to attract asset protection trust business. Asset protection planners no doubt realize that creditors, especially lenders, are aware of asset protection trusts and the potential for losing unsecured assets transferred to such trusts that would otherwise be available to pay a claim. As an alternative, many planners have started venturing off into the world of LLCs to immunize assets. After Delaware enacted a divisive LLC statute, law firms representing creditors immediately began warning lenders to change their loan documents and processes to account for the change. In Florida, an attempt was made to change the tenancy by entireties laws to provide retroactive classification for improperly formed tenancies by the entireties – which could apply to LLC interests held as TBE. The Florida Bar's Bankruptcy/UCC Committee in the Business Law Section immediately identified the danger to lenders and the proposal was rejected.

## Notice to Creditors

Lenders must be vigilant in their lending practices to account for these debtor-friendly changes in long-standing law and public policy. For example, the law of another jurisdiction might cut off the lender's right to recourse under a shortened statute of limitations for fraudulent transfer purposes.[5] At least one

4. New Falls Corporation, Plaintiff, v. Soni Holdings, LLC, Kunal Soni, Anjali Soni & 632 MLK Blvd Jr LLC, Om P. Soni, Soni Capital Resources, LLC, Kanwal Kapur, Weanona Hugie & Richard Spears, Defendants., No. CV19449ADSAKT, 2019 WL 4015170, at *12–14 (E.D.N.Y. July 5, 2019).

5. *See TrustCo Bank v. Mathews*, No. CV 8374-VCP, 2015 WL 295373, at *12 (Del. Ch. Jan. 22, 2015), where the Court of Chancery of Delaware was asked to apply Delaware's statute of limitation under its Qualified Disposition in Trust Act. The Court of Chancery refused to do so, however, lenders should be aware of the attempt to transfer assets into a trust that is governed by law which mandates a shortened statute of limitations. The Court explained why it refused to rule: "First, little case law interpreting the QDTA exists and some of the issues implicated here appear to be ones of first impression. Second, after conclusion of the briefing on the motion for partial summary judgment currently before me, the Court of Chancery rejected the argument that the QDTA requires suits to avoid a qualified disposition to be brought exclusively in Delaware. Third, whether Ms. Mathews maintains impermissible control over the assets transferred to the Three Trusts such that the QDTA's restrictions would not apply presents a material question of disputed fact not appropriate for summary resolution on the current record." (Emphasis added.)

court has held that a generic statement that transfers were made for "estate planning purposes" started the one-year discovery rule. In *TrustCo Bank v. Mathews*, the debtor argued that statements sent to the bank put the bank on notice of a fraudulent transfer, thereby extinguishing any cause of action under the one-year discovery rule:

> Defendants also note several significantly earlier dates when Plaintiffs allegedly received information about the ITRAX Transfers that should have put them on notice. In connection with the discussions leading up to the first modification of the StoreSmart Loan, Ms. Mathews submitted a net worth statement to TrustCo on March 25, 2008, that reported her net worth at $11,773,446. On April 11, 2008, Ms. Mathews supplied a revised net worth statement to TrustCo indicating her net worth to be $5,578,857. That revised statement included the annotation: "I am the discretionary beneficiary of each of the 3 Delaware trusts that have been established as part of estate planning." As part of the loan modification process, Ms. Mathews wrote in a May 6, 2008 email to Paul Steenburgh, a TrustCo Assistant Vice President and one of TrustCo's Rule 30(b)(6) deponents, that TrustCo had requested that she either "guarantee the loan with all 3 Delaware Trusts or put up another $1MM in collateral." At his deposition, Steenburgh recalled receiving this email and stated that Ms. Mathews's description of TrustCo's position was correct. The final terms of the first modification did include an additional $1,000,000 in collateral, as well as several other conditions, such as opening a $250,000 escrow account with TrustCo. The first modification to the StoreSmart loan closed on June 27, 2008. The accompanying closing binder included a copy of Trust II's Trust Agreement.[6]

Consequently, lenders must be aware of proposed pro-debtor legislation introduced in states where loan transactions might be impacted. Lenders in states that have already adopted DAPT legislation should review their lending forms and practices to preserve their rights and avoid the issues encountered in *TrustCo Bank v. Mathews*. Lenders must not only be cautious of an APT, but also for an APT variant typically reflected by an agreement with a nondescript name.[7] Disclosures that include asset protection trust are obviously more likely to raise a red flag than transfers to a family trust.

Further, lenders should be aware of their own exposure to creditors by accommodating a debtor/borrower's requests. In *Kruse*, the bank was named as a defendant in a fraudulent transfer action by creditors against the debtor/borrower. The creditors attacked the bank's lending practices as part of a scheme to hinder other creditors. "If the Bank's sole motive was self-preser-

---

6. *TrustCo Bank v. Mathews*, No. CV 8374-VCP, 2015 WL 295373, at *3 (Del. Ch. Jan. 22, 2015). (Emphasis added.)

7. Common titles include irrevocable trust, family trust or irrevocable trusts for the benefit of certain family members. *See In re JODELL M. ALTIER, Debtor. GOSHEN MORTGAGE, LLC, Plaintiff, v. JODELL M. ALTIER, Defendant.*, No. 6:15-AP-00156-KSJ, 2017 WL 1011416 (Bankr. M.D. Fla. Mar. 15, 2017). ("In 2012, Debtor conveyed the Properties to Jennifer Sandman and Jill Altier as successor co-trustees of the Altier Family Irrevocable Trust U/A DTD 7/9/2002 (the "Altier Family Trust"). *** Debtor concedes the Properties were transferred to Grande Legacy in 2013,11 and the transfers were specifically for asset protection purposes.")

vation and good-faith protection of its senior security interests, the discrepancies and irregularities present in the transaction are unusual because they would not have been necessary to effectuate a refinancing through ordinary banking practices."[8]

## Estate Planning with Collateral

If loans involve certain types of trusts,[9] extreme caution must be exercised; all documents involved in the loan transaction, including the underlying planning documents, should be hardwired (and consistent in approach) to produce protection and effective remedies for the lender. Additionally, and considering loans involving exotic asset protection structures (to the extent the lender wishes to accommodate the borrower and/or guarantor), consideration must be given to the type of collateral involved, the classification of such interests, as well as enforcement of security interests under the Uniform Commercial Code.

Ordinary, run-of-the-mill lending transactions are not immune from fraudulent transfer issues. A lender that has a system of checks and balances will be better equipped to avoid issues, such as characterization as a transferee:

> Defendant Provident Bank has moved for summary judgment, claiming that this was a relatively routine transaction, in which the bank followed all of its normal protocols, without any knowledge or reason to know that there might be something untoward about the transaction. The motion relies on an affidavit from Ms. Sabino, nominally a vice president of Provident at the time and the loan officer actually involved in the process of approving the mortgage loan to Blue Mountain (with Carmela Cannavo as guarantor).
>
> In response, while effectively conceding that in the absence of some actual or constructive notice of impropriety the mortgage would remain valid and enforceable, the plaintiff contends that there were numerous "red flags" or "badges of fraud" that were known or should have been known, sufficient to create a material issue of fact as to whether the bank's mortgage interests can be rendered void by characterization of the loan transactions as fraudulent conveyances/transfers. The plaintiff relies on an affidavit from current co-counsel authenticating a number of documents, as well as New York counsel, authenticating additional documents supplemented by a lengthy narrative.
>
> *2 In somewhat more technical terms, the plaintiff acknowledges (perhaps grudgingly) that even if the transfers of the parcels from Western Greenwich to Blue Mountain might properly be characterized as fraudulent transfers with respect to a creditor such as the plaintiff, any claim by an allegedly defrauded creditor is subject to the interest of a good-faith purchaser for value (a bona fide purchaser) of an interest in the transferred properties, as

8. *Kruse v. Repp*, 2020 WL 1317479, at 10 (S.D. Iowa Mar. 20, 2020).

9. Such trusts may include, but are not limited to, self-settled trusts. A trust agreement may incorporate features under state law that provide for self-settled trust protection but are not readily apparent from the wording of the statute or at the time the trust is created.

set forth in applicable common-law decisions and statutory codification (Chapter 923a of the General Statutes). There is no question that the defendant bank provided value for the mortgage interest it received, such that the focus is on status as a good-faith transferee.[10]

## Importance of Tracing Assets

Tracing a debtor's transfer of assets is important for two reasons. First, a creditor may potentially seek relief as to any transferee in the chain of transfers. Second, property that is claimed as exempt or immune may not actually be exempt or immune due to a defect in transfer formalities. For example, the immunity granted to property held as tenants by the entirety under Florida's common law may only exist if certain unities are established. Consequently, a debtor's claim that an LLC interest is held with her husband, as tenants by the entirety, could be challenged if the debtor transferred her sole interest from herself to herself and her husband as tenants by the entirety. This is so because time and title may be absent in the creation of the purported tenancy by entireties.[11]

Titling may be critical, as simply replacing "and" with "or" on the asset title can result in a subsequent fraudulent transfer. Creditors must investigate title (vehicle registration, bank account signature card, etc.) to see if a debtor has expressly designated the form of ownership that conflicts with an asserted defense (e.g., exemption.) In Florida, if the form of ownership is ambiguous, a rebuttable presumption arises as to property being held by husband and wife as a tenancy by the entireties. This does not end the inquiry, as a creditor may show a tenancy by entireties does not exist if one of the requisite unities (possession, interest, time, title, survivorship, or marriage) is missing.

## Solvency Analysis

Creditors will often encounter the argument that a debtor did not make a fraudulent transfer because the debtor was solvent. It is a common myth among some wealth planners that a creditor cannot bring a fraudulent transfer claim if the debtor was solvent at the time of the transfer. In some cases, a potential red flag may very well be the existence of a solvency affidavit. This affidavit is often required for transfers made to asset protection trusts. The affidavit should

10. *SR Holdings I, LLC v. Joseph Cannavo*, No. FSTCV166027598, 2018 WL 2973475, at *1–2 (Conn. Super. Ct. May 15, 2018).

11. This defect in asserted asset titling might have been the impetus behind a proposed Florida statute that would have abolished the time and title unities. A TBE status would permit a debtor to transfer the LLC interest to an asset protection trust since the LLC interest would not be an "asset" under applicable fraudulent transfer statute. From there, the trustee of the APT may decide to transfer distributions to one spouse to the exclusion of the other, or to remove the spouse as a beneficiary if the spouse separates or divorces the other spouse. As a result, what was once a marital asset becomes transformed into separate property, often under the guise of tax planning.

produce a clue to the creditor that a transfer might have been made for purposes of creditor avoidance, thereby triggering potential application of an actual fraud analysis.

Proving solvency may also require the assistance of a forensic accountant. This task should not be underestimated, as the assumptions made by the debtor might not have been true. Further, the qualifications of the expert should be carefully examined; otherwise, a court might disregard the expert's report.

## Loan Provisions

Traditional loan documents should be reviewed to determine whether they address sophisticated forms of wealth transfer, including the development of pro-debtor legislation in certain jurisdictions. For instance, statutes enacted permitting the division of LLCs, use of a civil law foundation, use of self-settled trusts, powers of appointment, etc., all need to be considered if these tools are present in a borrower/guarantor's existing asset plan prior to a loan as well as during any loan modifications or permitted uses of collateral. Consideration should be given to the liberal use of waivers, not only as to state exemptions, but also as to sophisticated planning techniques, and the use of such waivers should be reviewed to ensure compliance with applicable state law providing for the waiver of exemptions.

## Family Law & Personal Injury Lawyers

The personal injury bar must be even more attuned to the erosion of creditors' rights in the form of modern estate planning laws. Whereas a sophisticated lender might be able to deal with obviating the cost of litigating relief under fraudulent transfer law through lending practices and contract, the personal injury victim has no such luck. The same can be said for spouses and children of a debtor, as some spouses unwilling to pay spousal settlement or support payments entice their unwitting spouses to sign away rights through sophisticated trust agreements.

CHAPTER 12

# What Comes Next?

> "'Twill be wise to cultivate and foster private Credit by an exemplary observance of the principles of public Credit, and to guard against misuse of the former by a speedy and vigorous administration of Justice, and by taking away every temptation to run in debt founded on the hope of evading the Just claims of Creditors."[1]

Long before Alexander Hamilton set forth his views on the vital role credit plays in the birth and stability of the United States, history demonstrated the important role of credit and mechanisms to protect its integrity. At a time where the United States has been rocked by the devastating effects of a global pandemic, and where it has been called to provide aide to those in need, the principle that "man must be just to his creditors" is especially meaningful.

Debtor-creditor battles over the transfer of wealth illustrate why creditors (and those who represent them) must stay at the forefront of legislative developments impacting creditors' rights and identify potential avenues of relief before it is too late. Notwithstanding the new and sophisticated strategies that can impact creditors' rights, fraudulent transfer law is flexible enough to look through form and focus on substance.[2] While wealth transfer planners strive for black and white results for planning purposes, the facts and circumstances presented by a client's unique situation often paint a picture that is varying shades of gray. Consequently, those who orchestrate the transfer of wealth cannot ignore the broad application of fraudulent transfer law to wealth transfer planning and must consider all the facts and circumstances in the process. Most

1. Alexander Hamilton, January 16, 1795, Report on a Plan for the Further Support of Public Credit, Philadelphia, January 16, 1795, as abridged by Richard Sylla and David J. Cowen, *Alexander Hamilton on Finance, Credit, and Debt*, Columbia University Press, 2018.

2. *Canon Latin Am., Inc. v. Lantech, S.A.*, No. 08-21518-CIV, 2011 WL 13101029, at *8 (S.D. Fla. July 26, 2011). ("The Uniform Fraudulent Transfer Act, on its face, evinces a policy of protecting creditors from debtors who prefer paying one creditor over another. And it prevents debtors from fraudulently avoiding their obligations. Florida's policy is a weighty one.")

importantly, consideration must be given to fraudulent transfer law in all its sources, both under statute and the well-developed common law.

In summary, the transfer of wealth, as sophisticated as it may be today, can still be challenged successfully using centuries' old fraudulent conveyance law. As demonstrated in this book, a vast amount of case law provides ample opportunity for creditors to analyze new strategies by analogy to old tricks. Conversely, wealth transfer planners can plan for their clients successfully but must navigate complex fraudulent transfer laws to ensure the effective transfer of wealth.

# Table of Cases

## B



## C

## D

## E



## F



## G

## H



## I

## J



## K

N



O



P

## Q



## R



## S

## T

## U



## V

## W



## Y



## Z

# Index